D0216339

Polish
Americans

Polish Americans

SECOND, REVISED EDITION

Helena Znaniecka Lopata

With a new chapter by
Mary Patrice Erdmans

Transaction Publishers
New Brunswick (U.S.A.) and London (U.K.)

Library of Congress Catalog Number: 92-41516
ISBN: 1-56000-100-3
Printed in the United States of America

Library of Congress Cataloging-in-Publication Data
Lopata, Helena Znaniecka, 1925-
    Polish Americans / Helena Znaniecka Lopata.—2nd rev. ed.
        p. cm.
    Includes bibliographical references and index.
    ISBN 1-56000-100-3 (cloth)
    1. Polish Americans.   I. Title.
E184.P7L66   1993
305.891'85073—dc20

                                                              92-41516
                                                              CIP

Helena Znaniecka Lopata gratefully acknowledges Prentice-Hall, Inc., Englewood Cliffs, New Jersey for permission to use portions of *Polish Americans: Status Competition in an Ethnic Community* in this second, revised edition.

Dedicated to
Eileen Markley Znaniecki
and the other
Poles
Americans
Polish Americans
Americans of Polish Heritage
in both Mary's and Helena's Families

Contents

Tables and Figures

Tables

Figure

Preface

I wish to begin this second, greatly revised, edition of *Polish Americans* with an expression of gratitude, this time to Charley Moskos and Irving Louis Horowitz. I was on a panel with Professor Moskos at the Polish Copernicus Center in Chicago: I talking about Polonia and he comparing the situation to that of the Greek Americans, whom he studied. He suggested that evening that I do a revision of my 1976 *Polish Americans: Status Competition in an Ethnic Community*, as he had revised his Greek Americans when Dukakis was running for president of the United States. The more I thought about this, the more I became intrigued by the idea. After all, there have been tremendous changes in Poland and Polonia and in the relations of both with America since the 1970s. Poland regained her independence; its charismatic leader Lech Walesa, a Nobel Peace Prize Laureate, started to change the country from a communistic to a democratic form, from a state-controlled to a privatized economy. A Pole became pope of the Roman Catholic church, which certainly could have helped the Polish American self-image.

Polonia also experienced dramatic changes with the influx of a third cohort, or wave, of immigrants starting in the late 1970s, after many decades of Poland's closed frontier behind the "iron curtain." Its changes were visible in the mass media, as new radio, television, and press programs emerged, organizations were formed or revitalized, and new joint ventures were started in Poland. On a less intellectual level, I kept hearing about "my nice Polish cleaning lady who does not know a word of English."

I wrote to Irving Louis Horowitz with the suggestion that Transaction Publishers might be interested in a revised *Polish Americans*, since they published the second edition of *Greek Americans* and, sure enough, he was interested.

This whole project turned out to be much more complex than I had anticipated. I learned soon enough that it was impossible to just incorporate the changes by adding a few pages to each chapter, and not only because so much has happened recently. I had to rewrite much of the basic manuscript due also to a knowledge explosion about Polonia. Polish scholars have turned their attention to the Polish Americans; many coming here to study communities, churches, and parish schools, farmers and urban workers, and the theater. There is a whole journal devoted to Polonian matters coming out of the Jagielonian University in Krakow. Joint ventures between Poland and Polish American scholars have produced congresses, conferences, and volumes of books. American scholars of Polish background have also been busy, publishing numerous works and presenting results at meetings of the Polish Institute of Arts and Sciences in America and the Polish American Historical Association. All in all, there is an enormous growth of knowledge about Polonia. In the meantime, I had learned from Hal Orbach (1992) that Thomas and Znaniecki, authors of *The Polish Peasant in Europe and America* (1918–1920/1958) had planned two volumes on the Polish American intelligentsia and bourgeoisie that had never come to fruition. Had these works been published, the world's view of Polonia would be much more complete. No one else has been able to accomplish a similar job, and without these volumes it has been impossible to reconstruct this subworld.

Reentering the world of Polonia through its publications, radio, and television; through interviews and organizational meetings, I became fascinated with the complexities and directions of the changes since the 1970s. At that time the fraternals were still active but losing in membership, and there was relatively little liveliness in Polonia compared to what I was finding in the 1990s. None of the scholars studying Polonia in prior decades could have predicted Poland's independence, the influx of the third cohort into America, and all the repercussive changes.

New thanks are also due now. In the first place, I am exceedingly lucky to have found Mary Erdmans. Colleagues familiar with the Northwestern University scene kept telling me about a Ph.D. candidate studying the Poles who have just recently come to America and their relations with the established organizations. A fifth-generation Polish American who had to learn Polish in order to study Polonia, Mary moved into the neighborhood and lived around the "new Poles," as she calls the third cohort, for four years. I have enjoyed our many conversations and was very pleased when she agreed to contribute a chapter to this book on the interweave of political activity on behalf of Poland between the new cohort and established Polonian organizations. I have also gained much from reading her dissertation, focused on Polonian life from a social movements perspective. Mary continues to study the Poles in America, concentrating right now on the black market care of the elderly and sick.

Another person who has helped immensely is Bozena Nowicka, an assistant vice president of PEKAO, a trading corporation. She is also head of their consulting division for cooperative investment in Poland and executive training of Polish bankers, and so is familiar with Polish matters on both sides of the ocean. I also talked again with Robert and Lili Lewandowski, active in the Chicago radio and television world. It was a pleasure to learn much about different Polonias from folklorist John Gutowski, and historians Dominic Pacyga, Ted Radzialowski, William Galush, James Pula, Stanislaus Biejwas, John Bukowczyk, Donald Pienkos, and Leonard Chrobot, as well as sociologist Barbara Les (who translated the first edition to Polish). Thanks also to Michal Kuchejda, editor of the *Dziennik Chicagowski* and *Gazeta Polska* and to Maryla

Kostrzewska, and indpendent contributor to the newspapers. Walter Zarnecki, a lawyer living in Jackowo in Chicago, helped me understand some of the legal problems facing new immigrants and especially the wakacjusze, while Wiesia and Maciej Znaniecki introduced me to some of the Solidarity emigres in New York.

My colleagues, including some very nice recent additions to the department like Fred Kniss and Anne Figert, have been highly supportive. Judy Wittner, Peter Whalley, Richard Block, Phil Nyden, and Kirsten Gronbjerg kindly listened to all the problems and often helped solve technical computer glitches.

Again thanks to Richard Lopata for his advice on economic matters involving Poland, for so patiently going through the whole manuscript, and for lugging resources back and forth between Chicago and Delavan, Wisconsin.

Preface to the First Edition

I find it impossible to write a personal preface within the normal space allotted for such presentations. After all, it took years of several lives to collect all the data and, hopefully, insights.

Much of the literature on the immigrants to America, ethnic communities, assimilation, the hyphenated-Americans, and so forth, has been simplistic and biased. This applies to the writings of early sociologists just as much as to the various commissions appointed to investigate the situations early in the twentieth century (see Jones 1960). A major source of the bias among sociologists was an idealization of an allegedly stable village or small community, of Gemeinschaft or primary relations, and of total cooperation involving good, happy and passively adapted people. From such a vantage point, what was happening in the centers of American cities as they were filing with millions of former villagers was bewildering, even repugnant, warranting predictions of disaster and doom. The sociologists who studied the newly forming ethnic communities in America came from other backgrounds: Park from a small town and a newspaperman's interest in deviancy and dramatic evidences of disorganization, Wirth as a refugee from intelligentsian Germany far removed from the Russian-Jewish *Ghetto*, Thomas with a concern for maladjusted people, Znaniecki accustomed to relatively stabilized cities of Poland, and Zorbaugh, Thrasher, and the many other urbanologists with attention focused on problems such as the contrasts depicted in *The Gold Coast and the Slum* (Zorbaugh 1929).

Most observers of immigrant communities in the early years of this century were not looking for a social structure or a gradually emerging fabric, but only for indices of a lack of organization and even of disorganization of prior social systems. Thomas and Znaniecki's major theme of 1918–1920 revolved around this point, but so did the works of other men. Sociologists who followed were really more concerned with the type of life described in the *Street Corner Society* (Whyte 1955) and the processes of assimilation (Drachsler, *Democracy and Assimilation* 1920; Smith, *Americans in the Making* 1939), than in the overall social system the groups had created. Wirth's *The Ghetto* (1928) was a partial exception to this generalization in that it concentrated on the community. Of course, the sociologists were not the only ones concerned with the problems of immigration and the ability of the American society to absorb numbers of people whose behavior diverged dramatically from accepted middle class or at least formal Protestant norms. The sociologists, however, certainly helped create a strong and consistent picture of disorganization among immigrants. Societal concern was so strong, and its justification so well documented in the writings of our fellow social scientists, that the flood doors were closed by the quota laws of the 1920s and everyone breathed a little easier with the optimistic hope that these "barbarians" would settle down and assimilate, *soon*, and without untold problems. There were some social scientists like Hourwich (1912) who tried to convince the American public that the immigrants were not the cause of economic problems and that the industrialization process itself resulted in numerous dislocations (see the discussion in chapter 5), or Taft (1936) who examined criminal statistics in an effort to calm fears about the crime-ridden immigrants, but their voices were not sufficiently strong. Over the years, besides surrounding the ethnic communities with "benign neglect" and telling each other that it was good for "those people" to be in there, sharing warm primary relations along with the good and smelly foods, Americans of nonethnic identity, or at least of forgotten or allegedly superior ethnic identity tried occasionally and sporadically to "assist" the immigration process. Park (1922) recommended ways of controlling the foreign press, which was judged as dysfunctional to assimilation, and Edith Bowler (1931) advised the National Commission on Law Observance and Enforcement on methods of controlling the foreign-stock crime and juvenile delinquency; but other sociologists turned their attention elsewhere as the depression and World War II emerged on the scene.

The "black is beautiful" and "black power" movements, followed by the "white backlash" in *The Rise of the Unmeltable Ethnics* (Novak 1972) have brought forth another tendency in the sociological perception of American ethnic communities, the tendency to lump them together. The process by which ethnics are seen as a single mass of people with equal status (see even Kramer, *The Minority Community* 1970) has several forms. Seen from the perspective of *The Sociological Eye* but in a simplistic manner that Hughes (1971) would never employ, the ethnic minority-status communities are presented as internally homogeneous, except for generational and social class differences due to the fact that not everyone moved the same distance or at the same rate up the traditional American status ladder. In addition, several ethnic communities are combined along two lines of demarcation, social class, and religion. Novak's (1972) work equates the "unmeltable ethnics" with working-class people and norms, as does much of the literature concentrating on the working class in general. The third form of combing ethnic groups is a consequence of the continuing concern with the "melting pot," somewhat more diversified than in the original version, thanks to Herberg (1955), Glazer and Moynihan (1970), and Kennedy (1952) in *A Triple Melting Pot*. In spite of Gordon's (1964) insistence on the importance of studying the social structure of each ethnic group, much of the current literature slides into discussions of this supposed triple melting pot, without testing its application for many groups. The ease with which the theory was accepted is due to two factors. One is the use of individual behavior, particularly of intermarriage as an index of assimilation, the other is the fact that much of the literature generates from the Jewish case whose peoples of different ethnic flavor, which was acquired through centuries of life in various national culture societies, melted into a single "Jewish" ethnic community. The other immigrant groups are then combined by the writers into one of the two remaining religious classifications, thus denying their ethnicity entirely.

Catholic Americans have been attracting more attention in recent years, and some of it is not only a result of being lumped together but is also due to class bias. The ethnic communities are seen as problem-ridden, teeming with criminals victimizing ignorant and passive ethnics. This class-biased view of the ethnic community is similar to the one illustrated by Davis, Gardner, and Gardner (1941) about the class perceptions in a community in the *Deep South*. From the vantage point of the intellectual or at least professionally competent sociologist, the ethnic enclave with a Catholic base and its second- or third-generation "minority" community is thus seen as homogeneous, and mainly concerned with its position vis-à-vis similar groups in American society. It is not seen as having a life of its own or a social structure weaving members together.

Much of the recent attention given ethnicity in America uses a theoretical framework dating back to Park's days. Assimilation is being examined from the standpoint of what items of past ethnic culture individual or family units preserve, without reference to the web of social relations or new cultural items being developed. Seeing change as nothing more than a loss of prior items oversimplified the ethnic scene.

Other approaches to the ethnic community emanate from other biases. In the case of Polonia, for example, the members of the national culture society who come from Poland, immediately react to Polonia's lack of Polishness by their definition (Nowakowski 1964 and many others over the years) and predict its demise for this reason. Other intellectuals, visiting or in refugee settlements (Janta 1957; Symmons-Symonolewicz 1966, 1969 and others of the second emigration), decry Polonia as a representative of Polish culture because they regard it primarily as a folk community with only traces of national culture. People who were brought up in this community often view the changes within it from individual assimilationist vantage points; they predict assimilation because of generational or class deviations from the basic folk culture they knew, which was limited to the food, dance, costume, and religious ritual combination (Janta 1957). The Roman Catholic church has always seen Polonia as a problem, while other observers look for future attempts at increases in political power as in *The White Ethnic Movement and Ethnic Politics* (Weed 1973).

Thus, ethnic communities including Polonia have in the past, and with variations in the present, been examined as social problems, breeding places for social problems, ghettos with all the negative connotations that term elicits, masses of people with the same status position, having identity from their minority position only, having identity from their religion only, centers of primary relations of village-style harmony, containing too rapidly assimilating, or too slowly assimilating people, and so on, but usually not as social structures with lives of their own. The "hyphenated-Americans" have usually been treated individually and examined through census and other surveys for unique characteristics of patterns of change. In such studies they are not examined as members of social structure, let alone of complex social structures. They are seen as objects of curiosity, as objects of discrimination and prejudice, or as containers of future behavior emanating from current attitudes. Above all, in spite of Novak's (1971) claim in *The Rise of the Unmeltable Ethnics*, they are seen as passive and undifferentiated, except for some variations in Christmas customs. The trait of passivity permeates the very image of the immigrant, valiantly but passively adapting to the problems of his environment (unless he [*sic*] is a rebel), holding back the flood of disorganization with temporary measures only if pushed by necessity, gradually but inevitably having acculturated with the hope of eventual assimilation just to be slapped with prejudice and, now lacking a distinctive culture, turning with his children and grandchildren to others of the same background to create a minority community of psychologically scarred people. The ideal end of this process is seen as a relatively happy adjustment of still passive people, within a "pluralistic" society, living in harmony and peace with fellow ethnics (or at least fellow Catholics, Protestants, or Jews).

It is this image (drawn perhaps a bit dramatically since this is the preface in which such an excess is permissible) that I hope to at least partially dispel, taking literally Gordon's (1964) admonition to study the social structure, not just "the social-psychological sense of peoplehood" of the ethnic group.

> By the structure of a society I mean the set of crystallized social relationships which its members have with each other which places them in groups, large or small, permanent or temporary, formally organized or unorganized, and which relates them to the major institutional activities of the society, such as economic and occupational life, religion, marriage and the family, education, government and recreation. (Gordon 1964: 30–31)

We will study the structure of the patterned relations over time, within the community and in its relations to the two broader national culture societies of Poland and America (see also Znaniecki 1952, 1965). In this work, we can benefit from some of the recent contributions to the study of ethnic communities.Gordon's (1964) analysis, entitled *Assimilation in American Life*, provides many theoretical guides to understanding the complexities of the process of integration and internal differentiation of the ethnic groups. The concept of "ethclass," by which the ethnic community is divided into social classes within which primary relations and interaction are maintained, is a very useful sociological tool (see definitions of concepts in Gordon 1964:118, chapter 6). Suttles's *Social Construction of the Slum* (1968) also provides insights into the ways different groups organize life within adjoining, and even overlapping territories. Also of help are the studies of other ethnic groups, particularly those in this Prentice-Hall series.

Many different methods and techniques were used to research and prepare this study of Polish Americans. These methods involved immersion in the community's activities at several local levels and the superterritorial level at two, or really three, different periods of time. The documents contained within Thomas and Znaniecki's (1918–1920) *The Polish Peasant in Europe and America* serve as the first immersion, since the letters, diary, and commentary present detailed pictures of daily personal and group life in the years before 1918. I became immersed in the community on two occasions, first between 1950 and 1954 for my dissertation, and then between 1972 and 1974 for this book. The primary sources that I used included verbal and written communications by community members and groups, as well as newspaper and other periodical accounts, with participant observation supplying much data on ways in which events are carried forth by different companionate circles. Much of the data contained in this volume come from secondary sources, in which other authors have analyzed primary data and organized their presentation (see references).

Any author trying to summarize Polonia in America is bound to be accused of relying too heavily upon Chicago's Polonia. This dependence is partly due to the fact that it is the largest local community and the headquarters of so many organizations. A major library containing materials on Polonia, records of various organizations, and a "morgue" for periodicals spanning many years is located in this city. One of the few remaining dailies in the Polish language is published here and Chicago has been the residence of the researchers connected with the Znaniecki family. Attempts were made, however, to cover events and maintain contacts with the Polonias of other locations, and there are several studies of communities in other parts of the country.

What remains to be stated are the thanks, to the Americans, Poles, Polish Americans, Americans of Polish descent, Americans of Polish heritage, and Americans of other heritage with whom I have discussed at great length the intricacies of ethnicity including the Lopatas, Owsiaks, Burns, Kents, McClures, Benoliels, Jacksons, Kellehers, Goldsteins, Schwartzs, Brehms, Petersons, Petersens, Winchs, Greers, Wayne Wheeler, and, naturally, my multi-identity mother, Eileen Markley Znaniecki.

There have been several other sociologists, in addition to those mentioned above, to whom I owe thanks. Of special importance are Everett Hughes, Louis Wirth, and Herbert Blumer, forming the dissertation committee that sent me out into Polonia after taking one look at my name, and all the faculty from whom I learned sociology at the Universities of Illinois and Chicago. Professor Abel, Felix Gross, Eugene Kleban, Richard Kolm, Danuta Mostwin, Stanley Piwowarski, the Terleckis, Alexander Janta, and others of the Polish Institute of Arts and Sciences in America with whom I have met on several occasions in conferences and with whom I hope to work in an extended study of Polonian communities have also been of great help, as have the Polish sociologists, Nowakowski, Szczepanski, Piotrowski, and Kurzynowski. Thanks also go to Andrew Greeley and his associates for the work they are doing from which I have been able to learn much about the Polish Americans. I am grateful to Hobby (Robert Habenstein) and Charles Mindel for forcing me to do chapters on the "Polish American Family," thus pushing me back into contact with Polonia, and to Milton Gordon for enlightenment, encouragement, and editing.

Of course, this study could not have been started so many years ago or revitalized now without the help of many individuals and groups of Polonia. My information for the dissertation was collected in the years between 1950 and 1954 with the help of Sabina Logish and George Walter of the Polish Roman Catholic Union Library, and the data obtained in recent years with the help of Father Bilinski and his staff. Fathers Ziemba and Chrobot, and Robert Geryk of St. Mary's College and Orchard Lake Center for Polish Studies and Culture, Jan Librach and Franciszek Puslowski of the Polish Institute of Arts and Sciences in America helped me find materials on Polish Americans. The Polish American leaders who have been specially cooperative include Alojzy Mazewski, Roman Pucinski, Judge Adesko, Mitchell Kobelinski, Adela Lagodzinski, Kazimierz Leonard, Robert Lewandowski, the Drs. Rytel, Father Madaj, and Eugene Kusielewicz. Also helpful were the members of the Legion Mlodych Polek (Legion of Young Polish Women), particularly Anna Migon who assisted me on several occasions, the members of the Polish American Congress, the Polish Arts Club, the Council of Polish Arts Clubs, the Polish American Historical Society, the Stowarzyszenie Samopomocu Nowej Emigracji, the Polish American Commercial Club, the Polish Army Veterans Association, the Club Mielec, the Polish Roman Catholic Union, the Polish National Alliance, the Polish Women's Alliance, the Queen Kinga group, Spojnia, the Polish American Club, the Polish Falcons, and the Polish Institute of Arts and Sciences in America.

Eileen Markley Znaniecki aided me in many ways during the early stages of the research, including corrections of my phrasing and spelling, after Everett Hughes OK'd my dissertation with the comment, "Please find someone who knows English; you do not spell of course off course." Milton Gordon, Ed Stanford of Prentice Hall, and three anonymous readers helped with their comments on an earlier draft and Richard Lopata assisted me with the painful process of cutting 130 pages from the "final" draft. Lucille McGill and Carla

Christianson helped to get the printed page in final form and Monica Velasco has earned undying gratitude by the fantastic job she consistently does in juggling everything and meeting deadlines (in spite of the fact that I had promised her that she would not have to be involved in this venture so that she could manage the other projects of the Center for the Comparative Study of Social Roles).

1

Background to the Study of Polonia

This book analyzes the history and current life-styles of Polonia, the structurally complex ethnic community maintained by Polish Americans for over a century with the help of changing ideologies and a highly developed status competition. Several basic sociological concepts form the framework for this analysis: national culture society, political state, country, ethnic community, ethclass, life-style, social life space, and status competition. These are applied specifically to Poland, America, and Polonia.

National Culture Society, Political State, and Country

Polonia, as the Polish American ethnic community is called, is involved in the life of several types of societies. Florian Znaniecki (1952:10–21) developed a fourfold classification of societies that is of special relevance here:

First, *the tribal society,* designated by a distinct name, united by a belief in common ancestors from which its culture was originally derived, and possessing some degree of social integration. Its culture is traditional and non-literate. A tribe occupies a given territory, although it can change it by migration.
Second, *the political society* or state, which has a common legal system and an organized, independent government controlling all the people who inhabit a definite territory.
Third, *the ecclesiastical society,* which has a common and distinct literary, religious culture and an independent, organized church.
Fourth, *the national culture society,* which has a common and distinct secular, literary culture and an independent organization functioning for the preservation, growth, and expansion of this culture.

The concept of tribal society is inappropriate to the present society. We will discuss the ecclesiastical society when analyzing Polonia's relations with the Roman Catholic church.

Polonia is an ethnic community located in the American national culture society with the United States as its political system, but it was founded on the

1

Polish national culture society. Poland existed as a national culture society without its own political state on several occasions. During the long period of 1795-1919 it was partitioned, its territory occupied and its people dominated by three other states, Russia, Prussia, and Austria. The people of the occupied lands defined themselves as three provinces of the Polish nation, while the Polonian community in America considered itself to be the fourth province. The identification of Polonia as the "fourth province of Poland" many years prior, during, and after World War I had a great deal of influence upon the immigrants and émigrés and the formation of their communities. Poland also functioned as a national culture society without a legitimate local government during the Nazi occupation in World War II, the government in exile being located in London and its armies being attached to the armed forces of other political states. Finally, many Poles considered themselves to be without a legitimate government from the "socialist" (communist) period following the war until very recently.

Nationalism is the term usually applied to identification with a national culture, to feelings of solidarity with others who share the same national culture, and to awareness of having such a common bond (Znaniecki 1952). It is accompanied by a resistance to denationalization, that is, to being acculturated into other cultures or assimilated into other societies (Gordon 1964). Societies with a strong national consciousness wish to transmit the shared culture to new generations and sometimes even to people originally from other cultures. This wish is particularly strong among nationalism—developing or defending countries whose leaders try to discourage identification with tribal, folk, or religious units and encourage identification on a national cultural level. Nationalism creates a "common ancestry" for the members of the society (even in the face of inevitable and known biological mixture), and a "national character." Nationalism idealizes the language, customs and total institutions, history, land, and other geographical features of the territory occupied and worked by generations of ancestors. It creates, selects, and symbolizes objects of art, science, literature, architecture, and other tangible or ideational cultural traits created by "our people." It identifies and idealizes heroes, presenting them as typical examples of national character (Schwartz 1987). Nationalism has been intensified in Poland by the partitions, the attempts by the Prussians to Germanize the people, the wars, and the communist control.

Identification with the political state is being referred to here as "patriotism." Political states are usually controlled by a political party or another group that centralizes power through organized agencies (such as the army, the police, the courts, etc.) and that demands loyalty of citizens. The combination of patriotism and nationalism can be a powerful source of social organization, especially when assisted by mass education into both identities, national and state. National culture societies also often try to obtain control over an existing political state or create a new one, and then to solidify this control by increasing the number of members through birth incentives or conquest of neighboring territory. The situations in the former Soviet Union or Yugoslavia are perfect examples of such action. Political states gain support by convincing their members that patriotism is the best means of maintaining the national culture. Both political state and national culture society expansion in recent centuries have used psychological pressures as well as political force to develop nationalism and/or patriotism among populations judged as rightfully belonging to the units and to change conquered peoples. Both ideologies are products of upper classes (socially or politically). For example, the "intelligentsia" of Europe created and defined the national cultures, and, when they had the power, controlled the educational systems by which previously locally educated lower classes became national-ized. According to Thomas and Znaniecki (1918-1920), premodernization Polish peasants limited their identification to the *okolica* or area within which their reputation resided. However, modernization trends of industrialization and urbanization, combined with mass education during independence years have broadened identity of most Poles from the *okolica*, or region, to the national culture society. The conflict between this identity and the actions of the com-munist political state has been continued until the recent victory and attempts to build a new government.

Modern national culture societies and political states are so complex that the common cultural overlap may be only a minor part of any subgroup's life. This is particularly true of peoples not sharing all of the dominant national culture because they are deemed ineligible or unwilling to embrace it. They are often assigned minority status. According to Wirth:

> We may define a minority as a group of people who because of their physical or cultural characteristics, are singled out from the others in the society in which they live for differential and unequal treatment, and who therefore regard themselves as objects of collective discriminations. (1945:348)

The Polish political state as well as the territory occupied by the national culture society contained many minority groups, the most significant one for Poland's history being the Jewish population. We will return to this subject later.

The United States of America is a political state and the national culture society has as its only identifying label "America," much to the discomfort of some Canadians and Mexicans. However, there is simply no other term by which to identify the society and its people. Although there is some debate as to the presence of an overall American culture because of the ethnic heterogeneity of its population, sociological texts have no trouble identifying its basic values. The activities of the political state influence who enters it and what laws apply to both citizens and aliens. The attitudes and activities of the dominant segments of the society influence many aspects of the life-style of immigrants. The language itself forms either a barrier or a facilitator for people entering both units. The United States contains many groups of different origin and depth of ethnicity and racial identity.

The concept of "country" will be used here to refer to the combination of national culture society and political state. There are several concepts used in connection with the migration or movement of peoples from one territory to another. The simple term *migration* does not identify the ownership of the territory. Migration refers to movement within the same country, emigration is used by a country when some of its people leave its territory, and immigration when people of another country enter its territory. These terms are usually identified this way by a political state, but they can be meaningful to a national culture society, such as Poland during its occupation by foreign states. Wygocki (1992:3) makes a very clear distinction between emigration and refugee status: "An emigrant is one who knowingly and voluntarily leaves the fatherland to temporarily or always remain in a foreign country." In the case of post World War II Polish ex-combatants, he then states that the concept *emigrant* does not apply because they left the country involuntarily due to the invasions by Nazis and Soviets and did not return due to communist control following the war. In addition, they still refuse to return because of the continued involvement of communists in the recent Polish government. In general, ex-combatants and others in a similar political situation can be identified, and identify themselves, as refugees. Their choice of host country is of secondary importance to their refusal to return to the home country.

The Ethnic Community and Ethnicity

The concepts connected with ethnicity have been debated by social scientists over the years, changing meaning with changes in the peoples. However, it is possible to combine the characteristics discussed by various authors into a set of associated concepts (Ware 1931; Gordon 1964; Kramer 1970; Breton 1964; Etzioni 1959). An ethnic community consists of:

1. A group of people, rather than a demographic collectivity, who share a culture, a consciousness of kind, and a web of relations
2. Sharing an ethnic culture, distinctive from and marginal to the dominant culture, independently developed and limited to this community alone, based on a national culture of a society living elsewhere, but modified by adaptation to a new environment and changing over time
3. Identifying with this culture and with each other through various forms of solidarity
4. Living in a society dominated by a different national culture, or several different cultures

5. Being relatively concentrated in residentially distinctive communities, although not necessarily in a single location or set of locations, some members even scattered outside of community centers
6. Sharing a network of organizations and informal social relations of varying degrees of institutional completeness so that members *can*, but do not necessarily need to, limit their significant and important interactions to its confines.

The point about the independence, or at least relative independence, of the ethnic community from local territoriality by requiring member concentration and institutional centralization and control is an important one in terms of the American society (Etzioni 1959). Gusfield (1975:44–52) pictures communities of "my people" as arenas of situated action with communal networks. These can be extended over territories occupied also by other groups, with various forms of social contact.

We can distinguish the following ranges of residential and organizational subunits in the Polonian community. In the first place, there is the local *neighborhood* having a more or less strong concentration of Polish Americans, with some form of institutional network tying together the parish, the local clubs, the social services, and so on. People living in the same neighborhood often come into daily contact with each other. The next type of ethnic concentration is the *settlement*, which is generally made up of more than one neighborhood and usually has greater institutional completeness. Several such settlements form a *local ethnic community*, that is too large to operate on the basis of face-to-face contact alone, causing it to develop more complex forms of communication. Between it and the total *ethnic community* within a single society there may be *regional* groupings of several local communities and of isolated settlements that are not part of a local community. Polonia thus contains what Hunter (1974:12) identifies as a "natural" local community social structure in combination with a "proliferation of purposively organized local community voluntary associations which serve to integrate members into the social structure and symbolic culture of the local community." I do not agree that the voluntary associations replace the "natural" structure, at least not in the case of Polonia.

American Polonia is united by ties of organization, mass communication, and personal relations and interaction. When Poles in Poland talk of Polonia in general they are referring to all the communities of Poles settled outside of the territory occupied centrally by this national culture society. However, the Polonias in different parts of the world have developed different relations with the mother country, depending on mutual interests and its definition of how far they have drifted in culture and identity away from the national ideal. American Polonia is differentiated from, for example, the Canadian or Australian Polonias in that the society in which it is located adds special flavor because of its national structure and culture. From now on, reference to Polonia will be to the one in America, unless otherwise indicated.

Polonia does not have the cultural or structural completeness typical of a national or regional culture society. Nor does it have the political power of a political state, since it is dependent upon the dominant American society and state. However, it has a life and vitality of its own, and it is possible to study it and those Poles and Polish Americans who have contributed to this life.

Ethnic Americans

Polonia is an ethnic community created and maintained by Poles and Polish Americans. However, not all people who could be so identified have been involved with and contributed to Polonia. The questions of who is an ethnic and what is an ethnic population have bothered social scientists for years. In general, certain conditions appear to be needed in order for "ethnic Americans" to exist as a researchable entity. In the first place, there must be an identifiable ethnic community, with a culture floating between the home national society's culture and that of America or any of its other ethnic groups. In the second place there must be, in the symbolic world of people in the larger society as well as in the community, an ethnic identity such as Polish American (Italian American, Jewish American, etc.). It is usually summarized in a label and by indicators, a package of presumed characteristics that serve as a means of identifying persons to whom the label can be attached by the self or others. In American society, the package usually contains a name, sometimes speech and behavioral patterns, customs and rituals that make the persons different from representatives of other ethnic groups, and an assumed position in the society at large. Physical appearance that differentiates people from the dominant group can produce instant labeling, even if mistaken, as in the case of many immigrants from the Far East (are they Koreans, Vietnamese, Chinese?). Identification by the name of country of origin, or by answers to ancestry questions are also used to place people in an ethnic identity. However, an ethnic culture can be quite heterogeneous, differentiated for example by social class, what Gordon (1964) calls "ethclass." In the case of Polish Americans, there has been a strong division between folk and national cultures, exemplified by language and knowledge of Polish history and artistic achievement. There are also regional divisions, although they are not as strong. However, there are many questions that remain unanswered in discussions of ethnic Americans. One wonders if people identify themselves as Yugoslav Americans in modern times, or even in the years of the existence of that political state. How much of a folk or nationally based ethnic culture must be experienced and evidenced by people before they can be identified as belonging to that ethnic group? What about newcomers in America who come from the home country but do not identify with its ethnic community and do not share the variations produced in the original culture by its life? When does the ethnic identity wear so thin as to be meaningless in daily life? In other words, what are the boundaries of ethnic identification?

Social scientists have frequently found a gap between what the "insiders" of an ethnic group consider is true of themselves and what "outsiders" assume to be true. A typical situation in America is that outsiders impose negative, demeaning character upon people identified as ethnics of a certain group. The people so labeled who are aware of the characterization may respond in several ways, if possible: build and stay within their own self-image, withdraw from contact, ignore those aspects of interaction in which the negative identity is introduced by others, or fight the stereotype. Of course, some people can change their ethnic identity if there is no outward sign of it. The Nazis had to put arm bands on Jews, because they could not otherwise identify them. Changing names is a frequent means of passing out of an ethnic group.

Self-identification with an ethnic group can become part of a pervasive identity that cannot be ignored, like gender or racial identity. It can lead others to assumptions of whole personality and enter all social interaction, with those assumed to be similar, and those assumed to be very different. Being labeled a "Polish American" may affect how a person acts, the traits he or she calls forth in the self, and the behavior offered to or received from others.[1] We are concerned here with identifying Polish Americans because of our interest in Polonia. The content and consequences of ethnic identity upon life-styles are discussed in chapter 5.

Of course, social scientists and members of ethnic communities are always interested in the population of potential members. Unfortunately there have been no uniform methods of determining the parameters of such populations, since they depend on the nature of the questions, which vary from study to study. Americans have had problems identifying their potential ethnics due to the failure of the U. S. Bureau of the Census and other information-gathering sources to include relevant questions. Until recently, residents have been asked only place of birth of self, of father, and of mother. In 1979 and 1980 the census finally included an ancestry question. Respondents were asked to list all national identities and multiple or mixed responses were coded (Lieberson and Waters 1988: 6–7). An instruction guide clarified the question:

> Ancestry (or origin or descent) may be viewed as the nationality group, the lineage, or country in which the person or the person's parents or ancestors were born before their arrival in the United States. Persons who are of more than one origin and who cannot identify with a single group should print their multiple ancestry (for example, German-Irish).

This simply provides a listing of ancestry that respondents wish to identify. Lieberson and Waters 1988) devote considerable analysis to the results. The total number of persons listing Polish ancestry in the 1980 census is 8,228, 000 and 78 percent of these reported a mixed background (Lieberson and Waters 1988: 34, 45). Polonian leaders had used the inflated figure of 12 million Americans of Polish descent in political pronouncements (Mazewski, quoted in Zmurkiewicz 1972:10). We will discuss these figures in greater detail in chapter 3.

Definition of ancestry obviously does not insure membership and active involvement in an ethnic community. There are thus "layers" of ethnicity possible in America. The most ethnic would be a person proclaiming specific ethnic identity, active in community affairs, associating with co-ethnics, observant of cultural events and norms, reflecting the ethnic culture in personal relations, having a working knowledge of the home language with its local variations, sharing knowledge of both the folk and the national culture of the home country, and cognizant of the position of the ethnic community in the wider society. The least ethnic would probably be a person who identifies him or herself as of a certain ancestry but does not carry this any farther.

Luckily for social scientists, and for those who are interested in ethnicity in America, there is a wealth of information in the historical and current descriptions of the life-styles of many Americans with ethnic identity that can be used here. It is contained in studies of specific local communities undertaken by historians, political scientists, and sociologists, and in a variety of publications, newspapers, magazines, and radio programs produced by ethnic organizations.

The Polonian Ethnic Community

Certain factors contribute to the fate of an immigrant group in the host society. The major one is physical difference from the dominant group, both discardable differences, such as clothing, and permanent ones such as skin color. Next is the degree and form of cultural difference. Both influence consciousness of kind as well as the attitudes of the dominant society, often the amount of prejudice and discrimination. The larger the size of the immigrant waves, the more the newcomers are able to create institutionally complex ethnic communities that serve to protect against change, and the greater the probability of negative treatment. The more recent their arrival, the less likely they are to have acculturated, that is, absorbed the local culture. The composition of the migrant wave is also important, as evidenced by the "golden" early migrants from Cuba. The more educated, urbanized, and "modern" the people, the easier it is for them to assimilate structurally, even if they retain their national culture (Gordon 1964). Ties to the home country can influence orientation to the host country, especially if they are based on the assumption of return.

Several characteristics of the Polish Americans make them similar to, as well as different from, other ethnic groups. Although there were political émigrés during the early years of America's history, the majority of the Poles who emigrated here during the years of the first wave (1880–1920s) resembled other European migrant groups of high immigration in that they came from lower-class rural and agricultural areas, had little formal education, lacked familiarity with the cosmopolitan world, were confronted with a very foreign society, and had no "calling cards" guaranteeing positive social contact and interaction with the dominant groups. Most Europeans had a physical advantage over black and oriental immigrants in that their physical characteristics of clothing and manner were easily discarded; they were able to blend in with the general population through the acculturation process (Gordon 1964).

Like many other immigrants, Poles tended to huddle together in urban subcommunities that had clear physical or social boundaries isolating them from the rest of society. Also, like all other immigrants, the Poles were unable to reproduce the social structure and way of life of their homeland, so these communities developed and maintained a new product: marginal to both the country of origin and that of settlement. Polonia was thus created.

The Poles in America are different from other ethnic groups in several ways. First, they entered the United States in three waves that varied considerably in social class and nationalistic identification. The first wave came here between 1880 and the 1920s.[2] These people are for the most part no longer alive, and their descendants are called by various labels depending upon generation. The second wave, or *nowa emigracja* consisted of peoples displaced by World War II. The labels "Displaced Persons" (DPs) and "refugees" contain their own meanings within Polonia. Those who have come most recently are identified in different ways, depending on historical time in Poland and America's classification system. They are quota immigrants, refugees, and nonimmigrants on temporary visas. The importance of the distinctions will become apparent in following chapters. In general we can call these the newest wave, or cohort, or as Erdmans (1992; see also chapter 8) does, "New Poles." The presence of a very large number of these recent short-term and other new cohort Poles has strongly influenced the community.

Polonia as the ethnic community is also unique in the history of its relation to the home country.[3] Many political émigrés and temporary residents reflected the nationalistic activity in Poland during times of foreign occupation or in consequence of communist control. They entered as refugees or came to obtain Polonia's help for political and military activity for Poland. Generals Pulaski and Kosciuszko were of the first type; the pianist, Paderewski, was of the second. The political émigrés were, and are, rather numerous. Although the traffic back and forth to and from Europe was brisk, those who paused in America helped develop a complex ethnic community, with multiple publications and organizations.

In general, whether identified as political émigrés or economic immigrants, most Poles came for what they defined as a temporary stay and did not plan on becoming "Americanized."[4] The great waves of economic migrants came to earn money, invest in property, and wait for the right opportunity to return to Poland and buy land there that would assure them a desirable social status within the familiar world of a limited reference group. A large number of them actually returned to Poland during the interwar years. The presence of economic emigrants is still visible in the 1990s, as we shall see. Of course, immigrants from other societies often dreamed of returning to the homeland, but unlike them, the Poles displayed an unusual lack of interest in American society and in acquiring traits that could gain them a higher social status in America. Since all the ills of life in Poland could be blamed on foreign occupation, the emigrants did not even resent the Polish upper classes as much as the immigrants of other European countries detested the top layers of their home countries. Their relation with the mother country has been, in fact, unique; the contact has been constant, multileveled, and of great importance to Polonia's life. Poland as an independent political state has attempted to exert other types of influence upon its Polonias, but with less effect than when those living outside could claim to represent and perform political and humanitarian actions on behalf of the national culture society lacking a state structure. This is an important aspect of Polonia's relations with Poland.

Another unusual feature of this ethnic group is the internal heterogeneity of the culture brought over by each of the three waves, by social class, province, urban-rural residence, and characteristics of the society from which they came. The Poland that the first wave left behind was very different from that of the second and especially the newest waves. Until the middle rungs of social structure was filled out, the early Polish immigrants brought with them two major subcultures, that of the gentry and that of the peasants. The ethnic community evidences the effects of these two subcultures, both in the way it integrates them and in the internal conflict among persons and groups focusing on variations of the folk or of the national (urban, educated, "modern") culture.

The combination of factors enabled the Polish Americans to build a complex and inwardly oriented ethnic community, while they were unsuited for immediate involvement in the larger society and easy interaction with its members.[5] Polonia contains thus several adult generations from two of the waves plus young people of the third. The coming of political émigrés of the second, World War II wave and of the newest "wavelets" revived Polonia's vitality.

The cultures that the Poles brought with them to America diverged considerably from those already established here. An example of the difference between the Poles, even with the complexities of internal variation, and American culture can be seen in religion. Although their major religion was Catholic, they had their own saints, spoke Polish during ceremonies and confessionals, and had special ways of celebrating important events. In America, they immediately entered into so strong a conflict with the Roman Catholic church that part of the community broke away to form a Polish National Catholic church.

The very size of the Polish immigrant group contributed to its social isolation from the rest of society in two ways. In the first place, the numbers made possible the creation of relatively self-sufficient local ethnic communities. In the second place, the combination of size and community isolation increased the prejudice and discrimination from other groups. They were also the last of the Europeans to enter in such large waves (with the exception of Italians in some areas of the country).

The complexity of the Polish American ethnic community, founded upon the original and continued heterogeneity of the immigrant and temporary resident population, was assisted by what may be one of the major characteristics of Polonia: a highly individualistic status competition. Polonia not only developed a complex status competitive structure, but also it has been able to motivate even second, third, fourth, and fifth generations of Polish Americans to concentrate their energies and concerns in its direction. This competition reinforces other community-binding characteristics, feelings of "peoplehood," of minority status, of uniqueness, and of sharing a difficult life in the country of settlement (Gordon 1964). It also reinforced internal focus and prevented the use of status-gaining resources of the dominant society if they were not part of the community's sources. Thus, Polish Americans neglected until recently the use of higher education, in contrast to Jewish Americans, who took advantage of this important means of gaining status.

Status Competition

Sociologists have long recognized the presence of status hierarchies and status competition among different social units, individuals, families, organizations, and even nations. They have been mainly interested in the effects of such competition upon individuals and the macro social structure.[6] Status competition serves as a useful organizing concept in analyzing Polonia because it forms an important part of community life, with both positive and negative consequences. This does not mean that other ethnic communities lack such a motivating force, only that I find it strong among Poles and Polish Americans, and so do the Polish Americans themselves.[7]

American literature dealing with status competition is often negatively oriented, contending that it is "undemocratic" or dysfunctional to human happiness and the social system (see Packard 1959, 1962). In fact, though, such competition can hold a community together and give life meaning to its members. This appears to be the situation in Polonia.

Social status may be defined as a location assigned to an individual, a social group, or other social object by a larger social unit in a complicated prestige hierarchy. In order to have a status system we need the following conditions:

1. A set of criteria of prestige characteristics; for example, it is more prestigious to own more expensive, larger things than to own things that are small and inexpensive
2. A set of items, such as cars, homes, and pay checks, that can be measured by the degree to which they have the prestigious characteristics
3. A hierarchical ladder with defined rungs
4. A sufficiently precise method of measuring the degree to which a given item possesses the measured characteristic to determine its location on a particular rung in the hierarchical ladder
5. A method of communicating such locations to relevant persons, who can then combine this knowledge with information on how that item fares in other status hierarchies based on other sets of criteria.

A person can be located in a particular status position from her or his location in a combination of the following hierarchies: the prestige of the family into which he or she is born, prestige of associates, education, occupation, income, residence, age, gender, race, organizational membership, ownership and use of material objects, family behavior, and general life-style.

In all societies and their subunits, even villages—in spite of the simplistic view of peasant communities so typical of our nostalgia for the past—the various sources of status available to any individual or family within a single social class are sufficiently complex and flexible to enable a competition for what may be called "status points" vis-à-vis other individuals, families, or larger social groups within the community, nation, or cosmopolitan world. Even when the personal status is dependent upon the status of the family unit through generations, an individual may acquire status points or insure the loss of some by others against whom she or he is competing through the use of established sources. Often the competition is facilitated by cooperation from close associates who benefit from the rise of the principal status achiever. Families, employees, friends, and neighbors may combine efforts to help an individual raise his or her social position vis-à-vis others within the group in which the competition is significant, permissible, or possible. Some groups are out of range for such competition.

The "products" of status ascription or achievement include: a personal and family "reputation," that is, an overall status as a community-known crystallization of ranks in several status hierarchies; specific advantages (or disadvantages) in daily life and within each social role that come from the overall position; influence or power in interactional scenes that is not based on role-related authority; access to certain roles, objects, and experiences that are status related; and life chances of children.

The process by which a person is placed into a more or less crystallized location is dependent on several social variables. In the first place, there must be a community within which her or his "reputation" is known, that is, a community of people who share status hierarchies and know him or her well enough to undertake the process of ranking and of communicating the ranks to each other (called *okolica* in Polish). This is one of the major functions of gossip, the better known one being social control. The dissemination of knowledge about a person, accompanied by the weighing of criteria and gradual crystallization of personal status, always in comparison with other persons, is assisted by gossip. The basic unit of status may be a family or group or a town, but there has to be a broader unit that is able to compare the universe of subunits, which are going through the ranking procedures. If we stick to the criterion of "reputation," we see that there is no need to limit status competition to territorially bound communities. Another prerequisite for the status competition is the willingness to enter it and to go through the process of classifying other members of the community.

We should keep in mind that people use only those sources of status that are developed and acknowledged within the community. The fact that other sources of status are available in the broader society, or that the sources used internally are not acceptable to other groups (and can even become sources of prejudice against the community) is evident in any study of intergroup relations. The dominant group establishes its status hierarchies by selecting some aspects of life for positive and others for negative evaluation. What is prestigious among the people of India's Brahmin caste, for example, may not be a source of high status in America. Many an immigrant has been dismayed when the new society found his or her status symbols meaningless or, worse still, repulsive.

Polish Americans are very much interested and involved in status competition on all levels. The complexity, breadth, and decrystallization of traditional status roles has made it possible for most members of the community to compete at different levels. Participation is possible for the immigrant woman who does not speak English or literary Polish, and whose whole life is restricted to her neighborhood. She has many sources for accumulating status points, competing not against men or upper-class women, but against her "almost" peers. The presence of Polonia as a superterritorial ethnic community enables people to obtain reputations within it and even venture out to gain reputations in the Polish and/or American societies directly or as representatives of the community.

Life-Style and Social Life Space

Each family unit and each independent person weaves the aspects of daily life into a fabric sociologists define as life- style. A life-style is exactly that, the "style" with which individuals or families go through life, which places them into one of several, sometimes overlapping, societal strata and companionate circles of association. As Form and Stone (1970) have pointed out, people and groups vary considerably in the symbols they use to build and identify life-styles, but alternate patterns of styles emerge within communities of more than a few families. These patterns are known to inhabitants, and are used as a criteria for judgment and association. Components of life styles include place and type of work; the sources and amounts of income; the rhythm and relative proportion of direction of expenditures; use of consumer objects such as homes, furniture, cars, or boats; use of time and recreational activities; community involvement and relationships to others; rituals connected with eating, loving, and playing; ways of rearing children; deference and demeanor vis-à-vis other people; values and worldviews; and so forth.

The social life space of a person covers the territory within which she or he moves during involvements in all the social roles that form the role cluster. The boundaries of the social life space are at the cutoff of the web of social relations. The space can be institutionally flat, as when the person limits main role involvements to one institution (e.g., the family), or multidimensional, encompassing several institutional areas.

Having defined our basic concepts and given a brief background of Polish Americans, we can now examine the socialization processes of Poland and the relations that Polish immigrants developed, maintained, and modified with that national culture society after arriving in America. We will then analyze the life and social organization they developed in their own community Polonia, and their relationship with American society. Ethnic communities that arose out of a migration from a national culture society into another national or political society must somehow work out all three sets of relations, with the mother country, among themselves internally, and with the host society and its other subunits.

Notes

1. In recent years sociologists have become convinced of the need to change the sexist nature of the English language, which has consistently neglected the female half of the human species. Although techniques for de-sexing it have not been fully worked out in mutual consensus, I consider it of sufficient importance to use one of the suggested versions in my own publications.
2. The internal labeling identifies these as "stara emigracja" or old emigration. Note the term *emigration*, which accentuates the process of leaving the home country rather than entering a new country.
3. Few other ethnic groups have been so influenced by the home country as have the Polonians. For example, Fallows (1979) devotes only a very short paragraph to "ties with Ireland," claiming that most Irish Americans do not even know their family ties, let alone ties with the political state or the national culture society.
4. Although other immigrant groups, such as the Italians, also felt some reluctance to declare permanent settlement in America, observers of the Polish peasant in America report a firmness of their original commitment to return to Poland (Thomas and Znaniecki 1958, 2: 1496). Of course, the declaration of planned return helps assay

guilty feelings over leaving friends and relatives, or "deserting" the homeland. This has been particularly true when the emigrant's country was in a difficult situation, as in recent years in Poland. The Jews coming from Russia or Russian-occupied Poland were not pulled in two directions; they settled in America for good (Goldstein and Goldscheider 1968).

5. The Polish Americans definitely distinguish the "old emigration," that came to America prior to World War II (which means mainly around World War I), from the "new emigration," that arrived here during and after World War II.

6. There is an extensive literature on status decrystallization, summarized by Burton (1972) in an unpublished dissertation entitled "Status Consistency and Secondary Stratification Characteristics in an Urban Metropolis." The concept of identity decrystallization follows the same line of conceptualization.

7. Stress upon status competition is also an important part of my theoretical framework, while it is not used as much in analyses of other ethnic communities, within which some of the same patterns emerge.

2

Home and Host Countries

In order to understand an ethnic community, especially Polonia, we must have some familiarity with the national cultural society upon which it was originally based as well as the one in which it developed: Poland and America.

Poland

The historical relationship of national culture society and political state makes Poland a sociologically interesting country. The two types of societies—national and political—do not necessarily exist at the same time and in the same place (Znaniecki 1952). The Polish political state has extended over many different tribal, folk, and later national culture groups. The national society has survived without any political state on several occasions. People scattered among many nations and political states have identified with Poland's national society and have interacted with each other across borders and oceans. This phenomenon strongly affected what happened in Polonia.

A Brief History

Szczepanski (1970:6-13) identifies four major periods in Polish history prior to 1772: the *Kingdom Period* (960 to 1138), during which Poland became organized as an independent nation; the *Duchy Period* (1138 to 1320), during which the kingdom dissolved into smaller units lacking a central power; the *Empire Period* (1320-1572), known as Poland's "Golden Age," when the kingdom was unified, beginning with the reign of Casimir the Great and became the third largest in Europe (see also Tschan et al. 1942:664); and the *Period of Elective Kings* (1572 to 1772) when Poland experienced the first partition. The country was weakened in the years prior to the partition by the introduction of the *liberum veto* in the Sejm (Parliament), allowing any deputy to stop the passage of any bill.

The first partition of Poland between Russia, Prussia, and Austria took place in 1772 and the second in 1792. The final partition in 1795 wiped it from the map of Europe as an independent political state. During the period of foreign occupation both Prussia and Russia made efforts to de-Polonize the people by forbidding the use of Polish language in schools, restricting education, and, in the case of the Germans, devising various means of getting the Poles off the land. Austria was more lenient with its Polish sector, but the area suffered from a great deal of poverty. As a result of the oppression and poverty, extensive emigration of political refugees, peasants, and landless laborers took place in the years prior to World War I.

During the period of foreign occupation, the national culture society was maintained with the help of the nationalistically conscious intelligentsia and a flexible social organization tying together the Poles in the three provinces and those living as political or economic émigrés abroad. Numerous uprisings against the occupying powers were followed by political emigration and the formation of two competing governments-in-exile. Each side defined one of the two major enemies, Russia or Prussia, as the lesser evil with whom cooperation was possible in the struggle for independence. Polonia abroad also had to take sides with one or the other camp.

Poland did not regain political independence until after World War I in 1918. It then immediately plunged into war with Russia to regain lands it considered Polish, settling down to rebuild the country in 1920. In the interwar years between 1920 and 1939 the Polish government made gains in education, industrialization, and land reform, but the country was not militarily strong enough to stop the Nazis in 1939.

World War II tore Poland apart in many ways:

> Poland paid the highest price of all the belligerent nations: of the 35 million prewar citizens of Poland, over 6 million perished; that is 220 out of every 1,000 were killed. . . . Only about 66,000 Poles, however, were killed in active battle. The rest died in bombed cities, in prisons, and, above all, in concentration camps. (Szczepanski 1970:34)

The Nazis considered *untermenschen* all "non-Aryans," in which category they placed both Catholic and Jewish Poles. They organized a complex system of extermination in concentration and death camps of two categories of Poles: the intelligentsia and approximately 3 million Polish Jews. In addition, they forcibly transported Poles out of the area they incorporated into Germany, and used Poles for labor in several camps in Germany, while "political prisoners" were held in prisons and concentration camps.

Zubrzycki (1956:51-61) lists two main forms of population movements affecting both military personnel and civilians during the war years: the voluntary movement of refugees, and the forced expulsions and transfers of people by the conquerors. "To the first category there belongs, to begin with, a mass flight of the Polish population before the rapid advance of the German army in September 1939" (51). Many of these refugees crossed into Rumania, Hungary, and Latvia. Using figures of the International Labour Office and one of the main histories of World War II in Poland, Zubrzycki estimates that there were 32,000 Polish civilians and 70,000 soldiers interned in those countries by the end of 1939. The voluntary movement also included many young Poles who escaped in following years to join the Polish armed forces fighting in other parts of the world.

The mass expulsions and forced transfers included those carried out by the Germans, which "until the end of 1940 affected about 1,500,000 persons (1,200,000 Poles and 300,000 Jews)" (Zubrzycki:52). "The second mass transfer of this sort was organized by the Soviet Union in the Eastern Areas of Poland between October 1939 and June 1941" (52). "The Polish government in exile estimated the number at one and a half million, while the Institute of Jewish affairs in the U.S.A. put it at two million, of whom 600,000 were Jews." Finally, an estimated 3.5 million Poles were deported to work in Germany.

Much of the country was destroyed during the World War II invasions and the movement of the Germans across Poland in their attack on the Soviet Union and subsequent retreat. According to Szczepanski (1970:34), 800,000 Poles died in Warsaw, comprising two-thirds of its prewar population, during the battle at the beginning of the war and the two uprisings. In spite of their losses, the Poles, accustomed to fighting the occupying forces, organized an underground army of 380,000 which was reputedly one of the most efficient in Europe (see Karski 1944, *Story of a Secret State*). The émigrés formed a government-in-exile, located first in Paris, then in London.

After the war, Poland was taken over by a communist (socialist) government, organized with the help of the Soviet Union and opposed to the government-in-exile. As a result of this political move, many of the refugees, displaced persons, and ex-combatants refused to return to Poland, having very strong feelings against the Soviet Union for its action early in World War II and nationalistic dislike for Russia dating back to the czarist period. The purposeful extermination of peoples and the refusal of the émigrés to return, left Poland short of young people, particularly young men, and the top social classes, particularly bourgeoisie and the intelligentsia.

Poland underwent two political subperiods since World War II, the first under a harsh and highly restrictive Stalinist atmosphere behind the "iron curtain." Poles were not allowed to emigrate or even to travel outside the communist countries, and the society had many characteristics of a police state. Uprisings of workers, plus changes in the Soviet Union and Polish political scenes, resulted in a partial "thawing" of the political control over the society, starting in 1956.[1] Contact with the West increased, facilitated by the traditional Polish orientation in that direction. One indicator of increased freedom was the reintroduction of sociology into universities. However, censorship continued and the communists definitely remained in power (Davies 1984: 593).

Industrialization was pushed at great speed through centralized planning, often at the cost of the environment. Urbanization was rapid and free education, albeit in only a communistically approved, authoritarian style, received high priority (Davies 1984:603). The Roman Catholic church has been a very strong influence in the country, being both a symbol and an organized force against the communist party and the government. Revolts against the system occurred in 1968, 1970, 1976, and 1980. A number of people left the country at these times, many coming to the United States.

Stefan Nowak (1981:49), an internationally noted Polish sociologist, published in the *Scientific American* the results of 25 years of surveys of Polish social values and attitudes. He and his colleagues found a homogenization of these with little change over time, due to the strength of the educational and communication systems, starting in the Stalinist period which he defined not as a melting pot but a "grinding mill." Organizing the population into four occupational categories, of unskilled worker, skilled worker, nonmanual worker, and intelligentsia, they found all groups giving the following hierarchal order of values: the self, the family, friends, and the nation as a whole. No group existed between the primary and the broadest identity. Freedom of speech was also highly valued and most people expressed great frustration, political irritation, and social apathy due to their inability to reach their social ideals. Synak (1990:6) defined the early 1980s as a crisis of legitimacy. It was under these circumstances that Solidarity developed and gained strength. Nowak (1981:53) credits the movement with "elimination of the feeling of powerlessness and [in] the restoration of people's dignity." Although the government tried to squash it through the imposition of martial law in December 1981, Solidarity finally won, with the "round table" agreements of 1989 between the government and the opposition allowing for "almost" free elections ("almost" because a block of seats in the Parliament were reserved for the communists [Erdmans 1992a]). Poland was the first Soviet bloc nation to win independence from communism and, indirectly, Soviet control. Other Eastern European nations followed, and the Soviet Union collapsed soon after.

Synak (1990:7) and many other observers note that the transition from "state society to civil society" and to market economy and privatization has been very difficult due to a number of factors, including psychological anomie or the feeling of meaninglessness inherited from the past. The proliferation of political parties, each with its own leadership and solutions for problems, indicates that the status competition is still strong.[2]

Both the political and the economic problems have driven many Poles from the country, in temporary, permanent, or indefinite emigration, often to the

United States. Of course, it is often difficult to determine the major base for emigration and immigration. Political states usually make the classification on the basis of their definition of the situation, evident in the process by which passports and visas are issued. For example, Poles were not allowed to emigrate during much of the communist period and those who found a way to leave were classified by the United States as political refugees. Now that the communist system is officially gone from Poland, the immigrants are classified as coming for economic reasons.

Composition of the Population:

The inhabitants of Poland were not all of Polish extraction during the years of emigration to the United States:

> In round figures, as of January 1, 1939, Poland had 35,500,000 inhabitants, which included approximately 5,000,000 Ukrainians, 1,900,000 White Russians, 800,000 Germans and 3,400,000 Jews (about 400,000 of the latter listed themselves in the census as being of the Hebrew religion, but of Polish nationality). (Ehrenpreis and Kridl 1946:391).

Generally speaking, the changing political boundaries of that part of Europe, and the strength of political, religious, and national loyalties resulted in an uneasy relation in Poland between the dominant segment composing two-thirds of the population and the different minority groups. The Jews "were granted an asylum in the more tolerant Polish principalities under charters such as that conferred by Boleslaw the Pius of Greater Poland in 1264" (Boswell 1950:105). A large number of Jews with a variety of backgrounds immigrated to Poland in the ensuing centuries (escaping persecution in countries such as England and Spain), resulting in a highly diversified minority. Prior to the great migration to the United States, Poland contained "four-fifths of world Jewry" (Davies 1984: 240). Their relations with the dominant group and other minorities went through vicissitudes of cooperation and hostility, depending on historical events and on their location in rural or urban areas, within the social class hierarchy, and in the different regions of Poland.

Scattered in villages or the shtetls of small towns, Jews were visibly different and retained the posture of strangers because of the functions they performed for the non-Jewish community.[3] Jews often undertook commercial and other money-exchanging activities forbidden to the Poles and marginal to the Polish peasant culture, as did the Chinese (Fallers 1967) and other groups entering a society to become its middle-men and merchants, operating between the upper and lower classes.

Fictional and sociological descriptions of village life in Poland (Reymont 1925; Thomas and Znaniecki 1918-1920) often made reference to the marginal position and function of the Jews. The Polish peasant usually distrusted and feared the person upon whom he or she was or could be economically dependent. Political officials and the gentry often used the Jews to impose their taxes or enforce the purchase of their products. Both *The Slavonic Encyclopedia* (Roucek 1949) and *The Cambridge History of Poland* (Reddaway et al. 1950) state that the poverty of the peasants in eastern Poland became so severe at one time that the

> results of such a situation were the disastrous happenings after 1658, when the peasants of Eastern provinces joined the Cossacks, who were better off, being armed, and a part of them receiving government pay. Together they started a massacre of the gentry, the Jesuits and the Jews. (Bruckner 1950:566–567)

Hostility against the Jews was particularly strong in the eastern part of Poland when under Russian rule. The Russians had not allowed Jews within their borders in prior centuries and did not know what to do with the vast numbers that came with the territory that they had acquired with the partitions of Poland. Starting in 1881 with the reign of Alexander III, "physical assaults," and "expulsions and limitations of rights of Jews became the order of the day and led to great expulsion from Moscow, 1891 . . . and strict segregation within the limits of the Pale of Settlement," or district within which the Jews were forced to locate (Roucek 1949:553). Another factor contributing to the hostility of the Poles toward the Jews, according to *The Slavonic Encyclopedia* (Roucek 1949) was the activity of the Catholic church which, through its councils and parishes, pushed for restrictive legislation.

The Jews living in partitioned Poland under Austrian rule had more rights than did Jews elsewhere. Gradually, more and more Jews moved into cities, contributing to the expanding middle classes along with those Poles who had been freed from the medieval restrictions on their occupations. As late as 1939, only "about 10 percent of the Polish Jews, however, regarded themselves as part of the Polish nation and used the Polish language in everyday life" (Ehrenpreis and Kridl 1946:392). Thus, the vast majority of the Jews was not well assimilated.[4]

The hostility between the Christian and Jewish Poles is apparent from their failure to form joint ethnic communities in America. The Jews tended to settle with other Jews, regardless of their country of prior settlement. The other minorities in Poland (the Ruthenians, Ukrainians, and Germans) were also alienated from the Poles in America. Only among the intelligentsia in America did the lines of difference and hostility between the Jew and the non-Jew from Poland lessen (Gordon 1964).

Social Class Structure in the Twentieth Century

Prior to World War I, there were two separate class systems in Poland, one in the country and one in the city (Thomas and Znaniecki 1918–1920/1958:128–

40). The country hierarchy was still the more important of the two because Poland was an agrarian society. It was made up of:

1. *"A few families of great nobility."* Some had royal or aristocratic titles, but these were obtained from political or religious sources outside of Poland, which operated as a democracy of the nobility and the clergy
2. *"Numerous middle nobility"*
3. *"Peasant nobility,"* a class found only in Poland, characterized by coats of arms and some political rights, but lacking the financial resources such as serfs or extended lands of the regular nobility:
   (a) "village nobility"
   (b) "bed nobility" (referring to their small beds of land)
   (c) "grey nobility"
4. *"Peasant farmers,"* including:
   (a) "crown peasants" (almost completely free but having no political rights)
   (b) "church peasants" (under control of the church)
   (c) "private serfs" (of landowners, mainly nobility)
5. *Landless peasants,* called *komocniki,* who hired themselves out to work on the land of others; regarded as highly inferior since they lacked economic independence.

Szczepanski (1970:23-26) shows how the country hierarchy was woven into a national society hierarchy with the city strata in the interwar years:

1. *Estate owning nobility* were "highly conscious of their long-held historical role as the leading class of the nation," which includes the first two classes of the country nobility
2. *Owners of large and medium-sized enterprises,* industrial, commercial, and financial; members of this lower-upper class had arrived in this urban strata relatively recently
3. *The intelligentsia* "was a highly differentiated and stratified class composed of all kinds of white-collar people and intellectuals
4. *The middle and lower middle class* (petit bourgeoisie) "were the owners of small enterprises—handicrafts, commercial shops, and all kinds of service establishments (11 percent of the population)"
5. *The peasantry* was "the most numerous class in Polish society during the interwar years"; included owners of all farms up to 50 hectares (52 percent of the population)
6. *"The working class,* in the Marxist sense of the term—that is, gainfully employed manual workers possessing none of their own tools of work and getting their living from selling their labor"—included 20 percent of the population, counting families:
   (a) skilled workers, (few in number)
   (b) semiskilled, (the most numerous)

    (c)   unskilled, (mostly domestic servants)

    (d)   farm laborers on farms and estates, (9 percent of the population)

7. *Various marginal elements,* beggars, vagrants, the permanently un-
employed, the mentally retarded who were not under treatment in medical
establishments, and the like; their numbers have never been accurately
ascertained.

Special mention must be made again of the intelligentsia and the peasantry
and the relation between them. The intelligentsia, different from the American
intellectual class, played an important function in the formation of the Polish
national culture society through the selection, creation, and integration of
cultural items and complexes, through dissemination of this culture to other
classes of society, and through the building of national consciousness and
solidarity (Znaniecki 1952). The national culture so developed contained two
images of national character, one for the intelligentsia, the other for the peasantry, which influenced the relations between these groups not only in Poland but
also in America. The intelligentsia's image focused on "the cultured man,
participating widely in the nation's cultural heritage, a man with knowledge of
history, literature, the arts and good manners" (Szczepanski 1962:408). Other
qualities included individualism, a highly developed feeling of honor and
personal dignity, "intransigence to subordination," and inability to organize
collectively for any long-term efforts. The image also included a strong emphasis on status competition, patriotism, and national pride, with an overlaying
romanticism of the tragic hero who cannot save his country from defeat.

Although these traits define the Polish national character in upper-class
terms, the peasant image also contains an emphasis on individualism, intransigence, and status competition. The similarity did not help bridge the strong
gulf and social distance between the peasant and the intelligentsia (Benet
1951:33). The peasant classes were generally anti-intellectual; education and
knowledge were the provinces of the upper classes.

As stated above, the activities of both the Nazis, during their occupation of
Poland in World War II, and of the Soviet Union, at the same time and later,
decimated the intelligentsia and especially young men. Those who remained
alive in other lands, but refused to return when the communists took over, were
also mainly young men from the armed forces. The communistic system was
very suspicious of anyone with middle- and upper-class family backgrounds.
Hence, the people who ruled Poland until the last few years were mainly
lower-class party members, called *nomenclatura* or bureaucratic functionaries.
Even universities were controlled and censored by members of the party.
Peasants were now called farmers and the mass media were used to educate
them about more modern agricultural techniques. One of the interesting
phenomena in communist Poland was the refusal of the farmers to collectivize.

After 1956–57, in fact, there was a dramatic decrease of collective farms, "leaving 83 per cent of the arable land in private ownership of small, ill-equipped, horse-drawn peasants" (Davies 1984:596). These farmers managed, however, to feed the nation and export (without much choice) to the Soviet Union. There has also been a trend for the farmers to take employment in factories and towns, leaving much of the agricultural work to women (Tryfan 1976). In the meantime the urban middle class expanded dramatically.

Status Competition in Poland

Movement between the two main Polish social classes was a rare phenomenon. However, the internal structure of a village was socially complex. The Poles developed a set of interwoven relations knit into overlapping networks (Bott 1957) that were very different from the popular image of a simple village life. The usual portrayal of peasant life in "gemeinschaft terms" of "warmth, intimacy and closeness" (Greeley 1969b:5) ignores the status competition within the *okolica*, or the area within which the person lives and interacts, the social life space that contains his/her identity Thomas and Znaniecki (1918–1920; see also Reymont 1925) .[5] The *okolica* of the peasant includes the family, home, lands, the village of families, and sometimes other villages. It also contains a relatively complicated set of social hierarchies of status sources enabling individual and family competition. Each person is born into a family with a certain position vis-à-vis other families within this social area. This status is cumulative and competitive; points are won by the acquisition of new prestige items and lost by the dissipation of such items. Each competitive family member depends upon his or her family to provide him or her with a suitable background, to help acquire objects needed for status competition, and to continue working for the acquisition of new points. Thus, to the extent that each member was locked into the village and could not "make it on his or her own" and the extent to which daily life and exceptional events were made public through gossip, family solidarity was a necessity, and strong measures of family social control were used to prevent deviations that might shame the family.

The Polish peasant had several means of acquiring status. The most prestigious material object was land, which could be obtained only at a loss to other people, since all that was available for cultivation was already owned by others. Next were the more durable goods—houses, barns, and major tools of work. Third came the less durable possessions such as stock, smaller tools, and clothing. Finally came "income" goods, such as eggs and milk, or home-crafted products that could be sold at market or exchanged for durable goods (Thomas and Znaniecki 1918–1920/ 1958: 156–57).

Marriage was a means of uniting economic units. It created a new family linked bilaterally with both families of orientation, into which each of them born.

This new unit was expected to start at the economic status level that the marital partners enjoyed prior to its formation. This was accomplished with the help of both families of orientation through dowries and gifts for daughters and land for sons, if possible. Marriage was not a matter of love, but an arrangement guaranteeing the best status and economic position for the unit.

The final source of status was personal reputation in terms of efficiency, specialization in an admired craft, personality, looks, and behavior within the village, which reinforced the individuality and independence of each person, who was aware of his or her importance as a contributor to the family's status. The importance of the personal reputation made the function of shame and continued self- and other-control very important in village life. As Finestone (1964) emphasized, a member of a Polish family had to continually earn his or her right to belong to a family.

The Polish nobility also stressed land and related objects but gave great importance to appropriate life-style and knowledge of Polish and cosmopolitan cultures. This, then, was Poland as a national culture society at the time of the first, great emigration to the United States. Feudal in social organization until very recently, partly as a result of policies of the occupying forces, but partly because of the political strength of the relatively numerous landed nobility or gentry, its class system was polarized between the various strata of peasants and the *szlachta* or gentry. Its village life was complex and individualistic, containing a family cooperative system of status competition within a geographically circumscribed *okolica*. In the years prior to World War I the situation within which the peasantry and the nobility were living, particularly under the Russian and Prussian occupation, and the poverty problems of both the Russian and Austrian provinces led to a mass and heterogenous emigration. The political exiles tended first to go to European countries, while the peasants and other émigrés went to the United States. However, as Polonia in America became more established, more and more migration was directed toward it by Poles living elsewhere.

Poland of the interwar years became more urbanized, the class system filled with more urban middle-range groups, such as a "mushrooming" bureaucracy, and the landed nobility weakened. The democratic characteristics of the republic gradually withered as Marshal Pilsudski gained authoritarian power (Davies 1984:423) until his death in 1935. Few Poles emigrated during those years, and the American quota system prevented all but a few from coming here. The Communist party attempted after 1945 to create a classless society, except for its privileged bureaucracy. However, as documented by Nowak (1981), Szczepanski (1962), and other sociologists, the class system continued. The opening up of free education, however, enabled descendants of even peasants and blue-collar workers to reach the top rung of intelligentsia, although, its nature and values changed.

Effect of Emigration on Poland

The history of Poland contains a great deal of movement of peoples, due to the actions of political states and voluntary migration. A perfect example of the former are the frequent shifts of boundaries, such as in the partitions and following World War II and the Yalta agreement between the Allies. Political states also moved vast numbers of people to Siberia or Nazi labor camps. Emigration took various forms. At all levels of the society Poles moved around Europe, in permanent settlement, but usually while awaiting political changes or seasonal work (Davies 1984; Kula et al. 1986; Thomas and Znaniecki 1918-1920; Walaszek 1988, 1992).

Polish scholars have consistently been interested in three aspects of emigration: the characteristics of the emigrants, the effects of emigration upon the communities and peoples left behind, and the emigrants and their Polonias. (Miodunka 1989:5). This chapter examines only the effect upon Poland of having so many varied peoples leave the national culture society and the political state. At present, the concern is over the "brain drain," the emigration of more educated people. Earlier, Florian Znaniecki, who had just earned his Ph.D. from the Jagiellonian University in Crakow, took on the position of director of the Society for the Protection of Emigrants (SPE) in Warsaw. In that capacity he published a periodical from 1910 to 1911, issued bulletins, and collected a mass of data on the area from which emigrants were leaving (Lopata 1976d). Dulczewski (1992:73-74) describes it as follows:

> The Society for the Protection of Emigrants was an organization that aimed at giving comprehensive advice and help to those, who decided to leave the country, both those in search of seasonal labor, as well, as those intending to settle abroad.

According to Dulczewski (1992: 74) and other sociologists, the aim of SPE was to discourage emigration of its most enterprising members. On the other hand, the local economic problems made it more likely that SPE simply tried to help emigrants avoid common "corrupt practices" of those "praying on the ignorance of simple people." It is at the SPE offices that W. I. Thomas met Znaniecki, which resulted in a major collaboration, at the University of Chicago in America, on a set of volumes entitled *The Polish Peasant in Europe and America.*

Emigration to North or Latin America often affected families negatively, especially in cases where the communication across the ocean was severed. Kula and associates (1986) have recently published a set of letters from America and Brazil that were never delivered, because the czarist government censors simply kept them. These letters often contained money or tickets to enable relatives to join the emigrants. Whole villages could be deprived of the young during the times of the great migrations.

On the other hand, those who emigrated seasonally, to Germany or other European countries, brought money, objects, and ideas back home. Even those who moved further usually planned on returning, and hence, they sent, or upon return brought, money home to buy more land, or build or fix up a house. Walaszek (1992) studied the economic effects of the migration upon the area of origin and claimed they were minimal in spite of the amount of money involved. For example, in 1902, Austrian Galicia received from America alone $3.5 million in money orders, and $4 million were brought back by returnees. An additional $3.5 million was sent to Russian Poland and he estimates that another $12 million was probably sent in private letters. However, according to Walaszek (1992) the money was mainly used to meet immediate needs, particularly during winter and emergencies. Most of the knowledge gained abroad was also of little value, not being relevant to life in Poland, or resisted by the local population. Wyman (1989:47), on the other hand, reports that the influence varied according to person and community. He states that estimates by American statisticians show that 30 percent of the Poles returned to the "old" country in the years between 1908 and 1914. That is a lot of people. Monies have continued to move from Polonias to Poland over the years. One needs to only drive around village Poland of recent decades to see what are called "American homes," built with the help of money earned in America.[6]

America

Since most of the readers will be American, I will only highlight those aspects of this society that have a direct relevance to immigration and international policies as they influence Poland and Polonia. A late president of the United States of America, John F. Kennedy (1964), called this country *A Nation of Immigrants*, but Taft and Robbins (1955:370) pointed out that, "Technically, immigration began with the Declaration of Independence" because a political state had to exist before people could officially immigrate into it. Prior to the formation of such social units, people simply permanently changed their residence without meeting groups that controlled boundaries. They either moved into uninhabited territories or they conquered inhabitants who were unable to defend themselves against the invaders. Taft and Robbins (1955: 19–20) classified population movements into five types:

1. Invasion—movements en masse, involving the whole or a large part of a tribe, and usually includes warfare
2. Conquest—attack and control, often with few conquerors, with the exception of "soldiers, traders, adventurers, and missionaries," actually changing residence
3. Colonization, "a movement in which a well-established and vigorous state sends bodies of its citizens to settle in a specific locality under its political

control, or within a politically weak state," a peaceful movement with often devastating effects on the colonials

4. Free immigration . . . a movement of people, individually or in families, acting on their own initiative and responsibility, without official support or compulsion, passing from one well-developed country (usually old and thickly settled) to another well-developed country (usually new and sparsely populated) with the intention of residing there permanently.

5. Compulsory migration and exchange of population—such as slavery, indentures, and other forms of compulsion and forced labor.

The United States of America has experienced all these forms of migration, to the extent that Indian tribes invaded each other. It conquered territories that belonged to other nations, such as Mexico. Its original political history included colonization by Britons who benefited from the production of commodities by the colonizers. While many people came there of their own free will, American colonies were also used as "a dumping-ground for undesirables," until the revolution (Jones 1960: 21). After it became an independent political state, it attracted voluntary immigrants and brought in slaves and indentured servants. Thus, its history involved a wide variety of peoples who came at different times, in different ways, and for different reasons. According to Taft and Robbins (1955: 370), "There were about two million whites in the thirteen American Colonies in 1776," but about one-third of English stock. Although there was some attempt to make German the official language, the English language predominated.

The name United States of America was first used in the Declaration of Independence in 1776 and then in the Constitution in 1787, replacing the previously used "The United Colonies" (Andrews 1962: 974). The Revolutionary War freed the colonies from Great Britain's control. The original population of the continent within which the colonies were located consisted of various tribes of Indians. The so-called Great Migration from England in the early seventeenth century (1629-1640) (of 60,000 people) involved mainly political or religious Puritans, but also people who came for economic betterment (Andrews 1962: 412).

As larger and larger waves of immigrants came from a variety of countries, the descendants of the initial settlers became uneasy, fearing that their "race" would be overwhelmed by the newcomers and worrying that they would no longer be able to meet their own needs. Although labor was badly needed in the rapidly expanding agriculture, especially on the plantations of the south and the factories of the north, prejudice against certain types of immigrants increased over time. Initial restrictions by the colonies were not directed toward nationalities, but toward "religious affiliation, economic status, and moral standing" (Jones 1960: 44). The antagonism was then directed at the Scotch-Irish, later toward the Germans (Jones 1960: 46–47), and finally against any group that came in large numbers and settled in ethnic communities. Racial nativistic feelings soon expanded, as evidenced in the Chinese Exclusion Act of 1882 which "suspended Chinese immigration for a period of ten years, forbade the naturalization of Chinese and imposed other restrictions on them" (Jones 1960: 249). The act was renewed in 1892, and by 1902 all Chinese immigration was suspended. California passed many policies directed against Orientals, in fear of "The Yellow Peril" (Jones 1960:264).

In spite of the fears and attempts to restrict immigration, Jones estimates that between 1815 and World War I, "no fewer than thirty million" immigrants came from all countries of Europe in gigantic waves; a variety of reasons pushed them out of the old world and pulled them into the new. Many American firms were involved in locating possible emigrants, convincing them of all the advantages, and facilitating their passage. They took monies from the emigrants and from companies needing workers. The situation at entry points such as Ellis Island was confused and identification of people often incorrect. Few of the immigrants spoke English and their village- or region-bound pronunciations and intonations resulted in misunderstanding even with agents speaking their national language. Some immigrants could not identify the political or national society from which they had come, being limited in their knowledge to a region or even village. In addition, the American government changed the identification base by which it classified all immigrants several times. The immigration recording and reporting agency was moved through the years from one department of the government to another, and the data selected for reporting and the method of presentation were modified by new personnel who rejected prior methods.

As industrialization, and interurban and cross-country railroads moved westward, so did the immigrants, sometimes directly, but often in secondary settlement as demands for their labor shifted. The numbers and cultural differences of these masses increased concern by the established populations. "The dedication ceremonies for the Statue of Liberty in October, 1886, took place, ironically enough, at precisely the time that Americans were beginning seriously to doubt the wisdom of unrestricted immigration" (Jones 1960: 247).

Anti-immigration sentiment became so intensified by the 1920s that the federal legislature finally passed a number of acts, all of which considerably restricted the number of persons admitted from Eastern and Southern Europe. The initial quota act of 1921 restricted immigration to only 3 percent of the "foreign born persons of such nationality resident in the United States as recorded in the 1910 Census" (Hutchinson 1949:16). The act also called for the establishment of tests to determine if the applicant met standards of admission. In 1924 the law was revised to be even more restrictive of non-Britons: as made the base year, and only 2 percent was the proportion allowed ationality.

The next revision of the quota acts, which went into effect in 1929, was based on the 1920 census, but the proportions were dropped. The quotas it established formed a "flat one-sixth of one percent of the population of that nationality present in the United States in the 1920 Census" (Bogue 1969:806). The discriminatory and prejudicial features of the quota act were a sore point for many Americans who attempted to change it over the years. Finally, in 1968, the quota act was replaced by a uniform limit of 20,000 people per year for each independent country in the eastern hemisphere. Close relatives of people already settled in America had been favored, 75 percent of the quota being reserved for them until 1972, when it was dropped to 50 percent (Cross 1973:22). Non-Europeans have faced a variety of restrictions over the years, often depending on whether they were classified as coming for economic rather than political reasons.

The U. S. government has made many exceptions to its immigration policies in response to world conditions. For example it passed eight special acts allowing many people displaced by World War II and the extermination and concentration camps of the Germans, estimated at 12 million, to find asylum here (U. S. Department of Justice 1969: 45). The Refugee Relief Act of 1953 allowed 214,000 refugees to enter within a 41-month period (Jones 1960:286). The strong anticommunistic stance of the government resulted in the opening of the gates to people from countries identified as under such control to seek refuge here. Of course, there are also many illegal people living and even working for money within American borders. We shall see later on in this chapter how the various governmental policies have affected the Polish immigration over more than a century.

The Refugee Act of 1980 tried to solve some of the problems of uneven flow of people wishing asylum (Daniels 1990: 345). The 1956 Immigration Act tried to establish a numerical maximum, so the various U. S. administrations "stitched together ten makeshift parole programs" for Asians and the need for a general refugee law was made apparent. The final law was also inadequate in terms of numbers, but introduced a new legal category of refugee, an "asylee." The U. S. government's definition of refugee accepted the United Nations definition, which focused on fear of persecution by the country of nationality. An asylee "is a person who applies for entry into the United States while already here, either legally, such as a person who came in as a student or visitor's visa or . . . arrived illegally" (Daniels 1990: 346).

The greatest change in the immigration policy of the United States since the liberalization of 1965 occurred in October 1990 (Przezdziecka 1990: 2). The major change was the repeal of the "numerically limited immigration" concept by which each country was assigned a limited number or quota. A worldwide cap of 675,000 by 1994 on total immigration was substituted, giving preference to families of residents and individuals with "skills/professions that the U.S. lists as in demand" and special individuals who petition for a visa.

One of the problems facing the United States has been the large number of illegal people entering by simply crossing the border, such as Mexicans, or by extending their stay after coming over on a visitor's visas, such as many Poles have done. The 1986 Immigration Reform and Control Act, identified as the amnesty bill attempted to solve this problem by allowing spouses and minor children of legalized aliens who arrived in the United States on or before 5 May 1982 to receive "a stay of deportation and work authorization." This meant that they can stay and work in the United States. A whole set of procedures was developed to transform an illegal resident into a permanent one. The other side of the act was the threat to punish employers for hiring illegal workers. This has had some interesting recent repercussions as Americans nominated for major political office have been rejected for having hired illegal immigrants. One of the innovations in the immigration system was the lottery system for visas, introduced in 1992 and modified in 1993.

Consequences of Immigration

It is difficult to estimate all the consequences of immigration to the United States. The society's population is composed of conquered native Indians, Mexicans in territories obtained through various means from other governments, voluntary and involuntary immigrants, and their descendants. It is a large, complex, and heterogeneous social unit.

Americans already established in this society have responded to the presence of the less established groups in many different ways. Welcoming attitudes may have been representative of employers desperately needing workers, but neighbors of different backgrounds usually felt and expressed strong prejudice, which resulted in discrimination. The society in general tried to control the entrance and life of such people and, once the tide was cut off, to understand what was happening to itself because of their presence. The first major perspective was assimilationistic. America was seen as a "melting pot." Given enough time, the strange and unpleasant characteristics of the immigrant groups would vanish as they learned the superior American culture and adjusted to its life. Irritation was felt only at the slowness with which some of the groups dropped old habits and acculturated. Given physical similarity to the dominant group, the immigrants, or at least their descendants, could become part of the mainstream. It helped if they changed their names to more pronounceable ones. However, a new view of America has emerged recently—or is still in the process of emerging: that of a pluralistic, multicultural society consisting of groups that retain some of their unique characteristics. In between these two theories existed one of religious or class meltdowns. The persistence of certain "non-American" ethnic, racial, and religious groups could not be ignored. There was an attempt at one time to lump ethnic groups by religion. Kennedy (1952), studying intermarriage trends in New Haven, found a "triple melting pot." Herberg (1955) followed this conclusion with *Protestant-Catholic Jew*. All Hispanics are now referred to as of one background.

While observers were trying to classify American society, the civil rights movement of the 1960s and 1970s produced a reaction from what became defined as the "Euro-ethnic American." Novak (1971) published a popular book, *The Rise of The Unmeltable Ethnics*, identified mainly by social class and racist reactions toward societal efforts to assist African Americans. The U. S. Commission on Civil Rights was sufficiently worried about the feelings of unfairness on the part of these ethnics to hold a "consultation" in Chicago in 1979, which focused on the *Civil Rights Issues of Euro-Ethnic Americans in the United States: Opportunities and Challenges*. Social scientists and representatives of numerous ethnic organizations presented papers describing various areas of life, such as housing, education, social services, employment, intergovernmental relations, the situation of ethnic women, and the biases of the communication media, in which they believed American Euro-ethnics were deprived of their rights. Horowitz (1979:53) explains that, although "the new ethnicity is a statement of relatively deprived sectors seeking economic relief through political appeals," each ethnic group has its own heritage and consciousness. Thus, united attempts to gain status do not mean a melting down of the differences into a single class unit in the main spheres of life.

In fact, Horowitz (1979:62) points out that most ethnic groups, having an overseas origin and concern with what happens in "the mother or father country of origin," attempt to influence U.S. foreign policy. However, they have had relatively little influence because of several factors, a major one being inter-ethnic group rivalries.

The pluralistic view of American society has grown with the recognition of the persistence of differences between ethnic and racial groups. Mindel, Habenstein, and Wright's (1988) *Ethnic Families in America: Patterns and Variations* has gone through three editions. A look at this edited book gives us a picture of the major groups in this society. Under European ethnic minorities can be found the Polish, Catholic Irish, Greek, and Italian families. Next comes a section on Hispanics, including Mexicans, Cuban, and Puerto Rican, then one on Asians, Korean, Chinese, Japanese, and Vietnamese families. The chapters in the section entitled "Historical Subjugated Ethnic Minorities" describe African Americans and Native Americans, while the section on "Socioreligious Ethnic Minorities" describes the Amish, Jewish, Arab, and Mormon families. This is quite a variety, and it includes only the major groups that have been studied. Many other European, Asian, African, and American societies are represented in this pluralistic country. The current multicultural emphasis goes one step further, stressing the importance of groups of non-European identities.

Population Composition

As of the 1980 U. S. Census, 22 percent of the Americans declared themselves to be of English ancestry, 22 percent German, and 18 percent Irish (Lieberson and Waters 1988:34). Other European backgrounds accounted for much smaller percentages. Blacks or African Americans constituted 12 percent of the population. Although there has been a large recent influx of Asians in recent years, the size of the country is so enormous that they do not as yet form a significant proportion of the total.

> The nation's population in 1979 is not only overwhelmingly of native birth, it is also primarily a population with at least three generations's residence in the nation, 81 percent were born in the United States of parents who were themselves both born in the nation. (Lieberson and Waters 1988: 43)

The authors expect the proportion of at least three-generation people to increase rapidly in the future, due to restrictions on immigration and the size of the population base.

Social Class Structure and Mobility

Most Americans identify themselves as belonging to the middle class. With some exceptions, migrant groups enter at the bottom, not having the knowledge of the culture, especially the language and the necessary skills to establish themselves at a higher level. However, upward mobility within the second generation was relatively frequent, given the absence of strong barriers, as in the case of African Americans. The main means of upward mobility has been education, which enables higher occupation, income, residence, and life-style. The life-style of parents provides life chances for the next generation. Although many Americans and outside observers assume that money is the only criterion for social class placement, it is the combination of education, occupation, types and sources of income, residence, style of work and leisure, and membership in voluntary associations and in companionate circles that forms this life-style. On the other hand, there are definite ceilings or boundaries between the so-called underclass and the so-called working class, as well as between the upper-middle class and the upper class.

A number of social scientists have concluded that downward mobility is much more frequent in recent years than in the past, due to many economic factors and the unwillingness of some members of new generations to work as hard as, or harder than, their parents did to obtain the same life-style (Ehrenreich

1989; Newman 1988). Those descendants of immigrants who used higher education as a means of upward mobility, such as the Jews and the Japanese, were most likely to succeed, with some complications of status produced by prejudice and discrimination.

General Characteristics of the American Society

In spite of the heterogeneity of the population, American society has developed some general characteristics that differentiate it from other societies. Many of its traits, including language, are based upon its English heritage, and only in recent decades has it removed vestiges of the British common law restricting women's rights. It also has a unique legal system based on precedent, and an educational system that separates church from state but is under local rather than national control.

The society has entered the postindustrial, postmodern stage of social development, defined in a variety of ways by different observers. It became urban with the help of technology, which enabled, or forced, most people to move off farms as those became incorporated into large units of agribusiness. Smoke stack industry decreased in importance, while

> business has been organized into stabilized giant corporate bureaucracies which have replaced the earlier and more primitive forms of entrepreneurial business organizations. Hand in hand with this development has been the bureaucratization of all other institutional areas in American life . . . assisted by federal budgetary support. (Bensman and Vidich 1971:vi)

The postindustrial nature of the economy means that most of its activity centers on information production and communication. Most jobs are of the white- or pink-collar variety, automated manual work going offshore where nonunionized labor is much cheaper. This does not mean that there is an absence of an unskilled labor market, only that the jobs that it now contains are so marginal and so low-paying that only illegal or very poor legal workers are willing to take them. The fact that such workers are allowed to cross illegally into the states indicates the continued need for such labor. This situation leaves a large contingent of previous industrial unskilled workers, often first or second generation immigrants and members of other minority groups, without jobs.

The American value system, which differs rather dramatically from that of more traditional societies and social classes from which many immigrants had come, includes individualism, the privatization of the family, and the Protestant ethic of hard work, success, and progress. The ideology of a two-sphere world with the public sphere controlled by men and of higher importance than the private one, which belongs to women, has resulted in gender stratification and segregation both in family and in the occupational/economic/political arena

Emphasis on the economic institution has allowed "greedy" organizations to demand total commitment of men and the "greedy" family institution to demand the same of women. Many Americans have changed their ways of family composition and life away from the traditional ideals of work-oriented employed husband, full-time homemaking wife, two children, and a dog in a suburban home. Sexual permissiveness, premarital pregnancy, single parenthood, divorce and multiple marriages, lesbian and gay relationships, and intermarriage across ethnic, religious, and even racial lines have all become more frequent than in the parental generation. Intergenerational conflict is especially likely to occur if the parental or grandparental generation was socialized in a different culture, as in the case of immigrants.

The Poles: Emigrants and Immigrants

A major factor in the successful establishment and maintenance of an ethnic community in America is the sheer number of people who become its members and their continued arrival from the mother country. This can be seen in the case of the Poles, who emigrated to the United States in large numbers in three waves or cohorts: that of mass migration, that produced by World War II, and the newest, which is actually of multiple experiences.[7] The immigration figures themselves are difficult, if not impossible, to establish precisely for several reasons. First, Poland was under foreign political domination during most of the periods of immigration to America. Second, the U. S. Immigration and Naturalization Service changed its forms of identification of Polish immigrants several times. Third, there was heavy back and forth traffic between Poland and America, even though "immigrants" were technically people who declared their intention of staying permanently in the host country. The tendency of Poles who entered as temporary residents or as nonimmigrants to change their status also confuses the picture. Fourth, Poland's minority groups, upon arriving in America, inconsistently identified themselves, or were wrongly identified by the immigration officials. Finally, the problems of enumeration facing all ethnic communities in America also confront Polonia. As new generations appear of the scene, who is to be included under the classification of Polish American? Should only the foreign stock, those born in Poland and their immediate descendants, be included, or can anyone with an ancestor from that country be included, or is it necessary to ask people how they identify themselves?

As noted above, immigration to the United States was extensive at the turn of the twentieth century, the Immigration Bureau's working conditions were far from adequate, and the policies of identity assignment shifted frequently.[8] This was particularly true of the Poles due to their nation's political situation.

Methods of Recording Immigration

Over time, three bases for classifying all immigrants have been used by the U.S. Immigration Bureau, providing unmatched data, unsystematically applied: "country of birth," "races or peoples," and "country of last [and future, in cases of emigration] permanent residence." Country of birth did not mean national culture society but political state. Feeling that this information was insufficient during the height of immigration, the bureau introduced the new classification of "races or peoples."[9] Both methods were used for recording immigrants from around the turn of the century till 1932. After 1932, the Department of Labor (which was then housing the bureau) seemed to lose interest in many of the more detailed figures on immigration. It dropped the reporting of nonimmigrants and all references to "races or peoples," or reported them only sporadically. Country of last permanent residence has been used occasionally, particularly in recent years, possibly because of quotas and restrictions by country of origin. During some of America's history the outflow of emigrants was also of interest to the bureau, which recorded the number of people leaving the United States and occasionally the country of future permanent residence.

Poland did not appear as a major country of immigration in the U. S. Immigration Bureau's *Annual Report* until 1885. The changes in recording and reporting policies since then provide us with a very mixed set of data on Polish immigration. From 1885 until 1898 Polish immigrants were listed by country of birth. However, "Beginning in 1899 Polish immigrants have been included in the country to which they belong," which meant the state that was occupying their part of Poland (U. S. Department of Justice, *Annual Report* 1902: Table X). In fact, it is quite probable that instructions to reclassify Poles went out to port officials even earlier than 1899, in view of the otherwise unexplainable decline in the immigration numbers of the prior time. Even the Census Bureau was instructed for two decades not to record Poland as a country of birth of American population.

Luckily for students of Polish immigration, the classification of "races or peoples" was added about the time that Poland as a country of birth was dropped, so some data are now available as to the numbers who entered, as well as for those who left. By 1920, Poland officially reemerged as a political state and the Immigration and Naturalization Bureau reported both "country of birth" and "races or peoples" figures for Polish immigrants. In fact, the immigration figures for the years between 1920 and 1932 are extensive. However, the dropping of the second method of classification in 1932 leaves us with only "country of birth" or, in some years, "country of last permanent address" to fall back on in estimating the number of Polish immigrants from that year to the present. The main complication in comparing "races or peoples" and "country of birth" figures is that many people leaving Poland as a political state did not identify themselves as Polish in national identity and did not join Polonian communities. Many of the people who stated their country of birth as the Russian, Austro-Hungarian, or Germanic empires, or later, Poland were Jews, Ruthenians, Bohemians, Germans, and so on. The number who identify themselves as Jews when given the opportunity of doing so is very large, but the proportion that they, rather than non-Jewish Poles, form of the total emigration varies by year and by country. This problem of being unable to separate peoples who would identify as Poles from Polish Jews who would not so identify is a major one for the student of Polonia.[10]

Later Immigration Policies Affecting Poles

Thus, the total number of immigrants from Poland who could have become involved in Polonia has been affected by America's policies as well as by world conditions. The 1921 quota act was based on the U. S. population of 1890. This would have resulted in only a trickle of Polish immigrants since the number of people giving Poland as their country of birth in 1890 was so small. According to the 1927 quota law, Poland was allowed 6,488 of its nationals per year.[11]

The U. S. government made exceptions to its immigration policies, even prior to rescinding the quota system, by allowing entrance to many specially classified Poles and other nationals following World War II. The displacement of the Polish population during the war was extensive and subject to sympathetic humanitarian action. According to one Polish author (Wicislo 1959:86), "There were 12,000,000 displaced persons liberated from extermination and concentration camps by allied armies in 1945 . . . 3,201,000 of them were Poles." The American government passed eight special acts resulting in the entrance of 162,462 Poles between 1945 and June 1969 (U. S. Department of Justice 1969:45). According to Mostwin (1971; see Erdmans 1992: 265) there were 140,000 Poles, including

> former prisoners of war and ex-servicemen from Germany and insurgents from the Warsaw Uprising (20,000); ex-servicemen from Great Britain (20,000); families of ex-servicemen (25,000); displaced persons from West Germany (35,000); and immigrants from Poland from 1956 to 1968 (40,000).

An additional complication in estimations of Polish immigrants arises from the fact that the category of a person entering the United States depends on this country's classification system and the entrants often change their intention upon settlement.

Immigration Figures

There are several ways people can enter the United States legally. First, they can come as immigrants, which means as persons intending to settle permanently. Since 1929, Polish immigrants have been classified either in the quota or nonquota categories. Nonquota immigrants include relatives of Poles already settled here, or persons admitted under special provisions, such as displaced persons and refugees. Second, people can enter the United States as nonimmigrants if they are representatives of governments or other official bodies, students, travelers, visitors, or in transit. In recent years (since 1952), people with temporary visas have been listed separately by the Immigration and Naturalization Service in its *Annual Report* (U. S. Department of Justice). In the case of Polish entrants, the nonimmigrants are mainly tourists, called *wakacjusze* by the community, or people who claim to be only tourists or vacationers. Most of them then get jobs, illegally since they do not have a "green card," in order to earn dollars for apartments, weddings, cars and other expenditures upon return to Poland. They have often overstayed their visas and had not been too carefully monitored because America hated to send anyone back to a communist country. A new problem of dealing with these illegal nonimmigrants has been the overthrow of the communist regime in Poland. The nonimmigrant entrants are now seen as coming to America for economic rather than political reasons and subject to deportation. As we shall see later, many of those who arrived before 1982 have recently been given amnesty and made legal residents.

A third category of entrants are refugees. Before the Refugee Act of 1980 such people were admitted on an individual basis or under special acts following World War II.

> After 1965, refugees were admitted as a seventh preference of immigrants, given 6 percent of the total slots available to immigrants. The Refugee Act of 1980 eliminated this category and began admitting refugees on a uniform basis . . . [with] admission ceilings. A refugee is "a person residing outside his or her country of nationality who is unwilling to return to that country because of a well-grounded fear of persecution based on race, religion, nationality, membership in a particular social group, or political opinion." Asylees are similar to refugees except that at the time they apply they are residing in the United States or are at a port of entry. (Erdmans 1992a: 342)

Immigrants, nonimmigrants, and refugees can also, of course, leave this country. The U. S. government has occasionally been interested in this traffic of peoples, keeping a record of entrances and departures from 1908 until 1932, when it was concerned with border crossings and naturalization.[12] However, immigration authorities disagree as to the actual number of Polish immigrants entering the United States. Some of the numerical confusion is due to differences in the dates and years being grouped together by the examiner. The various sets of figures are presented in table 2.1.

The *Annual Report* of 1950 summarizes prior decades, and the numbers are added for the 1950s and 1960s. The figures in table 2.1 are, however, highly questionable, in spite of constant use (Emmons 1971). Schermerhorn

(1949:265) pointed out that there were 174,365 Polish immigrants in the year ending June 1913 alone. The underreporting during the 1890s, the blanks during the time when the immigration was highest, and the contradictory figures given in different sources warranted an examination of each *Annual Report* available in several major university libraries.[13] For the purpose of this discussion summary figures will be used, which establish the parameters within the actual numbers of Poles who came to the United States as immigrants and who remained here are apt to be located. The totals of Poles listed by "race or peoples" can be used as the minimal parameter since we know that these people can be counted as first-generation Poles in America (see table 2.2). Table 2.3 offers the total numbers of Polish immigrants to, and emigrants from, the United States identified by country of birth.

TABLE 2.1
Decade Summary of Immigrants Identified as Polish by the U.S. Immigration and Naturalization Service Between 1820 and 1970

Decade	Number of Immigrants	Decade	Number of Immigrants
1820	5	1819–1900	96,700
1821–1830	16	1901–1910	_____a
1831–1840	369	1911–1920	4,813b
1841–1850	105	1921–1930	227,734
1851–1860	1,164	1931–1940	17,026
1861–1870	2,027	1941–1950	7,571
1871–1880	12,970	1951–1960	9,985
1881–1890	51,806	1961–1970	73,391c
	Total	1820–1970	505,682

Source: U.S. Immigration and Naturalization Service, *Annual Report for Fiscal Year Ending June 30, 1951* and *1970* (Washington, D.C.: Government Printing Office, 1951, 1970): 60–64. (See also Emmons 1971:38.)

a. The immigration officials were instructed to list Poles under the political state Austria, Prussia, or Russia within which their community was located.

b. These figures must be due to changing policy in 1920.

c. The figures are not accurate; they do not add up to the total and are different in different tables. The 1961–1970 total on pp. 60–61 of the *Annual Report* is 53,519; on p. 64 the total is 73,286; by adding and subtracting I come up with 73,391.

The totals in Tables 2.2 and 2.3 offer us the maximum parameter of 1,670,536 for the number of Poles who immigrated to, and stayed in, the United States from 1885 to 1972. Of course, Polonia as a community has been strongly influenced even by the temporary presence of 297,590 immigrants who later returned to Poland, and the 669,392 nonimmigrants and temporary residents who lived in America for varied amounts of time of Polonia's history. They were probably some of the more educated and cosmopolitan participants in American life but were also highly dependent upon the Polish community for personal contact, thus serving as a bridge between it and the societies of origin and settlement. The outflow of Poles from the United States was, at times, sufficiently larger than the inflow to result in an actual loss of persons to the community, particularly immediately following World War I. All in all, there were 592,568 Poles departing from the United States in the years between 1908 and 1932, when the continuous record of departures ceased being reported. This includes both immigrants and nonimmigrants.

TABLE 2.2
Total Numbers of Polish Immigrants to and Emigrants from the United States Identified by "Race or People," as Recorded in the Immigration and Naturalization Service Annual Reports

Years	Immigrants	Emigrants	Total
1899–1907	556,025	_____	556,025
1908–1919	677,620	174,602	503,018
1920–1932	90,815	120,824	-30,009
	1,324,460	295,426	1,029,034

Source: H. Z. Lopata. *Polish Americans: Status Competition in an Ethnic Community.* Englewood Cliffs: Prentice-Hall, 1976:38.

TABLE 2.3
Total Numbers of Immigrants to and Emigrants from the United States Giving Poland as Their Country of Birth as Recorded in the Immigration and Naturalization Service *Annual Reports*

Years	Number of Immigrants	Number of Emigrants	Total Immigrants
1885–1898	131,694	_____	131,694
1933–1946	46,573	_____	46,573
1946–1972	301,709a	_____	301,709
1947–1972	164,292b	2,766	161,526
1885–1972	644,268	2,766	641,502

Source: H.Z. Lopata. *Polish Americans: Status Competition in an Ethnic Community.* Englewood Cliffs, N.J.: Prentice Hall, 1976: 39.
a. Includes immigrants.
b. Includes displaced persons and excompatants.

What is important for our understanding of Polonia's life are the numbers and types of Polish entrants since World War II. The second, or war refugee cohort, and the third or recent communist-reared and temporary *wakacjusze* cohort have helped to revitalize the community. The political situation of Poland during and after World War II is reflected in the reports of the arriving and departing immigrants and nonimmigrants who gave Poland as their country of last (or future) permanent residence. Only a trickle of persons came directly from, or were going to, Poland during the *prethaw*, or pre-1956 years. Poles were not allowed to leave the Polish political state for the United States, and they were definitely not leaving America for Poland, from 1945 to 1956 (see Lopata 1976b, table 7). Of course, the quota system would have kept the number of immigrants down all this time, before and after. In 1957, the year after the Poznan revolts, 11,225 immigrants entered the United States, but only 3,300 were on the quota, the remaining ones joining families and coming for similar reasons. That is the highest number of nonquota immigrants in the years between 1947 and 1972.

Table 2.4 documents the size of the second and of the third wave Poles coming to the United States. Between 1948 and 1972 there were 301,709 immigrants, most coming under the quota limitation, and 348,284 nonimmigrants, the majority of whom were admitted as "temporary visitors for pleasure" (rather than for business or other declared reasons). The number of refugees does not match that of the second cohort. There is really no comparison, given the unusual circumstances of the war refugees. Starting with 1973, we find that the proportion of immigrants entering under "numerical limitations" or the quota system dropped from 79 percent to 24 percent in 1989. Erdmans (1992:343) explains that

> total immigrants include both new arrivals and those who adjusted their status to permanent resident. Immigrants not subject to numerical limitations include refugees and asylees, as well as parents, spouses and children of U.S. citizens. Between 1965 and 1988, only 47 percent of the non-quota immigrants were refugees and asylees; however, between 1980 and 1988, 62 percent of the non-quota immigrants were refugees.

The really dramatic increase of Poles in America is among the *wakacjusze*, the temporary visitors who declare their desire to be tourists while they actually come to earn money for a better life back home. Up until the overthrow of the communist government, American dollars bought extensive benefits. Their value has decreased, however, due to Poland's current economic changes. From 1973 to 1979 the percentage of wakacjusze, out of the total number of nonimmigrants admitted to the United States, increased from 61 to 78. These people for the most part do not know English and are thus dependent upon the local Polonias for their illegal jobs and life's necessities.

Table 2.4
The Number of Immigrants, Including Those Under the Quota System
and the Number of Nonimmigrants, Including "Wakacjusze" and Refugees
Entering the United States from 1948 to 1972 and from 1973 to 1990.

YEAR	Immigrants All A	Quota B	Nonimmigrants All C	Temporary D	DP* Refugee E
1973	4,914	3,874	28,046	17,041	
1974	4,033	3,083	38,258	24,483	
1975	3,941	3,042	42,242	28,411	
1976	4,765	3,332	41,080	26,605	
1977	4,010	2,948	38,974	26,312	
1978	5,050	3,646	49,439	34,467	
1979	4,413	3,270	41,638	31,450	
1980	4,725	2,827	41,450	32,900	
1981	5,014	2,986	41,392	34,390	
1982	5,874	3,412	15,040	11,127	6,312
1983	6,427	2,259	22,517	13,947	5,520
1984	9,466	2,304	36,236	27,110	3,794
1985	9,464	2,916	51,867	42,113	2,806
1986	8,481	2,777	57,376	50,125	3,617
1987	7,519	2,500	55,831	45,373	3,737
1988	9,507	3,382	58,433	45,139	3,670
1989	15,101	3,633	69,093	54,042	3,792
1990	20,537	6,771	75,226	57,399	1,883
Total 1973–1990	133,241	58,962	804,178	602,434	35,131
Total 1948–1972	301,709	256,643	348,284	259,088	164,292
Grand Total	434,950	315,605	1,152,462	861,522	199,423
A+C	434,950 + 1,152,462 = 1,587,412				

Sources: H. Z. Lopata, "Polish Immigration to the United States of America: Problems of Estimation and Parameters," *The Polish Review*, 21 (1976): 85–108, table 7. M. P. Erdmans, "Emigres and Ethnics: Patterns of Cooperation between New and Established Residents in Chicago's Polish Community" (Ph.D. diss. Northwestern University, 1992).
* Displaced persons

When we add all the immigrants and all the nonimmigrants we have a grand total of 1,587,412 Poles who have come either in the second wave, many of whom are still alive, or in the third wave, which consists of young adults; it is easy to see why Polonia in America has not vanished.[14]

There are other ways of determining the size of the population that could identify with Polonia. Estimates of the total Polish stock in the United States in 1970 (including the foreign born and the native born whose parents, one or both, were of Polish birth) range from 2 to 3 million. We will examine the figures and the known characteristics of these Polish Americans in chapter 5. In the meantime, the 1980 U. S. Census did ask for national ancestry, as mentioned in chapter 1; the Lieberson and Waters (1988:34) volume *From Many Strands* contains basic facts regarding the answers to this question. According to their analyses, 8,228,000 people listed Polish ancestry in their background. Seventy percent, which is relatively small, have been here three or more generations and 54 percent are of mixed ancestry.

The Immigrants

The United States Immigration and Naturalization Service (as it is now called) defines an immigrant as "an alien, other than a returning alien, admitted for permanent residence" (U. S. Census 1969:87). A profile of the immigrants from Poland at different periods of Polish and American history indicates changes in their basic characteristics, and thus in the characteristics of the population from which Polonia could draw its members.

Taking only certain years as examples of the composition of the three cohorts, we find that there were over 77,000 immigrants entering the United States in the fiscal year ending 30 June 1909 who were listed as Polish. Three-fourths of them were farm laborers and servants. Only one-seventh were women and children without any occupational designation. Thus, very few immigrants of that time represented skilled occupations and those who did were typical of village economies: blacksmiths, carpenters, locksmiths, miners, dressmakers, shoemakers, and tailors. There were only 66 professionals (U.S. Department of Justice 1909:41-46). These people brought with them resources for starting service establishments in the newly developing Polonian communities. Few urbanites or farm owners were included in the immigrant group, because they had more invested in staying in Poland. Most of the immigrants were young males between the ages of 14 and 44 and the outflow of almost 30,000 people officially declared immigrants or visitors was also heavily male dominated. The inflow was accompanied by over 8,000 visitors, who were generally more sophisticated than the farm laborers.

The U.S. Immigration and Naturalization Service in those years was worried about the ability of immigrants to sustain themselves in this country, so it asked the entrants several questions including the amount of money each carried with him or her. The service reported that only 3 percent of the Polish immigrants were entering with $50.00 or more in their possession. Most of their money was used for the purchase of transportation, since only one-fourth had the cost covered by someone else, usually relatives. All but 14 percent of the entrants were going to join relatives, with 13 percent joining friends and a few others venturing forth as pioneers or at the initiative of people whom they had not known from the homeland. Although economically destitute, only about a third to a fourth of the immigrants did not know how to read or write (U.S. Department of Justice 1909: 22–23). Unfortunately, the language skills they had were not suited to American society.

As the years went by, immigrants came with greater occupational and financial resources, reflecting what was happening in Poland. In 1929, however, they were still heavily rural in background. There were far fewer people coming that year than in 1909 (3,500 compared to 77,000) and their arrival was somewhat offset by the number who were leaving to return to Poland. The highest proportion of emigrants to immigrants, 89, had been in 1926. By 1929 this proportion was down to 66, although this is still a significant number (U.S. Department of Justice 1929: table 90:202). The occupational distribution shows an almost doubling of the proportion of nonfarm immigrants from 20 years before, and a sizable number of "no occupation" wives, children, and even some older parents (U.S. Department of Justice 1929: table 33:90). The entrants carried with them more money than that of their 1909 predecessors, half of them having $50.00 or more. More had their passage paid by relatives than by themselves. This distribution shows the greater affluence of the American-based relatives of the 1929 entrants than of the 1909 immigrants, and the difference in their connection to the people already settled here. The earlier group came to stay with other male relatives or pioneer families; the 1929 immigrants came to join their families of procreation or orientation. Thus, the 1929 immigrants were brought over to fill family units, although there were still a few pioneers and returnees who had tried life back in the homeland and decided that they liked it better in America after all. Very few of the 1929 immigrants could not read or write (4 percent), reflecting the expansion of mass education by the independent Polish government.

The refugees who were admitted by special acts of the American government in the years between 1945 and 1969, totaling more than 160,000, were even more different from their 1909 predecessors. Many, as Wygocki (1992) found, did not really define themselves as emigrants, since they were forced out of Poland and refused to return because of communism. They were much more educated and more of them had an urban background (Mostwin 1991: 19). They had been soldiers, students, or seasonal workers caught outside of Poland at the beginning of the war. For example, the 1949 influx of 27,000 included almost half with "no occupation," indicating a movement of whole family units, usually ones with young children. Only 7 percent of them were listed as operatives, household workers, nonhousehold service workers, farm laborers, and laborers (U.S. Department of Justice 1949: table 8, no page). An additional fourth had been farmers or farm managers. Professionals, sales workers, clerical workers, and craft workers composed the rest of the immigrant group. Thus, in terms of occupations and other characteristics, the Polish immigrant group was heterogenous and changing over time.

Mostwin (1991) conducted two studies of the two newer cohorts of Poles in America, the "transplanted family" in 1970 and political émigrés in 1984. Actually, both samples identified themselves as political emigrants, although 50 percent of the latter group had came at the invitation of relatives. Many had gone to technical or vocational schools, typical of Poland and many other European countries. This was generally the first generation educated in socialist Poland. Less than 10 percent came from villages and 65 percent listed large cities as their home (Mostwin 1991:50). Those Poles in Mostwin's sample who came between 1974 and 1984 were young, that is, under 40 years of age. Many were not, or were no longer, married, although 80 percent had married at some point in their lives. They resembled earlier immigrant waves in that many did not speak English at all (68 percent; Mostwin 1991:52). That is, however, better than in 1909 when none spoke English. Only 13 percent had become American citizens; 65 percent were permanent residents, leaving 22 percent being neither.

Erdmans's (1992:326, see also chap. 8) sample of third wave Poles living in Chicago who were absentee voters in the Polish elections contained a high proportion of professional (23 percent) and skilled (45 percent) workers. This was particularly true of permanent residents. More of the temporary residents, with valid or invalid temporary visas, were in unskilled jobs, mainly because they could not speak English and were often working in cleaning or construction jobs. Interestingly enough, from 44 percent of the youngest (18–29) on up to 80 percent of the oldest of her samples intended to return to Poland. However, the younger the respondents, the more likely they were to be uncertain as to whether or not they will stay here (49 percent for the youngest and 15 percent for the oldest).

"Estimates are that half a million Poles left Poland in the 1980s. ... In 1989, the United States Consulate in Poland issued 80,000 visas to Poles, but they also refused 60 percent of the visa applications" (Erdmans 1992b:8). Sakson (1989) explained that the "mass emigration" from Poland of the 1980s presented a brain drain in that it consisted of many highly educated people in technical or professional occupations.

This mass emigration has worried both Solidarity and religious leaders. The Polish primate of the Catholic church tried to discourage people from leaving because of their moral duty to the nation, since it weakened the supply of highly educated and skilled people (Erdmans 1992b: 10). Even Pope John Paul II "urged Poles to stay in Poland because of national duty" (11). However, economic and political conditions in Poland had gotten so bad in the 1980s that the emigrants preferred freedom and the possibility of earning housing and a better standard of living to remaining in their home country, even though they felt guilty for "deserting" their nation. Solidarity activists either had to leave in return for being released from jail in 1984 or found a loss of status during martial law that disbanded the union. Those who did accept the compromise of leaving the country in return for release from prison have had the hardest time adjusting to the new country; ". . . while these activists were in the eye of history's storm in Poland, in America they were but refugees from history bearing heavy psychological burdens" (Blejwas 1992: 83).

Erdmans (1992b) also interviewed immigrants in America as well as those who decided not to leave Poland. Both groups were aware of the fact that they could not achieve the same status in the United States due to the nontransferability of skill and weakness of language. Those who did not emigrate could not get visas, had family ties in Poland, and had no ties to anyone who could help them in America. Many were fearful of "status degradation" (Erdmans 1992b: 19). A few mentioned national loyalty. Not only did the "Solidarnosc" cohort have trouble adjusting to its new status within the broader American community, but it also had trouble relating to the established Polonia (see chapters 7 and 9).

Summary

American society has become populated through invasion, conquest, colonization, and free and compulsory immigration. The Polish immigrants came by choice or under personal or other adviser influence. They entered from other political states and nations, with a variety of backgrounds. The country from which they came has had a complicated and difficult history, that has had strong repercussions upon its emigrants.

Poland has been a buffer state between two political states that have become increasingly centralized and expansionistic since at least the seventeenth century. Having experienced a "Golden Age," the Polish state weakened through political inaction following a complete democratization of the upper classes in the Sejm, or Parliament. Each member of the nobility and clergy could stop any official action through the use of the *liberum veto*. Partitioned by Russia, Prussia, and Austria, it remained under foreign occupation for 125 years until after World War I. The national culture society was maintained during this time by the political leaders and the nationalistically oriented nobility. Life in the villages, where a high proportion of Poles were living, involved a complex system of status competition, with multiple sources of status and individualistic personal reputation assisted by strong family solidarity. However, poverty and oppression by the occupying powers led increasing numbers of peasants to economic emigration, first to other parts of Europe and then, before the turn of the century, to America. Simultaneously, the politically active gentry, and some of the urban dwellers were pushed out of the country, so that the emigrants and temporary émigrés who came to the United States were a heterogenous lot.

The host country for the emigrants, the United States of America, has been very ambivalent toward its immigrants, trying to control who came and in what numbers. Prejudice levels rose with the increase of numbers of people with sociopsychological, economic, cultural, and physical differences from the dominant group. At the same time, the rapidly expanding economy needed workers, especially during its industrializing stages. The volume of peoples strained housing, health, and welfare resources of the society to such a point that the government finally closed the gates, with policies decreasing numbers and also discriminating against unwanted groups.

The American social structure and culture have changed dramatically in the past one hundred plus years since the heavy migration began. Each wave of newcomers also came from a changing homeland, although the rate of change was likely to be slower and of a different quality than that experienced by the Americans. The probability of conflict and strain in acculturation of the immigrants and their ability to retain some characteristics of the home culture and develop their own ethnic way of life has resulted in a recent recognition of the pluralistic nature of America. There is still an uneasy lack of balance between tolerance of diversity and the wish for homogeneity, as evidenced, for example, in the argument over language in schools and public settings.

The very heterogeneous three cohorts of emigrants from Poland to the United States form the base upon which Polonia was built and maintained over the years. The early emigrants from Poland primarily represented the various strata of peasants, but enough professionals and skilled craftsmen came to help in the formation of a relatively self-sufficient community. They were then joined by more and more professionals, skilled workers, and the new intelligentsia, first represented by priests and political émigrés. The "new emigration" of World War II was dramatically different from the old, being more urban, industrialized, and representative of all social strata and occupational skills. This is true even more so of the newest immigrants, many of whom first work in menial jobs but then learn English and move up. There is a sizable group of entrepreneurs among them who are helping to set up joint ventures in Poland. In recent years there has been an increase in temporary emigration, composed of young people who are working illegally while on temporary visas. However, they are not active in most of Polonian life.

Notes

1. Although Stalin died in 1953, it was not until 1956 and the Poznan riots that the "thaw" was actually felt in Poland (Bethell 1972:194, 202).
2. But then, one can find the same competition in the political life of Italy and France. Also evident are the problems of creating a new social system after decades of dictatorial control among all the former communist countries. As of July 1992, three years since the fall of communism, the fourth Polish prime minister failed to form a coalition government. There were then 29 parties, down from over 60, in the 460-member Parliament (or Sejm) (Myers 1992:5).
3. And yet, the nonurban Pole and the nonurban Jew lived very similar lives, particularly in the Russian-occupied part of Poland. *Fiddler on the Roof*, as a play and movie, captured this feeling of life, and the Europeans who flocked to see it and sat with tears in their eyes were not just Jews. "The shtetl was a collection of ramshackle houses and mud streets in which several hundred or several thousand people huddled together, excluded, prevented by law from engaging in all normal occupations, yet rubbing elbows with the local peasants, who might be huddled in their own ramshackle houses just a street or two away" (Yaffe 1969:16). Going through the daily routine of a harsh life, the two groups crossed paths, sometimes with genuine respect, but more often with disdain and even open hostility. They shared many values—disapproval of education for women, patriarchal emphasis on the importance of man's work, strong negative attitudes toward the *prosty zyd* (plain Jew) or landless peasant, internal status competition that excluded each other's community, poverty, and insularity (the Pole was surrounded by fields and a larger structured society outside his range of identification; the Jew was surrounded by the Poles). They differed in several ways: in their attitude toward religion and its representatives, in their method of socializing children, in their view of analytical and literary knowledge, and in the value placed on physical labor and family norms. The Polish peasant at the turn of the twentieth century had no tools for freeing himself from the class position and subsistence economy into which he was born. The Jewish child could gain high status within the community regardless of family background by proving his ability to learn and think. Both had an avenue of escape from the grinding and anxiety-ridden life—emigration—and both used it.
4. According to Celia Stopnicka Heller (1973:221–37), author of "Assimilation: A Deviant Pattern among Jews of Inter-war Poland," there was a group of assimilationists in Poland:

   No exact figures exist but one can attempt an estimate on the basis of census data. Thus, I have arrived at the estimate that the assimilationists constituted one-ninth to one-tenth of the Jewish population, which numbered over three million (270,000–300,000 assimilationists). However, this figure has been considered too high by a few historians whom I have consulted; they think that it was between 150,000 and 200,000 but emphasize that there is no way of arriving at an exact figure.
   The estimates of what proportion the assimilationists constituted in the

various strata of the Jewish population are even looser than the above, for no census or other figures exist as a base. Assimilationists were especially prominent among artists and the top Jewish intellectuals; the latter were among the most prominent intellectuals of Poland. On the basis of the interviews I conducted, I should estimate that as many as 90 percent of the top Jewish intellectuals were assimilationists. Another stratum in which they were proportionately over-represented was that of the very rich Jews. I should guess that about half of them were assimilationists. But assimilationists were virtually non-existent among the workers, the small traders, and the poor, who were minimally acculturated. Thus, the great distance between the assimilationists and the bulk of the Jewish people was both a class and a cultural distance.

5. Diaz and Potter (1967) do not make such assumptions. "Life in most villages is certainly not a rustic communal paradise. Communities frequently are rent by bitter factional disputes, whether they are between political parties, different lineages, different castes, or merely different clique groups around strong men" (163). But they ignore the possibility that status competition leads to such conflict and alliances.

6. American homes can also be found in Ireland and Yugoslavia, as I can vouch from personal travel in these countries.

7. I am using here Erdmans concept of cohort as a group of people who have gone through the same experience (see Chapter 8).

8. The situation at the ports of entry to the United States was subject to many investigations during the years of the heavy influx. This was particularly true of Ellis Island where "the annual number was over three quarters of a million" and "the number passing through within a single day was five thousand or more, an average of two per minute" (Heaps 1967).

9. Jones (1960) identified the Immigration and Naturalization Commission's reports on the new immigrants and the classification of the entrants by "races or peoples" as highly questionable and reflective of the commission's biases, but there is no clear-cut definition of procedures by which people were so classified. The concept of *race* was popular at the time since careful anthropological analyses had not yet dispelled the myth that people such as Poles or Jews formed a biologically homogeneous separate species of mankind.

10. In only a few years of the immigration history we can separate those who identified themselves as Polish (see Lopata's *Polish Review* article, 1976a) from those who identified themselves as Hebrew. Emmons (1971:54) quotes Saul Kaplan, Director of Research at the Jewish Welfare Federation on Chicago, who "estimated that at least 80 percent and perhaps 90 percent of the Russians in Chicago are Jewish, although no reliable data are available." Emmons found in a University of Illinois, Circle Campus, survey of the population of Chicago that 10 percent of the Poles gave Judaism as their religious preference.

11. President John F. Kennedy (1964) was instrumental in changing the quota system. See the preface (written by Robert Kennedy) in *A Nation of Immigrants* (published posthumously).

12. Turn-of-the-century immigration officials tried for several years to make official a policy of recording departures. In 1902 the report included the following statement: "The Bureau can only reiterate with emphasis arising from an additional year of experience, its recommendations of the past three or four years with regard to keeping a record of departing aliens."

13. For details of the immigration, see Lopata (1975).
14. I will discuss the influence of these differences in life style in chapter 7 and Mary Erdmans will detail differences in political activity in chapter 8.

3

Creating and Maintaining an Ethnic Community

Creating and Building Polonia

The Early Years

The foreign-born Poles settled in a few New England, Middle Atlantic, and North Central states, particularly in Connecticut, New York, New Jersey, Illinois, and Michigan (Hutchinson 1956:41) in highly concentrated communities (Lieberson 1963). They were also one of the most urban of the immigrant groups in their manner of settlement; over 86 percent of them were found in cities, the percentages not varying much over the decades (Hutchinson 1956:26). The location they chose for settlement in this vast land was not haphazard, but followed the migration chain established by early pioneers who had been successful in finding residence and employment. Villagers in Poland heard (via letters, potential fellow migrants, agents of steamship companies, employers looking for cheap labor) of opportunities in America where equal or less effort produced economic benefits far outweighing what they were able to wrest from the homeland (Curti and Birr 1950; Thomas and Znaniecki 1918–1920/1958). Young men were usually first to venture on the long journey overseas. They had a better chance of finding employment than older men and were freer to experiment than were men bringing their families over. Young single women also came to stay in homes of relatives, but they were much fewer in number.

A young man usually left Poland in the company of other men from the same family or village and headed for the American town or city in which he knew someone already established. Upon arrival, he obtained work in a factory, steel

---

This chapter is limited to the establishment and all but recent years of Polonia. See chapter 6 for changes.

mill, mine, or other industrial organization accepting unskilled labor. Foremen or other workers served as marginal links between the foreigner and the American system. The young Polish immigrant usually boarded with friends or relatives. The few women who were part of the early migration waves ran such boarding houses. This was considered women's work and highly appropriate for those who were married because it allowed them to stay home while contributing to the family income. "The boarders were frequently brothers or other near relatives of the husband or wife, or fellow townsmen from the old country, and so the household was something in the nature of an enlarged family" (Zand 1956:79). Strangers could find boarding houses through local newspaper advertisements. As a man became economically stable, he went back to Poland to help his family migrate, or sent for a few family members at a time. Some men deserted their wives and children in the homeland, making new alliances in the host country, but there are no figures as to the frequency of this practice.

The immigrant family unit focused around the initial male migrant. The family tended to settle near the friends or relatives it had initially joined, gradually building a community of Poles from the same village, or at least the same region. Eventually, the community became so large as to attract new immigrants from other parts of Poland or Poles from other parts of America. These local ethnic settlements were located near large industrial work sources and in the poorer sections of the city; the newcomers could not afford better housing or higher transportation costs. The history of Polonia records much movement among the localities, accompanied by repeated family separations as the men sought greener pastures in other parts of America. Hamtramck, Michigan, for example, attracted Poles from other settlements during "the first and second decades of the present century as the automobile industry expanded its needs for unskilled workers" (Wood 1955:16).

The absence of resources to which the Polish immigrants had been accustomed back home, and presence of needs arising out of the new circumstances of life in the rapidly industrializing and urbanizing foreign country encouraged many members of the Polonian community, even those with limited funds, but with special skills such as shoemakers or dressmakers, to open businesses and provide services. This contributed to the growth of an increasingly complex, diversified, and self-sufficient economic and social structure. The immigrants were unable to transplant from Poland all they needed to build a new life. As a result, they had to: build their own churches; import their own priest (since the Irish one assigned by the Roman Catholic hierarchy in America was usually not to their liking); start and staff schools in which their children could learn their language and culture; organize mutual aid societies for emergency needs; insure that objects necessary to traditional life were available in stores where Polish was spoken; find doctors and lawyers who understood their needs; even find scribes who could write letters and read the replies if a member were illiterate.

In addition, at all times and in all places, they needed to locate translators to mediate between them and the strange world to which they had migrated.

Building a Social Structure

The Polish Americans have built a complex and organized ethnic community, with sufficient institutional completeness (Breton 1964), that has lasted more than a century, although its local subunits vary considerably in size and complexity. This community consists of several layers of social order:

1. The *local neighborhood* is often organized around a parish; it allows direct contact, personal knowledge of the lives of others, and the use of informal methods of social control and social integration. The neighborhood uses gossip to crystallize reputations (see Thomas and Znaniecki 1918–1920) with sufficient flexibility to allow for de- and re-crystallization of status with the addition or loss of major clusters of status points. Social mobility is made possible through the dynamics of change in status packages. People see each other as neighbors, customers, parents, spouses, earners, participants in religious ceremonials, students, contributors to and leaders in local associations (see also Suttles 1968, 1972).

2. The *settlement* is larger than a single neighborhood; it contains a greater institutional complexity or completeness and has a definite boundary in which a single ethnic group is dominant. For example, there were originally three main Polish American settlements in Chicago: the near northwest, the "back of the yards," and the south side near the steel mills. Each contained several neighborhoods and "community areas" (see the *Local Community Fact Book of Chicago* series of volumes, originally compiled by Louis Wirth et al., in 1938; see also Emmons 1971:56–58).

3. The *local ethnic community* consists of all members of the ethnic group who participate in the superstructure at any level. Members may even be dispersed over several noncontiguous neighborhoods, settlements, or even ethnic boundaries. Thus, there are local Polish American communities in Detroit, Chicago, Buffalo (New York), Erie and Scranton (Pennsylvania), and Panna Maria (Texas), for example.

4. The *regional* or *district ethnic community* consists of several local communities but shares some form of organization and communication. Many, but not all, ethnic communities are organized on a regional basis. The regional Polish American groups hold meetings and facilitate inter-group communication as well as regional reputations.

5. *Polonia* is the ethnic community itself; it encompasses all those who identify with it and are engaged in some form of interaction and activity contributing to its existence. The members can be scattered in a variety of work and residential centers; the community is maintained through superterritorial

organizations, mass communication, and personal contact (see Thomas and Znaniecki 1918–1920 for the concept of superterritoriality). As mentioned before, our concern here is only with American Polonia. The lack of unification and similar life-styles among Poles living in America, England, Australia, and other areas of the world makes it more realistic for us to refer only to American Polonia and to shorten its designation to Polonia.

An important factor contributing to the Polish Americans' ability to build a complex social structure, locally and superterritorially, was their need to innovate in order to meet the demands of life in a foreign country. American society allowed social experimentation, not really caring what the Polish Americans did among themselves as long as they continued to provide labor and did not cause too many problems. Accustomed to the oppressive controls of the Russian and the German occupations, the first wave of immigrants welcomed this internal freedom. They were uninterested in the American scene; thus, they directed all their attention to building their own world on the new ground.

Another factor contributing to the creation of Polonia was the relatively rapid affluence gained by peasants who had been merely surviving on a near subsistence level in Poland. As Abel (1929:216) explains:

> The ability of the immigrant to establish himself so quickly and to pay off staggering mortgages in a short time, was owing to the cheap labor offered by a numerous family, and to the willingness to do hard work and to his low standard of living.

They did not spend money on luxuries in order to maintain a competitive standard of living with non-Polish neighbors; rather, they depended on the status symbols learned back home. As soon as they became sufficiently free of the mortgages, they bought more land and contributed to the building of "Polish houses."

The main base for the formation of Polonia, granting the facilitating factors, was the combination of heterogeneity of population with the strong heritage of status competition. Although most of the immigrants were originally of peasant background, they were internally heterogenous, belonging to all the substrata of the peasantry discussed before, and varied in many other ways. Regional differences were strong, since the German occupied territories were more industrialized than were the Russian, and the Austrian area was poorer but less oppressed. Accents, vocabularies, and styles of life varied considerably. There is still much joke-telling and teasing in Polonia along regional lines. Villages differed not only in size but in degree of urban sophistication. Villagers varied by leadership skills. In fact, there was sufficient leadership ability among the peasants to start many social groups, mutual aid societies, parish clubs, and so forth (Thomas and Znaniecki 1918–1920). In addition Polonia contained, permanently or temporarily, many other immigrants and political émigrés. Socialists came to revolutionize the communities; intelligentsia refugees started a wide range of periodicals; nationalistic leaders organized to prepare for the liberation of Poland; priests started Polish parishes; and restauranteurs provided opportunities for an exchange of ideas and organizational plans.

Because of the interest in status competition and the individualism within each subunit of Polonia's communities, there developed a proliferation of groups of all sizes, functions, and complexities. These gradually became united with similar units into larger federations and, at all levels, provided experiences and training to new members and new leaders. Local leaders, who started local groups and then trained other members in organizational procedures and leadership roles, were themselves being trained by more sophisticated organizers at community-wide or even superterritorial levels. Local groups sent representatives to neighborhood, settlement, or national congresses, and to social events that were being organized at every level of the developing social structure. They learned, and in turn, brought back information about new activities or procedures for undertaking cooperative action. To this day there is a great deal of attention paid during organizational meetings to formal rules of procedure.

Certainly the effects of the more nationalistically inclined residents of and visitors to Polonia contributed to its creation. The ex-villager probably did not have the organizational *savoir faire* needed to form a Polish National Alliance, a Polish Roman Catholic Union, or any of the other superterritorial, literary, or economically based groups. However, the community included enough people who were able to develop these organizations, build an ideology justifying their existence, and convince the parish-bound peasant to join the local branch and contribute time and money even to abstractly idealistic causes. A major factor contributing to the success of these groups was Poland's genuine need, a need communicated in many different ways by the leaders to the mass of immigrants. Few ethnic communities in America have experienced this highly dramatic ideological justification for building a complex social structure, or the opportunities for such a large segment of their population to gain interaction skills.

Status Competition in Polonia

In addition, of course, the former Polish peasant was willing to invest so much time, money, and effort in active participation in the social structure of Polonia because of his or her interest in the status competition. Status competition in American Polonia was even more engrossing than it had been in Poland at all levels. The many and expanding opportunities for gaining status vis-à-vis other members of this community has served as a motivator not only in establishing Polonia, but also in maintaining it for a century. The strong interest Polonians have had in status competition, and their ability to use available resources to build numerous status hierarchies have provided them with many of the characteristics of social movements: an *esprit de corps* and a source of morale. The status competition gives meaning to daily and more dramatic activities, a justification for action, institutionalization of internal conflict, and a certain *joie de vivre*.

What is sociologically interesting is that the status competition and the complex structure of the community have served an integrative function throughout Polonia's history, while the ideological base has been able to shift from religious identity, to national identity, to ethnic identity. Even the criteria for the status competition have varied with Polonia's changing ideologies, as the people involved over generations in different companionate circles have varied. Throughout, however, the competition itself has supplied a meaning to life, a means for feeling important as an individual being, and a method for keeping strangers outside of interest boundaries. The success of Polonia as an ethnic community had been to a major extent due to its flexible ideological base—it is not the content of the ideology itself, but the status competition that gives it vitality. The changes in Polonia over the years within which the community has been developing, maintaining, and justifying its existence have been extensive, so that its continued existence has surprised many observers not cognizant of the complexity of its structure and its status foundation. It has changed from a basically two-class folk and national culture-based community, into one devoted to a very acculturated but not assimilated ethnic community to the extent that many of its members find their status competition within their static or mobile companionate circles interesting enough to prevent them from moving out into the broader society. The newest immigrant wavelets form their own competitive arenas, being rather disdainful of the existing ones; and the temporary residents usually do not have the time or energy to join groups and participate in the community.

Developing Institutional Completeness

A major criterion of ethnic survival is the institutional completeness of its community (Breton 1964; Gordon 1964). Let us examine the contention that Polonia's organizational activities are local variations of the major institutions in total societies.

There are six basic types of institutions in human society: religious, educational, economic, political, family, and recreational. In addition, there are (in varying degrees of complexity) language, the scientific-technological institution, welfare, and art (see Hertzler 1961). Together, these provide the foundation and organizing structure for the community's culture and activities.

An ethnic community must always operate within a broader national, religious, or political society. Very few communities have been independent enough to meet all of their own individual and group needs. The Amish may come closest, but even they are dependent upon the broader society. Although Polonia's web of social relations contributes to the distribution and consumption of economic goods, few of its communities produce consumer objects from their own raw materials, using only Polish American workers who are paid with local currency that is then spent for locally produced goods or services. On the other hand, Polonia does adapt American practices and build them into unique packages, typical of Polonia alone. For example, there are many Roman Catholics in America, but Roman Catholicism in Polonia is unique to Polonia. Many people in America dance the Polka, but it has a distinctive meaning for members of the "Polka Federation," who use this dance for social and competitive purposes and weave it into a whole folk culture (Emmons 1971). Let us now look at the six major institutions in Polish American communities.

The Religious Institution

Religious organizations were the first organizations to be developed by the Poles in America and they formed a base for the social structure that brought them into immediate conflict with American society. A Polish version of Catholicism was combined with pagan and magical beliefs in animated natural objects and spirits by Polish peasants (Thomas and Znaniecki 1958, vol. 1: 205–88). Their beliefs were strong and important to their lives. In Poland, they took for granted their church buildings and sacred objects for whose maintenance they did not need to sacrifice heavily. However, there was some ambivalence in their attitudes toward the priest who was a stranger, a representative of outside powers of the ecclesiastical society, and a member of the intelligentsia. On the one hand, the priest was central to community life; he mediated on behalf of his people with the heavenly system and held power useful to any villager in the status competition. On the other hand, his power created strong negative feelings whenever the highly independent and competitive villagers felt that the priest "overstepped" his bounds by trying to control secular matters (Reymont 1925). Also, the very nature of Roman Catholicism contributed to much of the latent and manifest tension with the villagers because of the doctrinaire insistence on conformity to norms that were interpreted by the priest. Two additional tendencies emerged in village life and were transmitted to Polonia: anti-intellectualism, and disregard for theological ideology and norms if they interfered with other beliefs or status competition.

The mixed feelings of the peasants became more complicated when they settled in the United States. The Roman Catholic church had an already established hierarchy and version of rituals and beliefs. The Poles were assigned priests of other nationalities (usually Irish) against whom feelings often ran so high as to prevent the religious personnel from carrying out their duties. Part of the refusal to cooperate resulted from the difficulty in communication due to language barriers, but the feelings ran even beyond this aspect (Buczek 1976). The Poles have consistently felt underrepresented in the church hierarchy and resented its often obvious attempts to Americanize them.

Eventually, ethnic parishes were created, Polish priests and nuns were imported, and schools were developed to train religious personnel in Polish Catholicism. According to Radzialowski (1975, 1990), the Polish Americans founded seven religious orders. The Felicians, transplanted from Poland in 1854, became a very active order, providing women with education and with an alternative to marriage or domestic work. The orders worked in parochial schools, hospitals, and orphanages.

In the early years of Polonia's life the parish served more than religious functions—it combined the parish and the *okolica* as a community and was the focus of life within the neighborhoods (Thomas and Znaniecki 1918-1920). Often it was developed with much sacrifice since, in addition to contributing financial support, the people literally had to erect the buildings themselves without state support (Les 1981). These were then owned by the Catholic hierarchy, not by those who invested labor and money in them. These efforts to build the church, parish house, and parochial school, however, provided the former peasants with an important training ground for organizational and leadership abilities. The priest could not manage everything; he had to delegate authority. While the structure was taking shape, a web of social groups was being formed and prepared for leadership roles. Once trained to be leaders, the former peasants started competing with the priest and resenting the structure of the church that gave the lay members little actual power. Thus, as is typical of Polonia, the strong unifying bond of religion also became a source of conflict. Much of the conflict was due to the status competition and the stubborn individualism that the immigrant brought with him to America. The protest against the power structure of the Roman Catholic ecclesiastical society (see chapter 1) took five major forms. The first of these protests took place on the local level. Many of the parish mutual aid societies had joined the Polish Roman Catholic Union (PRCU), organized in 1873. The PRCU focused on the religious institution to the extent of giving priests the right to "free admittance to all meetings of the church societies, . . . to approve all candidates for office and membership in these associations . . . and to approve each decision in matters not anticipated in the constitution of the Union" (Haiman 1948:85). Many groups broke away from the PRCU because of these provisions. Others did not join, preferring the more nationalistic Polish National Alliance (PNA).

A major protest against the Roman Catholic control over parishioners was the formation of the Polish National Catholic church (PNCC) in the years between 1897 and 1904. The organization of the PNCC, which was so popular that it even spread to Poland in a rare example of reverse diffusion, illustrates the sources of friction between Polish Americans and Roman Catholicism. The power of each parish is located in the combined hands of lay leaders and elected priests, who can marry. The top governing body, the Synod, consists of six priests and six laymen. Polish rather than Latin is the official language and the doctrine of papal infallibility was replaced by the doctrine stating that each man [sic] has the right to interpret the Bible for himself. Hell was abolished from the belief system (Fox 1957). In spite of these changes, Galusz (1977: 91) found that only about 5 percent of Polish Americans joined the Polish National Catholic church.

In addition to the formation of a competing church, the Poles protested by individually leaving Roman Catholicism for American protestant denominations. For example (Les 1981) studied a Polish Baptist congregation in Chicago.

Another illustration of protest not only against the Roman Catholic hierarchy in general, but also against the authority of the Polish religious leaders, has been their inability to unify Polonia on a community-wide level. Polonia's history is replete with the long, strong, and eventful competition between such leaders and those focusing on nationalistic themes. The most dramatic example of this competition is the relationship between the Polish Roman Catholic Union and the Polish National Alliance. The PRCU was organized earlier on religious themes and grew quite successfully on the foundation of the local parish groups. The PNA was founded in 1880 around a nationalistic theme. The competition was so extensive between these two groups as to amount to open conflict, with the PRCU losing its position as the main unifying group to the PNA. Over the years, these groups have reached a compromise, mainly because they realized by the 1930s that both themes were needed to maintain Polonia and draw the youth to it. The PNA is now the much stronger of the two superterritorial groups.

There have been many other attempts to unify Polonia along religious lines, including several lay and clerical congresses whose aim was to improve the position of Polish clergy in the American Roman Catholic hierarchy. The competition among groups, and the clergy's lack of defense against pressure from above to decrease such activity, led to a lack of effective protests (Bukowczyk 1987). Even today, the Roman Catholics among the Polish Americans complain over the lack of representation of their ethnic group in the hierarchy. As of the late 1960s, there were "only seven bishops and one archbishop of Polish descent" (Wytrwal 1969:74). The headquarters of Roman Catholicism in Rome is seen as a source of power with which the Polonians hope to influence the American hierarchy. One of the forms of protest by the clergy itself and other community leaders was communication with the Vatican, requesting greater representation in the hierarchy. Of course, having a Pole become the pope, head of the worldwide ecclesiastical society, led to great expectations of increase of power among Polonia's Catholics. A cover story in *Time* magazine (Bernstein 1992), entitled "How Reagan and the Pope Conspired to Assist Poland's Solidarity Movement and Hasten the Demise of Communism," showed that the pope has been very active in Polish political affairs. His election certainly brought pride to both Poland and Polonia, but the latter seems to have been helped only indirectly.

Thomas and Znaniecki (1918-1920) found 70 organized groups in the Chicago parish of Saint Stanislaus Kostka. There are still numerous Polish parishes in the United States. The *Informator Polonii w USA 1980–81*, published by the *Daily News* in New York, identifies parishes as Polish in a number of localities in each state. The names of the priests and the locations would indicate that at least some parishioners identify with this national or ethnic group. For example, it lists a Polish bishop, a Dominican sisters convalescent home, and 65 parishes for the city of Chicago alone. There are, according to this source, 29,143 children in the parish schools. In addition, there is one high school connected with the church with 444 students (*Informator* 1980:165-169). The Polish National church, headed by an "ordinary bishop" of the western diocese, maintained in 1980 a cathedral, one chapel, five churches, and one parish without a church.

Barbara Les (1981), who studied a Polish Roman Catholic church, a Polish National Catholic church, and a Polish Baptist Church of Chicago in the late 1970s, found that all three had become Americanized to a great extent.

> Stating that the initial character of Polonia religious institutions and organizations was Polish, I mean here that in spite of the fact that they existed and functioned in American industrial centers and formally belonged to the American Churches, they worked in the Polish language and preserved some elements of the Polish culture, including the religious one, as well as the fact that they formulated and disseminated Polish ideologies. (Les 1981: 289)

By the 1970s, she found many American characteristics, including the use of English in rituals and records, the decrease in number of members, especially those of a Polish background, and so forth. However, the large influx of the newest cohort of Poles has revitalized the churches. St. Hyacinth, which was her Roman Catholic case study, now has four Polish masses on Saturday and Sunday and draws an estimated 2,000 parishioners who have scattered throughout the city and suburbs, but who return to the old neighborhood, which is identified by the nickname of the church, *Jackowo*.

Mostwin (1991:176) concluded from a study of a sample of the latest immigrants, obtained mainly through parishes, organizations, the press, and radio, that there is a "need for a new model of a Polish priest working with the Polish Immigrants in the 1974-1984 United States." The new immigrants are different, coming from cities and towns, forming a new intelligentsia who knows English and will simply not accept the authoritarianism of the old-style priest. According to her, a new-style priest-patriot should be imported from Poland and prepared for missionary work, educated in psychology and sociology. Speaking fluid Polish and English he must conduct a pastoral mission not only to the parishioners in his own church but also to other needy Polish immigrants. He must "understand the trauma of transplantation of newcomers and serve as a contact with American social agencies which can help serve the Poles in America."

The Educational Institution

Education has long been closely associated with religion in Polonia. Most Polish Americans found American public schools unacceptable in terms of their emphasis on American culture, language, history, and geography, to the exclusion of Polish culture. Also, the immigrants were more concerned with discipline and the learning of moral virtues than they felt American schools were teaching. As late as the 1960s, Obidinski (1968) found the Polish Americans of Buffalo still firmly convinced that parish schools provided a superior education than public schools. Polish Americans, therefore, have entrusted the education of their children to the Catholic parish schools in spite of the financial costs to the community and to individual families, and in spite of their ambivalent feelings toward religious personnel. The early schools were quite restricted, being mostly concerned with transmitting Polish Catholicism and morality (Bolek 1948; see also Miaso 1971). Little emphasis was placed on the teaching of Polish or American secular, literary, national cultures. The curriculum was often unstandardized, the schools inadequately equipped, the teachers relatively uneducated, and the students poorly taught. The Polish peasant had little interest in formal education, desiring instead the strict moral upbringing his children received in the authoritarian classroom. [1] The nonpeasant-based Polish immigrants made other provisions for their children, very often sending them to public schools.

Around 1918 the United States government began to pressure Polonia to accept the standardized schedule of classes and to use English in its schools, charging that too many young men in the armed services did not understand or speak English. As it was, some schools were already beginning to convert to English. This trend increased as fewer children came to school with a background in Polish and as the need to function in the American work and school systems increased. The curriculum eventually phased out all Polish subjects and language training, which was taken over to some extent by the Saturday or "continuation" schools, usually organized by the major voluntary organizations.

Because of the parental insistence that their children attend Polish American schools, the community has supported a relatively large number of such educational establishments. By 1920, every Polish parish in Chicago and its suburbs had an accompanying school, with 60 percent of youth aged 7 to 17 attending these (Kantowicz 1984). There was also a St. Stanislaw College, which became

Weber High and Gordon Technical schools and a Holy Family Academy for girls.

Recent figures are unavailable because of the dispersal of the children to nonethnic parishes, but as late as 1942 there were 585 grammar schools, 72 secondary schools, and 58 institutions of higher learning that were purely Polish American, as well as 300 grammar, 17 high schools, and 37 "other" schools that had major courses of relevance to Polonia (Bolek 1943). In the late 1950s there were an estimated 250,000 elementary school students being taught by Polish American Catholic nuns and over 100,000 students registered in special programs, the largest of which were catechism classes (Sister Tullia 1959:603).

The influx of third-cohort Poles into America has revitalized some of the schools, even led to the organization of new ones. *Glos Nauczyciela* (Teacher's Voice), a nicely presented quarterly that began publication in 1985, describes such schools in locations as diverse as the city and suburbs of Chicago, Los Angeles, Holyoke (Massachusetts), Brooklyn (New York), Doylestown (Pennsylvania), and Silver Springs (Maryland).

The "first Polish American institution of higher learning in the United States" was a Polish seminary (Radzialowski 1978: 462). This became the complex of Orchard Lake Seminary, St. Mary's College, and a high school in Michigan (Wytrwal 1969a:75). The seminary has gone through several stages, first teaching Polish future priests and lay students in the Polish language. The second-generation Polish Americans were also taught Polish in spite of the fact that most Polish churches by then offered mass in English. The priests needed to use Polish in their contacts with parishioners in generationally mixed parishes. In recent years the seminary has again drawn men from Poland, and Mostwin (1991) recommends that they should be taught to perform different functions than in the past, due to the higher level of education of Polish Americans. As of the late 1960s, 23 percent of the students at St. Mary's School in Orchard Lake never spoke Polish at home and 39 percent spoke it rarely (Chrobot 1969). The seminary and related schools of Orchard Lake also contain a Center for Polish Studies and Culture, formed in 1969, offering courses in Polish, a library, and an art gallery. The latest addition in the complex is the Polish American Sports Hall of Fame, begun in 1973 (Radzialowski 1978)

The Polish American Teaching Sisterhoods, especially the Felician Sisters have a four-year senior college and three junior colleges (Radzialowski 1978: 471). The Sisters of the Holy Family of Nazareth also have a liberal arts college and a teacher training college (473). However, these as well as the college of the Bernadine Sisters of the Third Order of St. Francis, do not offer any Polish language, literature, or culture courses.

A recent move in Polonia has been to pressure American schools of higher education for the inclusion of Polish language and literature courses. Columbia University housed an Adam Mickiewicz Chair of Polish Culture from 1948 to

1954 (Blejwas 1991a: 323). There was a great deal of controversy concerning this chair during the cold war years in American society because it was funded by the Polish communist government and because of the characteristics of the person who was appointed to fill it. The Polish Americans of the second cohort were particularly opposed to this support, and the chair vanished, replaced with only a few visiting professorships, after Columbia University refused further support. It was not till 1971 that another Polish chair was created, this time the Alfred Jurzykowski Chair of Polish Studies at Harvard University (Blejwas 1991b: 446). Forty-eight American universities and colleges and sixty-eight public secondary schools offered Polish courses in 1957 (Miaso 1971:38). The pressure on the universities has an uneven flow, often dependent on the availability of faculty. It has intensified in recent years with mixed reports of success. Many schools have started such courses only to quickly remove them from the curriculum for lack of students.

Other groups have contributed to Polonia's educational institution by creating or disseminating Polish and Polish American culture. These efforts are directed toward Polish American adults, Polish American youth and/or American society. Almost all the multifunctional groups include a youth division aimed at educating descendants of the immigrants in the Polish language and culture. Some organizations, such as the Harcerze (Polish Scouts), are aimed at the youth audience exclusively. The Polish Falcons combine physical and national culture development of their members. The American Council of Polish Cultural Clubs sponsors many "cultural events" (see chapter 7 and the list of associations in appendix B). The American Institute of Polish Culture has, in addition to seminars, concerts, poetry readings and scholarships, a permanent traveling exhibition of "One Thousand Years of Polish History and Culture" and one on "Polish Music Today" (Gale 1992: 1111).

The history of Polonia records many cultural and educational associations that have not survived into the 1970s or that went into a dormant period until revived recently. The 1970s are significant in the community's life due to the aging of the second emigration while the third wave had not as yet become numerically and socially significant. The exception to the above statement is the Kosciuszko Foundation, founded and remaining in New York since 1925. The foundation devotes most of its funds and energies to assisting historical, social and natural scientific work through the exchange of students and scholars between America and Poland. In addition, it grants stipends, supports students and others working on special scholarly projects, and publishes the products of such work. Polonia's main lay institution of higher learning, Alliance College in Pennsylvania, closed down in the 1970s. The Polish People's University, founded by Polish Socialists, with branches in several cities, which drew audiences of as many as 1,000 Polonians, had only one remaining branch on the East Coast in the middle 1970s (Radzialowski 1978: 477). Polonia's Esperanto club for people interested in building a cosmopolitan culture was no longer active. The Polish People's University, the Esperanto Club, and the very active Polish Socialist party usually drew the same people to their events, forming a substratum of intellectually oriented Polish Americans that was likely to be socially isolated from members of the village parish clubs.

Most of the currently active organizations dealing with the development and dissemination of Polish culture were founded during and after World War II by a combination of the intelligentsia of the second emigration and the descendants of the first emigration. Members of the third cohort have contributed to their revitalization. The Polish American Historical Association, founded in 1942, meets in conjunction with the American Historical Society and publishes *Polish American Studies,* a scholarly journal and a newsletter, both in the English language. The Polish Society of History and Museum of America, founded in 1943, has as its main function the maintenance of the Polish Museum of America that was created in 1937 in the Polish Roman Catholic Union building in Chicago's old Polonian neighborhood. The museum houses archival and artistic products of Polish and Polish American culture, and is connected with a library and a periodical collection. The society and the museum have become quite active in recent years with numerous artistic exhibitions, concerts, and celebrations in honor of visiting dignitaries, under the leadership of the third cohort intelligentsia.

The Polish Institute of Arts and Sciences in America (PIASA) was formed by refugee scholars in 1940, on the model of the very prestigious Polish Academy of Sciences in Poland. It is headquartered in New York with branches in the Midwest and Canada. It publishes *The Polish Review* and a number of books dealing with Polish subjects. It also holds periodic scientific congresses and cultural events. In fact, it organized three international congresses at universities, the last one being at Yale the summer of 1992. The rectors of the major Polish Universities and the ambassador of the Republic of Poland were among the speakers, as were Polish American scholars. The Joseph Pilsudski Institute of America, founded in 1943, devotes itself to research in the modern history of Poland. Its functions are similar to those of the PIASA. The Polish Institute of Science and Culture, affiliated with the Polish University Abroad (PUNO) in London, was opened in the late 1980s in Chicago. In the form of an "invisible college" (Crane 1968), it provided diplomas and the kind of knowledge impossible to obtain by newcomers with a weak familiarity with English, which kept them from American universities. However, it closed down in the middle of 1992.

This history of Polonia's development of its educational institution beyond the parochial school indicates that, although the majority of Polish Americans have not used schooling as an important criterion in status competition and have even been hostile to the intelligentsia, there has always been an intellectual element in the community that has increased in size and influence in recent years. There are several factors contributing to Polonia's increased emphasis on the development and dissemination of Polish national culture and on higher education of its youth. First, the second and third cohorts are less anti-intellectual and more oriented toward achievement through education than the old emigration had been. Second, Polonia is becoming more interested in status competition with other ethnic communities in America. Third, Polish Americans are becoming more willing to use American criteria of success. Finally, Polish Americans are becoming increasingly aware of the disadvantage of being ignorant of the culture of the national society of their origin. These points will be developed in future chapters.

The Political Institution

Political institutions are sets of procedures by which a society or community regulates its internal relations and its relations with other groups. Observers of Polonia in America have noted two main tendencies in its political life: internal strife and conflict, and a lack of unified involvement in the political life of the larger society (Thomas et al. 1921/1971; Park 1928; Wood 1955). Thomas and Znaniecki (1918-1920) observed and predicted increasing social disorganization, evidenced in conflicts on individual, family, and community levels as the traditional forms of community control typical of the village dissolved and were not replaced by sufficient control from agencies outside of the community. Poland, the country in which the emigrants had been socialized, lived under very strong social controls imposed on all classes by the occupying powers, so that deviation brought reprisals, and escape was possible only through emigration. Most villagers were not involved in protesting this externally imposed social controls, but were controlled by a system of locally developed norms. Socialized into a shame culture by families demanding continued contributions to their reputations in the status competition, most villagers lived within narrow behavioral limits (Lynd 1965). Socialization into a shame culture results in minimal deviation because of fear of having things known and used against one's reputation, rather than because of internalization of norms and self-control.

Thomas and Znaniecki (1918-1920) expected people dependent on a small, highly controlling village to become "hedonistic" and morally disorganized when these controls were weakened by the immigration process and by many characteristics of American society, including its size and democratic norms. Observing conflict within the communities and families, they interpreted this as evidence of, and a contribution to, social disorganization. In other words, they expected families and the community itself to become disorganized. They did not see the structures that were emerging. The point being made here is that the political institution that emerged in Polonia was built upon competition and conflict to such an extent that these very characteristics had a community building rather than destroying consequence. Alliances were created, break-away organizations formed in competition with established ones, and interest in community life focused attention inwardly rather than pushing members into assimilation. The structures were built with the help of many layers of Polonia's community and have been strong enough to pull in members of even new generations of the first cohort of immigrants, the World War II cohort, and, though to a much lesser degree, the newest cohort.

The internal conflict was itself an outgrowth of status competition, which is a competition for power, for economic goods, and for reputation. The conflict occurs when the competition becomes so strong as to result in open action between the competing parties. The history of Polonia is replete with numerous, publicly expressed schisms within groups in the struggle for leadership roles or a voice in the formation or reformulation of organizational goals and procedures. The mass communication media constantly carry stories of such conflicts, and letters by people denouncing their political or organizational opponents have appeared for as long as there has been a Polonian press. The groups formed this way continue involvement in the community, competing now with their former "enemies." This is one of the main reasons for the proliferation of groups in Polonia. The same is true of conflict-ridden families and other social units.

The institutionalization of conflict as part of the status competition in Polonia and the neglect of reputations outside of its boundaries is evident in the external social control agencies used by many groups and individuals to enforce con-formity of one's own group. Thomas and Znaniecki (1918–1920) expressed shock over parents who took their own children to court for failure to contribute to the family's economic status base. Wood (1955) made frequent reference to the use of courts and mass media to settle "squabbles" among politicians in Hamtramck, a predominantly Polish American subcommunity of Detroit. The leaders' struggle for political power as a means of acquiring status was combined with an utter disregard for the poor reputation Hamtramck gained in the larger society for its political in-fighting. Each candidate for office tried to discredit and disenfranchise all opponents through all possible means. The American political scene at time of campaigns for office bears resemblance to this process. To a lesser degree, other Polish American organizations have tried to force their competing opponents into submission or cooperation through the use of courts and mass communication, even at the cost of lowering the community status in the society at large.

The status competition within Polonia has had another effect on its political life and that is the avoidance of the recognition and assistance of the deviant. Finestone (1964) found that family members who shamed the unit by criminal behavior were simply ignored while in prison and had to reestablish their relations with each family member separately upon release, on the promise of contributing positively to their status in the future. Public avoidance of the deviants is seen in the lack of admission that they exist and in a lack of social agencies designed to help them reintegrate into society (Thomas and Znaniecki 1918-1920; Park 1928).

The internal focus on status competition has contributed to a lack of unified involvement in the American political scene in two ways: through a lack of interest in committing resources to striving for political office, and in an unwillingness to unite in support of a particular candidate. Hamtramck, for example, has had an extremely large turnout of voters for many of its elections, but the competition leads to a splintering of votes among the numerous candidates (Wood 1955:72). The same is true of Chicago, as we shall see in a later chapter.

The political life of the community has been deeply dependent upon the actions of organizational leaders who formulated policy and provided the backing for the few candidates for public office, who are members of Polonia or who promise to support its causes. These leaders have changed as members of the first generation have retired or died and have been replaced by second-generation members. These newer leaders are apt to have an educational background in law or economics and often lack knowledge of the Polish language and Polish culture. Fishman and Nahirny (1966) found strong generational differences among leaders of four ethnic communities: Polish, Ukrainian, Jewish, and German. The new generation represents "organizational" rather than "cultural" leadership.

> This shift from personal involvement in ethnic cultures to involvement in ethnically-peripheral organizations is of crucial significance here. It prompts us to conclude that native-born leaders, far from being ethnic *cultural* leaders, should be more properly considered ethnic *organizational* leaders. Of course, by actively participating in ethnic organizational life native-born leaders may be trying to reassert their attachment to ethnicity. But organizational participation does not necessarily lead to personal and creative involvement in the ancestral culture. In point of fact, native-born leaders are largely de-ethnicized (both linguistically and otherwise) while, at the same time, they remain extensively involved in organized ethnic life. (Fishman and Nahirny 1966:178)

These authors are saying that the native-born leaders are not apt to be members of cultural associations in their community. There is evidence, however, that Polonia's political leaders may have changed their orientation toward the importance of ethnic, and particularly national, culture. Ever since the spread of "Polish jokes" in the early 1970s the main leaders have developed a policy of attacking them and trying to change the image of Polish Americans by stressing and idealizing Polish national culture. This emphasis has been strengthened by the presence of the more nationally oriented third cohort of immigrants.

Even during the times of the highly competitive political activity, the Polish Americans have been able to unify not only vis-à-vis external agencies, but also in many joint humanitarian efforts. Events in Europe called for help in the form of food, medicine, clothing, and other needed items. As we shall see in the next chapter, the raising and use of enormous sums of money and direct involvement in Poland's political life brought Polonia's organizations together during the wars and the early years of independence following World War I. The Polish American Council (Rada Polonii Amerykanskiej) organized relief efforts during World War II.

The most important interorganizational, political association has been the Polish American Congress, formed in 1944. Its political activities have been focused on both Poland and the United States. For example, in 1948 it organized the American Committee for Resettlement of Polish Displaced Persons, which was able to work with the U.S. Displaced Persons Commission and many other relief organizations to find Polish refugees throughout Europe, and locate them with housing and jobs in America. This effort definitely involved numerous members of Polonia, organized in 26 State Division Commissions as well as local groups (Jaroszynska 1987: 69).

The Polish American Congress (PAC), the main politically active organization of recent years consists of established, rather than third-cohort, Polish Americans. It identifies itself in part in the following way in the *Encyclopedia of Associations* (Gale 1992:1976):

> Promotes qualified Polish-Americans in government, business and other professional fields. . . . Works with the U.S. State Department regarding Polish and Polish-American matters. . . . Committees: Anti-Defamation; Cultural Promotion; Polish-Jewish Relations; Political Action; Refugee and Immigration; Youth Commission.

This statement shows areas of concern within Polonia's political life, including status problem (as reflected by Polish jokes, against which the PAC has been actively opposed), relations between the Polish and the Jewish communities, and problems of immigration.

Thus, although Polonia's press and local gossip stress the individualistic and competitive nature of its life, the community has been able to rally around important issues under the influence of a few leaders. This does not mean that there is a lack of conflict over who has the right to represent the community to the outside world, only that Polonia has been very politically active in trying to influence both the home and the host countries. The competition is evident in the failure to elect Polonian representatives to the governing bodies of the United States, mainly due to the unwillingness to support competitors.

The Economic Institution

Mutual aid has been very important in maintaining Polonia and was central to the development of fraternal insurance organizations. Although most of the superterritorial associations (including the Polish Roman Catholic Union and the Polish National Alliance) started with ideological goals, they added insurance within a short time. This function has contributed to the maintenance of at least 18 such groups as powerful, multimillion-dollar business enterprises. The money collected in insurance is used for loans, mortgages, and stocks and bonds; each investment brings in additional capital. These insurance groups are sociologically interesting because they combine a multimillion-dollar business and a large voluntary association with numerous functions.

The stability of the voluntary association is maintained in two ways. First, the top officers form a bureaucratized *cadre* or nucleus of trained personnel, and retain their positions for long periods of time. They are paid officials and managers located in the central headquarters of the organization. Their continuity of office is due in part to the unwillingness of members to trust neophytes with large sums of money. The leaders prefer to remain in office as long as possible since the salaries are good, and the status benefits of the positions are high. Few social leaders are willing to enter positions of such responsibility for short terms of office, since they are full-time jobs and require temporarily dropping former occupations (with possible reentry problems after being voted out). Generally speaking, these leaders are very visible on the political scene, which brings reflexive status to the members, who thus continue to vote them into office.

Second, the business itself is so complex that it would be very difficult to dissolve. For example, the Polish National Alliance has 332,962 policies, each one guaranteeing membership, and assets and loans in the millions. Unraveling these would be such a tremendous task that once such an insurance group passes a certain financial size, it tends to perpetuate itself.

Economic functions are performed by many organizations. Any group can serve as an economic support system for its members by providing information about sources of economic goods, be they jobs or excellent buys. Such groups can help members become established in professions or occupations by providing sponsors in the form of already established colleagues. As Hall (1975) points out, men's careers—and probably women's, although they are not discussed as often—are strongly influenced by the people they know and the opportunities these people make available to them. Medical, dental, legal, and other professional organizations have a referral system by which a new professional gains a set of clients. Many professionals with Polish backgrounds chose to practice within Polonia because of the status benefits coming from affiliation with the ethnic professional group. Other organizations provide economic opportunities directly or in the form of exchange of services. Polish immigrants of the first cohort were employed in mines, factories, packinghouses, and steel mills (see chapter 6). However, it did not take long before a small business class emerged.

> Poles clustered in two . . . types of business—small artisanal or retail shops like
> bakeries, butchers, or saloons, or businesses that met specialized immigrant needs
> like printshops (Polonia's intellectual and political nerve-center), the retail of
> religious and patriotic goods, or Polish funeral parlors. (Bukowczyk 1987:36)

Another "type of Polish business operator, the successful immigrant
entrepreneur" (37) emerged. As the decades went by, businesses owned by
Polish Americans expanded in number and size but the community could never
offer employment to most of its members. The expansion has been assisted in
recent years by the arrival of the third cohort of emigrants from communist and
privatizing Poland, as will be discussed later.

The Family Institution

There is no single Polish American family type. The variations by social class
and region in Poland combine with the influence of location, cohort and
generation in America to create many different types of families. Not all families
are even Catholic, although Catholicism has influenced and been woven into
family roles and life. Poland, as is true of almost all other national culture
societies, was and is patriarchal but with major differences from the stereotype.
However, this fact does not result in passive women or children. One of the
characteristics of Polish status competition is the mutual interdependence of the
individual and the family for the combined "package." This is true of the major
social classes who migrated in the pre-World War II years. Unfortunately, we
know very little about the intelligentsia and the bourgeoisie, since their family
systems have not been studied as thoroughly as that of the peasant family. [2]

The traditional, stereotypical Polish peasant family was not only patriarchal, but
also limited the social life space of girls and women. [3] In a Polish village, the new
bride usually moved into or near the home of her husband's family, as typical of
many such systems (Benet 1951; Thomas and Znaniecki 1918–1920; Zand 1956).
Girls never inherited property unless there were no sons to take it over, and then the
arrangement involved an "adoption" of a son-in-law into the bride's family. The
woman's power within the family was very low at first and did not increase until
she was older and had children of her own (particularly sons), and until the
introduction of younger women into the unit relieved her of physical tasks and
elevated her to a managerial position. Her status also increased with the status of
her husband. However, this typical portrayal of the situation of women in patriarchal
families does not reflect reality. All agricultural families involved the interdependence of men and women, which made both indispensable to the family (Bloch
1976; Sanday 1974; see also Lopata 1988a).

> In matters of reciprocal response we find among the Polish peasants the sexes equally
> dependent upon each other . . . under conditions in which the activities of the woman

can attain an objective importance more or less equal to those of the man, the greatest social efficiency is attained by a systematic collaboration of men and women in external fields rather than by a division of tasks which limits the woman to "home and children" (Thomas and Znaniecki 1918-1920\1958: 82-83).

In addition, a woman's behavior and direct contribution to the economic and social welfare of the family unit were important for its reputation, so that although the patriarchal authority was absolute, her status was not as low as it might have been under such a system. Her husband and his family, and later her children, needed her constant contribution to their status vis-à-vis other families.

Marriage and parenthood among the Polish peasant were not normatively of the American "romantic love" type.

The bond [family] is not necessarily one of affection. . . . There appears to be as much concern for economic status and stability and for "face," as for emotional bonds. The family is an economic unit and it is also a social corporation, reinforced by the strongest traditional sanctions. (Benet 1951:144; see also Thomas and Znaniecki's description of village life [1918-1920], Reymont's [1925] *The Peasants,* and Finestone's [1964] analyses growing out of this literature)

The immigrant family could not recreate a similar pattern in America, since it settled for the most part in an urban area with no inheritance of land or other possessions. Zand (1956:77) claims that the immigration process itself resulted in female hegemony within the Polish American family for several reasons. Wives were often left back in Poland while husbands migrated to America, or were left in one city of the new world while the men sought better working conditions in another. They therefore became accustomed to leading and managing their families. The kinds of jobs the men were able to get often kept them away from home for many hours, six days a week; the children did not have much time with their fathers and turned, instead, to their mothers. The fact that each woman could establish her own household rather than having to move in with her in-laws helped increase her influence over the family. Being freed from the male kinship group, women acquired much more power than the young peasant women had traditionally enjoyed. Zand (1956) also indicated the possibility that, since there were so few single women among the immigrants, some of the single men married the daughters of more established families. In such cases, the woman's family had the major say over the new unit, particularly if the couple lived in her family's home until the husband became economically self-sufficient. In addition, American laws protected women and dealt with family members individually rather than as part of a unit. Thomas and Znaniecki (1918-1920) concluded that the Polish-American marriage, in fact, had little chance of survival because the woman could refuse to be coerced by the man and could resort to external control agencies in order to force him to do her bidding, punish him for transgression, and demand full economic cooperation.

Marriage tended to become, under those circumstances, a matter of civil and legal rights rather than subject to community and extended family controls. In fact, however, the divorce rate among the Polish Americans remained very low until recent years, families being dependent upon each other and Catholicism reenforcing the community's negative view of divorce and desertion. Entrance into marriage remained a matter for status matching and building.[4]

Social interaction between man and wife of peasant background was generally limited to matters of common interest, such as sex, household management, and child rearing. Men were expected to be concerned mainly with male matters, to seek the company of other men, and to use alcohol as a means of recreation and emotional release. Drinking on special occasions, such as pay day, Saturday night, or a wedding was traditionally heavy and accompanied by outbreaks of violence. Taverns formed an important meeting place for Polish men in the village and then in the American city (Thomas 1949).

Most foreign-born Poles married foreign-born Poles (except when newcomers married daughters of more established families), and the tendency to stay within the ethnic group carried over to their children. The immigrants generally had many children. However, the infant mortality rate for children of Polish immigrants was the highest of all white immigrant women in 1919 (124 to 87 total; Lieberson 1980: 45-47). Although the rate was halved by 1932, it still remained highest for any group but the blacks (62 to 58). The great decrease in the gap between the Polish rate and the total one indicates the speed with which the former peasant women learned hygienic methods of self and child care. Fertility rates for Polish women have dropped considerably over the decades. The fertility rate for foreign-born Polish women began to drop over the decades. The figures for women aged 35 to 44 dropped from 5,868 children having been born per 1,000 in 1910 (compared to 4,102 for all foreign-born white women) to 2,076 for foreign-stock Polish Americans in 1960. This was below the total foreign-stock rate of 2,195 (U.S. Bureau of Census, P-20, N.226, November 1971: table 8). Children were a valuable asset on farms back home, and even in urban settings in the host country. In addition to contributing to the family social status and family income, they were expected to support their parents in old age.

Regardless of the influence women have gained on American soil, each family exerted strong patriarchal control over the children, particularly the daughters.[5] A girl's reputation affected her marriage chances and the family status. Constraints were placed upon young women's involvement in school and employment.[6] Schooling was not valued positively for girls, and working a job away from the immediate neighborhood was equally undesirable.

Domestic service, while recognized as hard and humble in social scale, was valued for the training and experience it gave a girl. . . . Young men married a girl who had been in domestic service more readily than one who had worked in a factory, partly because they expected that she would be a better girl morally, partly because she would be a better housekeeper. (Zand 1956:85)

Factory work was less favored, but might be permitted depending on the kind of relations it involved.

The location was also a factor in the community's appraisal of the factory; if it was located within or near the Polish settlement so that most of the people who worked in it were Polish and the girl was, in a sense, under the eye of her friends and neighbors, the community approved it. The greater the distance and the opportunity for strange contacts, the less the community approved of factory employment for girls. (86)

Married women ideally remained at home to care for their husbands and children. The labor statistics of Polish American women until recent years reflect an unwillingness of the family to have them work outside of the home once they are married. This ideal could not be met in many circumstances, when additional income was needed for the family, as was true during the depression years (Radzialowski 1990). In addition, women contributed in major ways to the family income by keeping boarders and lodgers, as well as running small businesses such as taverns or grocery stores. Polish neighborhoods had a reputation for their large number of boarding houses, often housing newly arrived immigrants. Their contributions to the economic life of the community was evident in the work they did for schools, parishes, their fraternal organizations, and their building and loan associations. As was noted before, the community could not function without their active support.

As the immigrants reared the second generation, they came into conflict with them, primarily over obedience and economic cooperation. The traditional Polish culture was based on a negative view of human nature: "The Poles are a censorious lot and have little faith in the continence or general moral fiber of their fellows" (Zand 1956:79). Finestone (1964:126) concluded that "the Polish mode of interpreting experience is deeply imbued with the conception of sin; moral categories are widely applied in the judgment of human conduct." The result of such a mistrust of human nature was a system designed to rigidly control the behavior of children. Benet pointed out a contradiction inherent in the Polish family institution:

Unquestioning obedience was expected of a child; at the same time the child was expected to become self-reliant, strong-willed and independent of spirit. . . . The dual emphasis on unquestioning obedience and independence subjected the child throughout the formative period of his life to two opposing pressures, creating strong tensions that often resulted in serious clashes between parents and children. (quoted in Finestone 1964:150)

Children judged old enough to find means of earning money were expected to do so. Their earnings were then to be turned over to the parents to use wisely in helping the family live and maintain or even increase its status. Thomas and Znaniecki (1918-1920), were personally shocked by the behavior of parents and children toward each other. Describing the disorganization of the family, particularly the parent-child relations over economic matters, they state, "The parents, for example, resort to the juvenile court, not as a means of reform, but as an instrument of vengeance" (p. 104 in 1958 edition). Finestone (1964) feels that this is proof of a basic lack of affection among family members. However, the status competition may also motivate such behavior. Thomas and Znaniecki (1918-1920) for example, report a case in the juvenile court in which a father who had been asked to cooperate in solving the problem of his daughter who had been living in the streets answered, "Do what you please with her. She ain't no use to me" (p. 104 in 1958 edition). He was referring to her failure to contribute to the family economic status. Finestone (1964) also found that parents, spouses, and other relatives failed to visit or write to men who had been caught in criminal acts and sent to prison, unlike the Italians, who welcomed their exprisoners with a party and automatic help in reestablishment. Polish family members earn their right to belong to the unit through initial cooperation, but they must continue earning it throughout their lives by contributing positively to family status.[7] Those who dishonor or shame the family are either written off, legally disowned, or simply ignored as much as possible. Conflict with uncooperative children was emotionally charged since failures to take part in the competition created anger and even hatred (Thomas and Znaniecki, 1958: 104).

Not all Polish American parents were able to care for their children. There were orphanages in many communities. The Felician Sisters took care of about 7,000 children at St. Hedwig Manual Training School in Niles, Illinois. Some did not have living parents, others were placed there if their parent(s) "could not afford to raise them" (*Loyola World* 1991: 7). The orphanage was opened in 1911 and closed in 1960 as the number of orphans decreased.

One of the ways in which life in America affected the Polish immigrants and their families was through the decrystallization of sibling status. Each brother and, mainly through marriage, each sister established his or her own life, following economic opportunities or problems. Although they helped each other in the initial stages of settlement and sometimes in emergencies throughout life (Shanas and Streib 1965), many siblings became sufficiently status variant and involved with their own nuclear families to interact frequently with each other.

The Recreational Institution

"Recreation" refers to any patterned, stabilized set of procedures having no other primary function but leisure activity or companionate interaction. People have been known to convert a variety of activities from work to recreation and vice versa, but there are some traditional leisure activities. In Polonia, as elsewhere, recreational subinstitutions have been class stratified, each social stratum selecting an almost mutually exclusive aspect of the culture as a focal point for getting together and socializing. Common activities celebrate national events, such as 3 May, Polish Constitution Day. This is usually accompanied by a parade, bands, and groups of organizational members of surrounding and even quite distant communities marching in costumes to Polish music. Religious holidays, especially Christmas and Easter, are focal points of activity, bringing people into whatever neighborhood retains the church, restaurants, and stores displaying Polish foods. Christmas Eve mass is a long established tradition in the home country, replicated as much as possible here. The churches are usually decorated with flowers, smelling of incense, and packed with people. Easter foods require blessing from priests and the festivities are extensive with much visiting (Zand 1956, Obidinski and Zand 1987). Each organization has its social events, ranging from the White and Red Ball of the Legion of Young Polish Women and concerts of the Polish Institute of Arts and Sciences in America to club *pikniks*, the American term appearing in the Polish language announcements. Polish names are increasingly listed in memberships of country, golf, and other middle-class leisure clubs. These activities will be discussed at length in chapter 5.

Polish Americans turned to radio and television early in the history of the two media. Not long after the commericialization of radio (late 1920s) there were a number of radio programs originating from the Midwest and the East Coast. These programs (as they still do today) broadcast classic, folk and modern music, soap operas, discussions and interviews regarding current and historical subjects, polemic commentaries, and talk shows. In some cases program operators bought their own stations and used them as political vechicles to publicize their own political ambitions. Perhaps the most interesting days were in the 1930s when strong programs such as the "Polish Barn Dance" had live remote broadcasts from church auditoriums. Polish operas were also produced and presented by program entreprenuers. Regular Polish-language television programs existed throughout Polonia, but with an uneven history depending upon leadership and talent.

Developing Associational Complexity

Although each of Polonia's settlements has its own local groups, the community abounds with a variety of associations that weave the numerous smaller units into complex federated structures. There are three types of such superterritorial structures: those combining single interest groups, the multipurpose associations, and the interorganizational structures purporting to represent all of the community.

Single Interest Groups

Single interest groups can contain one category of people or can be devoted to a single type of activity (see appendix A). Some of the lasting voluntary associations of similar people have been the veterans groups, organized into local units by and for ex-combatants of either the Polish or the American armed services, with auxiliaries for wives and daughters. The Polish Legion of American Veterans is open to "American Citizens of Polish descent who served in the United States Armed Forces during World War I and II or the Korean or Vietnam Conflicts" (Gale 1972:101). The second such group is the Polish Army Veterans Association of America and it is open only to men and women who served with the Polish Armed Forces. There are associations of paratroopers, "ex-combatants," and former prisoners of war. These groups offer companionship to people who went through similar experiences, and take care of members who are hurt, disabled, or just elderly. Care of the veterans of the Polish armed services is particularly important and problematic since they are not recipients of help from either the Polish or the American government (see chapter 5).

The associations combining local groups named after specific villages or districts in Poland have also been long-lasting. The federations are mainly regional: the mountaineers have their own association, distinct from that of "Small Poland" or "Large Poland." Members of a group named after a particular village do not necessarily come from that village (Lopata 1954). The category of single purpose federations includes all those devoted to limited and specific activities, such as singing (Polish Singers Alliance), playing, dancing and listening to the polka, organizing cultural and artistic events, and so forth. There is a great variety of such organizations, including the Polish Genealogical Society, the Polish American Library Association, the Polish American Numismatic Society and the Polish-US Economic Council associated with the Chamber of Commerce of the United States. The Polish Scouts (Harcerstwo) have groups in several locations, while the Falcons, with 150 lodges or "nests" focus on building the body to support the spirit (Pienkos 1987). The Alliance of Polish Clubs in Chicago, which combines 35 different groups and consists of "about 2,500 Poles and Americans of Polish Descent," recently took over the organization of the events, uncluding the annual parade of the Polish Constitution Day of 3 May. The Polish American Congress had organized it in other years, but withdrew support in 1992.

The *Informator* (1980) listed the board of directors of 116 small groups in Chicago of the early 1980s. Each of these contains several leadership positions, some rotating over the years. This provides a lively set of activities, since most groups like to organize parties. Some join similar groups in other local communities, electing officers, holding conventions, and publishing newsletters. Chicago is the center of the governing bodies of the major nonfraternal organizations such the Polish Welfare Association, or the Highlanders Alliance with its many subgroups. Most of the groups emphasizing Polish national culture are located along the East Coast of the United States, in New York City, Maryland, Pennsylvania, or Florida.

The newest cohort of immigrants tends to form and reform more informal groups, centered upon specific events, such as the absentee voting for the Polish elections. A member of this cohort, who had been a very active Solidarity leader and now lives in New York with little hope of returning to Poland, explained the reluctance of this group to join associations, even to be involved in churches that demand set contributions, as a direct consequence of forced membership in so many groups in communist Poland. The formation of the Solidarity union and movement in Poland gave rise to several supporting groups on this side of the ocean, such as the Committee in Support of Solidarity, Friends of Solidarity, and Solidarity International. The third cohort has also organized small single purpose groups, such as the Centennial Gun and Bow Club, whose meetings and hunts are advertised in the *Greenpoint*, a Brooklyn newspaper.

Multipurpose Associations

The multipurpose federations of local groups usually have a unifying set of purposes with a variety of functions meeting the needs of different categories of members, organized either territorially or by function. The main ones are the Polish National Alliance, founded in 1880, the Polish Roman Catholic Union, founded in 1873, and the Polish Women's Alliance of America, founded in 1898 (see Appendix A). All three are headquartered in metropolitan Chicago, as is the Polish Alma Mater of America, the United Polish Women of America, and the Mutual Aid Association of the New Polish Emigration. There are several other fraternals headquartered in different states with a high Polish American population. All are insurance-based businesses, in addition to being ethnically oriented voluntary associations.

Most of the major multipurpose organizations started out as insurance fraternals, but others originated as idealistic religious or patriotic groups. The addition of insurance gave them a stable base, and they expanded their size by bringing into membership already existing local mutual aid "groups" or "societies"; later they assisted the creation of new locals. At the turn of the century, mutual aid groups had already mushroomed in the Polish neighborhoods, particularly in the parishes (Thomas and Znaniecki 1918-1920). Each such group insured its own members, guaranteeing a "nice funeral" or protecting them from the costs of lengthy illness. Each member would come weekly or monthly to a central location and pay the local treasurer a standard premium. The occasion provided opportunities for contact and socializing. When the mutual aid society joined the federated fraternal group, the contacts became more formalized and the tasks of the local office broader. The dates designated for the payment of premiums turned into business meetings. The money collected from the insurance premiums went to the central office, along with special "taxes" levied in order to maintain associational activities. For example, in 1906 the Polish Women's Alliance added a one-cent increase per month for each member for "cultural aims," half of this money going to the national headquarters and half remaining locally (Karlowiczowa 1938:50). The members of each group sell new insurance policies. Cash prizes have been periodically awarded to people bringing new "members" to their local group, membership being an automatic benefit of taking out an insurance policy. Actually, such prizes are especially beneficial to the organization since members serve as insurance agents without salary but with commissions.[8]

As Greene (1975) states, the fraternals and building and loan associations that developed in the early years of the first cohort's settlement in America provided the economic base to the community. The money collected by the insurance fraternals has been lent to members and groups to acquire property, a major interest of the Polish Americans. Building and loan cooperatives grew out of meetings held in a church or saloon where group members obtained home-buying information and organized a cooperative organization. Normally a member bought shares of the society regularly. At the end of a specified time (six years) contributions and the accumulated interest could be withdrawn. If extra funds were required to purchase a home, they could be borrowed in an amount up to two-thirds the value of the real estate (Green 1975: 54).

The expansion of the fraternal groups resulted in two types of organizational subunits. First, regional divisions integrated groups in the same district or region, depending on the density of members. These territorial units, still in existence, have served as intermediary links between the local group and the national headquarters, relaying communication and authority, helping to launch new groups, handling relations among the locals, and pooling resources for special events that most locals could not carry out independently. Second, functional or special membership divisions work through the existing local groups or set up specialty "societies." For example, women were given equal rights in the Polish National Alliance in 1900, and a Women's Division emerged with a set of women-only societies.

The superterritorial organizations have three channels of communication and integration for member groups scattered across the country. The house organ disseminates news of coming events, offers status opportunities for local and national leaders, trains and directs members in political action, crystallizes the associational ideology, and in general reminds members of all the benefits of being affiliated with such a strong and prestigious group. Personal contact with regional and local branches through tours by leaders or the telephone solves acute problems requiring joint decisions. One of the functions of associational leaders is to visit local and regional branches not only at times of crisis, but for special events of these groups. Neglect of that obligation creates indignation, because of the assumption that the offender did not consider the group "sufficiently important" to make an effort at attendance. Fortunately for the system, the hierarchical structure of status is generally known, so that the expectations of leadership presence are usually realistic. Problems arise only if there is a gap between the status that the group thinks it has reached and the personal attention it achieves from the appropriate hierarchical level of leaders.

A third method of integrating member groups has been through congresses. These perform a number of functions similar to those discussed by Durkheim (1915/1965) in reference to ceremonial events bringing members of a religious group together. They reinforce the "collective representations" the group has of itself, its ideology, and shared value. They afford opportunities for personal contact among delegates coming from a variety of locations and, through mutual socialization, they encourage group identity. The socialization also involves formal and informal training of new group leaders as they witness the very parliamentarian procedures, and the more sophisticated methods for handling strife and even conflict than those available by observation of smaller groups. In addition, they reinforce or, if need be, change and crystallize definitions of Polonia and accentuate the judgement of the organization as important by sheer size and complexity of the congress. Finally, the congresses serve to broaden the local member's awareness of the wider world, which is concerned with national policies and politics. The delegates later return to their home groups and disseminate all these sentiments to their fellow members, each of whom experiences the congress vicariously, or plans for the future to insure becoming a delegate. The local organization usually pays the costs of transporting, housing, and feeding the delegates, which contributes to their identification with the superterritorial organization and, therefore, with Polonia. The importance of the congresses, publicized months before and after in the ethnic press, should not be undervalued as a means of maintaining Polonia by crystallizing and shifting its ideological base.

On the other hand, the congresses can have dysfunctional consequences for the organization, in that they offer opportunities for any latent or sectional conflict to become manifest and to gain supporters. The public arena of the congress serves as a platform for opposing views of organizational functions or procedures and for the struggle for power. Splinter groups are provided a central location to engage in resource mobilization efforts and, if unable to obtain satisfaction from the central authorities, to leave the meeting place with their followers and form a new group. This has happened several times in Polonia's history. Fear of such events leads to tightly planned congresses, with strong control of the proceedings by the leaders, and a careful screening of delegates.

Because of the positive and negative consequences that can accrue from the congresses and the costs involved in organizing them, most associations have them infrequently, usually every four years. Conflicts over mandates of delegates and all conflicts in organizations are supposedly resolved internally, but the history of Polonia records frequent uses of external courts and mass media to settle them. Most of the larger organizations have judgment tribunals ostensibly formed to settle internal conflicts, but these usually consist of the representatives of the power elite within the group, and the conflicts are created by dissident groups attempting to change the power structure.[9] As a result, the tribunals are not used in really traumatic cases.

The presence of the Polish Women's Alliance is an interesting phenomenon in a traditionally patriarchal ethnic group, supporting earlier statements about the independence of Polonian women (see Lopata 1988a, 1988b; Radzialowski 1990, 1977).

> It is ironic that in 1975, leading newspapers in the United States heralded the establishment of a Women's Bank in New York City capitalized at 3 million dollars as a breakthrough for women at a time when the insurance and investment division of the ZPA, run entirely by women for decades, was worth about 40 million dollars. The Women's Bank subsequently failed but the ZPA has continued to grow and prosper to this day. (Radzialowski 1990: 10–11)

The Polish Women's Alliance publishes its own journal *Glos Polek* (The Voice of Polish Women) and is devoted to the education of Polish women and girls. It maintains a library at its headquarters in Chicago, conducts schools in Polish language, history, and culture, a summer camp, vocational schools, scholarships, and so forth. The newspaper devotes itself to news about Polish American women, but also famous Polish heroines and writers and women's rights in general and in different countries (Radzialowski 1990).

Interorganizational Associations

Attempts to unify Polonia behind a single federated organization have been unsuccessful or short-lived until recent years.[10] There are two major reasons for this problem. The Polish American community has been so heterogenous that it could not agree on goals that were important enough to warrant putting aside the status competition. Therefore, it did not establish an ongoing structure, in spite of creating many short-lived ones. Part of this lack of agreement on goals is an inevitable consequence of Polonia's marginal position. Lacking power in both the Polish and American societies, its members have often been hesitant to join groups taking a strong stand on subjects that may place them in jeopardy with the power structure. For example, organizations that were formed to exert pressure on the Roman Catholic hierarchy were unable to obtain the support of the clergy, let alone of groups that were strongly controlled by clerical groups. The powerlessness itself is a source of frustration and competition among groups, each convinced that it has the best solution for alleviating the problem.

Of course, the status competition itself has led to an unwillingness to subject one's own group to leadership by another. Each of the major associations within Polonia feels that it should have its leaders head the interorganizational association and its ideology guide the direction of the new unit.

There have been at least eighteen attempts to unify Polonia, starting with the Polish Roman Catholic Union in 1873 and the Polish National Alliance in 1880 (see Lopata 1954 for details). Neither succeeded, but no other interorganizational association has been able to survive without the cooperation of these giants in the community.

The longest lasting unifying association has been the Polish American Congress (PAC), formed in 1944 but somewhat dormant during the 1960s. It has recently become revitalized and its success is mainly due to cooperation among the Polish National Alliance (PNA), the Polish Roman Catholic Union (PRCU), and the Polish Women's Alliance (PWA). In fact, the president of the PAC is the president of the PNA, the most powerful group in Polonia. The PAC defines itself as a political organization aimed at influencing American society and American politics in favor of Polish Americans (detailed analysis of its activity will be given in the next chapter, and in Erdmans's chapter). The PAC is supported not only by powerful groups, but by individual Polish Americans who are very conscious of the importance of having their status raised in relation to other ethnic groups and in America in general. Members of Polonia have become increasingly concerned with presenting a united front to the outside. This does not mean that conflict is absent within the Polish American Congress or that the community is unified in its attitudes or actions, only that there is general agreement that the PAC should be a strong organization in order to have some politically effective means of pressuring the American society.

The Polish American Press, Radio, Television, and Theater

The foreign language press, radio, television, and theater have performed many functions in Polonia in addition to providing recreation. The press originally helped the nationalistic leaders to develop patriotism among the former peasants and at least an awareness of the Polish society, although it was not able to impart knowledge of the content of this culture. Periodicals devoted to Polish national culture existed, but their format drew only such readers as were already oriented toward intelligentsia subjects. Their numbers have increased dramatically in the last decade or so, thanks to the influx of the third cohort, which is educated and familiar with Polish culture, having been educated in that country. One of the functions of the early foreign language press was to develop a broader religious identification than is typical of village parishioners. In general, it facilitated the process of converting the villager into at least an "urban villager" (Gans 1962), though usually not into an urbanite, and helped his or her child to move even more in the direction of "urbanism as a way of life" (Wirth 1938/1970). The press also assisted in the development, crystallization, and change of the ideology explaining Polonia and its relation to Poland and to the American society. It introduced new ideas and reconstructed reality for community members, defining the world in terms they could understand. It helped the parents socialize their children into the rudiments of Polish language and its folk subcultures. Fiction published by the press described life in Poland and widened the readers' limited perception of the country. The Polish American press also helped to develop and record the new marginal culture and in its pages the gradual changes, for example in language, can be seen. In a way, even the Polish language media assisted in the assimilation of the immigrants and their descendants, by presenting news of American events and political activities, especially when they used English language in the stories.

Another important function of Polonia's press, radio, television, and theater has been the recording of community life, the record itself indirectly accentuating trends and building role models. People would read or hear that a certain family or group introduced a new form of social entertaining or succeeded in a new money-raising activity and would reproduce it, thereby adding new cultural items to Polonia's life. In these functions the mass media were assisted by, and in turn fostered, the active interest in status competition. Leaders at all levels could have their names listed as officers or organizers of an "event." Groups could compete by making known their successes in gaining members, carrying out their goals, or being honored by the presence of famous leaders. The press particularly provided an open forum for the competition when it reached conflict proportions by recording organizational strife. The press was used politically to encourage community members to support candidates or stances, or to refrain from such support. Candidates often used its pages to accuse opponents of all sorts of crimes and moral delinquencies—few internal struggles passed unnoticed.

The Polish-language media have reflected the heterogeneity of the community, not only in their source, but also in the content and even the language. For example, many of the daily and weekly papers and house organs catering to the lower classes had slipped into such a combination of regional, lower-class, and Americanized language by World War II as to shock the new emigration. There was a marked improvement in the "purity" of the Polish in papers when some of the war refugees with intelligentsia backgrounds joined their staffs. This had been dramatically evident as the third cohort started taking over the media, becoming editors or program announcers and even starting their own publications or radio stations. Other periodicals directed themselves to other audiences, the intelligentsia itself, a professional group of dentists or doctors, the "Polka world," or women. They existed side by side with newspapers devoted to mining or farming.

A high proportion of the Polish publications that did not survive for long were started by members of the intelligentsia who had no training in the business management of journalism, and the publications were sufficiently esoteric as to draw a limited number of readers. In addition, many were unable to obtain sufficient advertising to cover the gap between publishing costs and subscriptions. Many Polish American businessmen had small margins of profit and were accustomed to the word of mouth advertising typical of small communities. The social distance between Polonia and the rest of American society resulted in a neglect by English-speaking businessmen of the economic potential of advertising in the Polish American press or radio and television.

Most of the newspapers of the 1,356 Polish American Serial Publications that came out between 1842 and 1966 were weekly (325). The community also supported 51 daily papers during that period of time. In all, there were 388 newspapers, 81 parish bulletins and 887 "other publications." Monthly organizational organs (328) accounted for a great deal of the activity, with 94 annual publications (compiled from Wespiec 1968). Monthly and less frequent publications, such as *The Monthly Review*, were often directed toward companionate circles spread out all over the United States. The various types of publications—newspapers, parish bulletins, and other types of periodicals— were started at different periods in Polonia's history and at different locales. Illinois and New York competed in the number of publications, but other cities such as Detroit, Buffalo, Milwaukee, Cleveland, Philadelphia, and Brooklyn contributed their share in relation to their population (Obidinski 1977: 41–42). The period of 1940 to 1954 covers World War II and the intensive anticommunistic mood of Polonia as well as the strong attempts of the second cohort to propagandize its cause. The current increase is mainly due to the third cohort's attempt to bring its own culture to Polonia.

In spite of the high level of activity in Polonia's press, there has been a gradual decline of the number of separate publications, some of them being consolidated into more stable periodicals, but most of them simply dying without replacement. In 1925, there were almost 100 Polish language publications with a circulation of 1.32 million copies (Wachtl 1944:219). Fishman and his associates (1966:51–71) found a 56 percent decrease in the number of Polish language dailies between 1930 and 1960, accompanied by a decrease of 47 percent in their circulation. The number of weeklies decreased by 72 percent and their circulation by 74 percent. On the other hand, the number of monthlies increased 150 percent and their circulation 259 percent. An increase was also experienced in English language publications aimed at Polonia's members, and Renkiewicz (1969:58) estimates that the number of such publications the community supported in 1960 was proportionately higher than that for other ethnic groups. Although the Polish Americans formed only 12 percent of the people who spoke a non-English tongue, they maintained "22 percent of the foreign press circulation." The numbers are suspect, because of the difficulty of finding each publication, and the uneven history of their life span. However, the Polish American press has been extremely active, compared to that of other ethnic groups. By contrast, the 488 hours of average weekly Polish radio broadcasting in the 1960s were lower than that for other groups, forming only 6.4 percent of all foreign language broadcasting. I have no record of the current radio and television programing over the whole nation, although there is a great deal of radio activity reported in local papers.

Those periodicals that survived into the 1970s are most apt to have been supported by organizations. Obidinski (1977) classified the English language content of six major Polish American periodicals located at the Immigration History Research Center at the University of Minnesota in single issues in 1974 or 1975. The most frequent topics, in descending order, were: news of fraternals and "societies," Poland, sources of Polonian culture, discrimination and Polonian image, religion and morals, pop culture and "Polka world," personalities and honors, politics, patriotism in the United States, family values, and education. Of course, five of the six publications were organs of Polonian organizations, which explains the most frequent subject. Few Polish American publications were able to maintain themselves through subscriptions and advertising alone.

The Polish American ethnic theater, as Polish observers called any Polish language performance that did not use scripts for formal plays, operettas, or operas of the national culture society, has had an uneven but rich history in Polonia. There were a number of National Theater or Lovers of Polish Theater organizations in Chicago, New York, Detroit, and even less centralized Polonias. The first productions were connected with parishes and put on by amateur groups. These usually had religious themes. The attempts at more professional theater had to compete with these and were not subsidized; they often depended upon sponsorship by a wealthy Polish American or family. Most of the attempts at organizing a more stable theater took place in Chicago. The third cohort of immigrants has brought professional theater from Poland to tour the various Polonias in the United States and Canada. There is a sufficient number of Polish-speaking persons throughout these communities to provide sophisticated audiences. A one-man English language production, "I, Lech Walesa," was one of several shows that toured the area in 1992.

A "New Polonia"?

There has been a dramatic revitalization of an important part of Polonia, that not controlled by the "establishment" of the major fraternals and related groups.

Local Polonian communities have expanded their business and professional establishments and organizations in recent years, aided by the arrival of the third cohort of emigrants from communist and recently democratizing Poland. Many of the newcomers acquire rather rapidly sufficient knowledge of English to start their own businesses. In addition, the more established Polonian residents have been motivated to benefit from their needs for services and consumer items. For example the *Informator Polonii w USA of 1980–81* (1980) contains advertisements from over 20 law firms, written in Polish or with Polish-sounding names. They offer advice as to immigration law; the building, purchase, and sale of buildings; opening, developing, and liquidating businesses; formation of corporations and negotiation; divorce; testaments and wills; taxes; and any advice about staying in the United States needed by newcomers, including civil law. Many specify familiarity with Polish law, which enables the establishment of joint ventures and the return of property confiscated by the communists forty some years ago. The *Informator* lists 23 travel agencies, again written in Polish or with Polish names. Although some specialize in travel to Poland, their customers are now venturing to other parts of the world. The prolification of realty companies, of which 35 are listed separately is also evidenced by the presence of the Polski-Amerykanska Liga Realnosciowa (Real Estate League) with 39 members and seven affiliates. The motto of the league states "Swoj do swego dla wspolnego dobra," which means, in rather loose translation "fellow countrywomen and men go to fellow countrywomen and men for mutual benefit."

There are numerous banks and insurance companies that are interested in Polish and Polish American businesses, even matrimonial services. Polish bakeries, sausage stores, and shops selling jewelry and clothing give elaborate descriptions of their objects in Polish, with personal questions directed at holidays or other cultural events. A number of third-cohort Poles have gone into construction. And, whereas in the past there were only a limited number of common eating establishments, now restaurants abound.

The interest on the part of the recent waves or cohorts of Polish immigrants in America in doing business in the now privatizing Poland has resulted in the formation of new organizations, such as the U.S. Poland Chamber of Commerce. Founded on 24 March 1991, its motto reads "Promoting trade and investment between the United States and Poland" and the mission is to "build business opportunities by establishing relationships between businesspeople with similar interests and by facilitating access to information on business opportunities" (*U.S. Poland Connection* Fall 1991: 1–3). It declares itself to be an apolitical and not-for-profit organization.

A number of Polish American business and manufacturing owners are now interested in investing in Poland with the help of the Polish-American Enterprise Fund, which obtained $245 million from the United States Congress. The fund is authorized to lend money or take equity positions in organizations in Poland to stimulate private enterprise.

There had been a marked improvement in the purity of the Polish language mass media with the entrance of the World War II refugees who had intelligentsia backgrounds. This became even more evident in recent years. The *Dziennik Chicagowski* (Chicago Daily) has reappeared on the scene; *Gwiaska Polarna* out of Stevens Point, Wisconsin is going strong, as is the New York's *Nowy Dziennik* (New Daily). *Dziennik Zwiazkowy* is published by the Polish National Alliance; *Narod Polski* (Polish Nation), a semi-monthly entirely in English is put out by the Polish Roman Catholic Union of America. *Gazeta Polska* comes out weekly and the publisher has also published *ABC Emigranta* (the ABC of information for the emigrant). It contains information needed by newcomers, including maps, calendars, horoscopes, telephone numbers of services, and so forth. It is a local version of the *Informator*, which is published in New York. The third cohort, assisted by the technology of home publishing, has blossomed forth with numerous periodicals, often in slick covers and pages. Many of the monthly magazines, such as *Kariera*(Career), *Kobieta* (Woman), *Revia* (Parade, but the use of V is Americanization, since the Polish alphabet does not contain that letter), or *Panorama* come from the Chicago area. The most popular at the present time are *Alfa* and *Relax* (also a play on English language). All these are in modern day Polish. There is even a soft pornography style magazine *Goniec* (Courier). Most of these present news from Poland and Polonia, the United States, and other countries, with local advertisements and often fiction and/or humor.

Radio in Polonia is alive and lively, revitalized by each immigration cohort. *Polonia Today* (September 1992) lists over a hundred programs emanating from Chicago, Indiana, Michigan, Pennsylvania, and Wisconsin. The May 1992 issue listed "*Polka Radio*" programs in 15 states and Canada. The Polish National Alliance bought a station in Chicago to insure continued programming. The stations were very helpful, for example, in spreading information about the amnesty and the visa lottery policies of the United States government.

Polonian television exists today on a small scale when compared to the big city offerings in the Hispanic communities. One of the longest-running shows in Chicago has been that of Robert Lewandowski, a second cohort immigrant active on both radio and television. His Sunday weekly television program presented Polish and Polish American scientific and artistic talent. A third-cohort producer and newscaster is now active in the city. There have been any number of program offerings from program packagers for cable networks.

Summary

Polonia has developed as an institutionally and organizationally complex ethnic community with the help of a large number of Polish immigrants and their descendants. The first wave of immigrants came to the United States mainly in the years between 1880 and 1924. Most of them came from villages but they represented a variety of types of peasants, differentiated by subclass, degree of urban influence, and region. Most of the early emigrants used whatever money they were able to obtain to buy their passage, arriving in the United States with less than fifty dollars in their pocket. Most settled in urban centers, near other Polish immigrants, thus helping establish the local settlements. As these grew in size, Poles of other social classes and skills were drawn to them, and the institutional complexity began developing. Polish priests and nuns were imported, and later trained here, to take care of newly formed parishes. These parishes became the center of the *okolica,* not only of religious, but of total community life. Mutual aid societies and groups helping in the functioning of the parish and its school increased, giving opportunities for parishioners to develop organizational and leadership skills. Polonia's Catholics have had an ambivalent relationship, most often on the negative side, with the Roman Catholic ecclesiastical society, especially with its American division, due, according to Buczek (1976:61) to the latter's policy of Americanization and "benign neglect."

Nationalistic Polish leaders, many of them members of the intelligentsia, came to these centers, started other types of groups, and founded a variety of different periodicals and radio programs. Parents sent their children to Polish language parish schools, primarily hoping they would learn the rudiments of Polish Catholicism and moral values.

The ethnic communities developed some economic services for their members such as stores in which Polish was spoken and Polish goods were sold, doctor's and dentist's offices, legal and writing services, and larger businesses such as coal or sausage companies that employed Polish workers. Most of the immigrants, however, worked for American industry, as miners or unskilled and semiskilled steel and automobile workers. The Polish Americans did not involve themselves in American politics very extensively and the status competition within the community prevented unification vis-à-vis the rest of the society. The status competition institutionalized conflict and the use of all available resources, even external social control agencies in order to gain reputations, power, or other sources of status. The status competition, and even the conflict that splintered groups and contributed to the formation of new ones, helped prevent the extensive and predicted social disorganization that could easily have followed migration and settlement in a foreign country. The development of competing groups, clustered around competing ideologies and status-concerned leaders, with constant splintering to create new groups, each convinced that it was better able to meet the needs of the community than its competitors, has been the essence of the dynamism keeping the community together. The creation of a complex economic base under some of these groups helped their survival rate, but many other groups were able to survive without that base.

Most small groups have joined federations devoted to one or more functions and drawing either a special kind of member or several categories organized territorially or functionally. Attempts have even been made throughout Polonia's history to unite all the major groups but these failed until recent years. The forming and reforming of groups brought in new members and leaders, providing opportunities for participation in the community life and in its status competition for a very large segment of the population, including working-class and even lower-class people who are generally alienated from urban associational life. Even second generation, and in some cases, third- and fourth-generation Polish Americans have joined these groups, or formed new ones, as has the new cohort. This last wave of immigrants remained isolated in early years, feeling very alienated from the ethnic culture that the old immigrants had created in Polonia, which they found "archaic" and too low-class for the most part. Heterogenous to an extent exceeding even the prior immigrants and reared in a different kind of Poland then remembered or learned by the Polish Americans already living in Polonia, their presence and behavior had a profound effect on the community, increasing its interest in the Polish national culture society, changing the language in the Polish press, and shifting the content of the status competition. The same effect, even to a greater extent, is now being felt by the presence of the third cohort.

Throughout Polonia's history, the ideological identity and rationale for the community has shifted considerably from folk culture to Polish patriotism, from the "identity crisis" of marginality to increasing Americanization and back to stubborn forms of Polish Americanism and new Polishness. In the 1970s I (Lopata 1976: 67) wrote that

> The dynamism of the status competition and organizational flexibility and complexity carried it through the changes and has maintained it in spite of the fact that, at present, there are relatively few characteristics of this ethnic community which distinguish it from the larger society. Decreasing Polishness has not necessarily decreased the organizational and institutional complexity of the ethnic community. Yet, there are evidences of a decrease in Polish American involvement in Polonia, or at least a shift from daily concern to more specialized interest in the demise of the daily newspapers which are being replaced by English language monthlies.

These conclusions have been partially invalidated by the unexpected influx of the third wave of Polish emigrants, raised in communist Poland but escaping its system or staying in America allegedly temporarily to avoid recent problems and to obtain dollars to be used back home. It had already begun to arrive in the early 1970s, but their numbers and influence have grown considerably in recent years. The effect of this cohort is being felt thoughout the community and is threatening the "established Polonia." However, it has not as yet developed a base of power, not being accepted into the insurance, savings and loan supported fraternals, and not having built its own organizational and financial resources. We will learn more of this cohort in coming chapters.

Notes

1. This antagonism to formal education was typical of economic immigrants, partly because of its control by upper classes, and partly in self-defense. Squier and Quadagno (1988: 120), for example, found the Italians resistant to the educational institutions. The parents feared children learning "alien concepts" that might destroy the family unit and wanted them to seek employment and contribute to the household's economic situation. The authors also point to the negative repercussions of this hostility to schooling in terms of social status.

2. As mentioned in chapter 1, Thomas and Znaniecki had planned other volumes besides *The Polish Peasant in Europe and America* (1918–1920). According to Orbach (1993), projected volumes were to focus on the intelligentsia and the bourgeoisie. There have been several studies of individual Poles, such as Kosciuszko or Pulaski, or of the influence of Paderewski, but no general one (see chapter 5 on relations with America).

3. The concept "social life space" refers to the social territory within which a person moves during his or her involvement in all the social roles that form his or her role cluster. The boundaries of the social life space are at the cut off of the web of social relations in which he or she is involved.

4. Zand (1959) explained in "Polish American Weddings and Christenings" that the importance of status matching extended to the selection of couples to form the wedding party as bridesmaids and ushers. In choosing their attendants the bride and groom had to "match personality, appearance, social standing and wealth" (25). One reason for the concern was that "each couple was photographed separately at its own expense, with the man giving the girl six of the customary dozen photographs. Naturally, no one wanted to be thus immortalized in photographic print with a distasteful partner" (25).

5. Petras (1964) also concluded that the Polonian family was patriarchal. "Early studies characterized the Polish American family as authoritarian and extended, i.e., relatively unchanged from its form in Poland" (17). "In the period of 1927–1929 there was still a belief in the absolute paternal authority" (22).

6. Schooling beyond the requirement set by law was particularly rejected for women and "obviously the old belief that a girl does not 'need' much education is still active among Polish Canadian families" as late as the 1970s (Dunin-Markiewicz 1972:98). Dunin-Markiewicz found that "the females outperformed the males" in high school in Windsor, Canada, by getting good grades, "yet when it comes to planning a university education, the situation is completely reversed and the boys outnumber the girls fifteen to nine" (98).

7. Finestone (1964) repeatedly points to the difference between the Polish and the Italian cultural values, including the relation between role behavior and sentiment, emphasis on privacy, expression of interpersonal hostility, the relationship of work and play, and family membership.

> The criteria of membership were much more explicit in the Polish than in the Italian peasant family. Among the Poles, except for infants and the very young,

continued membership in the family presupposed that each individual would make a regular contribution to the material sustenance of this group. The application of this criterion tended to render ambiguous the position within the family of the deviant, the inefficient, and the aged. Within the Italian peasant family, in contrast, the terms of the transaction between individual and group were somewhat mitigated for the young, the aged and the deviant. A member could choose to sunder his tie with his family but it is unlikely that other family members would voluntarily impose such a condition upon him because of some disability on his part. (488–90)

In addition, "among the Polish peasants human nature was regarded as dominated by evil impulses and the human organism as fragile" (49).

8. The practice still continues to this day and most of the insurance companies sell their policies through their members, often in contest situations. For example, the Union of Polish Women in America had a "Very Important Member of the Year" contest, which involved the selling of insurance, with additional incentive in cash returns in proportion to the amount sold by each group (*Gwiazda Polarna*, 31 January 1974).

9. Many of the organizations try to prevent an open display of conflicts by forbidding such action in their constitution. The constitution of the Polish National Alliance states:

> It is treason to the Polish National Alliance for a member to incite or try to persuade other members, groups or departments to break away from the Polish National Alliance or violate its laws and rules; it is treason to slander the Alliance or to harm it by representing in speech or writing the aims, tendencies or interests of the Alliance in a false light. (Renkieawicz 1973:71–72)

The penalty is expulsion, which, in the case of successful "inciting . . . to break away" would be likely to happen anyway. Rather than stopping such action, this declaration gave the Alliance the right to expel the unsuccessful revolutionaries. In any case, this is a strong statement of loyalty demands. The 10th point is equally strong:

> No member, officer, group, committee, commission, department or part of the Alliance has the right of appeal to the courts of the country in affairs concerning the Alliance or any part of the Alliance until all the stages of jurisdiction and appeal within the Alliance, the diet included, have been exhausted. (in Polish, Renkiewicz, 1973:71–72)

10. Interestingly enough, while the Polish Americans consider themselves fragmented and uncooperative, assuming that other social groups are better able to organize or solve their problems, the Canadian Poles feel they are unique in cooperation difficulties (assuming that Polonia in the United States is integrated). Makowski (1967) states that the immigrants to Canada were so diversified that

> Complete unity was never really achieved because there was dissention between nationalists supporting the pre-war government, the liberals, the socialists and the clerics. In this regard the Poles in Canada differ greatly from their copatriots in the United States. In the United States a mass of Poles were,

and still are, united within the Roman Catholic Church, or to a much lesser degree around the Polish National Catholic Church. (176)

4

Relations between Polonia and Poland

A major function of an ethnic community, in addition to organizing itself and developing an internal structure, is to establish, maintain, and modify relations with both the country of origin and the country of settlement. Organized, patterned relations require an ideology explaining the position of the community in both societies, the initiation and maintenance of selected types of relations, and assimilation into the life-style of the society of settlement.

Both the formal and the informal relations of an ethnic community with its country of origin and country of settlement are affected by a number of factors. Emigration laws and policies, as well as the total situation in the home country, influence who leaves, when and how and, partially, where they go. Immigration laws and policies and the situation in alternative host countries influence where the emigrants go. The size and composition of the ethnic community, as well as the actions of the home and host societies influence the ideology it develops toward each and how this ideology is carried forth in organized activity.

This chapter is devoted to an examination of the two-way relations between Poland and Polonia, each trying to influence the other, ideologically and in practical action.

Poland's Orientation toward Polonia

There are many reasons and ways a home country can relate to those who leave it and settle in other countries. It can have mixed feelings about the emigrants themselves. The number of emigrants can be seen as a problem, especially in certain areas of the country. The people can be seen either as deserters or as "good riddance" (Erdmans 1992b). As noted earlier, the new Polish government does not want what is called a "brain drain." Judged as invaluable can be the educated and occupationally contributive or young men at times of war or in preparation for it. On the other hand, some of the Polish emigration has been welcomed, at times of economic crisis, and by those members whom the society judges as unnecessary to its functioning or undesirable. Of course, definition of desirability concerning who stays and who goes varies, depending on who is in power. The Nazis, for example, exterminated or relocated all educated and generally middle-class Poles and Polish Jews.[1]

The home country can simply be interested in what happens to its emigrants as a scientific concern. As mentioned in the last chapter, Polish scholars have not neglected the frequent and sometimes massive emigration of its people. The Poles started studying those who emigrated as early as 1889, with a conference devoted to the subject in Lwow. Znaniecki (Dulczewski 1992: 73) contributed to this research as Director of the Society for the Protection of Emigrants and editor of *The Polish Emigrant* from 1910 to 1914. The Polish National Academy created and funded (until recent times when it began to lack governmental funds), a "Committee on Polonian Studies" in Krakow which publishes *Przegland Polonijny* (Polonian Review; Miodunka 1989). Several congresses involving Polish and Polonian scholars who specialize in this research have been held in the same city and there is a vast amount of literature now on this subject.

Political leaders of Poland soon began to be interested in the emigrants for a very different reason than concern with loss of members of the society. Those who settled outside of the territory gradually became seen as resources, the communities as colonies concerned mainly with the welfare of the homeland. Poland needed Polonia several times in its history and set out purposely to influence its members into active involvement in its problems. Had the Polish state not been under foreign occupation at different times during its recent life, the Polonian communities throughout the world would not have been so strongly influenced by the activities of numerous, temporary, or even permanent, nationalistically oriented waves of visitors. More than most home societies, except maybe Germany, the Polish one tried consistently to influence Polonias all over the world. Interest by Poland's political leaders in American Polonia has been strongly affected by its location in a powerful state. In the meantime, the American society tried to do the opposite, decrease the Polish Americans' identification with Poland and increase their rate of assimilation into American culture, thus creating a negative reaction.

There have been many shifts in the orientation of Poland toward Polonia, due to its own political and economic situation and the estimation of its leaders as to the amount of assistance and influence on U. S. policy it would provide. Polonia's attitudes concerning this pressure, and the relationships between the two units have also gone through several major changes.

Early Orientation and Activity by Polish Leaders

One of the major reasons Polish leaders organized extensive efforts directed toward Polonia has been the composition of its population of the first cohort or mass economic immigration. Limiting ourselves again to American Polonia we find that the earlier, sporadic immigration of Poles had been of political émigrés following several aborted insurrections against the invading powers. Although relatively few in number, they established the foundation of nationalism. However, the early Polish Americans of the economic cohort identified not with the national culture society, of which they were not at all, or only vaguely, familiar, but with the *okolica* from which they came. Similarity of language, Catholic-based Polishness, community life, and the strangeness of American society provided bases for consciousness of kind. That did not necessarily require knowledge of Polish history and literary/artistic culture so developed and idealized by the intelligentsia and political leaders. An ethnic, folk-based, identification could not form a basis for organized, and self-sacrificing, activity on behalf of Poland. Thus, the nationalistic/political leaders of that nation, together with similarly oriented members and groups of Polonia concentrated their efforts in the years before, during, and immediately after World War I on nationalizing the Polish Americans. Studies by sociologists such as Greeley (1974b) or leaders such as Kusielewicz (1973) have concluded that this nationalism was still not of the intelligentsia type, since so few Polonians of those years or in following decades are really familiar with Polish history, and artistic and literary culture.

As the efforts by its nationalistic and political leaders to free Poland from occupation by Russia, Prussia, and Austria intensified prior to World War I, these leaders turned their attention to Polonia in America for three things: money, military forces, and political pressure on its political state. One reason they assumed concerted efforts to involve Polonia could bring these benefits is that the Polish Americans had been working hard in the expanding economic system and had been amassing funds that could be used in the fight for independence. Second, the emigration had been drawing young men away from Poland, thereby depleting the reservoir of men for the armed services when the expected war actually broke out and they wanted these men, or others like them, to join their armies. Third, the Polish Americans had allegedly already influenced President Wilson and they wanted him to force the European powers to re-establish Poland as a political state.

The political leaders of Poland capitalized on four characteristics of Polish American identification in their efforts to convince Polonia to make serious commitments to the fight for independence: identity with the people back home, their plans on returning to Poland once it regained independence, the ability to blame all past ills in the mother country on the foreign oppressors instead of the upper classes, and concern with status competition. Representatives of the social classes who had completely ignored the peasant as a conational in the home country and in Polonia's past now offered many symbols of attention and forms of status. Paderewski, an internationally famous pianist, played for Polish

American audiences after having visited President Wilson in the White House. Polish immigrants and their children were easily convinced that their status in the motherland would be improved by their known sacrifices during the struggle for political independence, and that they would have a free state to return to when they collected their new wealth. Even improvement of Polonia's status in American society was promised with the reestablishment of Poland as an independent European power. The emotional fervor aroused in Polonia by these arguments is documented in reports of meetings, the Polish language press, and constitutions and congresses of various groups.

In spite of the limited knowledge of the Polish national culture, the efforts of Polish nationalists were productive. The concentrated ethnic settlement made access to the Polish Americans easy for political leaders from Poland or living in exile in Europe. The complexity of Polonia as a community increased the ability of the leaders to exert their influence on small parish or mutual aid societies (Drozdowski 1990). The drama and worldwide aspects of its political situation added excitement to life as well as new sources of internal status competition. Communication and movement back and forth across the ocean, and the size of the group maintaining contact insured that what happened in Poland was part of the daily life of Polonia.

Poland's pre-World War I needs were mainly economic; money was needed to help support the government and the armed forces in exile. After war broke out, there was a need for men to contribute to the combat. Poland was in dire need of all kinds of assistance, from money to food and clothing as well as medicine, medical equipment, and means of rebuilding the infrastructure after it regained independence. During the interwar years, Poland lost interest in Polonia except as a source of economic aid, being concerned mainly in its own problems. World War II increased its need for all kinds of help, but the following years witnessed the "iron curtain," with little communication outside of its influence. The consulates were under U.S. FBI and other security observation; and protest from especially the third cohort of emigrants and practically all of Polonia was extremely anticommunistic. The formation of Solidarity and its relation to the communist government in the 1980s produced a vacillation of relations and the final overthrow of that government, to be replaced by one attempting democracy and privatization pulled Polonia back into strong involvement. This time it has been in the form of pressure upon the United States to assist in the financial rebuilding of Poland, and of joint venture investment in new Polish enterprises.

Polonia's Orientation toward Poland

The initial concern by economic immigrants with Poland was very personal. Most wanted to return to their own *okolica* with sufficient money, earned in the

United States, to buy land and status-producing goods. They were, however, nationalized by the activities of Polish leaders who settled or visited here to the extent of wanting an independent Polish state. They were willing to contribute a great deal of effort and their hard earned money to this cause. Polonia's organizations provided them with strong nationalistic statements at the turn of the century. For example, the Polish Women's Alliance stated in 1898:

> The purpose of the Polish Women in America Alliance is to establish a national soul, maintaining Polish ideas among the young generation by educating it in the history and language of Poland, and to demonstrate the need for constant contact with Poland so as to provide for it (the younger generation) in that manner the cultural strength which the Polish nation possesses. (Karlowiczowa 1938: 187; see Lopata 1954: 64)

The Polish National Alliance directed itself toward Poland's fight for independence:

> Since the Polish National Alliance can be regarded as having been formed by the will of the Polish nation in America, so, in the name of this nation, the central administration, as representative of this nation, will legally strive for the attainment of the independence of the Polish lands in Europe by all permissible means. (Zwiazek Narowowy Polski 1940: 108)

Polonia as the Fourth Province of Poland

Polonia prior to the 1920s identified itself as the fourth province of Poland, the other three being located in the other political states of Russia, Prussia, and Austria. Several groups tried to unify Polonia's help to Poland prior to World War I under that motto. The outbreak of the war finally resulted in the formation of the Polish Central Relief Committee, with headquarters in Chicago (Pienkos 1991: 429). It integrated relief activity throughout American Polonia, and then organized the Polish National Department, which was more directly involved in Polish politics.

Evidence of the identification with Poland comes from the formation of a Polish army in the United States, consisting of 28,000 volunteers, recruited in 1917 and trained in a variety of camps before being sent to France. The French government had given permission for the formation of the Polish army on its soil. The articles of formation included:

> Article I. An autonomous Polish Army under the highest leadership, fighting under Polish standards, forms in France.
> Article II. The organization and maintenance of this army is guaranteed under the French Government. (Lopata 1954: 78)

The Kosciuszko Legion, as it became called, also fought in Poland in its war against Russia to regain lands in 1919 and was then disbanded to return to the United States.

The Polish ex-peasants, most of whom entered United States with less than 50 dollars in their possession, also contributed millions of dollars both personally, by sending relief to friends and relatives, and through organized action of political groups. Jan Smulski, president of the Polish National Department, estimated that American Poles "altogether had channeled over $20,000,000 into all aspects of the Polish cause." This figure did not include the $67 million they bought in U. S. Liberty Bonds during the war (Renkiewicz 1973:21). The money went to support the governments-in-exile and the fighting when war broke out. Not only money, but military men were contributed by Polonia to Poland's fight for freedom. Finally, the political pressure, whether applied effectively by the Polish Americans or by the friendship that developed between Paderewski and American political leaders, resulted in President Wilson's decision that Poland should regain its political independence after the war (see Reddaway et al., *The Cambridge History of Poland* and Gerson's *Woodrow Wilson and the Rebirth of Poland 1914–1920*). The thirteenth of Wilson's fourteen points establishing the political world after the war read:

> An independent Polish state should be erected, which should include the territories inhabited by indisputably Polish populations, which should be assured a free and secure access to the sea, and whose political and economic independence and territorial integrity should be guaranteed by international covenant. (Gerson 1953:84)

Thus, from *okolica*-bound peasants, parish and mutual aid club members, the Polish Americans expanded their horizons in two decades to become identified as the "fourth province of Poland." They contributed to Poland's political rebirth through intensive effort and a willingness to part with money that was being saved for their most important status symbols—land and durable property. Their action was a reflection of political patriotism and an emotional response to dynamic leadership, despite the fact that they did not identify with the parties, ideologies, or internal struggle in Poland. They were simply interested in restoring Poland as a nation protected by a political state, in helping victims of the war, and in gaining status rewards in the process.

End of Identification as the Fourth Province of Poland

Polish Americans continued to send relief money to help Poland rebuild itself after World War I, investing $18,472,800 in government bonds and millions more in new businesses (Wachtl 1944). However, in the years following 1918, Polonia gradually became disenchanted with the Polish state and began to withdraw its identification and its economic contributions (Lopata 1954). The idealized "Poland," a vague unity, became a state, a government from which certain actions toward Polonia was expected and not met. A great number of delegates, some official, others with a variety of projects, came from Poland to the United States with only one purpose: to get more money in the form of contributions, investments, and so forth. These delegations tried to tell Polonia what it should do, and thus took away the feelings of importance of the local groups. Polonian leaders, in turn, felt they had the right to help determine the Polish government's policies and were taken back by the refusal to take advice. In addition, much of the money obtained from the sale of Polish bonds was used for political purposes, rather than for rebuilding the country. Soon Polonia resounded with the following statement: "close your pocket, boy (peasant), your money is going for political (party) purposes" (in Polish).

A major factor in the decrease of identification with Poland was disappointment in the response to Polonia's efforts before and during the war. Members felt they had been sacrificing their own life-styles and delaying their hopes for a better life. Instead of receiving gratitude, they continued to be inundated with requests for funds. Visitors or repatriates to Poland found themselves still treated as peasants even if they could buy status symbols. In fact, they frequently met with hostility and the difficulties of life in the homeland made many of the returnees disenchanted to the point of coming back to the United States. Those who returned brought back stories of poverty and a reality different from the ideal. The former members of the Polish armed forces were disappointed in their rewards. Poland lost interest in Polonia, turning to its internal problems. In fact, it underwent many political struggles over what leader and what party could best run the new government, struggles in which Polonia was completely uninterested. From the point of view of social psychology, this disenchantment was inevitable, but it was accompanied by much anger and bitterness.

Another factor in the separation of the fourth province of Poland from the rest of the nation was the impossibility of maintaining a similar life-style and worldview. The Polish Americans had been gradually, and often unconsciously, Americanizing and creating their own ethnic culture. Poland also changed, becoming very different from the Poland of the immigrant's memories. Polonia itself was having internal problems. Different groups were vying for leadership roles over the whole community. Concern was being felt over the Americanization of the younger generations, the lack of representation of Polish American clergy in the Roman Catholic church, and the community status in American society.

The shift of interest away from Poland was reflected by the motto of the third congress of the National Division in 1923, bringing together representatives of the major organizations: "Wychodstwo dla Wychodstwa," ("The Emigrant Group for the Emigrant Group"—the translation is difficult because the word Wychodstwo refers to more than just a mass of emigrants, implying a social entity). Now, declared the delegates, we are going to take care of ourselves. The withdrawal of identification with Poland was so complete that, during a 1934 convention of the World Alliance of Poles from Abroad, the demand that representatives of organizations in other countries swear allegiance to Poland was met with indignation by the Polish Americans. The delegation refused to sign such a pledge, declaring that Polonia was an "inseparable, harmonious part of the American nation, however tied to Poland by feeling, traditions and cultural ties" (Haiman 1948:427).

During the 1930s, Polonia maintained contact with Poland in three different ways. The first was personal interaction, correspondence, and, less frequently, visits back and forth of families and friends. Immigration fell below the Polish quota because most of the close relatives of earlier immigrants had already gone to the United States before that system was put into effect and because of the American depression. The second method of contact was through organized excursions aimed at familiarizing people with nationally significant symbols of Poland, allowing for personal contact, and obtaining official recognition. Third, various groups sponsored events involving both countries. The Polish Americans who returned to Poland after it regained political independence formed organizations to maintain contact and encourage participation in celebrations involving groups on both continents. Cultural and educational associations on this side of the Atlantic, such as the Kosciuszko Foundation attempted to retain contact and assist the exchange of students. The "harcerki" (Polish American girl scouts) asked for instructors from Poland. The most active group during these years was the Polish-American Chamber of Commerce, which arranged numerous cooperative ventures (Lopata 1954: 101).

World War II and Its Aftermath

World War II revived Polonia's interest in Poland as a national culture society, a political state, and a victim of Nazi persecution. Attempts were made by the intelligentsia to renationalize Polish Americans through such periodicals as *The Polish Review*. For example, its content idealized Polish culture and heroes and showed the suffering from the hands of the Nazis to increase humanitarian feelings. However, the nationalistic efforts were not very successful. There was much less direct involvement in helping Poland than there had been during World War I, reflecting Polonia's Americanization and concern with America's war problems. Arrangements were again made by the Polish government-in-exile with the U. S. government to recruit Americans of Polish descent to join Polish divisions attached to the French armed services. General Sikorski, chief of staff, who fled Poland during the invasion and joined the government-in-exile, and even the aging Paderewski (who died 29 June 1941) came to United States, touring Polonia and urging men to enlist. A training camp was opened to use for the planned Kosciuszko Legion in Canada, but the recruitment was not successful and only a handful of Polish Americans ended up in Europe as part of the Polish forces. This situation produced mutual recriminations and the strong attack by Polish leaders on Polonia simply angered the community. *Dziennik Zwiazkowy,* the Polish National Alliance daily newspaper, summarized the atmosphere by stating, "We have our own problems" (Wachtl 1944:421). It is probable that the Americanization process had been so extensive that few young men were motivated to join what was to them a "foreign army," speaking Polish, and sharing a cultural background different from that of the descendants of the immigrants.

The humanitarian interest of Polonias all over the world in helping their relatives, friends, and even unknown Poles resulted in intensive relief work during the war years. Millions of dollars of medicines and other medical equipment, food, and clothing were sent through all available channels. With the establishment of a communist government under the influence of the Soviet Union after World War II, official contact between Poland and Polonia practically ceased. Even the Polish governmental representatives in the United States were shunned, partly because of anticommunism, and partly because of fear of reprisals on relatives in Poland if anticommunist activities became known to the political powers in that country.

One of the situations that resulted in an increase of Polonia's orientation toward the Polish national culture society in the 1940s and 1950s was the presence all over the world of a very larger number of displaced persons and ex-combatants who refused to go back to Poland. Help to the displaced persons released from concentration and labor camps by the allied forces and to the ex-combatants and their families now living primarily in England and France operated on many levels. The most immediate was provision of food, clothing, and medicine. Second, the newly formed (1944) Polish American Congress put extensive pressure on the U. S. government, aided by the humanitarian appeal of the cause, to permit those people who were uprooted and who did not wish to return to Poland to enter this country. The government did respond with several specific acts, on the condition that an elaborate set of procedures were developed to screen out undesirable immigrants, those having dangerous or dependency- producing illnesses, and those known as communist sympathizers or activists. The entrants, who were not only Poles but other Europeans, needed guarantees from American residents. This condition created some problems, because many Polish Americans were afraid to sign such guarantees, and relief organizations had to take over the process.[2]

The arrival of refugees, displaced persons, and ex-combatants changed Polonia's orientation toward Poland and the internal life of the community in many ways. The new emigration was very different from the old one, having been brought up in an independent Poland, with a more urban and better educated population. Its members had undergone the uprooting experiences of the war, labor, and concentration camps, but they often knew English from years of residence in Great Britain. This immigration cohort was quite condescending of the members of established Polonia, seen as of peasant background, lacking knowledge of Polish culture and using archaic, folk, and Americanized language and social skills. They made the first cohort and its descendants realize how much they had already acculturated and also made them very angry. The term *DP* (displaced person), which was applied to the new emigration, acquired a derogatory flavor, implying brutalization by the war and a lack of sophistication in American ways. The common concerns of both cohorts of emigrants was anticommunism and an interest in Poland. The intelligentsia of the new emigration, shocked at the lack of knowledge of the Polish national culture, began a process of "educating" Polonia through the development of new activities and through the press. Although the new emigration created conflict and competition within Polonia, it influenced the orientation and continued interest in Poland, laying foundations for current attitudes.

Humanitarian efforts continued to be directed toward Poland after World War II, particularly after its political thaw of 1956. Many of Poland's families were dependent upon the food and clothing they received for many years after the war. In addition, Polonia organized a variety of other efforts. Some clubs and local groups "adopted" a Polish village or orphanage and sent money, tools, supplies, and equipment to it. Other organizations bought hospital equipment, school furnishings, and any other items needed to reestablish the basic activities of a society. Books were collected to replace volumes burned by Nazis or destroyed in the war. The rebuilding of Warsaw and other cities and towns was accomplished partly with funds from America. In all these activities Polonia's leaders and mass media kept emphasizing the separation between state and national culture society. These efforts were for the people and not to help the communistic state.

In the political arena, Polonia concentrated on three sets of activities: protests against the Yalta treaty, which gave lands considered by the Poles to be historically theirs to the Russians; efforts at pressuring American political figures to demand the "freeing" of Poland from the communist rule; and an arrangement for screening and processing Polish displaced persons, ex-combatants, and families who were allowed to enter the United States by special presidential or congressional acts. Feelings in Polonia during the years following World War II ran high and were heavily anticommunist; the community organized numerous activities in its attempts to get the United States to change its commitment to the Yalta treaty and to somehow rid Poland of its government. The efforts were not successful, in terms of their effect on governmental policy, but they unified the community on that issue, within its continued competition among groups. The anticommunism was reinforced by continued information, smuggled out or brought by escapees, as to the mistreatment of Poles under the system, especially during the Stalinist period.

Relations between Polonia and Pre-Solidarity Poland

As the Polish society resumed its functioning in rebuilt or newly created structures, in the 1960s and 1970s, the requests for help from Polonia began to shift from the basics of life to luxury items. Used clothing became redefined as less prestigious than new; doubleknit polyesters replaced nylon as desirable gifts; and American "Levis" and sweatshirts with American statements became very popular.

Some of the requests from Poland were met, and are still being met, with bitterness and anger by some Polish Americans. Puacz explained in 1972 that Poles still saw America as a wealthy uncle. Long deprived of luxury items, Poles in Poland felt that their rich relatives should not begrudge them. But the Polonians are irritated by the continuation of demands for such an extensive period of time after having sacrificed so much in emergencies. A New Yorker, part of the third cohort of emigrants, was angry in 1992 that a friend (not even a relative) complained that the $100 sent as an Easter present was so stingy as to embarrass him in front of neighbors (Lopata, field notes 1992).

In addition to obtaining luxury items, Poland has been recreating items of national culture. It rebuilt a famous palace in Warsaw with funds obtained from America and work volunteered by many Polish groups. The "thawed" communist government even encouraged and contributed to the rebuilding of churches—not as symbols of Catholicism but as tourist attractions and symbols of Polishness. With the gradual lifting of the iron curtain, contact with Poland in other than humanitarian ways became reestablished, with Polonia still insisting it rejects the government and accepts the nation. A brisk intercontinental traffic developed by the 1970s. Voluntary organizations arranged for "excursions" to Poland and numerous travel agencies have sprung up in the various settlements. Tourism has become a major industry in Poland, most of the visitors still being the emigrants and their descendants. The communist government encouraged this movement by removing the obstacles to travel, arranging for international scientific conferences, building additional housing and eating facilities, and rebuilding historical and cultural attractions. Summer became a season of completely booked hotels and congestion in restaurants.

Thus, contact with Poland increased considerably in the last years of the socialist regime. The government-sponsored Polonia Society united Polonians around the world. It held numerous congresses in Poland, with representatives from many organizations in the United States, Australia, Brazil, Canada, and France. Within the 1970s the Polonia Society gained 2,000 individual memberships from "civic leaders in 76 countries of the West" and it kept in contact with schools and the press in various parts of the world (*Dziennik Zwiazkowy*, 25 June 1973:3). Other contacts with Poland included tours for special purposes. For example, the Association of Doctors of Polonia of Detroit visited medical facilities in 1973, particularly those built and equipped with Polish American funds. Cooperative activity between Poland and the Association of Doctors of American Polonia included comparative research with the help of funds provided by the U.S. Public Law 480 (*Dziennik Zwiazkowy,* 30 June 1973:3).

The expanded contact between Poles and Polish Americans had resulted in a double-bind effect when carried out in conjunction with Polonia's official anticommunist stand. In the 1970s, the Polish American Congress still organized official protests, sent memorandums, and applied political pressure on the United States and the United Nations to change the Polish government (see details of activities in chapter 5). The motto of the newspaper that advertised all forms of interaction with Poland still reads "Remember that since the Polish nation is forced into silence, the *Alliance Daily* is its Free Voice." Anticommunist sentiment was still prevalent in Polonia and one of the most damning judgments of a member was that he was "pink."

The presence of this double-bind position in Polonia was acknowledged by its leaders.[3] Stypulkowski (1970:1) reiterated the Polish American Congress' stance against communism, distinguishing between the "ultimate goal" and the "practical propositions within the framework of the present international situation." "*[The] ultimate goal* for the overwhelming majority of the Polish community and for the whole Polish nation, consists in the recovery of external political independence and internal freedom."

A decision to separate the Polish nation and the communist government "imposed on it by force" was made at a conference of practitioners and theorists of politics, called together by the president of the Polish American Congress in Washington in 1970. These experts concluded that

> it would be wrong to overlook and deny the existence of the Polish state, which is the home of almost 33 million Poles and which, however circumscribed in its domestic and international activities, offers basic conditions for the nation's survival and for the protection of national interests. [Yet, the] PAC must continue to withhold its moral recognition and support of this regime, [by implication advising readers to refrain from political involvement]. (*Polish American Congress Newsletter,* 20 July 1970:7-8)

Polish Americans were affected by the increasing contact with visitors from Poland, in personal, official, or scientific exchanges during the years prior to the fall of communism. Such visits sometimes strained relations and produced ambivalent reactions. After all, there were many years and changes experienced by both sides. Criticism of America brought out the Americanized identity of Polonians and negative comments by Americans accentuated the Polish identity in the Poles. Polish Americans felt that the Poles do not understand them or America, while Poles viewed Polonia as a limited community with little remaining Polishness. Nowakowski, a Polish sociologist who spent several months in America, concluded that people on both sides of the ocean have mistaken pictures of each other, in spite of the expanded contact (1964:34-35). Many Polish Americans still visualized Poland as a poor and backward country with a nineteenth-century social structure. The Poles, on the other hand, according to Nowakowski (1964), expected Polish Americans as Polish patriots who are interested in coming to Poland's aid. Finding an absence of knowledge of even the Polish language, history, or culture Nowakowski concluded that any help that Polonia gave to Poland was not a result of nationalism (see also Tryfan 1973). The Polish Americans have been aware of the judgment by Polish visitors concerning their lack of Polishness. Personal contacts with the visitors, interaction at public events, and stories in the ethnic press provide such data. Usually, the judgments are met with anger (Lopata 1954), but they may also assist the leaders in their efforts to turn the community toward the Polish national culture.

Relations with Post-Communist Poland

The relation between Polonia and Poland changed dramatically with the overthrow of the communist government. Even before, as noted above, the force of communism had weakened, with the exception of the years 1981 to 1983, when it imposed martial law in reaction to the creation of the first free trade union, Solidarity. Polonia leaders allegedly convinced President Reagan to impose sanctions against the Polish government in response to this oppression (Pienkos 1991: 437) and a variety of events resulted in the lifting of martial law. The granting of amnesty to the numerous political prisoners resulted in the United States lifting the sanctions. By 1989 the Polish government officials finally recognized Solidarity and met with its leaders; the following elections resulted in the downfall of the Communist party.

This change in the political situation of Poland turned Polonia completely around into supporting both the government and the nation. The leaders on both sides of the ocean began exchanges of delegations aimed at helping the new state, especially in its economic needs. Numerous organizations were formed for these purposes, assisted by an economic base provided by the U. S. government in the form of equipment and training for democratic leadership, food aid, trade and development programs, debt reduction, the initiative of the Agency for International Development and the Polish-American Enterprise Fund (*New Horizon* 1991:26). Polish Americans have been involved in whatever activities have been relevant. The U.S. Poland Chamber of Commerce sponsored luncheons and other events for visiting Polish political and governmental leaders as a means of encouraging investment in that country, an unheard of activity prior to 1990. The Chamber's mission "is to promote trade and investment between the United States and Poland" through the provision of numerous services, such as business meetings, seminars and workshops; databases and a clearinghouse; referral to consultants, bankers and lawyers, newsletters, and so forth (U.S.

Poland Chamber of Commerce: n.d.: 2–3). Many of the speakers who come on behalf of Poland's economic needs are, by the way, members of the new and even of the old intelligentsia, as are most of the recent governmental officials, with the exception of Lech Walesa.

A number of projects involving members of Polonia or its groups in Poland are educational, preparing people raised under communism to try to work out a democratic system and private economic enterprises. For example, the National-Louis University of Chicago, which has been involved in many of Polonia's events, established the "first private undergraduate-level business school in Nowy Sacz with the cooperation of one of the senators of the Republic of Poland" (invitation for a fund-raising dinner, 29 July 1992). Obtaining funds from a variety of sources, a Polish American professor at Rutgers University has started three "Local Democracy in Poland" projects and a number of small pilot grants to teach people to "carry on through this transition period (*New Horizon* 1992b:10–11). The Kosciuszko Foundation has increased its summer program in Polish language, history, culture, literature and "issues of contemporary Poland" in Kracow, Lublin, and Warszawa for interested students from the United States (*New Horizon* 1991e: 21–22).

In addition to increased travel by Polish Americans to Poland, Poles are more frequently coming to America. Of great interest to many Polish Americans have been the performances of Polish sports teams in international competition or as they tour the United States in local competition. Concerts by leading musicians, operas, and theatrical performances draw large audiences in Polonia's local communities. The "temporary emigrants," who also increased in number in the 1980s and 1990s, entered as students or guests of relatives or other Americans. The U.S. government is cognizant of the fact that these visitors often come for extended times and work for money, although legally forbidden to do so.[4] Visitors to the United States are still required to have officially documented invitations; and a screening process by U. S. embassies prevents the entrance of "undesirables." Travel agencies in the United States and authorized dealers assist in making the necessary arrangements, such as invitations in proper form to relatives or friends for temporary or permanent stays. They usually provide such services as translation of documents, settlement of matters requiring knowledge of Polish laws, prolongation of passports and visas, and even arrangement for adoption of Polish children. They assist retired people in organizing their settlement in Poland with a guaranteed receipt of American Social Security payments (see *Chicago Sun-Times Midwest Magazine* 1983 for interviews with Polish American retirees in Poland). All these services reflect the dramatic changes in the relations between Polonia and Poland in recent decades.

Simultaneously, the same shift in Polonia's relations with Poland as developed in the 1930s appears in very recent times. The Polish daily *Dziennik Zwiazkowy* asked in 1989 "Will the concept of 'Émigrés for Émigrés' revive?"

(Bialasiewicz 1989). It is interesting that the very overthrow of the communist government actually deprived the main interorganizational association, the Polish American Congress, of one of its two main functions. The 1992 congress (it meets every four years) declared itself in the process of "constructing or fleshing out the concept it calls THE AMERICAN AGENDA" (*New Horizon,* April 1992: 17). A committee formulated for this purpose called for suggestions from members and an all-day conference was planned prior to the main congress to work out directions for action.

Poland is now reaching out to the Polonias all over the world. One method has been to bring people of Polish birth or ancestry to the country for special occasions. A Congress of veterans of Polish Armed Forces was held in Warsaw in August 1992 with great pomp and ceremony. Parades of former combatants in uniform brought emotional responses, pride of having fought for the country, and patriotic statements.

A very interesting event occurred later in August 1992 in Krakow, Poland. A new organization, Stowarzyszenie Wspolnota Polska (Association of the Polish Community), allegedly not government-controlled, called together a first congress of Poles and Polonias in Krakow. It was a very formal occasion, with speeches by the premier, Hanna Suchodcka, and the president, Lech Walesa, and a mass performed by Polish and Polonian bishops and priests. Walesa's speech, titled "We have Waited for You a Long Time," set the theme: "I know, that we can count on your hot patriotism. Although we live in different countries—we have to act together. Together we think of Poland as our joint goal. . . . Together we will create a political and strong lobby promoting our country" (Walesa 1992:3). People who had been afraid to come to the mother country just a few years before, were now greeted by major government officials. Poles living abroad were offered dual citizenship, enabling them to vote in Polish elections; and the leaders of Wspolnota offered to centralize news from their locations through its bulletin.

In spite of many sentimental speeches by those attending from many countries, including those from former Soviet Union nations, the congress did not meet its goal of uniting Polonias under the Wspolnota umbrella. The Polish Americans refused to cooperate under these conditions. There were two main problems. In the first place, the copresident of the congress headed a Canadian organization, the Rada Koordynacyjney Polonii Wolnego Swiata (the Coordinating Council of the Polonias of the Free World). This angered American Polonia, which is the largest and considers itself the most important. Of even greater significance, however, was the assumption by the Polish Wspolnota and the Polish speakers that American Polonia is so strongly identified with Poland as to be willing to be dependent upon its leadership. It became immediately apparent, at least to one *Dziennik Zwiazkowy* reporter, that the Polonias do not identify with the country of their ancestors as much as with their own community and the countries of their current life. Their goals are to gain a higher status and better life circumstances in the countries in which their ancestors began a new life; they are not solely concerned with Polish matters. They do not see themselves as representatives of Poland and its interests, but of their own ethnic communities or groups. Their observance of cultural traditions "and 'Polishness' as a heartfelt second identity should not be confused with their life concerns in Poland and taking an active part in its concerns" (loose translation of Wierzewski, 28–30 August 1992:5; see also Lewandowski's columns, fall of 1992). For this reason, the delegates felt no need for Polish citizenship, since they considered it improper to be involved in such events as elections. American Polonia's delegates, officers of its main organizations, definitely did not want to be dependent upon Poland or to have people in that country determine the use of their finances. The congress thus clarified the position of American Polonia vis-à-vis Poland: Sentimental ties, exchanges of culture and education, visits and congresses, but no return to being a part of Poland.

The aftermath of the congress reverberated throughout Poland and Polonia for months. Each side declared that the other did not understand it. The Polish Poles were greatly disappointed by the refusal of cooperation from the "Westerners" (mainly American Poles. They had hoped to bring the Polonias closer to their interests and felt insulted by the Polonian assumption that Poles were incapable of making democratic decisions and needed advice. The Polonians felt that the Poles did not want to learn about democracy, of which Polonians were more knowledgeable. One of the news reporters from Polonia concluded that Wspolnota simply wanted funds to maintain its building and staff, which the Polonians refused to pay for. "After the Congress in Krakow— Polonia in Deep Conflict" read a headline in the *Dziennik Chicagowski* (Jarmakowski 1992b; see also 1992a). Most commentators of the established American Polonia agreed with the delegates, led by Edward Moskal, president of the Polish American Congress and the Polish National Alliance, two very powerful positions. Moskal (1992:1,2,25) himself wrote very negative "impressions of Poland" not only from that trip but also from the time he and a member of President Bush's cabinet, Derwinski, accompanied Paderewski's ashes to Poland. Paderewski, famous pianist and former president of Poland, had died in America when Poland was under communist rule and had willed his ashes to be taken there when it gained independence. The trip was not a success because the Polish Americans were not greeted according to diplomatic protocol, as befitting their importance.

The third immigration cohort reacted differently to the events of the 1992 congress, accusing Moskal and his associates of handpicking the delegates in a way that excluded representation from the new groups. Its members felt that American Polonia should not be represented by the descendants of the first and second cohorts whom they consider too American to understand, and identify with, Poland.

The third cohort has its own problems of identification and feelings about Poland. As in prior times with other groups, the people, most of whom are in the middle years of life, are homesick and feeling guilty for not being there to help build the new society. Yet they do not want to return at the present time, what with the economic problems and upheaval of privatization, especially since life is increasingly comfortable in America. They express a combination of excitement over what is happening and disappointment that independence had not brought the paradise-like life they dreamed of while fighting, or at least surviving under, communism. These feelings are not shared by the established Polish Americans.

Summary

The relations between Polonia and the mother country have varied histori- cally, depending on events on both sides of the ocean. In the early years of its formation, the various settlements and superterritorial organizations were visited by nationalistic leaders seeking help for the government-in-exile; and they hoped for a world war that would bring independence in the form of a political state encompassing the national culture society. They and the nationalistic émigrés in America, mainly of the upper classes and intelligentsia, helped to convert the Polish Americans, previously identified with a limited *okolica*, into "the fourth province of Poland." This did not make these Polish Americans identified with the whole national culture, but only with folk and religious elements of it as well as with the Polish people. This identification weakened in the interwar years, as Polonia turned its attention to its own problems. World War II, with Poland as one of its heroic victims, again turned attention to the mother country; money and all forms of humanitarian help poured from Polonia. The takeover by the communist government cut off contact with the government, and Polonian leaders specified a definite division between the state and the nation. Identification with the nation continued, albeit in lesser form and degree than around of the time of World War I. The second cohort of immigrants following World War II had a different view of Poland and was much more oriented toward it than the established Polonia. The same is true of the third cohort.

The ambiguity and ambivalence of Polonia's feelings about Poland were crystallized by the recent congress of Poles and Polonias in which the demands for a union of all Poles abroad with Poland produced a strong reaction of independence. American Polonia, more so than that in Eastern European countries, declared its identification with the host country as stronger than its identification with the home country. Of course, this was the reaction of the delegates from America, who are mainly descendants of the early Polish immigrants, officers of the main fraternal organizations. The attitudes of the 400,000 or so people who were born in Poland and came mostly with the World War II cohort or in recent years are not recorded.

Notes

1. This I know from personal experience. The various branches of the Znaniecki clan were herded with others of the same social classes from the Poznan district into a concentration camp, then into cattle cars, driven around in winter until most froze; the bodies and survivors were dumped outside of the territory officially incorporated into Germany, not just occupied by that political state.
2. Most of these displaced persons were sponsored by voluntary associations within different nationality communities. Most of Polonia's work was channeled through the Polish American Immigration and Relief Committee, headquartered in New York but with an active branch in Chicago.
3. The president of the Polish American Congress explained the continued anticommunistic stances as helpful to Poles. "Some say that they are hurting our country by criticizing its government. This is a lie, thrown up by the communist propaganda. Our sisters and brothers in Poland want us to tell the truth to the world of their lot." (*Dziennik Zwiazkawy* 19 September 1973: 2). This Polonian leader feels that "pressure on the regime in Warsaw to meet its obligations to the people" is productive and has resulted in such achievements as an agreement to build more churches in new communities, relaxing of censorship of the press and publications, noninterference with the religious, education of the youth, conservation of historical monuments and artistic objects, lifting of censorship of letters, reduction of the tax on packages entering Poland, and return "to the Polish nation of the beautiful Panorama by Raclawski" (2).
4. Polonian leaders have historically accused the American government of discriminating against the Poles by refusing them visas in the embassy in Warsaw. Congressman John Dingell (1974) wrote to Secretary of State Henry Kissinger claiming that in 1969 only 865 visas were refused while in 1973 there were 6,853 such refusals (unfortunately no mention is made of the total number of applications). The State Department of the United States government had "alleged that a growing number of Poles on visitor visas have been apprehended working illegally in the United States, as well as attempting to change their status from visitor to immigrant," and referred to the situation as the "Polish problem." The letter did not deny the practice, but insisted that the visa refusals were discriminatory. It appears that the visa applications are currently continuing to be very carefully scrutinized, although Poland has recently lifted visa requirements for people wishing to travel from the United States (*New Horizon*, April 1991:18). Of course, there are different reasons for the travel, and thus different reasons for governmental action.

5

Polonia's Relations with the Rest
of American Society

"To gain influence and stature in the American society Polonia must involve itself in the mainstream of American life" (Piwowarski 1970:8). This conclusion, reached by a Polish American conference (Washington, D.C. 1970), and reiterated from time to time, reflected several aspects of Polonia's definition of its situation, particularly its status as an ethnic community within a larger society. First, it implies that Polonia has not been in the "mainstream" of American life, but that it should now move in that direction. (This assumes that the mainstream consists of ethnic communities rather than a core of nonethnic American life.) Second, it implies that Polonia wants to gain influence. This is reinforced by the following statement: "Another deplorable circumstance is the limited influence of Polonia in American political life" (Piwowarski 1970:8). Finally, it points to dissatisfaction with Polonia's stature in American society.

The Commission on Civic and Political Activities of the Polish American Congress reported in the PAC newsletter of 20 July 1970 the "shocking discrimination" against Polish Americans by the state government of Illinois, and by the federal government. Congressman Pucinski recommended that "all State Divisions [of the PAC] start a 'talent bank' which would give all of us a steady reservoir of capable Polish Americans who are willing to take on responsible positions, both in the Government and in the private sector" (*PAL Newsletter*: 12). Other stories focused on "anti-defamation" activities" and the concern that "There is so much to be done to uplift the Polish American image;" including "stimulating the interest of our youth in the Polishness" (*PAL Newsletter*: 3). The board of PAC was told of the "action and steps aimed at enhancing Polonia's standing and prestige in American life" by the organization's president.

The Polish National Alliance was less interested in the status of Poles in America at its initial constitution of 1880 than in the character of the population it served. Among the initial aims was the "material and moral advancement of

113

the Polish immigration in America" through the formation of the alliance, "to care for the needs of the Polish immigration in America," to "commemorate anniversaries that honor the Polish homeland," and "to promote moderation in the consumption of alcohol." Only one aim was oriented outwardly and that was: "To strengthen the immigrants politically as American citizens by setting up a Polish newspaper and to make contacts with the American press in defense of Polish concerns" (Pienkos 1984: 56). In 1991, PNA's description of its early aims read that it "was founded to form a viable union of early Polish immigrants and settlers and to facilitate their entry into the mainstream of America" (*New Horizon*, September 1991: 18).

The Polish American Congress was formed in 1944 mainly as a political interorganizational representative of Polonia and of Poland, "to speak on behalf of the Polish People enslaved in their homeland and assist them in their struggle for freedom and independence" (*New Horizon*, May–June 1992: 4). It lost one of its two main purposes with the overthrow of the communist government in the home country. It then revived its interest in the position of Polish Americans and of Polonia in the United States.

> While helping Poland in its fight for independence and sovereignty, PAC was not able to pay sufficient attention to the needs of people of Polish descent living in the United States. In the coming period, PAC should devote its energy and resources to fulfill its aims regarding millions of American Polonia, to secure their unity, their standard and position in American social, political and cultural life. At the same time, Polonia should strive [to improve] its knowledge of Polish history and culture and maintain its traditions. (*New Horizon*, May–June 1992: 4)

Its orientation toward Poland took the form of using "its influence on American society for its benefit in cooperation with the no-longer-communist govern-ment."

Bases for the Relationship

While Polonia was developing its unique structure and culture and formulat-ing its relations with Poland, it also had to interact with the American national society and the political state within which it is located. Relations of an ethnic community with the country of settlement can be on the community or in-dividual level (Gordon 1964).

Several characteristics underlie these relations on the community level. In the first place, Polonia is not an independent community, able to survive without interaction with the larger society. It is a functional component of the society, regardless of how much it has identified itself as a separate subsociety. The members of the community are influenced in their private and public life by the political, economic, religious, educational, and recreational life that is emerging, existing, and changing in the larger society and its other social groups. In spite of the ideology developed in Polonia in the 1930s that pictures American society as a mosaic of different ethnic groups with no central core, there *is* a distinctive American way of life. It would be hard to imagine anyone in urban America claiming total independence from American institutions and associations. The culture pervades the home through radio, television, and publications, as well as the actions and reactions of those members of the family who return home after participating in school or work roles on the outside. Although Polonia has developed a complex set of institutionalized alternatives to segments of American institutions (Breton 1964), the lives of its central core of organizational personnel and leaders are heavily American in structure and action. The recent revitalization of interest in Polish national culture rather than folk or ethnic culture, due to the presence of the newest cohort, does not negate the fact that Polonia is an ethnic community whose life-style heavily resembles the rest of America. Movement from folk or national Polish culture to American culture through the ethnic community has been gradual, but definite (see also Kramer 1970).

A second characteristic of Polonia's relations with America has been an underlying acceptance of the greater society and of the democratic political process (see also Symmons-Symonolewicz 1966). Whether applying pressure on the society, or objecting to some of its actions, Polonia has functioned as a reform group rather than a revolutionary group, aiming to change, not to overthrow. Unlike Poles living in Germany or Russia (who, for many years, organized extensive efforts to sabotage those states) Polish Americans identify with the system and operate within its political institutions, even when they feel angry (as over the Yalta agreement), or hostile (as over prejudice directed against them). Part of the general friendliness toward America has been due to the fact that the larger society left the immigrants alone to build their own community. The Poles came here voluntarily and the American society accepted them, made room for them in its cities and factories and allowed them to build their own churches and schools.

In fact, the third characteristic of Polonia's interaction with America has been a mutual neglect (not entirely benign) except at times of emergency. Polonia neglected the rest of American society in the early years first because of a lack of understanding, then because of an awareness of how difficult it was for the foreign-born and even second-generation Polish Americans to achieve high status within it. Only during wars and over peace settlements did Polonia's leaders attempt to change or direct the action of American society. In addition, there were some sporadic attempts to elevate Polish Americans to positions of higher prestige in the religious and political systems. This neglect of America has diminished in recent years due to the improved probability of positive responses and to the changing composition of the Polish American population (see chapter 6).

Anti-Polishness in America

An inflow and outflow of prejudice has colored much of Polonia's life. Since they first settled in America, Polish Americans have been aware of the prejudice of non-Polish Americans toward them. Prejudice against immigrants has a long history in America; Benjamin Franklin stated that although the country needed the Scotch, Irish, and Germans, he was worried about having so many of them and about their behavior (Cross 1973:4). Forgetting that they themselves had been the object of prejudice, or perhaps still reacting to it, the descendants of the groups who were now considered to be the "old immigration" expressed strong negative attitudes toward the "new immigration" from southern and eastern Europe.[1] In the first quarter of the twentieth century the Immigration and Naturalization Service and many nongovernmental agencies sponsored or conducted studies of attitudes toward immigrants of those years and found them defined as illiterate, often mentally deficient (see Mullan 1917, *The Mentality of the Arriving Immigrant*), and criminally inclined or victimized by their own people (see Claghorn 1923, *The Immigrant's Day in Court*; Thrasher 1927, *The Gang*). In addition they were said to be experiencing serious health problems (Davis 1921, *Immigrant Health and the Community*), individual and family demoralization (Thomas and Znaniecki 1918–1920, *The Polish Peasant in Europe and America*; Thomas, Park, and Miller 1949 *Immigrant Traits Transplanted*), and to be inwardly clannish and unwilling to Americanize (Park 1922, *The Immigrant Press and its Control*). Sociologists and other supposedly value-free scholars often expressed negative judgments regarding the new immigrants, a large number of whom were Polish. W. I. Thomas, an eminent American professor at the University of Chicago, used a policeman's stereotype as one of the reasons for wanting to study Polish Americans:

> They were the most incomprehensible and perhaps the most disorganized of all the immigrant groups. This may be illustrated by what the American police call "Polish warfare." A Policeman might enter a saloon where there was a noisy crowd of Poles and say, "You men be quiet," and they might subside immediately or one of them might draw a gun and kill him. This was due to the fact that the Pole in America has two attitudes toward authority. One of these reflects the old peasant subordination to authority. They were called "cattle" by the landlords and submitted like cattle. The other attitude reflects the conception that there are no limits to the boasted American "freedom." (quoted in Blumer 1939:104–5)

A very interesting sociological story concerning Thomas's interest in Polish Americans, repeated even in such scholarly works as Coser's (1977: 533) *Master of Sociological Thought* goes as follows:

One rainy morning while walking down the back alley behind his house, Thomas had to side-step to avoid a bag of garbage which someone was throwing from a window. As the bag bursts open at his feet, a long letter fell out. He picked it up, took it home, and discovered that it was written in Polish by a girl taking a training course in a hospital. It was addressed to her father and mainly discussed family affairs and discords.[2] (See also Janowitz 1966: xxiv)

Bias is also indicated in Thomas' report of his first contact with his future coauthor, Znaniecki, who

was in charge of the Bureau for the Protection of Emigrants in Poland,which means advising all who planned to emigrate as to the desirable destinations and guarding them again[st] exploitation, especially in South America. Incidentally, it meant also, as I understand it, keeping the best elements in Poland and facilitating the departure of the remainder. (Janowitz 1966: 105-6)

Even an American historian, Woodrow Wilson, advocated the reduction of Polish immigration to the United States:

But now there came multitudes of men of lowest class from the south of Italy and men of the meaner sort out of Hungary and Poland, men out of the ranks where there was neither skill nor any initiative of quick intelligence; and they came in numbers which increased from year to year, as if the countries of the south of Europe were disburdening themselves of the more sordid and hapless elements of their population, the men whose standard of life and work were such as American workmen had never dreamed of hitherto. (Quoted in Gerson 1953:55)

On the other hand, some social scientists questioned the validity of such portrayals of the new immigrants. Taft (1936, see also a more detailed discussion of his findings in chapter 6) analyzed criminal statistics of the 1930s and reiterated a prior finding that the foreign-born were not highly criminal, having rates lower than the native-born. He also concluded that the high second generation rates were due to the age distribution of the population. The new immigrant groups' second-generation males were highly concentrated in the "criminally significant" ages, as compared to the old immigration second-generation youth. Hourwich (1912) attempted to dispel the myths concerning the labor force and social behavior of the new immigration, including the Poles. However, their efforts were not very successful in decreasing prejudice against the Polish immigrants and their children, in the same way as they were not successful in decreasing the prejudice against other immigrant groups. From the point of view of sociology, the inability to change ethnic stereotypes is not surprising, given the cost of such efforts in an enormous society and the persistence of prejudice in spite of evidence to the contrary. The image of the poor immigrant bound to an unintelligible culture is carried into new generations and immigrations with the label of Polak, Wop or Dago, Hunky, and so forth.

Initial Reaction to American Prejudice

The Polish Americans could not be oblivious to the statements made about them nor to the significance of the quota acts, which were, after all, designed to keep people like them from entering America in any but minimal numbers.[3] They reacted at first by ignoring the society of settlement and turning their attention to Poland and to Polonia's internal life. Withdrawal from identification with Poland was very difficult for Polonia while it faced negative prejudice from Americans, and it took many years. Polonia's realization of its low status in relation to other groups was reflected in the anger and frustration of its pronouncements of the 1930s and 1940s:

> The great declarations of freedom in the United States are only empty watchwords. Statements are made by the Nordics: "You Pole are as good an American as I." However, when the same Pole wants to take a place on an equal level as this Nordic, then he meets another side of his character: "What, you foreigners want to be equal with us?" The Pole is supposed to be satisfied with slogans. That is why the [Polish National] Alliance must widen its services and waken the immigrant group to a recognition of itself and the role it has to play in the land of Washington. The Alliance must make the slogans become real. (Zwiazek Narodowy Polski 1940:27, in Polish)

Changing the status of Polish Americans in the American society was, however, very complicated. One internal problem was that the Polish immigrants of the first cohort and their descendants did not have a very positive image of themselves; in short, they suffered from a major inferiority complex (Kolm 1969, 1971a, 1971b; Nowakowski 1964). The prejudices of the gentry toward the peasants undoubtedly formed a foundation to a negative self-image, reinforced and accentuated by American attitudes. A perfect example of the problem is contained in a study conducted by an anthropologist, Paul Wrobel (1979), in a Polish American community in the Detroit area and the reaction to it. Wrobel found the men especially negative about themselves. Summarizing the findings in a paper presented in 1976 at a meeting of the American Association for the Advancement of Science he stated:

> Generally speaking, the men in this community view themselves as unintelligent factory workers unworthy of respect and incapable of accomplishing anything worthwhile except supporting a family through hard work and the ability to sacrifice (Wrobel 1979: 157).

Wrobel reported that the men did not want their sons to be like them, working in a factory in a socially downgraded job. They and their wives were willing to sacrifice their own life-style so that their children would have a better life. However, the children usually duplicated their socioeconomic level, since they did not continue with schooling. The process is the same as that experienced by working-class youth in England, studied by Willis (1977). The results of the sacrifices of parents are often painful in other ways:

> The pain, however, is caused by societal attitudes toward ethnicity and social class. For the sons and daughters of immigrants have been required to reject their cultural heritage in order to be successful in the larger society. And doing just that has made them ambivalent of their parents' way of life. (Wrobel 1979: 85)

Thus, the children reject the parents, yet do not reach the levels of success for which the parents worked so hard to make possible.

What was especially interesting about this study was the reaction it created in the American society at large, and the Polonian community's response to that reaction. Wrobel's point was that the stereotypes made by Americans had affected these factory workers to the extent that they believed them, in spite of the fact that their jobs and lives were complex. The society, through the mass media, eagerly picked up on the content of the self-concepts as proof of the rightness of the stereotypes. The Polish Americans themselves turned in anger upon the anthropologist, with letters to newspapers and vicious calls to his office and home. Although the middle-class Polish Americans resented his focus on the working class, the parish that he studied, for the most part, supported him, sympathizing with the misuse of his work by the mass media. Greeley commented on the role of the media:

> The national media latched onto every tiny bit of it [the Boston paper] which fit the existing stereotype of the dumb, passive Poles and ignored the rest of his work. The Polish community leaders, understandably but unfortunately also characteristically, also shot from the hip without bothering to read the Wrobel report. Thus they gave the stereotype even more publicity. (Greeley 1976)

Rather than dealing with prejudice through positive action, many Polonians simply became angry, withdrew from attempts to compete in American society, or dropped all ties and identities with Polonia and created a non-Polish family history (see also Novak 1972).

Ideological Responses

The inability of the Polish Americans to fight prejudice resulted in one Polish author (Kuniczak 1968) writing a book about them entitled *The Silent Emigration.* There is a double-bind problem involved in the situation. The leaders and organization members of Polonia do not want the people to gain status in the wider society by losing identification with the community, but by raising Polonia's status as a whole. Bishop Rhode pleaded, "If we forget our Polish heritage we become nothing but ships in the wind without anchors" (Haiman 1948:433). The Polish National Alliance kept telling the Polish Americans, "We can not change ourselves into hybrids, because then our worth would be completely lost. We must convince ourselves of the worth of our spiritual possessions and of our Polish history" (in Polish, Zwiazek Narodowy Polski 1948:35). And here lies the basis for the double-bind problem: which image of Polonia should be developed both internally and to the American society, that of the folk culture of the old Polonia or that of the Polish national culture?

The image of Polish Americans expressed by the Detroit men (Wrobel 1979) is an extreme of the negative view. The next level of self-image is that of the folk culture of dances, foods, and ceremonies. That level is partially shared by the second and third waves of immigrants. The immigrants from World War II Poland and thereafter do not reject the folk culture, but stress a completely different view of Polishness and wish to transfer Polonia into it. They consider the American stereotypes of the Polish Americans so wrong that they simply do not identify themselves in any way with them. However, they define the old Polonia in such terms and therefore distance themselves from it. Theirs is a Polish- and European-based self-identity, of equality among nationals, suffering, and braveness, with a touch of the old nobility romanticization (see chapter 1; Bloch 1982; Davies 1984; Giergielewicz 1979; Milosz 1968; Steven 1982). They find knowledge of Polish history and culture a prerequisite of civilized Polishness and it is this image they want to project to America.

A perfect example of the judgment of the old by the second cohort of Polonians is evident in the writing of Alexander Janta (1957). According to him, and most newer immigrants agree, the Polish Americans were hampered in their efforts to improve their self-images and their image in the wider society by their ignorance of Polish national culture. He concluded that the established Polonia of the first cohort and its descendants suffered from anti-intellectualism, which prevented them from breaking through this barrier of ignorance (Janta 1957): "At the root of this deficiency lies a profound misunderstanding of the meaning of culture among the majority of Polish leaders, and, consequently, among the masses as well" (83). Furthermore, "in spite of the efforts of a few national culture intelligentsia, . . . the overwhelming majority of Poles in America can express their 'Polonism' in relation to the American background by little more than costume, dance, or food" (86). Thus, according to Janta, old-wave Polish Americans have lived as a separate entity within the society, preserving the folk culture and the language, but ignoring the literary and artistic culture of Poland. The latter could have been of interest to Americans and might have helped change the image of Polish Americans and also of Poland as a limited and peasant-dominated land. "It is disappointing to realize that between the two wars too little was done to reverse this trend. No solid educational program has been conceived and developed [in Polonia] and no investment into its establishment was attempted from the Polish side" (Janta 1957:94).

One accomplishment of the leaders of established Polonia that assisted the preservation of the community was an ideology defining America as a pluralistic society as early as the 1930s, long before such a view became popular with the waning of the melting pot theory. This ideology looks at the United States as a group of subcultures—minority groups with no highly visible, permanent, and distinct majority (Bugelski 1952:3). Since Polish Americans cannot belong to another ethnic group, they might as well do their best with what they have and build it into a positive set of resources in competition with other groups. According to this pluralistic image of America, this society lacks a central core of nonethnics. In addition, each of the other ethnic and racial groups shares a consciousness of kind, is well organized, and has effectively concentrated its attention toward improvement of its relative status. Polonia has fallen behind such efforts to increase its status because of its involvement in Poland and in its own internal affairs. Within this frame of reference Polonia's low social position in the society is admitted, but is attributed to its long-lasting insistence on being the "fourth province of Poland" and its failure to work at establishing satisfactory status in this society, rather than to any "inherent" inferiority. The lack of "Polish power" (as it is currently being called) is thus reversible with proper effort and cooperation.[4]

It is here in the ideology, concerning Polonia's ability to unify, however, that some hesitation is voiced by all cohorts, the old, middle, and new Polonians. Many Polish Americans who still identify with their Polish background still believe in a Polish national character that makes sustained cooperation difficult, if not impossible (see chapter 1). The main features of this national character are individualism, independence, and competitiveness. The ideology thus provides a loophole for the lack of status achievement in the outside society. Not only were other groups more established on the status ladder to begin with than were the late-arriving Polish Americans, but they benefited from the absence of the "Polish character" that handicapped Polonia in its bid for superior or at least equal status in the past and is apt to do so in the future.[5] On the other side of the coin, the positive consequence of the national character is an internal appreciation of the dynamism of individualism and competitiveness. Feeling these sentiments and beliefs about themselves, recognizing their status in American society as low, and assuming a powerlessness to change it because of their very "character," the Polish Americans who continue to identify with Polonia have been concerned mainly with individual and family participation in community life and its lively and engrossing status competition. In sum, the Polish Americans of other than the Wrobel study do not believe the "dumb Polak" stereotype but attribute their low status in America to their inability to do away with the prejudice through cooperative antidefamation action.

The second cohort of Poles emigrating to the United States during and after World War II went in two directions. Some identified with Polonia and contributed to its literary life by forming organizations with Polish culture functions and by "cleaning up" the language of the mass media. Others dispersed into the American society, having relatively minimal contact with Polonia through such groups as the Polish Institute of Arts and Sciences in America.

The newest cohort has not had much influence on American society due to its lack of facility with the English language and interest in returning to Poland. The *wakacjusze* contribute negative images of "Polish cleaning ladies." Their educational and occupational background in Poland is unknown, again because they can not communicate with their employers.

Efforts at Participation in the American Status System

Polonia as a community has tried to change its status in America by capitalizing on events in Poland that gain positive world recognition and by drawing attention to contributions of Polish Americans to the broader society. It meets the latter purpose in three ways. First, it selects individual Polish Americans for dramatic publicity as positive representatives of the community; second, it repeats declarations of loyalty to the host state; and third, it tries to "enrich" American culture with elements of Polish culture.

The first of these activities is based on the assumption that certain types of people and certain activities are more highly valued in the society than are others. From early in Polonia's history, the two persons most often selected as reminders of Polish contributions to America were the Polish generals Pulaski and Kosciuszko who became heroes in the American Revolution. References to these men in mass communication media and the erection of statues of them attempt to anchor American memory of Polish contributions to the past, capitalizing on the society's idealization of its own history and length of residence or involvement by members on this side of the ocean. It also serves as a reminder of the historical presence of men of upper classes in a land from which most of the Poles who emigrated were of the lower classes. More recently, outstanding sports figures, film stars, successful businessmen, artists, and scientists have been chosen as representatives.[6] The publicity emphasizes that these individuals have achieved not only American but cosmopolitan reputations. Their idealization is expected to infiltrate the image of the total community.

Declarations of loyalty to America have also been used in attempts to change the image of Polish Americans as interested only in Poland. As one of the speakers at a 1938 joint Convention of the Polish Medical and Dental Association of the United States of America and the Polish Lawyers Association of the U.S.A. stated:

> Our first and most important duty is to be good Americans, take an active part in all phases of life here, and take advantage in full of all opportunities and privileges, as

are rightfully ours, not as a numerous minority but as mutual originators and participants in the common good of the American Republic. (Kostrzewski 1938:18)

One of the major obligations to America was defined as making it more knowledgeable about Poland. As Starzynski stated at the same convention:

Our second and no less important duty is to enrich our common American life and newly forming culture. This American culture is the total of contributions of all those national groups which live here. We can not be beggars, with hat in hand. We cannot take, giving nothing in return. (Starzynski 1938:18)

Several groups of Polish Americans of both cohorts, such as the American Council of Polish Cultural Clubs or the Kosciuszko Foundation (see chapters 3 and 6) undertook the selection, development, and dissemination of cultural items to the broader society. However, the effort increased dramatically in the 1970s with a direct attempt to change the image of Polish Americans. As far as can be determined from Polish leaders and the ethnic press, this effort started as a direct consequence of the "Polak" or "Polish" jokes (at least this was the symbolic focal point). The humor of these strongly negative stories centered on the lower class background and peasant culture of the immigrant. The increase of anti-Polishness was attributed in the Polish community, and by outside observers, to the upward socioeconomic mobility of the Polish Americans, which made the ethnic group more visible in the society. It has also been attributed to the anti-Polish sentiment of the Jewish community, many of whose members were writers and performers (*Dziennik Zwiazkowy* 1973, in Polish):

More and more Americans of Polish descent are complaining of the malicious anti-Polish articles written by members of certain Jewish groups, and to the constantly growing discrimination against Poles and Americans of Polish descent by these groups. The more judicious individuals of the Jewish community are ready to help in the goal of changing this situation, but they need facts on this subject. (12)

The Kosciuszko Foundation in New York asked the readers to send data documenting discrimination or prejudice with names, dates, places, and descriptions of the event. Although the foundation could not directly follow up each incident, it promised to find ways of helping other groups to do so.

Whatever the real and attributed reasons for their emergence, Polish jokes have had a profound influence on Polonia—more so, in fact, than all of Polonia's previous efforts at expanding the Polish American and American knowledge of its Polish heritage. The campaign against these jokes has been taken very seriously in Polonia for several reasons. In the first place, they were a jolt to a community that had been comfortably involved in its own status competition, only vaguely aware or responsive to prejudice from the outside. Second, success in acquiring American status symbols serves to increase interest in status competition outside the community. Third, the jokes affect not only the active members of the community, but *anyone* who identifies the self or is identified by others as Polish American. They have reportedly been told to people with Polish names as if they would be specially meaningful, even when the recipient considered himself or herself successfully acculturated and, in Gordon's terms, structurally assimilated. The jokes thus come as reminders of the imperfection of such assimilation. They also serve as a rallying point for those who want to retain Polish or Polish American identity. The leaders are now able to say, "I told you so. . . . You must support us and the community to change this prejudice." The leaders are aware that the jokes may have a beneficial effect in forcing the youth and adults to identify and cooperate with Polonia. They have thus provided a source of re-vitalization of community efforts, a specific goal, and sources for sentiments of peoplehood.

An official reaction to the low status of Polonia in American society was fully expressed in the report of the Committee for the Defense of the Polish Name (an anti-defamation committee) and stated:

> Slandered, ridiculed and misrepresented in the media as "dumb Polaks," Polish-Americans have, for the most part, remained silent. This silence, with all its implications of ineffectuality, fear and intimidation, is the greatest problem facing the Polish American community today.
>
> Too many of us are content to cart around for a lifetime the psychological and emotional damage that has been done to us by a continuing barrage of negative images, slurs and so-called "Polish jokes.". . .
>
> What the Polish-American community needs more than anything else is an effective process of consciousness raising. (Kowalski n.d.:3)

Polonian leaders developed five new ways of trying to change the image of their ethnic community in more recent years. First they consulted members of the intelligentsia (previously somewhat isolated from the community) to create ideologies and select cultural items that could be used outside the community to project a new image. A meeting of the political leaders and the intelligentsia at Cambridge Springs College in 1978 resulted in a set of recommendations as to such ideologies and items, and the methods to use in disseminating knowledge of Polish and Polonian culture internally and externally. Some of the recommendations were a push for high school and college courses in the language, history, and cultures of Poland and Polonia; teacher training programs at Orchard Lake Schools and Alliance College; publication of books and journals on the above subjects; a survey of attitudes of youths with a Polish background; excursions to Poland by the youths, the creation of speakers' bureaus; the hiring of a professional public relations expert; the collection and dissemination of information on all publications dealing with Poland and Polonia; and support of the Polish Museum in Chicago. A proposed study of Polish American communities and organizations by the Polish Institute of Arts and Sciences in America, which resulted in some local research, was a direct response to the recommendations, but many of the other ideas of the conference were not acted upon due to a shortage of funds.

While these proposals and plans were being crystallized in the minds of Polonian leaders, other members of the community were undertaking public relations actions. As one of the earlier actions, Edward J. Piszek, the Polish president of Mrs. Paul's Kitchens (a financially successful producer of frozen foods), decided to change the image of his ethnic group through direct advertising. The content of the advertisements was developed by the president of Orchard Lake Schools and Seminary. Together, these men devoted a year to an intensive publicity campaign, reported on the front page of the *Wall Street Journal* (Conderacci, 12 October 1973) as follows:

POLISH AMERICANS HIT
ETHNIC SLURS, PRAISE
THEIR CULTURE IN ADS
Was Copernicus Trying to Tell
Us Something? Yes, and It's
Far From a Joking Matter
By Greg Conderacci
Staff Reporter of the *Wall Street Journal*

ORCHARD LAKE, Mich.—Have you heard the story about the Polish Millionaire who spent $500,000 to help stamp out Polish Jokes?

It's no joke.

It's "Project: Pole," an effort to place a half-million dollars worth of pro-Polish advertising in newspapers across the country.

"Polish jokes should set up in a man a determination to prove they're not true," says Edward J. Piszek, president of Mrs. Paul's Kitchens, Inc. of Philadelphia and the man bankrolling the campaign. "In a positive way, it's an answer to the jokes—instructively. You eliminate the opportunity to originate the joke by proving it's not true."

So today a pilot campaign, in the form of a half-page advertisement will appear in Detroit newspapers with the headline: "The Polish astronomer Copernicus said in 1530 that the earth revolved around the sun. What was he trying to tell us?" The answer, Mr. Piszek says, is that Polish Americans are every bit as good as any other Americans.

A third form of action designed to change the image of Polish Americans was the joint celebrations of important Polish events. An example was the 1973 celebration by Poland and Polonia of the Copernican Year, declared as such throughout the world by business, religious, intellectual, and political leaders of Poland and its "colonies" in other countries. The celebrations took place in many cities (including Chicago and Philadelphia) and involved the unveiling of statues of the Polish astrologer. Many leaders of the larger societies as well as the ethnic leaders gathered for the ceremonies. The very erection of such statues, an expensive venture, involved concerted effort and a great deal of publicity and cooperation with various individuals and organizations. In addition, Polish Americans visibly participate in events significant to Americans. In trips to Jamestown and other American cities in connection with the bicentennial celebration, Polish American leaders stressed that "the Poles have been in the United States since 1608" (*Dziennik Zwiazkowy* 1973:7).

The final form of action aimed at changing the image of the Polish Americans has been the active protesting—by mass communication or through public representatives—of any known prejudicial statement. The antidefamation committee's guide specifies what data are needed to start a protest, the best methods of doing so, and the best methods for communicating with the committee so that it can reinforce the protest. For example, strong protests have been sent to NBC (the National Broadcasting Company) for sponsoring the television show "Laugh-In" because its comedians repeatedly use "Polak jokes." In fact, the case against the company was brought before the Federal Communications Commission.

The concern over the image the American public has of of Polish Americans has even been carried over to recent times. The April 1993 issue of *Polonia Today* carried "An Urgent Call for Unified Action" by a Polish American Guardian Society headquartered in Chicago. The call is for membership and donations so that the society can take legal action against the NBC [National Broadcasting Company] television network to prove that [the] stigmatized image has een deliberately implanted into the minds of the American public through the "Polish Joke" syndrome and negative stereotyping of the Polish American image during more than two decades by the television media (Polish American Guardian Society 1993:9).

Thus, Polonia has been actively involved in recent decades in efforts to offset negative images of Polish Americans from spreading in American society and to create its own positive images of Poles and Polish Americans, Polonian and Polish culture. And yet, the stereotypes and status of Polish Americans in the United States and their consequences upon self-identity and identification with Polonia and/or Polishness remain the two major concerns of the community and its leaders. Obidinski (1976) traced the status of Polish Americans vis-à-vis the British, German, Irish, and Italian ethnic groups in several American cities and found them first in income but fifth in occupational and education ranks in 1970 (see chapter 6 for changes). He (Obidinski 1988) thus concluded that there was some historical background to the stereotypes and that they have had very negative consequences upon new generations of "Americans of Polish descent," the vast majority of whom cease identification with Polonia or Polishness even to the extent of changing their names.

Participation in the Political Institution

There are two major forms of political participation available to interest groups in a democratic society: direct and indirect pressure upon outside public officials, and the election of their own members to political offices. Direct pressure may be applied if officials are dependent upon the interest group for their election or if officials have declared themselves in favor of the interest group's point of view. Indirect pressure involves convincing other groups, even in the cosmopolitan world, of the justice of an interest group's demand. The representatives of the interest group in public office have to use the same means of influencing their colleagues, unless there are so many of them that they can pass or kill important legislation without the cooperation of other legislators. Few, if any, groups are that well represented in as complicated a democracy as the United States.

Polonia has more often applied political pressure (the effectiveness of which is hard to measure) than it has elected its own representatives (an action with a more easily apparent consequence). Also, most of the pressure applied to high public officials has been on behalf of the Polish state and national culture society rather than on behalf of Polonia itself.[7]

The Use of Political Pressure

The two types of political situations during which Polonia uses pressure on public officials can be termed acute (or "event" focused) and chronic (use of relevant occasions to try to change a chronic undesirable situation or to introduce a change in policy). Available methods include personal contact and the use of mass media to influence a broad, national, as well as international, public opinion. Acute events frequently occur within a chronic situation and Polonia uses them to draw attention to the fact that the acute event would not have occurred had the underlying chronic situation been removed. An example of a chronic situation is the position of Poland in relation to its political state neighbors. Throughout its early history, Polonia tried to pressure the United States into forcing the three occupying powers to rescind the partitions and move back to their pre-1795 borders. During World War I there was extensive pressure on Congress, cabinet members, and President Wilson to this end. The interwar years involved some pressure concerning the "Polish question," which was the access to the Baltic Ocean, in terms of the narrowness of the "corridor." During World War II, Polonia again applied pressure on behalf of Poland. Pressure was intensified when the Yalta and Potsdam agreements were made public in Polonia; members were angry over the demands of the Soviet Union and the fact that the United States agreed to them. These treaties, and in later years other treaties, have been subjects of continuous political activity. The takeover of the Polish government by the Communist party, under obvious influence of the Soviet Union, had intensified the chronic situation, and anniversaries of historical events in Poland, visits of Soviet dignitaries to the United States, special international conferences and similar events brought forth acute activity directed at denouncing not only the event but also the chronic situation. Changes demanded of the Soviet Union and the Polish communist government through various forms of pressure on the American government included the withdrawal of troops from Poland, ceasing censorship of the press and the mail, and release of political prisoners. The formation of the Solidarity union in Poland called for American support, the imposition of the martial law for sanctions, the overthrow of communism, and the establishment of a democratically leaning government for economic aid. The Polish American Congress (the longest lasting of the interorganizational groups) had facilitated and routinized the application of political pressure. Although headquartered in Chicago, it has branches in many states; the Washington, D.C. office keeps track of current and projected programs, and other governmental actions that could affect Poland, Polonia, or Polish Americans. The office also helps in political lobbying. The presence of an interorganizational association has other advantages: first, it can claim representativeness in that it presents a unified front to the outside. Its leaders can begin all communications with a statement of voting power. For example, "We six [12] million Americans of Polish Descent." Second, its responses to acute events can be more rapid than can the pooling of responses by separate groups. Third, it can spend its time between acute emergencies in formulating basic ideologies and sets of policies. Since most acute events fall within chronic situations, such a crystallization of stances and procedures gives the leaders confidence to act rapidly and to communicate a call for action to Polonia without having to argue out the whole issue. Fourth, it has continuing operational budgets of sufficient size to cover most of its "normal" activity. Finally, it has a very broad, but definitely political, focus. The Polish American Congress was created in order to mobilize political pressure and it does not have distracting functions that might sometimes be given higher priority.

The methods Polonia uses to apply political pressure on the American government at the federal, state, and local levels have increasingly turned to personal influence upon selected leaders. Previously, Polonians sent communications to governmental representatives directly involved with specific bills in Congress of interest to Polonia; they publicized any bills that were favored or opposed by the community; and they used any means available for dramatizing their cause. Personal contact is being used by the second and third generations because of their familiarity with the American political system and many of its representatives, and their willingness to invest funds in such efforts.

However influential has been pressure by Polonia, rather than from other sources, the U. S. government has generally responded as desired. Lech Walesa was invited to speak before a joint session of Congress in 1989, while still an opposition leader, being only the second private person to do so. At that time he was already a recipient of the 1983 Noble Prize for peace. He was also invited for a state visit to the United States as president of Poland in 1991 (Bush 1991:5).

Many examples of economic aid to new Poland are now in place, including a cut in the Polish debt to this country, food aid, a "stabilization fund," the Polish-American Enterprise Fund for joint ventures of new businesses or recently privatized firms, environment and energy programs, help in labor market transitions, volunteers of the Peace Corps, trade and development programs, support of the World Bank loans for East Europe's redevelopment, and similar efforts (*New Horizon*, March 1991:25-27).

Polonia itself has been recognized by U. S. Presidents throughout its history. President William Howard Taft spoke at the dedication of the Polish National Alliance school in Cambridge Springs, Pennsylvania. Presidents Wilson and Roosevelt met with the leaders during the World Wars (Pienkos 1984: 407-8).

After World War II, every president met with the leaders of the PNA in their capacities as officers of the Polish American Congress and several took advantage to deliver public addresses to national conventions of the PAC. (Pienkos 1984: 407)

An excellent example of the fact that Polonia is recognized in the United States as representative of Poland took place recently when the remains of Ignace Paderewski were taken to Poland on 27 June 1992. The famous composer and pianist, who had also been the first prime minister of independent interwar Poland, died in America while his homeland was under communist control. His remains were temporarily interred in Arlington Cemetery until they could be moved to again independent Poland. President Bush conducted a Rose Garden ceremony in honor of Paderewski. Accompanying the body to Poland were the presidents of the Polish American Congress, the Polish Alliance, the Polish Roman Catholic Union of America, and the Polish Women's Alliance as well as the Veterans Affairs Secretary of the U. S. government, also a Polish American.

Political Action through Voting

The most effective method of exerting political influence in a democracy is by voting for people who can be depended to carry out the voter's wishes. Voters assume such a person will do so from statements made during campaigns, but also, and maybe even more so, if the candidate is a member of "our" group. In order to be effective, however, the vote must be sizable and predictable. This means that an interest group must be eligible to vote, must refrain from action countervening this privilege, must actually vote, and must vote as a "block." For example, the more Polish Americans there are in the United States and the more integrated and politically manipulative they are in their voting behavior, the more likely it is that their vote will influence public officials. A major problem of the Polish Americans has been that they make up only a small proportion of the total American population. However, their concentration in certain geographical areas could be of significance in local politics, though this potential influence has not been used effectively in Polonia's past. One of the factors contributing to this ineffectiveness was the immigrants' hesitancy to become naturalized; they planned to return to Poland and therefore wanted to retain their Polish citizenship.[8] Others did not pass the naturalization tests, being unable to speak English, having "incompetent witnesses," being ignorant of the Constitution, and lacking evidence of date of arrival since they were unaware of the importance of obtaining such evidence (Gavin 1922). For example, "In 1920 only about 35 percent of the 127,254 Polish immigrants in Chicago twenty years of age or over were naturalized" (Thurner 1971:122).

A later problem in influencing the American political system has been Polonia's internal status competition. The competition leads to a proliferation of candidates and split votes. Thurner (1971), for example, found the Chicago Polish American candidates independent, fighting with each other, and losing the position for which they ran because of a split vote.

> Like most ethnic groups in Chicago, people of Polish birth and descent developed various competing sub-groups, often openly antagonistic to one another. Although distinguishable by certain common cultural qualities, the Poles in Chicago were hardly a cohesive, well organized group bringing political pressure to bear for the advancement of their mutual interests. (20)

The status competition, an integral part of the life of the community, accounts both for the liveliness of the participation in politics and for the unwillingness to give up the competition for community gains vis-à-vis other interest groups in American society. The coming years will show whether the consolidating power base of the Polish American Congress and increasing concern with community status in the society will lead to cooperative backing of a few candidates chosen for political reasons rather than personal competitive reasons.

Political issues can swing the Polish American vote on the national level if they are sufficiently vital to Polonia's interests. For example, the Harris Poll analyzed the 1952 election returns and concluded that the Democrats had lost much of their support (estimated at roughly 70 percent) among Polish Americans because the latter believed that Poland had been betrayed at Yalta and in succeeding years. Several Polish Americans have made it to the House of Representatives of the American Congress and a few over the years have made it to the Senate. Most of those who have been politically active, such as Rostenkowski, came from Chicago. However, the Polish Americans have not been visible on the national level (Pastusiak et al. 1988). They have done better on the state and local levels, but not necessarily in proportion to their identified presence. For example, Chicago, the city second in size to Warsaw as to Polish population, has never had a Polish mayor, since the Irish have control over that and many other political offices, nor has the state had a Polish governor.

Kantowicz (1984:236) explains the underrepresentation of Polish Americans in Chicago politics as follows: "As in the Roman Catholic Church so in the Democratic Party, Polish leaders continued to nurture separate development and internal solidarity. They did not engage in bridge-building, coalitions, or broker politics." Detroit's Hamtramck was a Polonian enclave for years, but this did not translate itself into political office in the larger social unit. This is changing in recent years, especially on local levels.

All of the candidates for the U. S. presidency in 1992 did not take any chances and appeared at Polish American events, conscious of the large numbers of Americans claiming Polish ancestry in the 1980 census, in spite of the fact that few ethnic groups really vote in a block or influence elections.

Participation in Other American Institutions

As we saw in chapter 3, Polonia has been able to build and maintain a relatively complex system of ethnic institutions, which parallels the American system and capitalizes on many of its features. Maintaining the Polonian economic institution are those who provide services, such as doctors or lawyers, and objects, such as Polish American newspapers or foods. Most Polish Americans work for people of other ethnic groups or for nonethnic Americans and buy the society's products and services. But participation in the upper echelons of the American economic system appears to be limited, due to discrimination, according to Polish leaders. The Institute on Urban Life documented in 1970 the absence of a proportionate "representation of Poles, Italians, Latins, and Blacks in the executive suites of Chicago's largest corporations" (Ruggiero 1970:1). The conclusion concerning Polish Americans in particular was that "although Poles make up 6.9 percent of the metropolitan population, only 0.3 percent of the directors are Polish. One hundred two out of the 106 corporations had no directors who were Polish; 97 had no officers who were Polish" (3–4).

Polish Americans had been unevenly involved in labor unions, depending on the community and occupation. Napolska (1946) stated that "out of a Polish population of 300,000 in the state of Michigan in 1911, at best only 5,000 were union men" (39). She goes on to explain:

> There were several factors responsible for these condition: first, the inadequate knowledge of the American labor problems; second, the lack of adjustment of the Pole to the American system of organization; third, the unsympathetic attitude toward such organizations resulting from the inability of understanding the English language freely, and the consequent impossibility for looking into these associations depends often on the official policies of the parental organization.[9]

While the new immigrant groups were often used as strikebreakers, many scholars have documented extensive participation by Poles in union activity

(Lieberson 1980: 351). Their involvement in strikes in Pennsylvania's mines is part of that state's history (see Greene 1968).Morawska's (1985) historical analysis of the composition and activity of Johnstown, Pennsylvania brings out Polish involvement in strikes and attempts at organizing workers into unions. Pacyga found Polish workers very active in the 1904 and 1921 met strikes in the Chicago packinghouses, alongside other ethnic groups working in very difficult conditions (Pacyga 1982: 24). The most extensive documentation of union activity by Polish workers in America was done by Walaszek (1989), who found Polish Americans at various places and times, organizing and agitating with the American Federation of Labor, the Industrial Workers of the World, the Amalgamated Meat Cutters and Butcher Workmen, the Amalgamated Textile Workers of America, and many smaller unions or labor strikes. This includes Polish women, also found in Eisenstein's 1983 *Give us Bread but Give us Roses*. Frank Renkiewicz (1988) brings our knowledge of the organizations of workers of Polish descent in America up to 1980.

An excellent example of Polish, Polonian, and American involvements in a number of institutional areas is the Polish Welfare Association (PWA) of Chicago. Organized in the 1920s it became fully activated in the late 1980s thanks to new leadership. It served 11,634 Poles in 1991, which accounted for a "growth of almost 320% over the past five years. Our growth can also be measured in the increase of dollars to a record of $1,283,205" (Polish Welfare Association 1991:1). The funds were obtained mainly from the U. S. or Illinois government (67 percent), but also from private foundations, corporations, and organizations (13 percent), program fees (10 percent), contributions, special events, and the United Way (Polish Welfare Association 1991: 16). A major reason for the fact that it obtained so many grants is the concern of the U. S. government with its newcomers in the form of refugees and asylees, legal immigrants, illegal residents, and problem populations. The PWA serves as an intermediary between the Poles and the government in such situations. The most important way, from the point of view of Americans, and the most frequent, is help with immigration and naturalization (8,099 people in 1991; Polish Welfare Association 1991:2). As mentioned before, the political leaders of this society frequently introduce policies and laws that require the help of bridging organizations such as the PWA. One of the association's contracts, from the U.S. Department of State, provides funds to assist the resettlement of Poles admitted as refugees or given asylum. This involves assistance with document clearance, occupational retraining and help with employment, as well as prevention of public dependency. The Immigration Reform and Control Act of 1986, which provided amnesty to those illegal residents who had been here prior to 1982, also resulted in heavy activity for the PWA. Eight thousand Poles applied for amnesty and the PWA counseled 6,997 in immigration matters in 1990 alone(PolishWelfareAssociation1990:4).Legalization(i.e.,permanentreside-nce status with accompanying "green card") or permission for employment could be accomplished only if the person passed an English test or attended at least 40 hours of English-language courses, in addition to providing adequate documentation of residence. The state of Illinois administered the funds and provided PWA with a State Legalization Impact Assistance Grant. PWA informed the Polish-speaking population of this opportunity, offered classes, translated and processed necessary documents, took pictures and fingerprints, and provided the opportunity to take citizenship tests given by the U. S. Immigration and Naturalization officers in its own offices. Another contribution of the Polish Welfare Association to the situation of Poles in America concerned the U. S. government's rather unusual visa "lottery." It offered 40,000 visas to those wishing to enter the United States from immigration disadvantaged countries aside from the normal numerical allocation. Forty percent of these visas were reserved for Irish people. The requests of all others wishing visas had to be postmarked on a specific day. Members of the PWA staff drove the letters from Chicago Poles from Chicago to Alexandria, Virginia and stood in line for two days with the result that 6,000 Chicagoans won visas. People whose names were drawn had to go to the American embassy in their home country to obtain the visa, but that was a small price to pay for a permanent stay visa.

All this activity by the Polish Welfare Association demonstrates the dependence of immigrants and members of other ethnic communities upon American institutions and organizations. The PWA also performs the stand-ard welfare functions, such as assistance with family problems, including a shelter for battered women and children, as well as for homeless men. An alcoholic counseling program and a food pantry have also emerged. Senior citizens were provided with a drop-in social center and were "helped in remaining independent and self-sufficient" by a specialist who "cooperated with police in cases of elder abuse, made home visits, provided benefit information, outreach and crisis intervention" (Polish Welfare Assocation 1991:7). The basic contribution of the Polish Welfare Association is as an intermediary between American society and newcomers or those lacking necessary knowledge of English and of its regulations and norms. The majority of its staff performs an educational function. Offices provide information, translated into Polish, as to "Circuit Breakers" programs of the Illinois Department of Revenue. Such programs provide senior citizens and disabled persons with property tax relief and pharmaceutical assistance; they also provide help in cases of wife abuse, health problems, military service, "the green card," employee rights and opportunities, as well as financial help for university education.

Contributions to American Intellectual and Artistic Life

Polonia through its organizations, and individual Poles and Polish Americans have been involved in many scientific and "high culture" areas of American life, in its literature, music, art, theater, film, radio, and television (Kusielewicz 1988). There are several ways in which this has happened over the years. America has benefited from the presence of Polish political émigrés who were forced out of their homeland but continue their creative work in the host country. A number of these have been Polish Jews who identify themselves as such. The intelligentsia members of the second, post World War II cohort felt a "noblesse oblige" moral obligation to help Poland and Polonia's status by making the world familiar with its culture (Lopata 1976b, 1984, 1985). Some translated Polish classics, others wrote in English on "sacred" aspects of Polish culture, "symbols of higher ideals." These Polish intellectuals acted as defenders of Polish culture against the ignorance of the Americans, to which Znaniecki reacted to strongly in his 1920 anonymous article in the *Atlantic Monthly* (Dulczewski, 1992). Others felt that their main contribution to the home country was through scientific or literary work independent of Polish subjects, as long as they were known to be Polish (Lopata 1984, 1985).

Members of the Polish national culture society have also come over for temporary visits, giving concerts or exhibitions, at the initiative of artistic agents or the invitation from Polonian or other groups. In many cases, Polonian organizations make all the arrangements, including publicity which brings non-Poles to the event. Polonia itself is increasingly developing its own writers, artistic exhibitors, and performers who identify themselves through various forms of connection with Polishness. Poles in the home and the host countries also translate scientific, literary, and operatic works for English-reading audiences. All this activity has expanded enormously in recent years, with the weakening and final breakup of the communist government.

The Second Congress of the Intelligentsia (technically of the educated people) of Polish descent met in Krakow in 1979, and most of the sessions, as well as of the volume of published materials coming from it, was devoted to the contributions of such people not only to American society, but to the worldwide community, in all forms of science and art (Kubiak and Wrobel 1984; see also Lopata 1984).

Several aspects of Polish or Polonian folk culture have entered the American way of life, especially in the recreational institution. Restaurants and food stores advertise "Polish sausage"; and the polka, a dance rhythm, is often played at non-Polish social occasions.

Relations with Other Ethnic and Racial Groups

Besides stressing Polish contributions to American society and shared culture, Polonia's efforts at changing its image includes recently gestures of interethnic cooperation. The Polish Americans have repeatedly been accused of prejudice in relations with other minority groups, particularly those with which they are apt to have come in direct contact at community boundaries, in Poland, in America on a national level, and in local communities. This includes the Jews, Czechs, Slovaks, Croats, Ukrainians, Italians, the African Americans, and whomever they competed with for housing, jobs, and status symbols.

The history of relations between Polonia and the Jewish community dates back to the home country and has been one of mutual hostility. Attempts at cooperation have been relatively infrequent, although increasing in recent years. The Jewish Americans have memories and stories of anti-Semitism and even pogroms in Poland. The Poles remember stories of being taken advantage of by shtetl Jews whom they also feared for religious reasons. The relations between the Polish and Jewish communities in America have been complex and full of recriminations and accusations, at a high level of emotionality, but also full of attempts at understanding. Sporadic outbursts occur within chronic situations, such as the recent outbreak over the establishment of a Catholic convent in Poland near the locale of the Nazi Auschwitz death camp. Polonia's members have been increasingly angry over what they define as a deliberate attempt by Jews in mass communications media to prejudice the rest of society against them.[10] The most complete historical analysis of these relations from a pretty objective point of view can be found in Kapiszewski's (1988) chapter in *Polonia Amerykanska*. The attempts at understanding included a conference at the initiative of the Polish American Congress and the Anti-Defamation League of B'nai B'rith in 1970. In 1992, the Polish American press gave much publicity to the formation by Lech Walesa, the president of Poland, of a task force combating anti-Semitism. Poles have been honored by the Israeli "Righteous among the Nations" program (*New Horizon*, January 1992: 17; Kamm 1991: 11; see also Tec 1986). *The Polish Review* and other Polish and Polish American publications have published numerous articles on Polish-Jewish relations. *The Chicago Tribune* ran a story of attempts by Rabbi Byron Sherwin, vice president for academic affairs at Spertus College of Judaica, to bring together Polish Jews and Poles for seminars and serious discussions of their relations. The subject is of obvious importance to all involved.

The majority of Poles had never seen African Americans prior to emigrating to the United States. Most authors dealing with the subject of the relation between the Poles and the blacks in America refer to the fact that General Kosciuszko requested in his last testament that Thomas Jefferson sell his property, buy up the freedom of his slaves, and insure their education so that they would defend freedom and their fatherland (Radzialowski 1988: 674). Initial settlement of Poles in America placed them in virtual isolation from blacks (Lieberson 1963); but migration of the latter into northern cities and traditionally Polish neighborhoods soon acculturated the Poles into American prejudices against the blacks. The expansion threatened the status-invested property, their proof of success of upward mobility, so painfully gathered by the immigrants. The value of the property diminished as the black community expanded, due to panic selling and moving. The Poles, as well as the other central Europeans of communities such as Berwyn and Cicero in the Chicago area, for example, fought the movement of the blacks with every means they had, feelings running very strongly. The status loss created by the geographical expansion of groups that the Polish Americans considered below them in the American status hierarchy angered the Polish Americans, a did the black civil rights movement of the 1960s and the positive societal response to it. The Poles had worked hard to bring themselves up to their present, not yet very high, position and now society was threatening these gains by allegedly helping the blacks up to a similar position while they were losing money and property (see also Novak 1973; Wrobel 1979: 90). According to Radzialowski (1988:697), the most recent competition between the Polish and the African Americans is in the political arena. The Poles, for example, resent the fact that the blacks are succeeding in local politics, obtaining mayoralties in many cities in which the Poles are also numerous.

Aware, however, of the accusation of antiblack prejudice in, for example, Greeley's (1974b) work, community leaders have attempted both to decrease that feeling in Polonia and to develop and document instances of black-Polish cooperation. If fighting blacks did not benefit Polish Americans in the past, then cooperation in solving community problems deserved a try. An example of cooperation to solve common problems without a history of formal contact was the Black-Polish Conference of Greater Detroit—a combining of forces of two low-status groups to increase the status of both (Radzialowski 1988: 704). Many such groups do not have a long life, disagreements as to best means of reaching goals bringing their demise, as is so often true of voluntary associations. Several Polonian studies of local communities indicate cooperation between the groups, as when both send children to parochial schools (Radzialowski 1988: 703).

Polish organizations have met on numerous occasions with representatives of other ethnic groups for special events or in order to meet specific goals. For example, the Poles, Czechs, and Hungarians distributed 10,000 fliers with an open letter to the secretary general of the Soviet Communist party, Leon Brezhnev, demanding freedom for the "captive nations." The joint effort included the three countries that had tried to revolt against the Soviet influence or power in Europe (*Dziennik Zwiazkowy,* 29 June 1974:2). Other intergroup activities that have been institutionalized include participation in the Intercollegiate Council by members of Polish student groups, decoration of Polish Christmas trees in museums along with trees of other national groups, participation in ethnic festivals (Detroit), international trade fairs (Chicago), and singing and dancing competitions.

The popularity of the ethnic movement in America and the society's interest in it during the 1970s was documented by the Ford and Rockfeller Foundations' grants and governmental support of such institutions as Andrew Greeley's Center for the Study of American Pluralism and the Center for Immigration Studies at the University of Minnesota. The Poles themselves received a Rockfeller grant to study Polonia through the Polish Institute of Arts and Sciences in New York. This interest has guaranteed greater cooperation between Polonia and other ethnic groups and the society at large. Representatives of American society, in fact, are now coming to Polonia and to its organizations and leaders in order to photocopy their files of newspapers for permanent preservation and to obtain information as to its ethnic identity and the content of the ethnic culture.

On a personal level, of course, few Polish Americans lack contact with members of other ethnic and racial groups. As Pacyga (1991b:2) points out, using "the famous Hull House maps of the west side" of Chicago, ethnic segregation does not mean that 100 percent of a neighborhood is inhabited by the same group (see chapter 1). The Polish Americans move into neighborhoods dominated by other groups, and gradually the identification changes, even when others are still living within it. As a new group comes in, the process is repeated, as sociologists have found in numerous studies.[11] Records of local labor activity list participants coming from a variety of backgrounds (Morawska 1985; Pacyga 1991; Walaszek 1989). The most obvious consequence of personal contact that crosses ethnic and racial lines is intermarriage. There is a long history of such relations among Poles in America, not so much initially but increasingly in recent decades. Of course, European national societies were also not ethnically pure, due to wars, conquests, migrations, and other occasions for contact and intermarriage.

As noted in chapter 3, the Poles had very low intermarriage rates early in their settlement in America. The children went to parochial schools in which Polish was the predominant language, and the absence of mass media afforded little opportunity to learn English. Family insistence on an ethnically homogeneous social life resulted in pressure on the young to avoid other groups (Morawska 1985: 172). The pressures do not seem to have been as strong as among the Greek Americans studied by Moskos (1990:92-93). The anniversary issue of St. Hyacinth's parish documents, however, show an increase in cross-ethnic marriages over time. By 1980, as we shall see in chapter 6, the percentages of "mixed bloods" for those of Polish ancestry were very high.

Summary

Polonia as an ethnic community has interacted with the larger American society through official and individual action. The community has been maintained in spite of the fact that most of its members cross ethnic boundaries many times to enter the flow of economic, educational, recreational, and other aspects of American life. The community itself spent the early decades of its existence attempting to influence the American political powers on behalf of Poland. Engrossed in its own status competition, Polonia was unaware of, or at least ignored, prejudice against it and other new immigrant groups in the wider society. This lack of awareness usually resulted in a neglect of attention to what was going on outside the community boundaries, unless an acute event reawakened concern over a chronic situation such as the condition of the Polish national culture society or state or the underrepresentation in the American Roman Catholic hierarchy or the broader business and political arenas. Relations with other ethnic and racial groups were generally minimal or hostile if contact threatened each other's social position.

However, at two periods of its existence, the 1920s–1930s and then the 1970s, when interest in Poland decreased, Polonian leaders became increasingly interested in changing the image of Polish Americans in the larger society. The negative nature of this image was brought into focus by Polish jokes, and the community leaders in a variety of companionate circles have been organizing a concerted effort to change the stereotypes. Polish Americans have not been very active in American political life, underusing their potential influence because of an initial lack of citizenship or because of the status competition among candidates for public office. They have only recently organized on the national scale in order to use a variety of methods of political pressure.

The Polish Americans have also been underrepresented in the upper echelons of the American economic and voluntary association hierarchies, for a variety of background and attitudinal reasons. The antidefamation campaign, the attempts to change the Polish American image through new ideologies and cultural items, and dissemination of Polish culture internally and in the larger society may modify the position of this ethnic community in America. It is also probable that the changing demographic characteristics of Polish Americans, particularly their increasing use of American educational resources will assist this process. Thus, we turn to a description of the past and present characteristics of Polish Americans. For example, groups that identify with several European national culture societies have rarely combined anti-Soviet activities when that political state controlled their lives. In addition, some of the efforts of ethnic groups to change U.S. foreign policy go against the goals of this society, resulting in defeats and frustrations. As we shall see in the next chapter, another problem facing Poland, and thus Polonia, has been the political complexity and lack of homogeneity of goals and solutions to problems. Thus, pressure on the U. S. government from one segment of the ethnic community are often offset by pressure in a different direction by another segment. This situation is also true of other ethnic groups.

Notes

1. For example, Moskos (1990: 18) reports that "The reception accorded the new Greek arrivals by the larger community was generally hostile." The Lowell Massachusetts citizens "regarded Greeks as a 'quarrelsome, treacherous, filthy, low-living lot.'"
2. It is surprising that Professor Thomas of the University of Chicago would live in a neighborhood where garbage was thrown out of a window by an immigrant Polish girl. One wonders why the letter was not mailed and also why the story was so popular at the university.
3. Of course, the other ethnic minority groups faced the same prejudice and discrimination, and often believed the stereotypes of themselves in consequence (see Mindel et al. 1988 and any in-depth study of the immigrants).
4. The assumption that other ethnic groups are better organized and united than are the Polish Americans, and that this contributes to their alleged success in American society, was contained in pronouncements of the leaders of the "Wisconsin Plan" asking readers of the Polish American ethnic press to support "a candidate of your own choice for a congressional or senatorial seat" (*Gwiazda Polarna,* 16 February 1974: 5). Although indefinite as to the means by which the "Wisconsin Plan" will accomplish the goal of united action, the appeal for membership contains the following statements:

    > A more specific example [of united efforts which bring results] is the success story of the Jewish community in America. While small in numbers, they have become extremely effective through united action. . . . Americans of Polish heritage have built America, obeyed its laws, and contributed toward making it the great nation it is today, but they have been ignored. . . . Our brothers have labored long and hard to correct these injustices, but they have not been successful. Why? Part of the reason is that the average Congressman and Senator knows little about Poland and our problems, and probably cares even less.

5. The persistence of the idea that there is a national character and that it prevents internal cooperation is evident over decades. Tomczak (1933) states that the Polish Americans are considered clannish by others but that "a queer paradox is observed in this respect. For clannish though they might be, they are still divided among themselves. While distinctions and policies are not very sharply drawn, there is nevertheless an intense rivalry and competition between organization and between commercial houses" (70). Tomczak continues: "It is said also that the Poles are unable to self-govern, that they are by nature independent and self-seeking, and that their achievements in sciences and the arts are merely accidental and not representative of the people as a whole" (79).

    Aloysius Mazewski, president of the Polish American Congress and the Polish National Alliance referred to this "national character" in a speech entitled "The Poles—a National Group Full of Dynamism and Individualism" (Mazewski 1973:5) at a banquet following the unveiling of the Copernican Statue in Chicago: "It has been said and written many times in the past that Americans of Polish origin tend to weaken and fragmentize their strength and potential through internal discords." His argument was that although this "diversity and, at times, cross purposes, were the rule rather than the exception" in Poland's history, the presence of so many representatives of so many organizations and individually prominent Polish Americans in the audience is evidence of their ability to synthesize and reconcile.

6. The Poles and Polish Americans most frequently mentioned include pianist Artur Rubenstein; conductors Leopold Stokowski and Artur Rodzinski; harpsichordist Wanda Landowska; singer Bobby Vinton; Pola Negri and Gilda Gray of films; Helena Modjewska of the theater; Henry Sienkiewicz, author of *Quo Vadis, Portrait of America* and the newly translated *Trilogy*; Wieslaw Kuniczak, author of *The Thousand Hour Day*; sociologist Florian Znaniecki; political scientist Zbigniew Brzezinski; political leader Edmund Muskie; former Postmaster General John Gronouski; baseball stars Stan Musial and Carl Yastrzemski; and football players Ed Rutkowski, Larry Kaminski, and Bob Kowalkowski (Wytrwal 1969). Recent additions to the list are Jerzy Kosinski, author of *The Painted Bird* and *Steps*; Czeslaw Milosz, recipient of the 1980 Nobel Prize for literature; and Edward Derwinski, Secretary of Veterans' Affairs.

7. Krakowska (1955) emphasizes that the appeal these groups sent to President Wilson before the end of World War I on behalf of Poland contained a specific disclaimer of self-interest: "The Poles in America want nothing—they need nothing—but we beg you to keep Poland in mind when the opportunity comes" (16).

8. Manning (1930) reported that Polish immigrant women in Philadelphia and Lehigh, Pennsylvania in the late 1920s were not apt to be citizens. Only 18.2 percent were U.S. citizens and they were mainly in their thirties or forties; 51.9 percent were unable to speak English. There has consistently remained 20 to 30 percent of foreign-born Poles who have not become naturalized because they either hope to return someday to Poland, or because they are here for only a limited time according to their own plans. The American government forbids people who enter on a visitor or student visa to work in this country but those who come as immigrants can work even without becoming citizens. Eighty percent of the half-million foreign-born Poles living in the United States in 1970 were naturalized, with those remaining registered as aliens (U. S.Bureau of Census, Detailed Characteristics, 1970a: PC(1)-Di table 195).

9. The interesting thing is that the American society was very worried that the "new" immigrants were "radical" and would join or form unions and cause great problems for management. Hourwich (1912) defended them against this accusation and Rosenblum (1973) develops this thesis further. The immigrants were not radical; they just wanted a job and once here did not complain about wages. Although often not accustomed (from prior life) to wage labor, in fact they were against unionization that would be used to control the labor market. In addition, the immigrant did not identify with the society and its problems. "His contact with Native Americans was likely to be within an employment relationship and that relationship was predominantly rational, functionally specific, universalistic, avoidant and individualistic" (Rosenblum 1973:125). Also, the new immigrants often did not expect to stay in this country. Between 1908 and 1910 the "immigration commission found a greater rate of departure for new (73 per hundred admitted) than for the 'old' (13 per hundred admitted)" (125). They were thus unlikely to spend time and interest forming unions, preferring to work hard and live frugally.

We suggest that the failure of a major working-class challenge to capitalistic economic institutions to mature in the United States is partially attributable to that fact that a large portion of those in the lower reaches of the occupational hierarchy at the time mobilization was most likely to occur simply did not identify themselves with the society in which they carried out their work lives. (177)

Thus, the Poles were not the only ones to refrain from joining the American unions until they become established in the country.

10. Another situation that angers Poles and Polish Americans is the neglect in Jewish literature and conferences to acknowledge that half of the Poles killed by the Nazis were non-Jews. Most Americans do not know that non-Jewish Poles were killed for harboring Jews (the only country in which this rule existed) and themselves were sent to extermination, concentration, and labor camps (see Lukas 1986, *The Forgotten Holocaust; Poles under German Occupation 1939–1944*). Poles repeatedly ask in mass media and in private conversations why the anger over the Holocaust is so often addressed to them when they were so powerless under the Nazi regime which persecuted them both.

11. My husband, who grew up in Chicago, belonged to a Polish gang that had Italian members and had to fight his way to Lake Michigan's beaches through territory, "owned" by an Italian gang that had Polish members. See Suttles 1968 and 1972 for sociological analyses of territory, and Park and Burgess 1925 for theories of population succession.

6

The Polish Americans:
Patterns of Change

In the 100-plus years since the Poles started coming to the United States in large numbers, Polonia has undergone many changes in the education, occupations, social life-styles, and "ethnicity" of its members. In discussing these changes we must first ask, "Who is a member of the Polish American ethnic group?" Unfortunately, the inaccuracies and inconsistencies in the immigration figures (discussed in chap. 2) also confound census information. Early records were kept by country of birth and have lumped together Polish Catholics, Polish Jews, Lithuanians, and other groups. Neither the peoples, or races classification, nor the mother tongue are reliable sources of information.[1] The U. S. Census did not include a question on religion. This is particularly important when the country of birth figures include, for example, Polish Jews who do not identify with Polonia and who have gone in a different direction in educational and occupational achievement. Since 1969, ethnic origin, "determined on the basis of a question asking for self-identification of the person's origin of descent and is, therefore, a report of what persons perceive their origin to be" is included in the census (U. S. Bureau of Census 1973:3). Since 1980, people were asked in an open-ended question to list their ancestry and were allowed multiple responses (Lieberson and Waters 1988: 6-7). The changes in what is being asked in a census certainly complicates the determination of the population that can be identified as Polish Americans, from whom Polonia can draw its membership. We must remember that this analysis has thus far focused on Polonia as an ethnic community. This chapter focuses on the people who could participate in its life—which the vast majority does not. Because of the differences in sources of data, I will present the available characteristics of the population up to 1980, try to separate the first cohort and its descendants from the World War II cohort, and end with whatever knowledge we have of the third, newest cohort. The analyses of changes in the Polish American population will be discussed in the next chapter on life in Polonia's companionate circles and in Mary Erdmans's chapter on the intertwining of these circles in political activity.

The Polish Americans

Table 6.1 shows that the peak year for Polish "foreign stock"[2] in the United States between 1910 and 1970 was 1930, with a recorded total of over 3 million people. By 1950 the total decreased, indicating deaths of older members and movement into the third generation. The "new emigration," or second cohort, was not large enough to offset the continuing decline. Since table 6.1 is limited to the first two generations (as determined by country of birth rather than ethnic identification) and to mother tongue, we must look elsewhere to determine the parameters of the Polish American ethnic group. The special supplement to the census undertaken in 1969 asked for country of birth of grandparents and reported 1,776,921 third-generation Polish Americans (see U.S. Bureau of the Census 1970b: PC-2-1A). The three generational total, obtained by adding this figure to the 1970 foreign stock, is then 4,151,165. In addition, the number of people who gave "Polish" in response to the "ethnic origin" question since the 1969 census raised the total number of Polish Americans in 1972 to 5,105,000 or double the foreign-stock total for 1970 (U.S. Bureau of the Census 1973:T-41). This is probably the most realistic figure available. Other data on Polish Americans are unreliable since they come from smaller sample surveys of the American population conducted by a variety of scientific bodies. Conglomerate samples uniting several surveys conducted in a block of years camouflage changes over time.[3]

Keeping the problems of identification in mind, we can examine the makeup of the Polish American population in 1970. The original immigrants who are still living (most had died) had a mean age of 66.7, up considerably from 41.3 in 1930, and 57.3 in 1950 (U. S. Bureau of the Census 1973:T-41; Hutchinson 1956:17). The median age of the *total* Polish ethnic group, including succeeding generations was 32.9, indicating that younger people identified with this group when given a chance to do so by the census question. The ratio of second- to first-generation Polish Americans has been increasing at a rapid rate from 114 in 1920 to 224 in 1950, offset only by the "new emigration" arrivals (Hutchinson 1956:19). The ratio of men to women has also changed considerably: there were 131 men for every 100 women in 1920, 116 in 1930, 111 in 1940, 102 in 1950 (Hutchinson 1956:19) and 90 in 1972 (U. S. Bureau of the Census 1973:T-41). The ratio dropped between 1920 and 1930 due to the importation of families of the original male immigrants and between 1950 and 1972 due to differential death rates. Polish American men 65 years of age and over, formed 9.9 percent of the male component of this ethnic group in 1969; women of that age formed 13 percent.

TABLE 6.1
Total Numbers of Foreign-Stock Poles and People Listing Polish as
Their Mother Tongue in the United States 1910–1970, with Urban,
Non-urban Residential Details for 1970

| | COUNTRY OF BIRTH | | POLISH MOTHER TONGUE | | |
Year	Foreign Stock	Foreign-Born, White	Native of Foreign or Mixed Parents	Foreign-Born	Native-Born of Foreign or Mixed Parents
1910* Total	1,663,808	937,884	725,924		
1930* Total	3,342,198	1,268,583	2,073,615		
1950* Total	2,786,199	861,184	1,925,015		
1970 Total	2,374,244	548,107	1,826,137	419,912	2,018,026
Urban	2,138,531	512,522	1,626,009	385,567	1,743,121
Rural: non-farm	197,899	29,912	167,987	29,021	225,775
Metropolitan					
Total	2,098,912	502,245	1,596,667	376,572	1,713,997
Central City	1,127,853	331,543	796,310	223,596	790,473
Other urban	857,505	154,410	703,095	127,248	793,416
Rural: non-farm	98,386	13,751	84,635	13,453	113,943
Rural: farm	15,168	2,541	12,627	2,275	16,165
Nonmetropolitan					
Total	275,332	45,862	229,470	43,340	340,029
Urban	153,173	26,569	126,604	24,723	159,232
Rural: non-farm	99,513	16,161	83,352	15,568	111,832
Rural: farm	22,646	3,132	19,514	3,049	32,965

Sources: H.Z. Lopata. *Polish Americans: Status Competition in an Ethnic Community* (Englewood Cliffs, N.J.: Prentice-Hall, 1976, 89.

U.S. Department of Commerce, Bureau of the Census, Sixteenth Census Reports, *Nativity and Parentage of the White Population.*

U.S. Census of Population, 150, vol. 4, part #A, and 1960, vol. 1, table 36.

U.S. Department of Commerce, Bureau of the Census, United States *Summary, General Social and Economic Characteristics*, 1970, table 97–108 and table 136.

* *Historical Statistics of United States, Colonial Times to 1957* (Washington, D.C.: U.S. Government Printing Office, 1960), C185–217, pp. 218–83.

Geographical Persistence and Dispersal

The Polish immigrants and their children settled in the urban northeast and north central United States. Few immigrants went south or west.[4] As late as the 1950s, the heaviest concentration for foreign-born and second-generation Poles was in the New York-New Jersey metropolitan area. Chicago housed more Poles than any other city outside of Poland and the immigrants and their children also settled in Detroit, Boston, Buffalo, and in several cities in Pennsylvania and Ohio. More recently, they have moved to, or settled in California and Florida. There are also chapters of Polonian organizations in Arizona, Colorado, and other states, but the population base is very small. Within the major cities, they concentrated in their own communities and segregated themselves from both whites and blacks (Lieberson 1963).[5] In the 1960s, the foreign-born Poles were still highly concentrated in a few American localities in which they formed a high proportion of the total population ranking fifth out of 23 groups on their concentration scale (Fishman and Hofman 1966:48). Their local communities tended to be in central cities and, in spite of the recency of their arrival and the presence of a large number of persons who did not even speak English, they rapidly acquired home ownership (Lieberson 1963). The tendency to invest all money and efforts into home and land ownership is documented in a variety of informational sources.

Recent census evidence indicates that the Polish Americans are moving out of the central cities into other communities within the metropolitan areas (see table 6.1). Although the census figures recorded here are of the first two generations only, half of the children of immigrants were already living outside of the central cities in 1970, while two-thirds of their parents remained in the cities (see also Bukowczyk 1987). Relatively few Polish Americans live in rural farm locations of either metropolitan or nonmetropolitan areas.

Frysztacki (1986), a Polish sociologist, studied Buffalo in the 1980s and concluded that the city passed through four principal stages, allegedly applicable to other ethnic communities:

> The first is the emergence of a territorial community and its transformation into a strictly closed ethnic community with homogeneous and relatively simple manifestations of inner organization and integration. . . . The second stage is the strengthening and consolidation of this subcommunity with a simultaneous growth of internally differentiating factors. . . . During the third stage(when spatial grouping continues to be still prominent) the previous rules of internal functioning . . .become gradually more and more intertwined with those governing the surrounding environment. . . . During the fourth stage the demographic and spatial basis is weakened, which is accompanied by a simultaneous weakening of the previous manifestations of social integrity and distinctness. (Frysztacki 1986: 246)

As of 1990, 1,181,977 people of Polish ancestry, 89,874 of whom were foreign-born, were located in New York state (*Dziennik Zwiazkowy*, 31 July–2

August 1992: 3). They were distributed in a variety of communities, rather than in New York City itself.

On the other side, most of the 962,827 Polish ancestry, with 82,211 Polish-born who lived in Illinois were concentrated in Chicago and its suburbs. The next two largest concentrations of people of Polish ancestry are in Michigan (889,527) and Pennsylvania (882,348). However, there is a great dispersion of this population, nine states having more than half a million. This includes California, which is often a secondary location in the United States, and Florida, which is very unlikely to have been the initial settlement destination. New York and Illinois contain the largest numbers of foreign-born Poles, while many others settle in nearby eastern states. For example, New Jersey ranks third in newer immigrants, and fifth among the total figures. The newcomers can also be found in Connecticut and Massachusetts, while Texas has a relatively numerous Polish ancestry population, but very few foreign-born Poles.

Educational Persistence and Change

As we learned in chapter 3, there are numerous references in the literature to negative attitudes toward formal schooling among Polish peasants in pre-World War I Poland (Reymont 1925; Szczepanski 1962; Thomas and Znaniecki 1918-1920). The social class system of those years provided a foundation of nonintellectualism bordering on anti-intellectualism, which was accentuated by the great social distance between the peasants and the nobility. Although the upper classes idealized education as a necessary background of "the cultured man" (see chapter 2), the peasant classes did not adopt this idealization of education. Their anti-intellectualism is evident in the labeling of a person who enjoyed reading as a deviant, rather than as a wise man (Thomas and Znaniecki 1958, vol. 2: 1135-36). Traditional Catholicism did not encourage scientific curiosity or the love of learning; it was an authoritarian and dogmatic religion, and the lay person was expected to accept it without question. There was nothing in the village culture that would make learning, abstract thinking, or experimenting with knowledge a pleasurable activity. Nothing defined education as an important means of contributing to the vital spheres of life.

The attitudes of the Polish peasants toward education—which defined it as a waste of time at best, and as a dangerous thing undermining the traditional way of life at worst (Benet 1951:222)—were transplanted to the American soil. Ideally, the children of Polonia began working at an early age to help the family in its endless struggle for money. The U. S. Immigration Commission, which undertook an intensive study of immigrants in 17 American cities in 1911, found the children of Poles following this typical educational career: parochial school from the ages of 8 to 12, first communion, public school for two years, and then work (Miaso 1971:35). The idea of higher education was foreign to Polonia's first- or second-generation youth: only 38 men and 6 women of Polish birth or descent were studying in the 77 schools of higher learning in the United States in 1911. (See also Abel 1929:216–22.) Higher education usually did not refer to college, but to schooling above the minimal level required in the United States at that time.

Although a dramatic change in educational achievement among newer generations of Polish Americans has taken place in recent years, the median year of schooling for the total group is pulled down by first- and second-generation members (see appendix E). First-generation members born in Poland received very little formal education. The children born here suffered from having to go to work early in life. As late as 1960, Polish Americans aged 50 to 74 were ranked seventh out of eight major language groups other than English in median years of schooling, the only lower group being the Italians (Fishman and Hofman 1966:49). Only 9 percent had gone beyond grade school, 59 percent had attended primary grades, and 31 percent had never obtained any formal schooling.

These uneducated older persons handicap the newer generations when their median schooling achievement is compared to other ethnic groups. This is particularly true when the Polish Americans are compared to the total white population, most of whose members are already in the third, fourth, and later generations.[6] Greeley (1974a) noted that "among the English-speaking white gentile groups, the Poles are almost a year beneath the national average" (65). This deviation goes up to 1.1 years when the figures are standardized by geographical location since the Polish Americans are concentrated in large cities of the North "where there is more opportunity for education and educational achievement is higher" (66). However, age is an extremely important factor in understanding this deviation.

> The Italians over age 60 are almost a full year beneath their cohort mean in education, the Slavs a year and a half beneath the mean. The Italians and the Slavs in their twenties, on the other hand, are both about one-tenth of a year above the mean and the Poles about half year above the mean. (68)

The 1969 census, which first asked for "ethnic origin," further documents the expanding use of higher education on the part of young Polish Americans. Men and women between the ages of 25 and 34 who identified with this ethnic group had reached a median level of educational achievement of 12.7 years, second only to the Russians' amazing 16+ median (U.S. Bureau of the Census 1971 P-20:221). The Poles surpassed the English, the Germans, and the Irish— all of whom had a higher median than the Poles among the older age groups. The proportion of young people who had finished college was more than double that of older Polish Americans, and the proportion of young people who at least attended college was at least triple. Thirty-one percent of the younger Polish Americans had gone beyond high school.[7]

Educational changes in Polonia involve not only the number of years completed by the Polish Americans but also the source of this education. Most of the older people attended parochial schools and received training that did not guarantee knowledge of either Catholicism or Polish culture. Greeley and Rossi (1968:37) found that attendance at parochial schools did not increase the Polish American Catholics' knowledge of Catholic doctrine or respect for church authority, especially as a definer of moral issues; nor did the products of these schools fare well on a "general knowledge" index. One of the main leaders of Polonia has accused the clergy of inadequately educating the youth into Polish culture because of their own lack of knowledge about it[8] (Kusielewicz 1973:104).

If these allegations of inadequacy of parochial training in Polish American schools are true, then the movement of the young outside this system can be expected to produce a change in knowledge and attitudes. Findings indicate that the difference between parochial and public education does in fact have an important influence on Polish Americans. Greeley and Rossi (1968) compared Polish Americans who did and did not complete high school, and found that those who finished high school were more apt to have attended public (rather than parochial) schools for at least the last few years of education. Those who finished high school among all Catholic groups (Irish, Germans, Italians, and French) were different from their less educated fellow ethnics in many life situations and attitudes. But the differences between these two groups of Polish Americans were dramatic. The high school graduates were four times as apt to be in the top three occupational categories of the Duncan prestige scale, almost five times as apt to be among families earning $14,000 or more in 1962. The proportion of people reporting that they were happy increased from 22 percent for the less educated to 32 percent for the more educated; the probability of scoring low on an anomie scale increased from 38 to 50 percent. Although what Greeley calls "religious extremism" and "anti-Semitism" indices were considerably lower among the educated, the "racism" index was not affected by education. The latter set of attitudes reflects the late 1960s situation in Polonia in terms of status competition and anger of the type described by Novak (1971).

By 1980, 41 percent of Polish ancestry women and 33 percent of men born in the United States had finished high school. An additional 30 percent women and 43 percent men had obtained at least some college education (see appendix E; Lieberson and Waters 1988:107-8). However, hardly any of the women of several European groups finished college or went beyond. It is also interesting that a higher proportion of Polish ancestry men who received undergraduate degrees went onto obtain graduate degrees rather than end their education. The gender differences are very interesting and typical of many European groups in that women still received less education than did the men but the gap between men and women was highest for the Poles and the Russians. The highest levels have still been reached by the "Russians," who are overwhelmingly Jewish, many of whose families came from Russian-occupied Poland.

Interest in education, especially in Polish language and culture, is often reported in the Polish press but these appear to be isolated instances. *Polonia Today* (February 1992a:4) announced that

> a group of Polonians, led by Jan Wydro, is attempting to found a New Alliance College. . . . The founders hope to meet the needs of Poland and other free East European nations by offering degrees in International Business Administration, Environmental Engineering Science, and Nursing Education.

The student body is expected to come from Poland, Eastern Europe, and the United States. Northwestern University in Illinois is adding two courses on Polish history. The presence of the children of the third cohort of immigrants is evident in several activities featuring Polish or English subjects. The Polish Welfare Association "is offering a summer program of intensive English classes for children" (*Polonia Today*, May 1992: 3). The Heritage Club of Polish Americans announced the "Formation of a TEEN CHAPTER open to all teenagers, Polish American, Polish-Born or Interested in Things Polish, to meet at the Copernicus Center in Chicago" (*Polonia Today*, February 1992b:5). All in all, however, there is no dramatic evidence of a wholesale return to concern with Polishness.

Much of the educational activity in Polonia, as true of other efforts, seems dependent upon individual leaders. For example, the Chicago branch of the Polski Uniwersytet na Obczyznie (PUNO) (the Polish University Abroad, with headquarters in London, which had been founded in 1952), was first organized in 1978 by several university professors but limited itself for ten years to occasional lectures. It became highly activated in 1988 by a professor at the University of Chicago, recently migrated from Poland. The aim of Chicago's PUNO, and that of other branches, was

> to promote Polish culture, history and tradition beyond Polish borders, to carry forth independent scholarly studies, lectures, seminars and conferences in cooperation with other universities and scholarly institutes. The Chicago branch of PUNA also sets itself as a goal to help with the integration in American life of new waves of emigrants through the organization of vocational and English language courses, help with recognition of diplomas from Poland, as well as help with registration for studies in American universities (*Informator PUNO* 1988/89:5)

Professor Hubert Romanowski organized multiple courses in three divisions: humanities and economics, English language, and computers. PUNO was incorporated as the Polish Institute of Science and Culture with a not-for-profit status, and obtained several grants and gifts of space and computer technology. A numerous and qualified faculty offered several courses each semester. In addition, Professor Romanowski, in collaboration with the Polish Museum of America and the Roman Dmowski Institute, organized a conference for the "70th Anniversary of Independent Poland" in 1988. PINIK, or the Polish Institute, folded when Professor Romanowski moved to the embassy of the newly independent Polish government in Washington, D. C.

At the same time, a new American Center of Polish Culture was opened in July 1992 in Washington, D. C. with great ceremony including a letter from President Bush with wishes for success in providing Americans the opportunity to obtain a deeper understanding of Polish arts, literature, history, and music (*Dziennik Zwiazkowy*, 31 July–2 Aug 2 1992:7, loose translation from Polish). The idea for such a center first appeared in 1937 but only now did the community express enough interest in such an organization to fund it. The Polish American Congress also has offices in Washington but its focus is on political rather than cultural activity. The need for such a center was expressed by several intelligentsia leaders at the 50th Anniversary Congress of the Polish Institute of Arts and Sciences of America and the sponsoring organization was the American Alliance of Polish Culture.

Occupational Persistence and Change

Without knowledge of English and the "American way of life" and without industrial skills, the majority of Poles who emigrated to the United States were not equipped to enter the occupational structure at any but the unskilled level. They entered the Chicago packinghouses, the steel mills of Indiana, Detroit's automobile assembly lines, and Pennsylvania's coal mines much as any other immigrants had done before and would do after them. The second generation tended to put themselves at a disadvantage by limiting themselves to the occupations of their fathers. They did this partly because they were unwilling to use education as a means of learning new skills, and partly because the strong patriarchal family system provided entrance into the father's work place early in life. The unusual structure and culture of the American society almost guaranteed horizontal outward and even upward mobility for sons of immigrants. Yet Lieberson (1963:189) found the Poles were dissimilar to other ethnic groups, being below the expected rate of generational mobility. Duncan and Duncan (1968) used the 1962 census data on ethnic origin and concluded that second-generation Polish Americans started with a serious handicap in early life in that their fathers' occupations deviated more from the prestige mean of the total population than did any other group's included in the analysis. Additionally, they found that Poles "suffer a modest handicap" in achieving upward mobility from the first job to the current one (362). Occupational inheritance occurred more frequently among Poles than among other groups, not necessarily in terms of actual job but in level of prestige; that is, the occupational distribution among the second generation tended to be more concentrated than among the second generation for other groups. This reinforces Hutchinson's (1956) conclusions that second generation Polish Americans were held back by following their limited parental occupations while the country as a whole had moved away from such occupational inheritance.

The 1970 occupational status of Polish American men reflected the continued presence of the first two generations of the first, economic, cohort of immigrants in four occupational categories: craftsmen, foremen, and kindred workers (23 percent); operatives and kindred workers (19 percent); professional and kindred workers (18 percent); and managers, officials, and personnel (13 percent). These concentrations indicated a white- and a blue-collar polarity (U.S. Bureau of the Census 1971 P-20:249, T-7; see appendix C). This polarity deviated from Greeley's findings, based on a composite of ten years prior to 1973, and indicated a trend away from blue-collar jobs toward white-collar jobs. In general, most studies of those years showed that older Polish Americans of the old emigration had reached the top rungs of the blue-collar world, and recent generations moved to the lower rungs of the white-collar world. Increasing numbers entered the professions, shortcutting the traditional rung by rung movement of prior generations or maintaining the level of their World War II second cohort parents.

The percentage of Polish American women aged sixteen and over in the labor force was relatively low in 1970 (37.9 percent) when compared to the national female proportion of the same age group (44 percent)(U.S. Bureau of the Census 1971 P-20: 22; see appendix D). The lack of emphasis on higher education for women in Polonia was reflected by the fact that 36 percent were in clerical, 19 percent in operative, and 13 percent in professional jobs, while 16 percent were still in service occupations.

There were not many changes between 1969 and 1980 in the occupational distribution of Polish ancestry men who had been born in the United States except that even fewer were connected with farming. There were more sales workers and fewer craftsmen but the same proportion of laborers since the 1980 census combined the operatives and the laborers. Lieberson and Waters (1988:121) contrasted the percentages of men and women of different ethnic groups concentrated in agriculture and service occupations between 1900 and 1980. According to their findings, Polish men and especially Polish women (11 and 4 percent) were not likely to be in agriculture at the turn of the century. This contrasted with, for example, Norwegians, among whom 50 percent of the men and 14 percent of the women had been in agriculture. The Poles almost entirely moved away from farms by 1980 (2 and 1 percent). Comparatively many Polish men (31 percent) and women (34 percent) had been in service occupations in

1900. Only the Italian men had a higher percentage in such jobs (42 percent), while only half as many Italian women were in service occupations. The most likely to be in service jobs among the women of those years were the Irish (70 percent). By 1980, only 7 percent of the Polish men and almost twice that many of the women were in service occupations. Of course, the figures for the third cohort of Polish workers are not significant in that census.

In 1980 American-born Polish ancestry men were disproportionately apt to be bakers, tailors, and model/pattern makers. Generally speaking, there was relatively little change in the occupational distributions of Polish Americans between 1969 and 1980 (see appendix C). There is some problem with comparability because Lieberson and Waters (1988: 156) used slightly different categories from those used by the Department of Labor in the prior time period.

Intermarriage

A subject of great interest to social scientists as well as to members of ethnic groups themselves has been endogamous, or in-group, versus exogamous, or out-group, marriages. Gordon (1964), and others use intermarriage as a major indicator of assimilation. It often limits the amount of national or ethnic culture passed on to the next generations, although a person marrying into a strong family unit of a different ethnic group can become so incorporated that his or her ethnic background does not affect the life-style and socialization of children. One of the most famous studies of intermarriage in a particular community, Kennedy's (1952) "Single or Multiple Melting Pot: Intermarriage in New Haven," concluded that people marrying out of their ethnic group at least stayed within the same religion. One hundred percent of Poles married Poles in 1900, but by 1940 this had dropped to just over 50 percent and those who married out tended to choose Irish and Italian mates. Abramson (1973) used combined samples obtained by the National Opinion Research Center and found increased exogamy in ethnic marriages over generations. The Polish Americans in that sample tended to be most exogamous in New England, where the educational and mobility levels were higher and most endogamous in the North Central states.

Lieberson and Waters (1988) did an extensive analysis of marriage patterns of Americans of single and of mixed ethnic ancestry. Not surprisingly, in view of the presence of three and more generations of Polish Americans 54 percent are of mixed ancestry. The most apt to marry non-Poles are the young Polish Americans of mixed backgrounds. Forty-seven percent of the elderly, aged 65 and over, compared to 20 percent of those aged 25 to 34, marry within this ethnic group; and 25 percent of women with an all Polish ancestry, and 17 percent of those aged 25 to 34, with a mixed background, marry Polish men (Lieberson and Waters 1988: tables 6.1 and 6.3). The single ancestry women have a 9 to 5 ratio of marrying in to marrying out; those of a mixed ancestry have a 5 to 8 ratio. This means that the probability of the first category of women having married a Polish man is 9 to 5 while the second group is much more apt to marry out of the group. It is interesting to note that single ancestry women of that age group are much more likely to have married single ancestry men while mixed ancestry women marry mixed background men. This is evidenced in the following examples of percentages:

Wife Polish background	Husband single	German mixed	Husband single	Irish mixed	Husband single	Polish mixed
single	12	12	6	11	18	7
mixed	8	26	3	19	5	12

Life-Styles

Internal differentiation among Polish Americans makes it hard to describe their "typical life-style." Members of the old emigration had village and regional identities in common. World War II emigration Poles shared common experiences of displacement. Each group identified differently with Poland, America, and Polonia. Other important variables distinguishing one Polish American from another include generation in the United States, age, sex, marital and parental status, education, occupation, and presence or absence of an extended kinship group. These traits affect a Polish American's social class life-style; involvement in Polish, Polonian, and American variations of this life-style; and content of life. I will discuss the first generations of the old, the second, and the newest cohorts separately, and then deal with class and community variations of later generations.

Old Age of the First Cohort, First Generation

Few members of the first generation of the old emigration have survived until the 1990s and those still alive tend to have been brought here as children in the pre-World War I years or to have come to join relatives of already established family members after that war but before the imposition of the immigration quotas and other events stemming the immigrants tide into a trickle. Of course, in many cases it is only the accident of birth on the other side of the ocean that places them as first generation members of a sibling or age cohort, while their brothers and sisters born on this side of the Atlantic are considered members of the second generation. For this reason I am extending my comments to that generation that was born outside the United States or whose siblings were born outside the United States although they themselves were born of recent immigrants in this country.

The life-styles of the immigrants and their young children were heavily influenced by their class background, place of residence in America, sex, and age at migration. Their backgrounds were varied in that not everyone had been a peasant, and not all peasants were alike. Some came from small isolated villages, unable to read or write; many did not know how to prevent the spread of diseases in new crowded conditions (Davis 1921/1971). Others found cities such as Chicago almost barbaric with its wooden sidewalks and high crime rates, being accustomed to the more established communities back home. Most were taken aback by the great heterogeneity of peoples from all over the world and by the hostility they met because of their own behavior, which they considered normal. Although one-third of the Poles emigrating prior to World War I were illiterate, each local community had many temporary or even permanent residents who were relatively educated; these people started organizations, published newspapers, and helped develop the complex social structure. Community leaders at all levels wrote and read letters, taught the children, found jobs for others, and acted as role models for those trying to learn the best way of living in a strange new land. Reports of Poles in Detroit (Napolska 1945-46), Hamtramck (Wood 1955), Chicago (Thomas and Znaniecki 1918-1920), the Connecticut Valley (Abel 1929), and other local communities document the problems of rapid urbanization—long and very hard work, frequent victimization, and overcrowding as people shared quarters or rented rooms to help family income. But they also document lively interaction, status competition with increasing resources, organizational activity in each neighborhood, and mobility from community to community in search of better jobs and nicer places to live. These reports also document internal heterogeneity with many mutually exclusive companionate circles. Except for the few immigrants and temporary visitors who function partly or exclusively in the wider American society, the boundaries of Polonia were socially, if not always territorially, clearly drawn.

The children of the first wave immigrants were expected to take care of their parents in their old age. Wood (1955) found Hamtramck parents to be disappointed in the changes within their families brought about by Americanization. "After they finished school, they got married, and they are no help for the parents at all. They leave home and forget about their poor old parents" (215). The second-generation Polish Americans thus came into conflict with their parents as they adopted ways of relating to them that were not typical of the traditional obedient child role (Lopata 1988a). The American informality in intergenerational relationships often does not appeal to older generations who are focused on tradition. The demeanor of the young toward their parents and other elderly persons lost the quality of "respect" in the eyes of immigrant generation. Adult children became concerned with developing their own social status independent of their parents. In fact, those who moved upwardly in social status and outwardly from the neighborhood became unlike their parents, rejected their style of life, and did not even want them to help raise their children. Although the immigrants had been allowed to establish themselves independently because their families had been left behind in Poland, they now attempted to impose the traditional forms of control on their adult children. Conflict between the aging parents and the adult children, often over the way the grandchildren were reared, continued in three-generation households. Some parents retained contact with one child more than others by living in the same housing unit, in the same building, or within "soup carrying distance" (Lopata 1973b; Rosenmayr and Kockeis 1963; Townsend 1967). Contact with other offspring and their families became limited to holidays that had always been very important and gradually became the only items of Polish folk culture that younger generations experienced (Gould 1966).

One of the ways in which life in America affected the Polish immigrant and his family was through the decrystallization of sibling status. Each brother, and, mainly through marriage, each sister, established his or her own life following economic opportunities or problems. Although helping each other in the initial stages of settlement and sometimes in emergencies throughout life (Shanas and Streib 1965), many families became sufficiently divergent and involved in their own nuclear families to decrease interaction.

There are many older, first- and second-generation widows in the old Polish neighborhoods of Chicago that have become inhabited by different ethnic groups with their own community organization and "foreign" language churches (Lopata 1977). Their children moved away, often to suburbs, and the mothers did not follow for a variety of reasons. In most cases they explain this reluctance to move in with the children in terms of their own preference. The son is no longer held responsible for their care following the American patterns. The widows are able to maintain themselves economically with the help of social security and declare that they do not want to become periphery members in their married daughter's home. They anticipate conflict with that family, want to keep their own life-style, and do not want to go through another round of housecleaning and child caring. They like their independence, even if it means some social isolation and loneliness. Many are afraid of their own neighborhood or of venturing beyond it, unless picked up and brought back. This makes them dependent upon offspring, usually daughters. Even if their marriages had not been especially good, they fulfill the Polonian obligation to speak well of the dead, even to the point of sanctification.

The remaining members of the old emigration's first-generation Polish Americans are apt to be still residing in the older sections of American cities, while their children and/or grandchildren have moved to the outskirts or the newer suburbs. These older areas are often racially changing or mixed. The villagers' traditional fear of strangers combined with a lack of familiarity with people of different races (due to their absence in Poland) and the prior segregation of the Polish and the black communities from each other have resulted in mutual dislike and fear. The Puerto Ricans and Mexicans are also met with hostility since they represent different life-styles and are symbolic of the breakup of the old Polonian community. Studies of residential areas of elderly Polish Americans in cities present a picture of sadness, anger, feelings of abandonment by neighbors and family, and social isolation. The "Needs Assessment of Chicago Elderly" survey found that Poles have negative attitudes toward their neighborhoods at a frequency higher than that of any group but the blacks, and consider safety to be a major problem (Lopata 1975).

In spite of the limitations, the social life space of most of the old emigration's first generation had expanded with immigration to America. Polonia as an *okolica* provided greater variation of social roles than had the Polish village *okolica*. However, the difference was not dramatic. The lower-class Polish Americans tended to be limited in the geographical area of their social life space and the women still focused their major roles around the family institution. Men worked for large American organizations but generally refrained from active participation in those groups, preferring their own ethnic associations. Associational membership for both genders was high even among the working classes, with parish groups, mutual aid "societies," and village clubs being most prevalent. The higher the social class of the Polish immigrant, the fuller the social life space, with involvement in social roles in several institutions and the more apt was even the first generation man or woman to be involved in at least some American institutions outside of Polonia.

Life-Styles of the Second Generation

The second generation of first-cohort Polish immigrants is now in the middle to older years of life. Its members reputedly suffered much social disorganization because of their position as the marginal generation caught between the Polish culture of their parents and the American culture of the society around them (Park 1928; Stonequist 1937). In fact, most scholars predicted social disorganization in the community and the family, resulting in increased demoralization, "hedonism," and antisocial behavior among members (Claghorn 1923; Thomas et al. 1921; Thrasher 1927). Thomas and Znaniecki (1918–1920) expected this disorganization to follow the inability of Polonia to reproduce the Polish village culture and social organization, with its strong use of shame and other personal forms of social control.

The predictions of high rates of social and individual disorganization proved to be exaggerated. In fact, a few social scientists tried to convince the others that some of the indices of disorganization, such as crime rates, were being misunderstood and misused. Taft (1936:726–30) argued that "the foreign born as a whole are committed to penal institutions for felonies in proportion far below their normal ration," although the children of foreign-born parents had high rates. The main reason for this, according to Taft, was their disproportionate age distribution. Many second generation Poles fell within the "criminally significant" ages of 15 and 24. The age distribution of the Polish foreign born placed only 6 percent of them in these criminally significant ages in 1930 while the native born of foreign or mixed parentage of Polish background contained 63 percent between the ages 15 and 24 and an additional 33 percent between that ages of 25 and 44 (Taft 1936:726). The corrected rate, adjusted for population distribution, found Polish felons committed to state institutions in 1933 at a rate higher than that for the older immigrant groups but lower than that for Lithuanians, Greeks, Italians, and Spaniards (734). Thus, Taft's point was that the Polish Americans were not any more contributive to American crime rates than were other groups with a similar population age profile and similar newness of immigration.[9]

Unlike the Italian Americans, the Polish Americans engaged in little organized crime (Finestone 1964). Robbery and burglary were the most frequent causes of arrests and were usually "one-man jobs." The youth, on the other hand, were active in gangs; Thrasher (1927:9–10) reported that the main Polish business street in Chicago had "a gang in almost every block. The majority of gangs in Chicago are of Polish stock, but this may be due to the fact that there are more persons of Polish extraction in Chicago than of any other nationality except German."[10]

The Polish Americans also did not seem to have a disproportionately high divorce rate—the only real measure we have of family disorganization. In spite of the dire predictions of family disorganization, there is no outward evidence of it in the history of Polonia, except for the use of courts to force conformity on family members, or to punish them for failure to contribute to the family status. Thomas (1950) and Rooney (1957) have questioned the assumptions of family disorganization, but they unfortunately had recourse to only a limited amount of divorce data. The Greeley (1974b) composite sample also shows average divorce rates for the Polish Americans. Finally, the 1972 census showed that only 1.7 percent of the Polish males 14 years of age or over were divorced, a rate lower than the total American rate of 2.5 percent (U.S. Bureau of the Census 1972 PC(2)-4C:table 2). The female rate was 2.2 percent for the Polish Americans and 3.8 percent for the total population.

The low divorce rates for the Polish Americans do not imply the absence of family strain and conflict, but those phenomena are very hard to prove one way or the other.[11] It is one of the theses of this book that the internal structure of Polonia's subcommunities prevented and cushioned some of the conflict, or at least institutionalized it into the status competition. The first generation helped the second generation to develop its own status package by providing a good family reputation and by starting them on a level at least equal to the one on which they were reared. Furthermore, the same forms of social control that had kept families together in Poland operated in Polonia: parishes and mutual aid groups provided the foundation for status competition, and many status hierarchies were available in the social life of the community. It was also easy to gain financial success in traditional terms. All these developments allowed parents to socialize their children, in spite of conflict and rebellion, into a similar concern with the community they shared. Rather than living in an anonymous urban center visualized by Thomas and Znaniecki (1918-1920) as inevitably disorganizing to the person and the family, the second generation was born into and contributed to reputation-giving communities offering numerous rewards by decrystallizing and keeping flexible status packages. The young generation eventually broke from their parents but this does not mean that they became alienated throughout life. In spite of all the literature on assimilation, which claims a rapid "melting" of second generation ethnics, recent studies of Polish Americans indicate that the second generation is a "transitional" rather than a highly acculturated one (Gould 1966; Obidinski 1968; Sandberg 1974). Wrobel (1979) found the second generation of Detroit factory workers very much like their parents. Many changed their names, ashamed of the heritage. At the same time, some second-generation youth went to colleges and professional schools, becoming lawyers and physicians, often serving their fellow ethnics, especially if they had learned the Polish language. The continued existence of Polonia for over a century indicates involvement of the second generation.

Second-generation Polish Americans exhibit several different life-styles depending on whether or not they had been brought up in and identified with Polonia, had been able to synchronize family resources in striving for upward mobility, and also on their inherited position in their community. Those who remained in Polonia gradually became Americanized in their behavior and appearance, if not in all attitudes. Although they did not become involved in higher education, they began to look at it more positively for their children (Wood 1955). Their demands on the younger generation were much less severe than had been their parents' demands on them (Obidinski 1968). Much of their life centered around the community with varying levels of participation. Other Polish Americans moved away from the area of first settlement, but often to places where other Polish Americans lived (Agocs 1971). Commuting at first back to the old neighborhood to buy Polish foods, attend meetings, visit relatives, and even attend sacraments in the Polish parish, they gradually created their own neighborhood structure in the area of secondary settlement. Still other Polish Americans moved entirely away from Polonia, often changing their names and disassociating themselves from their ethnic identity.

Bukowczyk (1987) considers some of the blue- collar second-generation Polish Americans as reacting to the past and picking up on the "new ethnicity" of the 1960s and 1970s, much as did the succeeding generations.

[A]s second-generation Polish-Americans bought "Polish and Proud" bumper stickers, red and white T-shirts, and "Kiss Me I'm Polish" buttons and as they catapulted Bobby Vinton, a singer with a Polish Ancestry and an Americanized surname, to super-stardom during the years of ethnic revival, they revealed how the new ethnicity had become a purchasable and profitable commodity. (Bukowczyk 1987:118–19)

Other social scientists described the second generation as "the unknown Polonia" (Radzialowski 1986). As Radzialowski (1986:6) points out:

The drama of the immigration story is so powerful and so compelling, so heroic in its dimensions that it overshadows the experiences of the children of the immigrants. The first generation's accomplishment was to create a new society, an ethnic group and its institutions, in the space of a few decades in the face of enormous difficulties.

One characteristic of the second generation, said Radzialowski, a second generation Polish American himself, is that it also became migratory, moving off of farms, mines, stockyards, and ethnic neighborhoods to new areas. They created new social groups, focusing on sports and social clubs, special interest and occupational organizations, and became active in American unions (Radzialowski 1986: 11). Radzialowski's presidential address to the Polish American Historical Association urged his colleagues to study this generation. One of the interesting aspects of what we do know of this generation is the lack of information about the descendants of the middle classes and of the intelligentsia. It is possible that these are the people who either returned to Poland or assimilated, culturally and structurally into the broader American society and are thus unavailable for research. Only a detailed interview of a very large sample of Americans, or increased information as to family background by the U. S. Census could provide needed information, since they are not likely to be reached through Polish parishes or organizations.

The Second Emigration's First Generation

The first generation of Poles who came to America as part of the World War II emigration was an even more heterogeneous group than had been the old emigration. They were admitted by the special Displaced Persons Act of 1948 and subsequent laws. Many had spent up to five and six years in labor or other concentration camps and prisons in Germany. Others spent years fighting with the allied armed services in Europe or wandered the world after being deported by the Russians. Their background and the procedures they followed in resettlement were very different from those of the earlier peasant, middle-class, or intelligentsia immigrants. They had been reared in independent Poland, which had made more concerted efforts at mass education; they came from urban communities more frequently than from rural; and they had been involved in a variety of occupations. The intelligentsia was overrepresented among them, due to the German and Russian attempts at liquidating this segment of the population and its tendency to nationalistically participate in the underground government (see Karski's 1944 *Story of a Secret State*), and the Warsaw uprising, which resulted in its frequent dislocation. The experiences of uprooting, survival, and participation in the fighting inside and outside of Poland changed their outlook and concerns with world affairs. They had lived in other societies and their unwillingness to return to communistic Poland created a strong motivation for success in the adopted country. Their adjustment to American society was facilitated by a complex social system created to screen applicants in Europe, obtain guarantees of housing and employment or at least temporary financial support from sponsors, arrange for the trip, and obtain the cooperation of local communities in meeting settlement problems (Kolm 1961: chapter 7). The refugees were predominantly young, with a sex ratio of 119.3 males to 100 females and a much lower marriage rate than the American population (Kolm 1961: 225). Most settled in the largest cities of the Middle Atlantic, East North Central, and New England states.

All indications point to a more rapid and successful acculturation and adjustment of the new emigration than of the old (Kolm 1970; Mostwin 1971). The newcomers did not initially join in Polonia's status competition; they preferred to develop their own subcommunities or to turn instead to the American sources for self-establishment such as education, occupation in white-collar position, and residence in nonethnic neighborhoods. The most extensive analysis of this emigration was conducted by Mostwin (1971), whose respondents form a self-selective sample in that they were found through Polish American groups and only a relatively small proportion of distributed questionnaires were answered (143). Keeping in mind that the probability that the more educated and successful Poles were the most apt to answer the questionnaire, we can learn some aspect of their life-style from the 2,049 respondents. This was mostly a political immigration; few came for economic reasons. The majority were between 40 and 50 years of age at the time of the study, having come to the United States between 1948 and 1952. Mostwin (1971) found that

> The respondents who tend to be more satisfied with their living arrangement in this country are married, have longer years of residence in the U.S., immigrated to this country already trained in a profession, live in the suburb or in the country, do not live in a Polish section, have never lived in a Polish section, own their homes, and have comparatively low ethnic commitment. (196)

It is interesting to note that living in a Polish section of a city did not lead the respondents to residential satisfaction. Those people who knew English upon arrival, who had a higher educational achievement, lived outside Polonia, and developed a successful "American" life-style were apt to be satisfied not only with their residence but also with their employment. Employment satisfaction was related negatively to immigration for economic rather than political or familial reasons, living in a Polish neighborhood, low income, and strong ethnic commitment. The higher-status Poles of the new emigration were the most satisfied with all aspects of their lives. However, Mostwin found that although there were more upper-strata than lower-strata emigrants among her respondents in terms of status prior to the war in Poland, the two top classes paid a price in status drop for migration. In fact, it was mainly the middle class that suffered— over 50 percent of them moved downward to the lower middle class. Many had been owners of small businesses or required prolonged retraining made difficult by their age. The Poles who came directly from Poland after the 1956 political "thaw" were highly overrepresented among the professionals.

Although Mostwin's (1971:256) respondents reported that they had less conflict with their children than did the first generation of the old emigration, certain behavior patterns typical of American youth were picked up by their children which bothered the new emigration's parents. What bothered them most was "lack of respect for older people" (63 percent), "laxity in social manners" (56 percent), and "early dating(under 16 years of age)" (48 percent).

Like other social groups, the higher the social class of the new emigration, the fuller the social life space, and (even more than in the case of the old emigration) the more likely it was that this life space involved roles within the American institutional system. Contact with friends and relatives in Poland was maintained by many of the former displaced persons and excombatants, even during communist times and in spite of a continuing strong stand against its communist government. Polonian affiliation is strong among only a segment of the second emigration. The intelligentsia led a life typical of the American intelligentsia if they were affiliated with American organizations. There are many former members of the Polish intelligentsia of prewar Poland who were unable to reproduce this life in the American society and they tend to gravitate to each other in friendship patterns.

Of course, many second-generation Polish Americans were not reared in Polonia but grew up in nonethnic communities or those with only a scattering of Poles. An interesting life diversification by such children is reported by Mostwin (1971).[12] The children of the displaced persons, ex-combatants, and other refugees of World War II often live in two separate worlds: Polish and American, but not Polonian. Most second-generation, second-cohort children are antagonized by the lack of knowledge of the Polish national culture by the descendants of the old emigration. Contact with Polish American offspring of the old emigration tends to occur only among professionals or members of some politically oriented organizations. The second generation of the second-cohort immigrants who live completely outside of Polonia has not been sufficiently studied to know its distinctive characteristics. The same is true of the second generation of the third cohort.

Succeeding Generations of Polish Americans

Later generations of Polish Americans do not appear as a distinct unit in any collection or analyses of data on American society. We are thus limited to partial information from specific communities in which generational differences have been the subject of special studies. Fortunately, there is an increasing number of these studies (Emmons 1971; Gould 1966; Jurczak 1964; Mostwin 1971; Obidinski 1968; Sandberg 1974; Wagner 1964).

Obidinski (1968) found several important attitudinal and behavioral differences between second- and third-generation residents of Buffalo, New York, including increasing approval of ethnic intermarriages (38 percent to 64 percent respectively); decreasing support for a political candidate on the basis of Polish American identity (85 percent to 65 percent respectively), and decreasing preference for use of the Polish language during the entire Roman Catholic service (67 percent to 31 percent respectively). The third generation is much less active in voluntary organizations, both Polish American and purely American, than are prior generations. Fifty percent of the third generation belongs to a non-Polish organization. Of course, the differences between the second and third generations may be due to age differences. It is interesting that the less educated older generation is very active. Church attendance also varies by generation: the second was much more likely than the third to report going several times a week (36 percent of the second to 4 percent of the third generation). We can hypothesize that decreasing identification with Polonia in each succeeding generation may lead to a decrease of associational membership and community participation in general. That is, Polonia developed because of the active participation of the first generation of all social classes. It has continued with the help of the established higher classes of both emigrations. The third generation, although already in the middle class, seems to be less involved in the community life and status competition, and may simultaneously be decreasing organizational and community involvement in any community. The higher the class the lower the associational involvement; a reversal of American trends.

Both Obidinski's (1968) study and Gould's (1966) analysis of data collected by Jurczak (1964) indicate that third-generation Polish Americans have relatives and friends who are geographically more scattered in the community than are the associates of the second generation. The Polish Americans of the third generation in Buffalo, who tend to be young, are surprisingly more apt to live in the Polish area than are their parents. Obidinski (1968: 90) explains this by their inability to "rent or buy homes in the more expensive residential areas outside of East Side." In addition, many third-generation members are single and want smaller residential units. "Finally, younger respondents—both married and unmarried—may occupy the original family home with parents. Such joint residence in East side homes sometimes involves dependent elderly parents who retain title to houses" (90). However, both the second and the third generations have relatives scattered in the city and suburbs (42 percent and 34 percent, respectively) or living in the suburbs only (14 percent and 21 percent respectively). The same scatter holds for "best friends" except with greater concentration on the East Side for both generations (54 percent and 61 percent, respectively). On the other hand, the third generation in less satisfied with living on the East Side than is the second; although currently restricted to this area, they are suburban bound by preference.

While they are moving away from "ethnic islands" (Gould 1966), members are apt to be simultaneously moving up on the socioeconomic ladder as they approach middle age. Such mobility is assisted by formal education and by marriage outside of the ethnic group.

> There is upward mobility from the lower to the middle classes in the third generation and the third generation married to a non-Polish spouse has utilized education to a much more effective degree as an avenue of upward mobility than the third generation married to a Polish spouse. . . . The third generation still tend to marry a member of their own religion. (Gould 1966: 26)

The connection between higher education and marriage outside of the Polish group has many ramifications—most endogamous contacts were made in colleges and universities, and Polish American attendance at these institutions indicates at least partial independence from the community.

According to Sandberg (1974), the West Coast has tended to draw a more assimilated or higher-class Polish American into secondary settlement. In studying the Polish American community in Los Angeles, Sandberg found that with each generation of Polish Americans, membership in Polish parishes, and in any church for that matter, has declined. In general, there were few differences in ethnicity and behavior between the third and the fourth generations, and there was a similarity between the post-World War II immigrants and the second generation of the old emigration. The greatest amounts of decreasing ethnicity (as measured by Sandberg) were between the first and the second generations, modified considerably by ethclass.

Immigration and generational changes have not been strong enough to destroy the image of a strong patriarch in the Polish American family, even if his actual control over it has decreased. McCready (1974) found that "the Polish father has been able to maintain the image of the patriarch even during times of great stress and social mobility" (168). In fact, his being a "focus of attention" in the family resulted in a tendency for the mother to be "less salient for Poles than for the other groups we have seen" (168). By saliency he means relative importance of the mother to the father, as mentioned by frequency of reference.

> The young Polish women rate themselves high on domestic skills, attractiveness, and sex appeal, indicating that they do espouse the traditional values for women in society. . . . Their low saliency scores for mother indicate that they have received their values from their father rather than emulating their mothers as role models. In other words, they think of themselves as attractive competent women because their fathers told them they were. (168–69)

His conclusions are based, however, on the ten-year composite sample of the NORC studies and the data is not analyzed by generation, so it is impossible to determine if this image is undergoing any changes.

The Third Cohort

The third immigrant wave, that is, the cohort of entrants into the United States from Poland since 1965, contains, as discussed before, several types of emigrants. The typology is based on characteristics of those who emigrate from Poland and on the immigration policies of the United States (see tables 2.1–2.3 and Erdmans's chapter 8). There are the refugees and asylees, or those who left Poland for political reasons and who were acceptable here because of the American stance against the communistic government that dominated Poland. The immigrants join families or are admitted because of needed special occupational skills. The nonimmigrants come as business or political governmental representatives and as *wakacjusze* (vacationers).

Obviously, there is a great variety of third-cohort entrants, possibly even greater than that of the previous two waves. What they have in common is growing up in communist-controlled Poland, and being at higher educational, occupational, and urbanization levels than the first cohort had been. The political segment of the cohort shares some similarities with the second, World War II cohort. However, the segments of the third cohort do not relate well to each other, for several reasons, the most important being the illegal status of the *wakacjusze* and their overwhelming desire to earn as much money as possible for return to Poland. Many of these "temporary" residents are not involved in the political life that Erdmans describes in chapter 8. According to her figures, the proportion of Polish immigrants admitted under the quota, or numerical limitation policy, dropped from .83 to .24 from 1965 to 1989 (Erdmans 1992a: 343). The *wakacjusze* remained a relatively steady .75 to .78 of the total of nonimmigrants who were admitted during those two parameter years. This means that the other temporary entrants and the refugees did not represent the major population. However, the number of *wakacjusze* did vary considerably, building from 17,874 in 1965 to 69,093 in 1989. The proportion they reached of the nonimmigrant group peaked in 1986 and the totals for each category reflected what was happening in Poland: the formation of Solidarity, the imposition of martial law (state of war, as defined by opposition Poles), and the overthrow of the government. The numbers and proportions are important not only because size can influence the life of Polonia as a whole, but also because the life-styles of each segment of this cohort varies so considerably.

Political Émigrés and the Immigrants

Poles defined as political émigrés, that is, those accepted as refugees and those granted asylum when already here tend to be the most active politically in trying to help Poland directly or through attempts at influencing the U. S. government and the wider community (see chapter 8). They consider themselves heroes of the bloodless revolution, worthy of recognition by the established Polonian community, knowledgeable about Poland and trained into leadership. However, this is not how they are seen by the established community, which carries its former extreme anticommunistic stance into a suspicion of anyone brought up in Poland between 1945 and 1989. As noted before, relations between the remaining Polonian leaders of the second cohort and the descendants of the first are strained. Erdmans (chapter 8) documents chronic and acute situations in which cooperation has been successful or activities mutually exclusive.

The third cohort, with only partial involvement by the *wakacjusze*, has become more settled and legalized and has built a life of its own. Its members have resources in the form of friends from Poland who have already learned the ropes and who help find housing and jobs, as well as lending money for immediate needs. Working originally in a limited number of occupations, usually below those in the home country, they learn better English, get job training or take courses broadening their knowledge of American society, and move out of the geographical and occupational ghettos. Many start their own entrepreneurial business, even in conjunction with Poles in Poland. The imagery they present in the U.S. Poland Chamber of Commerce and similar groups is of young, (or middle-aged) successful businessmen and women. One does not meet those who have not succeeded in this country.

The Wakacjusze

The portrayals presented in the Polish press, literature, and even a new radio soap opera concerning life-styles of the wakacjusze are not as pleasant. Whether in sociological analyses (Rokicki 1989) or semi-autobiographical stories (Mierzynska 1990), the lot of those who come to the United States "for pleasure," that is, as wakacjusze, is fraught with danger and minimal life circumstances. They come, often at the urging of family members, to earn as many dollars in as fast a time as possible, and to send or bring this money to Poland for the purchase of usually very specific consumer items. These may include a tractor, an automobile, housing, wedding expenses, and so forth. They are greeted at the port of entry, which may be O'Hare Airport in Chicago, by relatives or friends from home. After a short stay in the home of such greeters, they end up in an illegal job and in the cheapest housing in a Polonian neighborhood. The job usually consists of cleaning homes and/or offices if the Pole is a woman, cleaning or construction for a man (Baraniak 1992). Often the person holds down two or even three jobs, working daytime, nights, and weekends. Alternative jobs for women include care of the elderly, the sick, or children, or live-in housekeeping. Language is the main problem, as is a lack of experience in such work, since prior occupations were completely different. Agencies have sprung up all over the United States where Poles can be located whose main function is to train the newcomers and serve as intermediaries between them and employers. However, the mass media and individual interviews by both me and Mary Erdmans indicate how unsatisfactory, even criminal, are such arrangements. The newcomer often has to pay in advance, if she or he has any money, or money is taken from the first week's or month's earnings. If the worker is taken to the job by a representative of the agency, it takes up to half of the daily earnings. A cleaning job in an office building in the Chicago Loop can cost as much as $1,200 at latest report, a house cleaning job with an agency as much as $300. In addition, the workers are allegedly dropped after a certain point of time, or the work is made so unpleasant that they drop out, to be replaced by even newer illegal workers with a down payment.

The housing afforded by a dollar-earning *wakacjuszka* (female of *wakacjusz*, which is male singular for *wakacjusze*) usually consists of a room, or part of one, in the basement of another Polish family, with limited bathroom and kitchen facilities (Rokicki 1989: 112). The Poles usually feel the need to save money even on food, and thus maintain themselves on an inadequate diet. They are willing to live in conditions observers find almost revolting. The literature written by the third cohort and published in magazines, newspapers, and books makes frequent reference to the shock expressed by new entrants to Polonia over the way their spouses or other relatives are willing to live (see, for example, Mierzynska's *Wakacjuszka*, 1990, a compilation of several volumes). The newcomers often remain unpacked for years, hoping to go back any day. Lack of understanding the English language results in fear and suspicion, especially in the areas of cities to which the newcomer is confined. On the other hand, women and sometimes couples who take full-time live-in positions can find themselves in pleasant surroundings with adequate living resources. One respondent told me that other Polish women were working in the neighborhood and they got together on days off to go to restaurants or movies. She was not as concerned about saving each cent as were others described in the literature. The disadvantages of such positions include distance from others of the same background, dependence upon a single employer, and the impossibility of earning money through additional sources.

The worst aspect concerning the situation of the wakacjusze is their illegal status. This subjects them to all sorts of exploitation and scams. Blackmail reputedly exists, the threat of being exposed to the Immigration and Naturalization Service making the newcomer willing to put up with harassment and low wages. Everyone in Polonia knows that they have money at any one time, not placed in banks but easily available. A lawyer in Chicago explains the situation:

> Most of my clients have more cash than the average American. You must remember that when an immigrant comes here he comes here to work hard. He rents a room in someone's basement and puts all his money under his pillow. He doesn't spend his money. Then, when something comes up, for example, if he's been working illegally and gets caught by the INS, he'll do anything not to be deported. What's a couple thousand bucks to him? He knows that if he gets deported he won't make any money. However, if I can get his permanent residency, he'll make up the money he paid me in a couple of months. So don't think that I'm dealing with impoverished clients because in most cases that's not true. (Worwag 1992: 10)

This is not an empathetic view of the client. At the same time, the "client" needs these services. The lawyers in Polonia perform multiple functions for the illegal residents, most of which require understanding and filling out forms needed for obtaining asylum or for permanent residency and thus the green card and, after five years of permanent residency, for citizenship. In most of the cases the Pole does not really need an expensive lawyer, but someone who can explain and fill out the forms. Deportation cases do need legal expertise, since the client has to be represented in the immigration courts (Worwag 1992: 12). A bilingual lawyer living in one of Chicago's Polonian neighborhoods with a knowledge of home and host laws explained that he had no trouble finding clients, he simply hung a shingle above a Polish American bakery. However, the legalization of so many clients, with the help of agencies such as the Polish Welfare Association has shrunken his clientele in the last years (Lopata, field notes 1992).

Stories abound in Polonia as to ways the wakacjusze and other newcomers are deprived of monies earned through extremely difficult conditions. Fly-by-night business firms promise to deliver automobiles or other expensive items to Poland but then vanish with the payment. Acquaintances and allegedly honest "experts" guarantee green cards, transportation of relatives to the United States, vacations, and anything else that the emotionally, socially, and physically starved Poles wish. Even contact with relatives in Poland can become a problem. In the past, due to censorship and the dishonesty of the "nomenklatura" in Poland, and to a certain extent now because of the inefficiency of the postal service, money and objects often do not make it back home. There is, at the very least, fear of such loss. People use each other as intermediaries to carry stuff from the United States to Poland, sometimes at a cost. A new problem has emerged recently, and that is the increasing demands of people back home. Each relative or friend visualizes the wakacjusze as living a life of leisure and comfort (after all, they are in America!), while they themselves are suffering back home. A cleaning woman who was brought to my apartment in Chicago by an agency explained that she has been in America for six years—in circumstances that sounded inhuman—because each time she wanted to return another child back home demanded what a prior one had already received.

It must be remembered that these entrants "for pleasure" left their children and spouses behind in order to earn money to make life better back home for all of them. Part of the frustration repeatedly voiced in Polonia, and reported in the mass media, is the misuse of the funds by those relatives. There is a great deal of resentment when the wakacjusze hear from "friends" or neighbors that the family is having a pretty good time while those in America are living under such restricted conditions.

On the other hand, the wakacjusze can form domestic arrangements here in spite of marriages back home. A man and a woman can enter a "Chicago marriage," as it is called, sharing household expenses and company rather than living alone (Rokicki 1989: 112). Some of these arrangements have their own dangers, since the money is easily available to the partner. The longer the people stay in America, the more they wish for recreation and sexual companionship. The wakacjusze become legitimated, more comfortable in their lives, and less willing to return, or send all their earnings back home. The prolification of restaurants, taverns and nightclubs, magazines, and the clothing of these Poles attest to these changes.

There is a very complex relationship among the various segments of the third cohort and between it and established Polonia. Most of the established Polonians resent the presence of the temporary residents. Having to work hard to increase their social status and that of the community, many Polish Americans resent the ubiquitous presence of "the Polish cleaning women" (they, rather than the men or Poles in other positions, have become symbolic of Polonia, probably because of the personal contacts so many Americans have with domestics; Rokicki 1989: 115). Although the Polish business community encourages everyone to "come to your own for both of our benefits" the wakacjusze and some of the other members of the third cohort feel that their own are exactly the people who take advantage of them. I have often been told that it is the "old Polonia" that cheats the new cohort, but it appears that the culprits are often members of the new cohort who have been here longer and learned how to take advantage of the need for their services (Rokicki 1989: 115). The symbiotic nature of the relationship is obviously reminiscent of that of other ethnic communities, not restricted to Polonia alone. However, one of the myths within Polonia is that these other groups protect and help each other. Almost invariably a respondent of the newest wave of Poles claims that the Jews offered much help to immigrants from the Soviet Union, while established Polonians refuse to help them, expecting these "snobbish" newcomers to work as hard as they did. At least this is the definition of the situation given by the newcomers. The newest cohort admits being given help, but feels that it comes from people in the same circumstances, not from established Polonia.

There is thus hostility between the third cohort and the members of the established Polonia. Even readers of *U. S. News and World Report* have learned of the attitudes of these groups toward each other.

> Leaders of the two groups ["Old Polonia" and "New Polonia"] have little in common beyond a lingering hatred of communitm and of each other. Edward Moskal of the old-line Polish National Alliance complains of "young malcontents" who grew up in a "privileged socialist atmosphere" and who, he claims, malinger on welfare rather than work hard like earlier immigrants. Jarek Cholodecki, a radio journalist and Solidarity activist who spent time in a Polish prison, counters that half the homes in Chicago have been rehabilitated by the hard-working Polish immigrants, who live in cramped basement apartments in Polish Village. He disparages Moskal as an "apparatchik" who clings to power to get his picture taken with President Bush. (Glastris 1992:23)

Now that the Polish government has changed and visas are no longer required of people traveling from the United States to Poland, the members of the newest cohort are free to return. Respondents in Chicago in 1992 constantly talk about returns, their own or others, using as an indicator of the probability of doing so whether the person sold belongings back home. As one woman explained to me: "I can not go back—I sold my home." Housing shortage in Poland can account for the firmness of this reply, but its meaning goes deeper than that. The current economic situation in Poland, struggling toward privatization but with enormous inflation is again providing a reason (not just a justification) for delaying the return. However, as with other cohorts and immigrants from other societies, the longer people stay in the United States, the less likely they are to return to the homeland, unless there are special circumstances drawing them back. Polish sociologist Rokicki (1989: 117), who studied wakacjusze in Chicago, concluded that the decision to return was hastened by illness or accident.

Ethnic Identity

In order to introduce this book I had to stick to the labels of Poles, Polish stock, Polish Americans, and Americans of Polish descent or ancestry, as they have been used by the U. S. immigration officials, the U. S. Census Bureau, or Polonians themselves, with just passing comments on variations among the self-imposed and other criteria for labeling or identifying people rather than for establishing identity (see chapter 1). In other words, we had to agree on some basic criteria for reference to people as Poles or Polish Americans. Now is the time to examine that elusive concept of Polish American ethnic identity. However, this is not an easy subject to investigate due to a lack of agreement over the dimensions, content, and pervasiveness that are "typical" or "necessary" (see Kolm's [1961 1969, 1971a, 1971b] extensive discussions of ethnicity in general). How "ethnic" does a Polish American have to be to be called an ethnic? Which traits of national culture or ethnic style of life does a person have to exhibit? How influential must such an identity be in the behavior of the person, in self-feelings, in the behavior of other members of the same ethnic group and of outsiders, toward him or her, before it is clearly identifiable? We will first look at some of the criteria used by other observers of the Polish American scene and then attempt to specify its components.

As mentioned in chapter 1, ethnicity began to interest Americans in the 1970s, possibly in response to the "Black is Beautiful" movement. In the past, they were mainly concerned with "Americanization" as a process by which distinctive folk, national, or ethnic behavioral and attitudinal patterns were dropped and American patterns substituted. Various observers noted different "symptoms" of delay or failure in the "melting pot" process (Drachsler 1920; Schermerhorn 1949; Smith 1939). Kennedy (1952) and Herberg (1955) used intermarriage as a basic criterion of assimilation. Polish visitors to the United States have defined Polish Americans as Americans with no Polishness to them on the basis of their lack of knowledge of the Polish language. Several sociologists focused on legal changes of Polish-sounding surnames as indices of a willingness to "pass" into the general society. Name changes end the last visible proof of identification with the ethnic group, breaking past family and ethnicity label ties, though not necessarily interactional ties (Zagraniczny 1963; Kotlarz 1963; Borkowski 1963).

Recent studies of ethnic persistence have developed more complicated lists of criteria, but perusal of the literature shows that there is no consistent pattern to the measurement of this identity. Each observer's criteria tap only limited phenomena, and in the case of studies of Polish Americans, these criteria are heavily based on lower-class Polish peasant or folk culture; they ignore other forms of Polish culture, the changes over time, and the creation of a distinct Polonian culture. As a result, studies of generational changes in ethnicity almost inevitably conclude that ethnic identity is fading since the children and grandchildren of Polish immigrants tend to score lower than the first generation on scales based on the folk culture of the first generation. This view of ethnicity—in terms of intergenerational loss of a limited number of cultural items—ignores the Polish national culture and the culture of Polonia. Some studies even neglect to look at relationships and memberships. However, other studies contain interesting contributions to a potentially more complex set of indices and they are of themselves reflections of the vantage point from which observers view Polonia. For example, a limited, folk culture-bound "ethnicity index" was developed by Jurczak (1964). The index asks about the frequency of serving folk foods, and uses an ethnoreligious practice subscale. Cultural habits that are used are limited to the sharing of the Christmas wafer, blessing of the Easter basket, and blessing of the home after the feast of Epiphany. It also inquires as to the use of Polish language but, unfortunately, not the vocabulary and the occasion for its use.

Obidinski (1968) used a more complex scale. His respondents were given a choice of identities including: (1) Polish, (2) Polish American, (3) American Pole, (4) American, and (5) some other nationality. He asked, "What phrase on the card best describes how you think other persons consider you?" without specifying the "other persons" (65-68). The interview asked about ethnic participation in Polonia's life, persistence of residence in the ethnic community, attendance at Polish language religious services, and membership in Polish and non-Polish associations. Ideational items included the possession of a religious (Polish Catholic) picture in the house, belief in selected ideas deemed typically Polish, and familiarity with the term "Polonia" and with the Polish American Congress as an organization.

Pienkos (1973) studied Milwaukee Polish Americans along several lines including: (1) self-identification (as Pole or non-Pole, religiosity, and friends); (2) extent of one's contact with the Polish homeland (place of birth, maintenance of contact and knowledge of Polish); (3) extent of one's own involvement in the Polish American Milwaukee community (knowledge of Polonia, identifying of its organizations, characteristics of primary education, and knowledge of Polish customs); (4) awareness of particular information or interest in subjects important to Poles (identification of Kosciuszko and Pulaski, identification of seven famous Polish historical figures, and mention of local Polish leaders and of Muskie as candidate for U. S. presidency); and (5) one's own personal orientation toward the country of Poland (personal feelings, nostalgia and pride, awareness, and negative feelings toward communist rule, and sadness about the Polish situation). This set of criteria covers both Polonia and Poland and is certainly broader than focus on loss of folk culture items.

Mostwin (1971) reflected her own involvement in the life of the new emigration by entirely ignoring Polonian ethnic identity. She developed a fivefold classification emerging from answers to three questions: How did the respondents identify themselves? How did they think Americans identify them? How did they think Poles in Poland identify them? (51-58). The only alternatives were "Pole" and "American" (55). Then there was the person who "thinks of himself as primarily Polish, but believes that the Americans and the Poles in Poland consider him American" (57). Finally, there was the person "with inconsistencies within [his] own ethnic identity."[13]

In addition, Mostwin was interested in the "transmission of Polish cultural values and selected patterns of behavior to children in the new environment" (251). She asked whether the parents talked to the children about their Polish heritage, sang Polish lullabies to them, and sent them to Polish-language schools. In relation to social class and ethnicity, Mostwin found that, "the higher the social class, the stronger the probability of 'passing' directly from the Polish to the American identity" (290). Some readers may say that this study is not relevant here because it does not deal with Polonian or strictly Polish American identity, but we must recognize that there are people of Polish birth living in America for whom Polonian identity is not a reality.

Just as Mostwin's (1971) study reflects the population she describes, Sandberg's (1974) ethnicity scale reflects the Polish Americans in the Los Angeles area who have a higher educational and mobility background than most of the older communities. Sandberg (1974) developed three complex scales, the first of which measured the importance assigned by respondents to the preservation of cultural ethnicity, including "Polish schools, centers, organization and the press . . . as well as the perpetuation of the language, music, dance, history and traditions of the group" (53-54). The religious ethnicity scale measured attitudes toward the Polish church, and the national ethnicity scale focused on the concept of "peoplehood," or ethnic solidarity.

> That scale probed at feelings of kinship, mutual responsibility, and a sense of belonging, with others of similar background. They also touched on the sensitive nerve endings of Polish identification, such as the concern with Polish jokes and the propriety of Anglicizing names. (64-65)

His scales are thus much more able to flesh out ethnic identity.

The problems with many of the scales used to measure ethnicity in Polonia are that they flatten the wealth of heterogeneity, oversimplify the content, and obscure the changes over time that consist of more than just the dropping of folk culture items. Only Sandberg's (1974) scale does not fall into this trap. There are many indications of revitalization within this ethnic community brought about by a broader source of identity harking back to Polish national culture as well as new items of Polonian literary and artistic culture. Future studies should tap the richness of the Polish American background more adequately so that we can better understand how its various components are brought together into different subtypologies if not limited to only a few items of the common denominator. We must keep in mind the three basic identities—Polish, Polish American, and American—and then see how these can be woven together into packages or typologies.

One characteristic of nearly all Polish Americans is a strong belief in a Polish national character that can be transmitted over generations. Although Americans consider it undemocratic, most Europeans believe not only in a biological or cultural transmission of national character but also in regional variations (see also chapter 2). Actually, the Polish Americans have two images of Polish national character—one of the gentry or nobility, and the other of the peasantry although there is some overlap. Super (1939) describes the characteristics of the Poles as including: an emphasis on equality within the two main classes (gentry and peasantry) with a strong sense of individualism; tolerance of other groups; religiosity of primarily Catholic identity; idealism, romanticism; love of the soil; a "knightly" tradition, with a sense of dignity and honor; intellectual culture; a strong family orientation; hospitality; interest in good food and drink of an international flavor; stress on courtesy, etiquette, and manner highly developed and strictly followed. The negative traits he defined as: restriction, until recent years, of the women to the home and to minimal education; lack of concepts of sportsmanship, fair play, team work, and efficiency; and a lack of directness of approach and openness in interaction. This view is more characteristic of the gentry, intelligentsia, and urban middle-class self-image than the peasantry, but even Reymont's (1925) descriptions of the peasants contain references to many of these items.

The overlapping characteristics involve the internal egalitarianism within each class although "the social cleavage between peasants and szlachta (gentry) was absolute and unbridgeable" (Benet 1951:33). Within each class, however, there is an almost fanatical insistence on the equality of individuals. "A Pole would rather bow to a foreigner than give authority to one of his own group" (33). Like the gentry, the peasantry had elaborate rituals of social interaction. "The Polish peasant is probably the most polite and well mannered man in Europe. Rural etiquette prescribes certain expressions and even certain dialogues for everyday life and it is not permissible to improvise substitutes" (Benet 1951:216).

At the same time, the peasant image of national character had some very strong negative features. It contained a negative and distrusting image of human nature, as prone to sin and evil action requiring a strong set of social controls, and the belief that shame was an effective means of socializing people. "Adult society is presented to the child as an arena in which social relations are determined by a constant and cruel interplay of domination and subordination" (Finestone 1964; see also Zand 1956). The peasant character was also portrayed as anti-intellectual and lacking the romantic, "knightly" traditions, which deflected the directness of the individualistic status competition among the gentry.

The Polish American judgment of the national character combines elements of both the gentry and peasantry portrayals. The Polish Americans have internalized an image of themselves as the most individualistic and the least cooperative of all ethnic groups in this country; they thereby assume other groups to be different. As stated earlier this set of traits is used to explain failures in cooperative action as a consequence of the national character.

In addition to the image of the national character, from which different traits can be drawn by Polish Americans, there are many other cultural items and group identity sources that can be incorporated in the identity packages. Part of the problem in studying ethnicity is the complexity of sources from which people can draw ethnic identities. There are basically three cultures and three groups of people who provide content for these identities. The cultures are the Polish and American national cultures and the Polonian ethnic culture that has grown from the merging of the national cultures and from its own dynamism (see chapter 1). Knowledge of these cultures can produce feelings of identity, as the feeling of Polish identification when hearing Chopin, or American identification when hearing the "Star Spangled Banner." Thus, part of Polish American ethnic identity can stem from the Polish national culture. As stated before, most Polish Americans have not expressed strong knowledge and identification with this literary and artistic culture developed and disseminated by nationalistic leaders and schools teaching Polish culture. Not enough is really known about the Polonian culture that has grown in this ethnic community to know how and when it provides sources of cultural, rather than group, identity. Cultural identity can be limited to a folk rather than a national Polish culture, as in the case of many Carpathian mountaineers.

Another major source of ethnic identity is the people. Again, there are three sets of people with whom Polish Americans can identify: the Poles, the Americans, and the Polish Americans. Such feelings of "peoplehood," of being a member of a group, can be very strong sources of a person's identity. This source can be complicated by divisions within the group, or by class, region of origin, and so forth. For example, a "new emigration" Pole who came from the traditional gentry class in Poland has a very different identity package than does the descendant of the mountaineer immigrant of the "old emigration." His or her child also has a different identity package than does the first-generation immigrant of either the old or new emigration. The Connecticut farmer sees himself as a Polish American very differently than does the official of a Chicago-based superterritorial ethnic organization.

It is quite probable that each Polish American combines these sources uniquely, drawing different items of Polish, American, and Polonian cultures and identifying with different groups of Poles, Americans, and Polish Americans in his or her ethnic identity package. This is particularly likely to have happened as generational, geographic, educational, occupational, and life- style mobility have decrystallized the identity packages typical of the many subgroups of the Polish immigrants who have entered America within the past 100 years (see also Gordon 1964; Mostwin 1971; Znaniecki 1952).

Summary

The old emigration of Polish Americans has progressed from the first generation of largely uneducated former peasants living in poor, urban ethnic neighborhoods, to the financially well-off second generation that did not use higher education as a means of upward mobility and thus stayed in blue-collar jobs and life-styles, to the increasingly educated third and fourth generations who can be expected to move up the socioeconomic ladder. The second cohort was more likely to adopt American life-styles, but to retain identification with, and knowledge of, the Polish national culture. The newest cohort is the most Polish and least apt to identify with Polonian life and culture.

Polonia has been able to survive the disorganizing and "demoralizing" effects of the migration, low status in American society and partial loss of Polish folk culture as a unifying force, with the help of the strong status competition in a background of individualistic need for cooperation from social unit members, the complexity of its organizational structure, and the constant infusion of Poles and Poland's needs. The new generations of Polish Americans are physically, and for the most part culturally, indistinguishable from the dominant groups, and the choice of items for continued ethnic identification will depend to a great extent on the new social movements in Polonia. Encouragement of ethnic identification by Polonia's leaders, especially by the intelligentsia of the newest cohort, could affect even those Americans of Polish descent who do not know or identify with Polishness, possibly converting them into "Americans of Polish heritage."

Most of the studies of ethnic identity among Polish Americans have been very limited in scope. They conclude that mobility through generations and upward through the socioeconomic class system diminishes ethnic identity because they measure it by old emigration folk or peasant culture criteria. Inevitably then, movement out of the culture of the peasant into more middle-class and upper-class identifications and life-styles must be defined as a loss of ethnicity. In other words, when Polish American ethnicity is measured by peasant folk culture criteria, those persons who are no longer, or never have been, peasants are apt to be defined as having lost their ethnicity. There is a need for in-depth studies of Polonian culture. One hundred years of its existence must have resulted in more than just a loss of imported characteristics and selective acquisition of American traits. What is Polonian culture, as a unique ethnic product?

If the activity of the intelligentsia and the organizational leaders in Polonia is successful, the whole base of this ethnic identity may change. We can assume that upward mobility will increase the social life space of Polish Americans, extending it through all three communities and cultures—the Polish, the Polish American, and the American—with a modification of the content of identity from folk to national, from generationally transmitted memories to an ideational ethnic community. If these trends are sufficiently strong, we would then need to change the content of the ethnicity scales being administered to the different generations of both emigrations of Poles, Polish Americans, and Americans of Polish heritage.

Polish names are increasingly visible in the mass media and on all but the top levels of political life. This upsurge may be due to three factors. One is the returning to original spelling and whole name constellation by Polish Americans whose ancestors (and possibly who themselves) went through name changes to Americanize themselves in the past (Kotlarz 1963; Zagraniczny 1963). The second possibility is that the descendants of the first two cohorts of immigrants are now moving up into greater visibility. The newest cohort of immigrants may also be increasing their involvement in the greater American society. Mostwin (1969, 1971, 1991) found fewer marital and parental problems among the second, World War II cohort of Poles in America. The parents' families were more likely to be educated at least beyond the equivalence of high school, and to be dispersed. The recorded violence of the peasant families is not evident in these studies. The rate of acculturation appears much faster among these families, and the items of Polish culture that are preserved are more on the national culture than on the village or folk level. Conflict with children mainly focuses on their absorption of American ideas concerning intergender relations and, in general, permissiveness.

Notes

1. More Polish Americans list Polish as their mother tongue than list parents as having been born in Poland. This indicates that some members of third and later generations are being raised in homes still using the Polish language (see table 6.1).
2. "Foreign stock" includes people born in Poland, and children born in the United States whose parents (one or both) were born in Poland. Many Polish families in the United Sates are still made up of immigrants (some of whom identify as "Poles") in addition to the second generations (usually identified as "Polish American" but occasionally referred to as "Americans of Polish descent") and the newest generation (to whom Polonia likes to refer as "Americans of Polish heritage").
3. Of special relevance here is the conglomerate sample developed by Greeley (1969b, 1971, 1974b) out of studies conducted by the National Opinion Research Center and the Michigan Survey Research Center.
4. There was an attempt to relocate "displaced persons in the Deep South" after World War II (Heberle 1951) and there has been a recent dispersal into the more leisure-oriented temperate regions of California, Arizona, and Florida.
5. Their index of segregation from the natives of native parentage ranged from 57.1 (out of 100 which would be complete segregation) in Boston to 70.5 in Buffalo as late as 1930 (Lieberson 1963).

6. This is the main reason for the deviation of the Polish American mean educational achievement scores in the Duncan and Duncan (1968) and Nam (1959) analyses of deviations from the non-African American national mean.

7. The Greeley analyses of the Catholics in America would indicate that this change is more than a reflection of the presence of Polish Jews in the census sample. Admittedly, I would feel more comfortable about the assumption that non-Jewish Polish Americans were contributing a major part of this increase if the table contained a Jewish ethnic origin group, since the Russian median is probably influenced by the presence of people socialized in the Jewish culture.

8. Kusielewicz (1973:104) specifically stated, "Is it any wonder, then, that our young clergy of Polish American background look upon their Polishness as a liability and that they reflect this view in the administration of their parishes and the schools attached to them." The teaching orders themselves, according to Kusielewicz, "suffer the same feeling of inferiority that is characteristic of the greater part of the Polish American community" (101). His point is that there is a vicious circle of ignorance of Polish culture being transmitted by the teachers of parochial schools to students, some of whom then become seminarians and future teachers of the young."

9. The American government was periodically concerned with the probability of its immigrant population contributing to the crime rates, particularly in its cities, and asked for investigations in 1911 and in 1931. According to Bowler (1931), the foreign-born Polish criminal rates were decreasing in the years between 1925 and 1929 from a higher level between 1915 and 1919 (83–193). In the late 1920s their rates were below the rates of the Mexicans, African Americans, native whites, Lithuanians, and, in some places, Greeks. In 1926 the Poles were underrepresented in relation to their proportion in the population, both in terms of total figures and in all categories but rape (154).

10. Certain Polish neighborhoods had very high second generation youth juvenile delinquency rates (Fleis-Fava 1950:11). The area around the settlement house began to be heavily Polish by 1899 and remained so until the 1920s. In the sixteenth ward, "80.7 percent of the foreign-born whites [were] Poles, while the Poles made up only 17.7 percent of the foreign-born white population in the city as a whole" (18). Crime rates were very high in those years.

11. Zand (1959:30) also states that "divorces and separations were indeed rare among American Poles, while desertions were more frequent" but she gives no statistics to support this contention.

12. See also Johnson's (1969) description of the youth of Polish parents in Australia and Dunin-Markowicz's (1972) study of Canadian children of Polish parents.

13. This last group falls into three subcategories:
1. the person who perceives himself as an American but believes that he is perceived as Polish by both the Americans and the Poles in Poland
2. the person who considers himself an American and believes himself to be an American in the eyes of Poles in Poland, but thinks that Americans consider him Polish
3. the person who considers himself American, believes he is perceived as American by Americans but as Polish by Poles in Poland (Mostwin 1971:56–57).

7

Life in Polonia

A careful examination of life in Polonia reveals the significance of several sociological principles: the presence of "ethclass" (Gordon 1964) and other complexities of social structures (Hughes 1934; Wirth 1928; Kramer 1970); the ability of an ethnic community to maintain itself in spite of territorial subdivisions and even dispersal (Etzioni 1959); and the overlap between the life of an ethnic community and that of the larger society (Lopata 1954). The concept of "ethclass" was coined by Gordon (1964) after an examination of the American scene, which concluded "With regard to cultural behavior, differences of social class are more important and decisive than differences of ethnic group," and "with regard to social participation in primary groups and primary relationships, people tend to confine these to their own social class segment within their own ethnic group—that is, to the ethclass" (52). Gordon (1964:51) thus refers to "the subsociety created by the intersection of the vertical stratification of ethnicity with the horizontal stratifications of social class as the ethclass."

Etzioni (1959) has pointed out to sociologists that ethnic communities do not have to be geographically or territorially bounded, with members of the same ethnic group inhabiting an area devoid of other people, or with all members living in such settlements. The community can function through interaction and identification by people who are territorially scattered, individually, in family units, or in many local communities and settlements. This is the main point of our definition of American Polonia as a superterritorial ethnic community.

There are several aspects of the Polonian situation that bear more detailed discussion. In describing life in Polonia we must limit ourselves to the activities of the community and its subgroups, not of people who could be identified as Polish Americans by descent but not by association. We focus our attention on people who belong to one or more of Polonia's organizations, participate in its web of polite companionship relations (Znaniecki 1965: chapter 8) and interaction scenes, and maintain a community "reputation" in that their status in at least one of its companionate circles is known and compared to the status of their peers, people immediately below and people immediately above. Each local parish, neighborhood, settlement, and local community has its own circles of companionate relations, drawing in life-style and interaction people of similar social status and involvement in Polonian life. Each level of community has its own set of hierarchies, depending on its size, length of establishment, internal differentiation, and location vis-à-vis other ethnic groups. The members of Polonia vary as to the size and complexity of the *okolica* within which their personal or family reputation is contained, ranging from the parish to Polonia as a whole, or even the cosmopolitan world.[1] People whose reputations are limited to a parish *okolica* are known only to a few people because they are not active in the web of organizational life beyond it, are not mentioned in the press of any but the parish newsletter, and have no other means of establishing themselves in a larger territorial and social arena. People with a Polonian reputation are active at national levels in the superterritorial organizations, have their activities reported in periodicals reaching members all over the country, and take advantage of many occasions for personal contact with local communities and other leaders.

Polonia's Companionate Circles

The *okolica*—not territorially but socially circumscribed—within which a person's or a family's reputation is contained consists of three companionate relations circles: the one in which she or he is involved, the one immediately below, and the one immediately above. A companionate circle is a loosely bound group of people from the same ethclass who interact with each other, belong to the same organizations, lead a similar style of life, and are identified by others as belonging to the same circle (see figure 7.1). The circle contains peers, or near peers with whom people feel comfortable in both primary and secondary interaction. The boundaries of companionate circles are penetrable, and status decrystallization allows for mobility and overlapping, so that Polish Americans can belong to two or more circles and organizations devoted to their needs and composed of their members. There are identifiable circles in Polonia, which are differentiated by life-style, personnel, and content of companionate activity. In general, the lower the social class, the more geographically limited are the companionate circles. The *okolica* is larger than the companionate circle because the circles at the upper and lower boundaries of that circle are usually aware of his or her reputation and membership within it.

The web of social relationships within Polonia involves Polish Americans at different levels of commitment and at different levels of community life. There is a core of organizational officials, people engaged full-time in its economic life through businesses or the professions, the mass communication media workers, the priests, and the active members of the parishes. Without them and their replacements the community could not continue to exist. There are other

Figure 7.1
Polonia's Companionate Circles

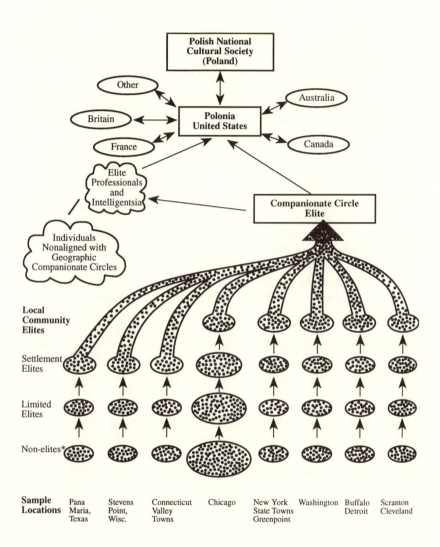

**Actually potential elites, in that the status competition, dependent upon status decrystallization, allows for mobility in the system at each level.

people who participate only at certain hours, while working or in leisure, or only occasionally. They come to the headquarters of the activity, the "Polish Home," or organizational club rooms, and informal meeting locales from other neighborhoods, for special occasions, to contribute their skills or objects, or to buy or witness the skills of others; or they meet in outside locations with people of similar interests. They keep the flow of events possible, sometimes moving it outside the community's remaining geographical core, if such a core exists. The open boundaries of the community mean that even people who have moved away from the traditional Polish or Polish American neighborhood are welcomed back at specific times or for acknowledged reasons. Some of those who participate in the community life never resided in localities with heavy concentrations of their fellow Poles or Polish American ethnics. The second generation Polish American doctor who lives in an integrated neighborhood and never contributes to Polonia's activities is simply not part of its life and we are not considering him here, but the doctor similarly located who is active in the Polish National Medical and Dental association is part of the community's life even if it is not a major part of his life.

Several factors influence a family's reputation and membership in a companionate relations circle. Most members of Polonia are not status crystallized—their positions in different status hierarchies are sufficiently inconsistent to prevent an indisputable and permanent status package. This inconsistency or "status decrystallization" is the necessary condition for building Polonia's engrossing status competition. The old emigration and temporary residents tended to be in one of two mutually exclusive, boundary maintaining, classes: the gentry and the peasants. The latter social class was, however, especially heterogeneous according to internal standards that affected their willingness to share companionate relations. The subclasses discussed by Szczepanski (see chapter 2) were extremely important, as was the place of birth in Poland. The peasant emigrants from German-occupied Poland and from larger villages or towns associated only with each other and looked down on the "more primitive" easterners and mountaineers. Due to the tendency of many Poles from the same area in Poland to migrate and settle together, personal and family reputations followed people across the ocean so that even small settlements in America contained their elites.

The first centers of community activity in America were the parishes (Thomas and Znaniecki 1918-1920). These served as the *okolica* or the areas within which reputations were contained for most of the emigrants. Gradually, with the development of nonreligious and territorially more expansive organizations, the community expanded the opportunities for social contact, drawing together those people who had common interests beyond that of neighborhood proximity or immediate needs. The internal differentiation of the community resulted in the formation of several loosely bounded or firmly overlapping memberships. Simultaneously, the uniting of neighborhoods into Polonia as a whole further broadened the scope of ethclass identification and association.[2]

In the meantime, of course, the original internal differentiation and the diversity produced by upward mobility of the former peasants and their descendants (Hughes and Hughes 1952) filled empty rungs of the social status ladder. The push into middle-class status was attained by members of the old emigration through higher education, business activity, or prestigious occupation. The second cohort of World War II reinforced both the higher level and the expanding middle level. Most of the Poles who entered at the higher status level were political émigrés of both emigrations who stayed long enough to organize the People's University, the Socialist party, or the Esperanto Club, and to start the national press (rather than ethnic press, which was limited to local Polonian interests). Some people, particularly of the World War II cohort, finally settled in America after years of expecting to return to Poland. Others of nonpeasant background participated in Polonia only marginally while generally living and keeping apart from the community that they branded as operating on a cultural level well below theirs. It is this feeling that has until recently kept the first two emigrations and even their descendants apart in different companionate circles, and is definitely isolating the newest cohort. The newest temporary emigration, made up of the *wakacjusze* who do not plan to stay after reaching a certain level of savings, has kept apart from the companionate circles of all three cohorts. These people are often of middle-class background, have higher education, and possess occupational skills that they can use if they know English. Many are young, meaning in their 30s, financially ambitious, and reject the life they see in the Polish American communities. How many will remain in America is hard to predict, as are their future relations with the other Polish Americans. Of course, the same difficulty of predicting permanence of American residence was true of prior emigrations, since so few Poles came with the declared desire to stay. This attitude seems to have also been true of the Greeks (Moskos 1990), but more so among the Poles, for reasons discussed earlier.

An important variable in all companionate circle interaction is, of course, the availability and convenience of contact. People who live far apart and who are not accustomed to using indirect forms of interaction may not be able to share much of their lives with others whom they consider their peers in Polonia. We will now examine the composition of several of Polonia's companionate circles.

The Intelligentsia

The intelligentsia forms probably the most geographically scattered companionate circle of Polish Americans. Some members (such as newspaper editors of the ethnic or national press) are located in the heart of the community, while others (those associated with various teaching, research, or artistic centers, and a variety of economic organizations) are apt to be living outside of the geographical confines of Polish American settlements. The circle consists of first-generation emigrants of the post-World War II cohort, the refugees and ex-combatants, or recent émigrés, plus the artists and other intellectuals of succeeding generations. Many members of the intelligentsia pride themselves in speaking literary Polish, but are necessarily bilingual if involved in American work organizations. Relatively few of the second-generation members are fluid in that language, specially in their fields of specialization, so conferences are often held in English. The intelligentsia tends to have a cosmopolitan outlook, keeping in touch with international events but retaining a strong interest in Poland, and its members read publications of fellow Polish intellectuals in other parts of the world. The intelligentsia is geographically mobile and meets with fellow nationals at scientific gatherings or "cultural events" such as concerts, speeches or meetings. Members also keep in touch indirectly through correspondence and through each other's visible products of work.

The intelligentsia can include people whose occupational status is not usually associated with intellectual or artistic endeavor. This is due to two main factors: the meaning of the intelligentsia in Poland (as discussed in chapter 2), and the presence of people who were forced out of a particular occupational background in Poland and were unable to transfer it to the American society. The Polish class system defined the intelligentsia not in terms of occupation, or professional and technical proficiency, but in terms of the combination of demeanor, knowledge of literary and artistic culture, and association with others of the "cultured man" or "cultured woman" class. This package of personal traits separated, for example, the businessman from a member of the intelligentsia even if the former had many more economic resources with which to buy artistic goods. It also accounted for the lower social position given to doctors, lawyers, and engineers. By the same token, a lawyer or businessman could belong to the intelligentsia if his life-style and demeanor were appropriate. Within the intelligentsia, the highest status was accorded to professors holding full academic positions in the universities.

The right and ability to retain intelligentsia status even when holding an inferior occupational position developed in Poland and has been institutionalized in Polonia. Involuntary emigration or forced expulsion from Poland often occurred, especially when the country was occupied by foreign powers. The intelligentsia was the most likely of the social classes to be taking an active part in political revolts or to be defined by the occupying powers as dangerous. (This is why the Nazis and the Soviets tried to remove that layer of the Polish society permanently and why so many who survived did not return to Poland). Often their occupations could not be transferred to the country of settlement because they were dependent upon language skills or because the bearer did not have high enough cosmopolitan status to be offered equivalent positions by the dominant society. Polonia, in America and elsewhere, simply could not absorb into its own institutions the large numbers of educated refugee Poles. Neither could America absorb refugees from other European countries affected by Nazism (Coser 1984). Many Poles had to obtain positions inferior to those traditionally identified with the intelligentsia (Mostwin 1971). Such immigrants have tried to maintain the life-style and circle of association that would retain their class identification, and the community has generally allowed such a status claim in spite of the occupational and often financial decrystallization.

In addition to the participants in the intelligentsia companionate circles described above, there are a few members of the clergy, but only if they share the "cultured" demeanor and life-style. The Polish American clergy itself is highly decrystallized in status, not so much in terms of the hierarchy in the Roman Catholic church, but in terms of education and cosmopolitan versus local orientation. The intelligentsia, although geographically dispersed, has been able to organize occasions for contact. Several major events have brought together members of this companionate circle: the congresses of Polish American Scholars and Scientists, meeting in North America, and the meetings of the Scholars of Polish Descent in Poland. The congresses have been organized by the Polish Institute of Arts and Sciences in America. The first congress drew 470 participants and 150 guests, some of whom were not of Polish descent (Zeranska 1971). Almost all, however, had been born in Poland. The tendency of the intelligentsia to cross ethnic community lines in America (Gordon 1964) is also evidenced by the presence of many Polish Jews who share Polish culture and scientific interest with Poles of other religions. The Fiftieth Anniversary International Congress of the Institute was held at Yale University in 1992.

The congresses of the Scholars of Polish Descent in Poland, organized by the Committee for the Study of Polonias Outside of its Borders, of the Polish Academy of Sciences, of the Society for Union with the Polonias, and of the Polish government have taken place on several occasions. The last one before the overthrow of the communist government involved cooperation of the American-based Kosciuszko Foundation and the Polish Institute of Arts and Sciences in America and drew Poles from various parts of the world. All four congresses used both Polish and English as languages of communication, but their products are published in Polish alone.[3] The latest conference, The World Assembly of Polonians and Poles held in August 1992 in Krakow, focused on Polish national culture and religious events. Its basic purpose was to develop and institutionalize ties between Poland and the various Polonias (see chap. 4).

Some members of Polonia's intelligentsia meet at the annual convention of the Polish American Historical Association, which is held in conjunction with the meetings of the American Historical Society. They also interact at other events sponsored by organizations devoted to their interests on less than national, but regional and local levels. Lectures, concerts, and art exhibits draw Polish

Americans to the Center for Polish Studies and Culture at the Orchard Lake Schools and Seminary in Michigan (*Polish American Congress News Letter,* 15 July 1969:7). Special events at the Kosciuszko or Pilsudski Foundation in New York, the newly reactivated Polish Museum in Chicago, or the American Institute of Polish Culture in Miami, can draw the intelligentsia from a wide geographical area.

Professional and Business Elites

The second type of elite in Polonia that forms its own companionate circle is the professional. Doctors, lawyers, and dentists are not given as much prestige in Poland as are the "cultured" intelligentsia (Szczepanski 1962) because their professions are considered technical rather than intellectual. However, they have acquired some of the prestige associated with such professions in America. In addition, some professionals claim intelligentsia status. The professional specialists in different activities, such as medicine, law, and education, have separate societies and publish their own journals.

A perfect example of a professional circle is that of the teachers of Polish language, history and related subjects. In the early years of Polonia's formation, these were mainly priests and members of Polish sisterhoods. The religious members of following generations lost their ability to teach in Polish and decreased in number, as lay teachers took their place. The second wave or cohort of immigrants contained numerous people who had been teachers or white-collar workers in education in Poland. They revitalized and changed the content of the schools, wishing their children to learn the Polish national culture, of less interest in the past. The third-wave teachers again revitalized the educational system, in the form of Saturday schools that engaged in many other "cultural" activities in the community. These professionals and related workers are organized under the auspices of the educational commission of the Polish American Congress and publish a quarterly, *The Teacher's Voice* (*Glos Nauczyciela*). The journal was first published in 1985 and the newness of the organization is attested by the fact that only the third such conference took place in 1989. It focused on methods of transmission of the culture in various centers. Teachers also belong to the Center of Polish Continuation Schools in America and the Association of Polish Teachers in America. In other words, there are many resources for Polish and Polish American teachers situated in a variety of locations to keep in contact with each other.

The business elites include a few millionaires, such as Edward Piszek, the founder of Mrs. Paul's Kitchen (consumer fish products), who has been so active in organizing "Project: Pole" (see chapter 5); some manufacturers, specifically heads of sausage-making firms; people holding high positions in insurance, banking, and similar ventures; broadcast media personalities; and travel agents.

Emmons (1971) studied the members of what he called the "Polish American Business and Professional Men's Association" in Chicago and found that most of the men were self-made (see also the Michigan State Chamber of Commerce's *Michigan's Challenge: The Polish Americans of Michigan* 1972). Emmons found a "marked pattern of upward mobility" among economic elites although few had fathers who "graduated from high school compared to adult white males and even other Poles" (205). Chicago's economic elite does not necessarily live in the ethnic community (where many have clients or customers). Although 96 percent of the members who responded to Emmons's questionnaire had been brought up in a neighborhood where the Poles were the largest ethnic group, only 47 percent are now living in areas of such ethnic preponderance (113). This means that the companionate circle draws people territorially scattered in their home life. This distribution exists in spite of the fact that the "Business and Professional Men's Association" members tend to be of foreign stock—17 percent were born in Poland, 65 percent were born in America of foreign or mixed parents, and only 19 percent were born in America of native parentage. Emmons concludes that

> normal class factors are operating to pull the elite in higher status ethnic roles away from the old neighborhood. This interpretation is consistent with eth-class theory, supports my contention that higher-status ethnic leadership roles contribute to mobility in the wider society, but contradicts my contention that upwardly mobile ethnic leaders show greater commitment to the ethnic group than do the general ethnic population. (115)

The last comment is based on the assumption that ethnic commitment would encourage the elite to remain in the ethnic neighborhood.

According to Emmons, the elite shared conservative attitudes toward the black civil rights movement, toward intellectuals (they tended to agree with former Vice President Agnew's "impudent snobs" comment), and toward "rebellious youth" (they felt that the United States "is leaning too much toward socialism") (124–28). These attitudes were judged much more conservative than those of a matched sample of non-Polish professional, technical, and managerial white males. Such attitudes are apt to both encourage and result from interaction and intercommunication.

There are now new, very active, and often interwoven business and professional elites in Polonia, consisting of members of the more established new cohort and young descendants of older cohorts. They are involved in such activities as real estate, law, banking, construction, publishing and other media, entertainment, food processing, and other retail establishment. Many participate in a variety of joint ventures in Poland.

Political and Organizational Elites

For the most part, Polish Americans have not been very influential in American politics until recent years. However, there are sufficient numbers of persons who now hold or have held political office to form a political elite. This group's members are often associated with the business, professional, or organizational elites because that was their initial status location before they entered politics. Members of this elite have had the sponsorship of the major organizations of their community, otherwise they would not have won office or been appointed. They spend a great deal of time interacting with people upon whose vote they are directly or indirectly dependent.

The organizational leaders form several levels of interactional circles. The top circle is composed of the presidents and main officers of the major organizations. In these top circles a person often retains his or her status even after he or she has left the office. Most of the officers of Polonia's major organizations are in their positions for many years. The first president of the Polish American Congress, for example, held that office for 24 years. Each organization and each locality has its own elite.

Parish Life

Thomas and Znaniecki (1918-1920) found 70 organized groups in the Chicago parish of Swietego Stanislawa Kostki (St. Stanislaus Kostka). The size and complexity of activity appears to have continued over the years. There are still active Polish parishes in the United States. The *Informator Polonii w USA* 1980-81, published by the *Daily News* in New York identifies numerous parishes as Polish. The names of the priests and the locations would indicate that at least some parishioners identify with this national or ethnic group. An unidentified number of the churches have gone back to using Polish in the masses to draw the third cohort, with the help of Polish priests trained at the Old Orchard Seminary. As stated before, St. Hyacinth in Chicago's Jackowo holds four Polish masses each Sunday, allegedly drawing over 2,000 people.

"Solidarnosc" and Other Third Cohort Circles

The recent arrivals from Poland to Polonia form their own companionate circles. Having lived through the dramatic changes of the 1980s and fought communism in a variety of nonviolent ways, they generally do not like what Erdmans (see chapter 9) calls the established Polonia. There is even some tension in relations with the World War II political exiles who had different experiences, in the underground and active combat.

One might have expected the large Polish American community to help ease the transition [of emigration]. Instead, there were tensions and conflicts. . . . The Polonia leadership was threatened by the arrival of the Solidarity immigrants, and did not know what to do with them. They were not welcomed as the heroes they considered themselves, and it can also be fairly argued that Polonia organizations and parishes should have provided more social services for the new arrivals. (Blejwas 1992: 84,85)

The newest cohort tried joining organizations such as the Polish American Congress, but were rebuffed and withdrew, claiming they "have nothing to say to each other" (quoted in Blejwas 1992: 85). Blejwas points out in his review of Krajewski's book, which contains interviews with members of Solidarity, that neither side really understood the needs of the other. The newcomers wanted to take over leadership positions in the old Polonia, but found these filled by people they considered socially inferior and lacking any knowledge of Polish culture. They, in turn, are seen as ignorant of American culture within which Polonia is, after all, located. The older cohorts, who consider themselves as successful in organizational life, feel the newest cohort needs knowledge as to business affairs in a democracy and is unwilling to listen. The hostility is apparent in interviews that Mary Erdmans and I conducted in Chicago, New York, and California. The new arrivals feel comfortable only with each other, having obtained most of the help from Poles in the same situation and not from the established Polonia. They tell each other horror stories about life in central parts of Polonia. One respondent in New York called Chicago's Polonia "brutal." Those members of the third cohort who are able to do so, stay away from the main centers, living relatively dispersed and returning only for church celebrations, foods, or services. One of the priests in Chicago has observed that the relationship between the newest immigrants and the church is different from that of the other two cohorts. The latest cohort tends to contribute for special occasions, but not to feel an obligation to support the church on a steady basis, resenting being told that it has to put in a certain amount each Sunday. They are much more likely to learn English and to be able to find occupations not too far below the level of those they held back home within five or so years, or, as noted above, to socialize on the basis of past status. Their social interaction tends to involve small groups of people with similar backgrounds. They are very much interested in what is going on in Poland, and tend to relive their experiences there or those of initial life in America. They are shocked at the ignorance of Americans and especially Polish Americans concerning Poland. They have started their own slick, "American Illustrated Weekly Modern Magazines" in Polish with news of Poland and other countries, comments on American events, sports, love, or immigration stories and a great deal of often ironic humor for which Polish culture is noted.

The same can be said of the *wakacjusze*, who tend to socialize with each other. They join relatives or others who have preceded them, much as have the previous migrants. Two major settlements draw these temporary visitors, Jackowo, or the area around St. Hyacinth's parish in Chicago, and Greenpoint in Brooklyn, although there is a scattering of such people elsewhere, wherever knowledge is available as to easy ways of getting a job. The local newspapers of such areas constantly run advertisements of jobs, even placing them in the Polish press with a national distribution.

The type of job they are able to obtain can determine where the temporary Poles reside and how they manage daily life. Contact with the family is made mainly through letters carried personally by intermediaries who are going to Poland. Packages and money are also delivered this way, especially during the communist control because of censorship.

The social life of most wakacjusze is limited to Saturday night, when they meet in newly formed dancing clubs or are out to meet members of the opposite sex. They often leave a spouse and children back in Poland and are lonely. Sunday is for going to church and then to a restaurant or each other's homes for dinner, one of the few special treats. According to Rokicki (1989: 115) their relationship with established Polonia, even with the third-cohort immigrants, is symbiotic; they are dependent upon intermediaries for jobs, housing, and other services. The stories told by them to writers and interviewers such as Mary Erdmans and me are full of being cheated, stolen from, and in general exploited by their "co-nationals" with great resentment—"our people are not supposed to cheat our people." The older cohorts, on the other hand, feel that the jobs the wakacjusze and other illegal workers take are lowering Polish American social status for which they have worked so hard. They repeatedly hear the same story: "the Polish cleaning ladies are so good—everyone has them." Americans of other backgrounds usually have contact with the wakacjusze only if they employ them as servants without knowing anything about them.

Other Companionate Circles

The middle range of Polonia's companionate circles includes religious personnel and ex-combatants, in separate groups. The ex-combatants form one of the most active and mutually interactive clusters of groups. Their members, particularly if they served during World War II and in the Polish Armed Services, tend to retain sufficient contact to form a definite companionate circle. The clergy, on the other hand, is internally highly differentiated, mostly by age and education. For example, the highly educated heads of major schools or specialists in scientific fields are part of the intelligentsia, as mentioned before, or are involved with organizational elites. The parish priests are often the leaders of their neighborhoods, especially in the absence of competing elites. The companionate circle of the parish priest depends not only on his personal status, but also on the match between his status and that of his parishioners. Some nuns who have acquired higher status than their orders are assigned in the community, due to their leadership positions, because they act as representatives of the religious circle, or because of individually acquired education or skills.

Emmons (1971) found another elite and companionate circle, made up of the top of the blue-collar classes in "the Polka world" which is still very active in the 1990s. The circle contains "personalities" connected with the playing, recording, or mass broadcasting of polka music, the bands, and their fans. Although most of the bands perform only as a second vocation, the "Polka world" involves a whole ideological and economic substructure. The performers are paid, belong in some cases to unions, play in lounges, at weddings, and, particularly during summer months, at numerous "pikniks" and other occasions drawing working-class Polish Americans together. The circle includes the fans, brought together not only by contact but by sharing a "working-class leisure culture with community values of happiness, merrymaking, nonviolence and ethnic-kin-peer loyalty" (Emmons 1971:173). The members of the Polka Federation communicate news of events in different localities through two periodicals and get together annually in Chicago for three days of festivities and competition. The members of the Chicago branch whom Emmons (1971) studied are much more apt to be third-generation Polish Americans than are members of the Polish Business and Professional Men's Association. Most of them were born in Polish neighborhoods and most of them still live in such areas, partly because their fans and clients are still so located, as are the lounges where they play or hear polka music (Emmons 1971:116). Most of the members have not gone beyond high school. They are the second- and third-generation Polish Americans who have risen to the top of the working-class community to become leaders in one of the few nonparish circles tied to folk ethnic culture. Interestingly, the polka world elite is not restricted to Polonia in organizational membership: the respondents to Emmons's, (1971) questionnaire list a median of three non-ethnic groups. (These memberships were not specified so we do not know if the groups were or were not composed mainly of fellow ethnics.)

Polonia Today of 1992 contains pages of polka news and polka radio information. For example a Polka Spectacular was held on Memorial Day in Chicago; two parishes in Dayville, Ohio combined forces to "provide two full days of family polka fun at a 'Polka Festival Weekend'"; and New London, Connecticut held an annual "Polkabration Festival." "If the number of new album releases indicates the health of the polka field, things are going well, indeed" (*Polonia Today*, June 1992: 19). The International Polka Association held a balloting for selection to the Polka Music Hall of Fame and the annual Polka Music Awards.

Interaction among Companionate Circles

Generally speaking, the Polish American intelligentsia does not get along comfortably with the political, economic, or organizational elites. One organization that brings the four types of elites together, and even contains some members of the less prestigious classes in some member clubs, is the American

Council of Polish Cultural Clubs. The member clubs arrange artistic events that draw both Polish and non-Polish audiences. Their activities vary considerably according to the composition of the club. For example in 1969 the Musicians Club of Phoenix presented a salute to Poland featuring women composers of that country. In 1972 the Polish Heritage Club of Grand Rapids, Michigan arranged a month-long exhibit of Polish Christmas customs (*The Quarterly Review*, January–March 1972:8), while the Washington, D.C. Polish American Arts Association in 1973 organized a puppet nativity scene based on Polish customs, speeches on Copernicus, an essay contest in conjunction with the U. S. projected celebration of its 200-year anniversary of independence, and so forth.

The various Polonian elites (mainly the white-collar ones) get together for special occasions that draw people from many organizational and even community sources. For example, the president of the Museum of Science and Industry in Chicago, who is not a Polish American, invited a number of university professors, members of the Polish Institute of Arts and Sciences in America, and organizational and mass communication leaders to the opening of a Copernican Exhibition at the museum. The Copernican celebrations all over the country drew local elites and the main banquet in New York drew them from all over Polonia.

The elites of the national scene and in the major settlements attend other social events, most of which are organized at regular intervals, such as the debutante or charity "balls" or dinner dances. The daily newspapers that service organizational members scattered throughout the United States announce and describe such events and the names of participants become known superterritorially. The professional elites, the associations of ex-combatants, women's clubs, and many of the other more prestigious associations have regular social events, inviting the members of other professions and companionate peers in other elites. The elite circles, and many peripheral members, including both generations of the second emigration and members of the third cohort, attend performances of Polish and Polonian artists, such as the Warsaw Philharmonic, the Mazowsze dancers, various theater groups, and concerts of individual pianists, violinists, and singers. Chicago used to have a permanent Polish theater, and even now it still musters together a cast for a special Polish play or operetta. For example, "Student Beggar," a play based on an important event in Polish history, was performed in both Polish and English in Milwaukee in 1973; a Polish-language comedy toured Polonia's local communities the next year. Plays written by Poles in Poland or located outside of its borders frequently tour the United States in the 1990s.

Interelite events that draw Polish Americans from many classes include the traditional 3 May celebrations of Polish Constitution Day (which usually consists of a parade with folk costumes and bands, and speeches by Polish

American and American political leaders). Such parades, similar to those of other ethnic and special interest groups, serve many functions, the most important being public recognition. Such recognition can have a two-directional benefit, increasing or at least maintaining identification with Polonia and possibly with Poland on the part of Polish Americans, and increasing or at least maintaining status within the general American society. A brief description of one such parade can serve as an example of many such yearly events. Aware of the importance of Polonia as a source of votes, the president of the United States of America proclaimed 11 October 1991 as General Pulaski Memorial Day and October 1991 as Polish American Heritage Month. A 55th Pulaski Day Parade was held on Fifth Avenue in New York City that year, with the help of many local and regional Polonian organizations in appropriate attire. This included the Polish American Veterans Association; Polish Army Veterans Association; Association of Polish Combatants; Pulaski Cadets; New Generation of Polish Falcons; Polish girl and boy scouts; women from the Krakow district; the Polish & Slavic Federal Credit Union of Brooklyn; the Highlanders; members of Liga Morska (Sea League); various sports clubs; New Polonia club from Bayonne, New Jersey; the Polish American Club of Toms River, New Jersey; the Holy Name of Jesus Parish from Stamford, Connecticut; the Bayway Polish Dancers; and the chorus of Polish Parish of St. Franciszek de Chantal. This partial listing shows the wide range of local communities and groups that contribute to an ethnic day parade. Add the friends and relatives who accompany them, and the Polish Americans in the New York area who come to watch the parade, and you have sizable evidence of the continued existence of at least some form of ethnic identification.

Another occasion for Polonian social events is the visit of Polish leaders. Cardinal Karol Wojtyla toured the major Polonian cities while still in the Polish hierarchy and returned later as Pope John Paul II. The Polish Primate Cardinal Glemp visited the United States in 1991, as did Nobel Peace Prize winner and president of Poland Lech Walesa. All such occasions call for banquets, mass in Polish American Catholic churches, and speeches to large crowds. Walesa's 1991 trip included Washington, D.C., New York, Brooklyn, Chicago, and Los Angeles.

Associations organize social events to bring together not only their members but peers in "sister" groups and other elites at the same status level. Those events are part of Polonia's life throughout the social structure. Invitations to such parties range from formal engraved invitations (typical of Copernican dinners) to the broad "all our friends in Polonia" newspaper announcements. Often, the middle- and lower-range groups list the names of officers of the higher levels of organizational structure and community leaders who are expected to attend a social event. As mentioned before, the social status of the hosting group is measured by the importance of the persons in attendance and there is strong feeling over the slight implied by the failure of the appropriate companionate circle members to attend. Local groups also compete for status as measured by the excellence of the band, the size of attendance, the extra activities, and the meeting of goals.

The associational style of events among the different companionate circles drawing upon their own members differs not only in the manner of invitation, but in the appearance of the guests and the hosts, the content of the activity and flow of action, the foods and beverages served, the manner of serving, and the closing ceremonies. The language spoken, the forms of humor, and the manner of deference and demeanor also vary considerably. The elites meet in country clubs, fashionable hotels, and independent restaurants. They wear formal clothing at major events, and dinner is preceded by a "cocktail hour" (adopted from American culture). Waiters serve French or American style foods at tables laid with a variety of crystal, china, and silverware. The working-class social events, on the other hand, are likely to take place in meeting halls with folding chairs, tables decorated by paper covers, mugs without saucers, liquor or "pop" bottles standing on the tables, and plain silverware. The serving is "family style"—the dishes are brought from the kitchen by women in cooking clothes and passed from person to person. The working class menu contains the standard peasant fare of potatoes, sauerkraut, Polish sausage, "pierogi" or dumplings filled with plums, cheese, cabbage or meat, and other dishes identified as typically Polish (see menus in most lower- or even middle-class Polish restaurants and recipes in such books as the Michigan State Chamber of Commerce's *Michigan's Challenge: the Polish Americans of Michigan* (1972:26–27).

While the Advocates Society, composed of Polish-American lawyers in the Chicago area, meets in places like French Lick, Indiana for a golf outing with formal evening events designed to please the wives, the summer schedule for working-class families includes excursions to youth camps or religious shrines, and the Polish-American version of the American "piknik." The "piknik" is usually held at a forest preserve or in a specially equipped commercial "grove" containing a place for the band, a dance floor, a bar, and lights for evening hours. If it is a major event in the local community, it is apt to have been described in the local press, with details as to special attractions, including expected guests. The attractions most often mentioned are music from one or more alternating polka bands, door and other prizes, sports or product contests, a cash bar, foods such as sausage available for purchase, or the right to bring one's own food and guests. The event is likely to last all day and involve people who have met for years in this style although they may belong to a variety of different clubs.

In the northern and older settlements of Polonia, life's ebb and flow varies considerably by season. Summer is a time for travel, ranging from visits to the "fatherland" to bus riding excursions to seminaries. Outings in country clubs, drawing elites from all over the country, are duplicated in "piknik" groves by other companionate circles. The fall reintroduces the "business" or function-oriented activity of associations, and clubs all over Polonia announce them regularly in the periodicals. Fund-raising events are carried out, representatives are sent to federated governing bodies or congresses, and long-range plans are formulated for the social events preceding and following Christmas and New Year's Eve. Christmas is a very important period in Polonia, one during which many Polish Americans act out the few remaining folk rituals or religious ceremonies. Even nonreligious members of the community or "Americans of Polish heritage" who really do not identify with Polonia will revive their remaining ties by putting hay under the table cloth, setting an extra seat for the hungry stranger, serving the dinner with the traditional thirteen courses when the first star appears in the sky on Christmas Eve, and going to midnight mass in a Polish church. Christmas carols will be sung in Polish, with even the youth formulating a few familiar words in response to the piano or the record from Poland.

Parties and organizational life continue until Lent when, for forty days, even nonreligious Polish Americans try to "give up something" as a symbol of sacrifice. Easter is also an important holiday in Polonia, although some of the traditional rituals are less often reported than in the past (Zand 1957). Spring increases outdoor activities and those "balls" and dinners that are not staged during the winter season. Organizations usually have end-of-the-year events. Of course, throughout the year the flow of interactional activity is punctuated by Polish and American holidays, political action such as protest meetings, and so forth.

Naturally, all of Polonia's life does not focus on organizational activity, although that is the structure holding the community together. People do get together informally, with friends or relatives at times of leisure. Lunches are shared, parties planned, and central meeting places draw members from the various companionate circles. Until recently, for example, the elites of Chicago's northwest Polonia were bound to meet in a central restaurant, coming there before or after events such as dances or mass, or arranging to see each other more formally. Restaurants still provide meeting places, as do the "Polish homes" built in various communities. The church is less of a community center than in the early years when it was studied by Thomas and Znaniecki (1918–1920), but there are still parishes that retain a Polish flavor and that even pull people who are geographically scattered, at least on special occasions (see Radzialowski 1974: "A View from a Polish Ghetto").

As in all ethnic communities, weddings, christenings, and funerals provide a guarantee of special events affording contact with intimates and acquaintances (Zand 1959). The Polish American wedding in stereotype is a prolonged and heavy-drinking affair, but the actual weddings vary considerably among the different companionate circles. Many are quite indistinguishable from weddings of similar companionate circles in other communities. In fact, as in much of ethnic culture, the lower the social class, the more common are cultural variations in religious and social events.

Functions of Cooperative Companionate Circle Events

In addition to offering opportunities for social interaction, the function of most events is to acquire funds for "charitable" or other projects. This is usually done by collecting "donations" instead of charging for tickets, a procedure enabling the event to be classified as tax free. Since groups compete not only in the format of their events but in the size of the contribution they make to the organizational or interorganizational goals, the money raised at the events is significant in many latent ways. For example, there was an obvious competition among associations in Chicago in 1973 in the amount each gave for the Copernican statue. Each major contribution was highlighted by press photographs, and the smaller or individual ones were listed in special columns of the daily or organizational press.

According to Puacz (1972), the funds raised in Polonia maintained thirty-four major special or ongoing activities in the community including colleges, hospitals, a museum, a religious shrine, the interorganizational political association and its activities, and the building of a variety of centers and statues. In addition, this money helped Poland in the rebuilding of its cultural symbols. During the 1960s and 1970s, there were from 2 to 3 million packages and nearly $15 million in cash sent to Poland yearly. Puacz also stated that $3 million to $5 million "flows yearly in letters and is given to Polish family members during visits. This does not count money taken by returnees or business transactions" (105). The political and economic changes in Poland of recent years have renewed Polish American financial aid to families and investment in new businesses.

Fund-raising activities and the monies collected perform more than just economic functions. The very method of raising and distributing the money is highly functional for the status competition so important in Polonia's life. One of the advantages of being an active member and especially an officer in any of the 5,000 collection and distribution groups (if Puacz's estimation is correct) is the right to organize fund-raising efforts in competition with other groups and then to sit in judgment over requests for contributions. Each bequest is then officially documented in organizational records and the contribution, when decided upon, is given a great deal of publicity. To centralize all the activity in an effort at efficiency, as some leaders have suggested, would deprive all the leaders of small groups of the pleasures of competition and the power of deciding which of Polonia's or Poland's special projects deserves some of the rewards of their efforts.

Companionate Circles and Local Community Life

It is not the function of this book to deal with all the local variations of the Polonian themes. It is important, however, to show how the history, manner of settlement, and ethnic composition of the immigrant stream have differentiated life in local ethnic communities. These patterns become apparent when we look at something like the *Informator Polonii*, published in New York. The large number of Polish Americans in New York state, the location of its publication, plus the fact that the publisher also puts out the *Nowy Dziennik* (*Daily News*) may account for the dramatically large number of pages taken over by New York State advertisements. A total of 561 pages contains advertisements of various businesses and professional services, as discussed under institutional completeness in chapter 3. In addition, groups that are interested in being known, and given the nature of the status competition in Polonia it would be surprising if most groups did not want to be known. place their names, addresses, and roster of officers in the advertisements. The large groups even took whole pages. Given the weaknesses of the data due to the location of the publisher, we still must conclude that Polish Americans and their groups and interested economic suppliers are located in a very limited number of states. Of the 561 pages of announcements, 405 are taken over by seven states: California (20), Illinois (37), Massachusetts (37), Michigan (20), New Jersey (64), New York (135) and Pennsylvania (47). Floridian activities took only 14 pages, in spite of the retirement migration of some Poles from northern states, and Texas only took 12, in spite of the very early settlement in Panna Maria. The remaining pages are devoted to Polonian businesses in other states. Polish American groups and services are scattered in the Eastern states, and more concentrated in Illinois and Michigan, with some suburban migration around the central cities.[4]

The communities discussed below (Chicago, Illinois; Hamtramck, Michigan; Buffalo, New York; Los Angeles, California) have been the subjects of studies that provide us with images of their life.

Chicago

Chicago's Polonia is quite large, heterogeneous by immigration cohort, generation, social class, and degree of involvement in the community. It was never concentrated in a single area, and it currently includes a widely and variously distributed population. One area is centered on the northwest side of Chicago, with a concentration of several major superterritorial and multifunctional organizations such as the Polish National Alliance, the Polish Roman Catholic Union, and the Polish Women's Alliance. A second area of concentration is centered around the meat packing houses: "Back of the Yards." The third area grew around the steel mills of the far south side (Pacyga 1982; Parot 1980).

Each drew a different segment of Polonia's population, and developed a different life-style. Pacyga (1982, 1991b) calls the steel mill and packinghouse areas "villages" or real neighborhoods with focal points around the church and taverns. The former met not only religious needs, but was a center for organizational meetings and general cultural activity. The latter were the meeting places of labor unions and political parties (Pacyga 1982: 22). The neighborhood was organized by blocks.

> The block was the area where primary relationships took place. The architecture of the Apartments and houses was conducive to an active street life. Families sat on the stoops in the evenings; children and adults used the alleys as playgrounds and short cuts. The block was like a small village and indeed often contained the population from the same village in the old country. Gangs became the military arm of the block and patterned themselves after adult organizations. (Pacyga 1982: 23; see also Gans 1962; Suttles 1968, 1972)

The early Polish Americans did not limit their interests to the family and the neighborhood, both men and women being very active in union activity in the stockyards (Pacyga 1991a: chapter 5). This involvement did not, however, result in political power in the city. The Polish-language papers blamed this upon the lack of cooperation and organization, a complaint heard often in Polonia communities (Pacyga 1991a: 197).

Parot (1980) described early life in the northwest side, when St. Stanislaus Kostka and Holy Trinity parishes were still Polish and the area was known as "Polish downtown" (1910-1950). Family life among the working class here included very high fertility and child mortality rates (Parot 1980:156). Housing conditions were unsanitary, since so many people had to be squashed into so little space without adequate facilities. The average population density was one of the highest in the city (157). The girls were taken out of school at an early age and were employed in the garment trades or "sweatshops." Dating and marriage were endogamous. In spite of all these disadvantages, "the predicted breakdown of the Polish family in the second generation did not occur" (175). Parot (1980: 175) ascribes this to the "tenacity, courage and spirit of thousands of unknown 'Beloved Mothers' in Polonia."

Although the working-class Polish immigrants of the first cohort and their children were living and working under very hard conditions, they organized and were active in numerous organizations. As noted before, Thomas and Znaniecki (1918-1920) found 70 organized groups associated with St. Stanislaus Kostka parish. The local lodges of the PNA, PRCU, and PWA were blooming, as were the regional and village clubs, the Falcons, and related groups (see appendix A for year of founding and location of headquarters of these multigroup associations). In the proliferation of local branches they were unlike most of the other immigrant and ethnic communities.

In addition, the various companionate circles at all levels organized events in the Chicago area. Business and professional groups were formed and the press and radio brought news of these events to the people. Changes were made in the life-styles and cycles in response to outside events, especially those in Poland and the Polish groups in exile.

Many of the second cohort of Polish emigrants came to Chicago, formed their own groups, especially those of ex-combatants, or joined the existing ones. They formed the Roman Dmowski Institute in 1961, which organized 57 public lectures, most on Polish historical subjects in the years between 1983 and 1989 (*Glos Nauczyciela*, December 1989:22-24). Only eight of these were in the English language. Although the hostility between the two cohorts was particularly strong in this city, their presence revitalized Polonia and retained its concern with Poland, especially after the communists took over. Then came the third cohort, with its different background and orientation toward Poland, America, and Polonia. Mary Erdmans's chapter 8 is devoted to an analysis of the political life of Polonia in Chicago.

There are pockets of business, religious, recreational, educational, and family concentrations in Chicago. The old areas, such as Jackowo (around St. Hyacinth's church), draws newcomers for residence and the more dispersed Polish Americans for services and consumer objects. The Polish Americans of the northwest side of Chicago have been moving out along Milwaukee Avenue and into the northwest suburbs.

Religious life has continued to be active through the decades. As late as 1969 St. Hyacinth was celebrating its jubilee of a 75th anniversary with great activity and an impressive commemorative volume. In it we can see some of the life of religious companionate circles, undoubtedly replicated, in greater or smaller degree of complexity, in other locales. The church was built by the Poles who no longer fit into, or lived near, St. Stanislaw Kostka, the largest Polonian church in the United States made internationally famous by the Thomas and Znaniecki (1918-1920) study entitled *The Polish Peasant in Europe and America*. The commemorative volume contains pictures of participants in the numerous parish organizations of 1969 in middle-class attire, including formal men's wear and long dresses of women. The Intra-Parish Council, which represented "all the societies, clubs and organizations" of St. Hyacinth, contained both genders. About 100 members each can be found in the pictures of Ladies Rosary, the St. Barbara, the St. Therese Soladities, and the Mother's Club. The Young Ladies's Rosary Soladity represented the younger generation, the Third Order of St. Francis the older one. Religious aims and assistance to the parish at all times were the aims of many other women's groups, while the men served as ushers and helpers on Sundays, and "encourage more zealous Christian life through participation in parish work and by receiving Holy Communion frequently and monthly in body with the society" (St. Hyacinth Jubilee Committee 1969:79).

The parish school had a grade school band, replete with uniforms and many members, and a teen club participated in "religious, educational, athletic and social activities for the high school students." The library was run with the help of many volunteers, and a choir performed in church, as well as at social events. The Liturgical Union of Lectors and Commentators assisted in interpreting changes in liturgical services introduced by the center of the Roman Catholic Ecclesiastical Society in Rome. Scout units were assisted by scout mothers and male leaders. Dancers in costume appeared for the silver jubilarian parades. Carnivals and bazaars are recorded in photographs. Of special importance to Polonia are the Easter holidays, including Palm Sunday and Ash Wednesday. The school was run by the Congregation of the Sisters of the Holy Family of Nazareth, the children all dressed in costumes. The jubilee itself was an extended affair, with a mass procession, a program of music by the choir and orchestra, a reception, and a formal dinner-dance.

The statistics for sacraments at St. Hyacinth's church from 1894 to 1969 reflect the Polish immigration and the stages of life cycle of the immigrants in Chicago. Baptisms were most frequent in the years between 1916 and 1925, ranging from 331 to 381. They went up again to almost the same frequency in 1947 (348), with the influx of the World War II cohort. The 1968 total was 208. The first communion followed, the highest numbers of between 302 and 355 falling during the 1924–28 period. There were 377 first communions in 1957 and the number fell to 117 in 1968. Confirmations were most frequent in 1924, totaling 791 people, and then went up again to 419 in 1960, falling to 151 in 1968. Marriages also reflect the ages of immigrants and what was happening in America. The lowest number after a high of 127 in 1920 was 50 in 1932, going up to 203 in 1947, and dropping to 55 in 1963 when few Poles emigrated. The 1968 number was 105. Finally, the number of funerals increased, with some variations over the years, until 1960, with 202 taking place then and 218 in 1968. Thus, we have a picture of the life cycle of the three cohorts. St. Hyacinth Church, has several Polish masses: one "Sunday mass on Saturday," four on Sunday, two daily and one on the first Friday of the month. There are eight priests, all with Polish names.

Chicago's population of Polish foreign stock, that is, of Polish birth or with at least one parent of Polish birth, has been aging. Most of the first generation of the first cohort is dead. By 1970, there were 191,955 foreign-stock Poles in the city itself, 71 percent of them were of the second generation, and 73 percent were 45 years of age or over. Twenty years later the survivors were 65 and over. There were 1.1 million Polish Americans in Chicago in 1989, according to a Pastoral Outreach program of the Polish Welfare Association (PWA, 1989). Of these, 115,000 were people aged 65 and over and 50,000 of these did not speak English. The PWA was interested in these figures because the only way such elders can be reached with vital information is through the Polish-language radio, newspapers, and mass or parish bulletins. A sample of 1,000 Poles aged 50 and over, obtained through a variety of religious and social contacts in 1991, provides additional insight into the presence of the three cohorts. The eldest came prior to World War I, or around 1948–49. The peak year of entry of the third cohort was 1989 and they tended to be between ages 25 and 45. Seventy-three percent of the sample identified themselves as Polish and only 27 percent as Polish American. In fact, 34 percent still have Polish citizenship. Although 59 percent identified the social background of their parents as working-class, 20 percent as farmers, and only 12 percent as intelligentsia or professionals (6 percent were craft or skill workers), the respondents were much more likely to identify themselves as intelligentsia (16 percent) or professionals (21 percent). Ten percent have been homemakers, 47 percent workers of various levels of skill, and 6 percent clerical workers. Interestingly, 62 percent identify their own social status as working-class and only 28 percent as intelligentsia/professional. The vast majority (82 percent) live in their own home. This is certainly a wide distribution of social class, considering that this is an older population of people with a Polish identity.

The social and organizational life of Chicago's Polonia went far outside of parish activities. For example, the February 1992 *Polonia Today* ran the following Polonia Datebook of events for the latter part of that month and for March:

> Exhibit of photographs "Old Polish Chicago, A Renaissance" at the Polish Museum of America; Installation Dinner of the Advocates Society of Polish American Lawyers, with Award of Merit to the Polish Welfare Association, at the Palmer House; Three separate People's Law School lectures sponsored by the Advocates Society (Polish), the Illinois Bar Association and the Copernicus Foundation at the Copernicus Center; White and Red Ball of the Legion of Young Polish Women, with presentation of debutantes at the Chicago Hilton and Towers; Mardi Gras sponsored by the Polish National Alliance for the benefit of handicapped and disabled children in Poland, at its Fraternal Hall; the 75th Anniversary of the Poslaniec Cerca Jezusa (Messenger of the Heart of Jesus) banquet for the benefit of education of new Polish Jesuits at the House of the White Eagle; Chicago Chopin Piano Competition, sponsored by the Chicago Chapter of the Kosciuszko Foundation, at the Chicago Musical College of Roosevelt University; Casino Nights for the benefit of the Copernicus Foundation, at the Foundation building; Spring Dance of St. Francis Borgia Parish (with corned beef and cabbage dinner?) at the Stokes Center. (February 1992b)

Chicago's Polonia often hosts political leaders of both Poland and the United States, especially at times of importance to those countries, such as economic investment needs in the case of the former and elections in the case of the latter. The headquarters of the major organizations hold a variety of meetings. Professional organizations of lawyers and physicians, local business groups, the U.S. Polish Chamber of Commerce and the Polish American Enterprise Fund arrange for presentations by delegates of Polish firms and associations. Regional Rotary

Clubs have restarted Rotary Clubs in Poland. The Polish Consulate has become quite active in helping Poles contact Americans of influence in order to increase investment in Poland, especially in joint ventures. It as well as other Polish governmental offices are finding themselves in an interesting situation. They are no longer seen as "the enemy," subject to demonstrations, but as representatives of the homeland. At the same time, they are very constricted in funds, as Poland struggles to convert itself to a market economy.[5]

In the meantime, the newly activated Polish Museum, the Copernican Center, the various art galleries, and the musical as well as theatrical presentations keep Chicago's Polonia busy.

Hamtramck

Hamtramck, Michigan a separate city—a political enclave surrounded by Detroit—has been inhabited mainly by Poles and Polish Americans until very recent years. The fact that it has been politically independent and able to elect or appoint its own officials was an important factor in its life. In fact, its political life and relations with other ethnic groups have drawn the attention of several social scientists (Wood 1955; Agocs 1971; Musick 1971; Radzialowski 1980; Wrobel 1979).

Hamtramck's political independence is obviously not complete, since there are many overlapping jurisdictions and interests of police, courts, and welfare; but it is closer to having institutional completeness and social isolation than any other local Polonian community. Hamtramck was an area of secondary settlement by the Poles who came in the first two decades of the twentieth century when, with the opening of automobile plants, unskilled labor was needed. They continued, as late as the 1950s, to work in jobs similar to the ones they first entered (Wood 1955). Hamtramck exploded in population before the 1930s. Then, during the depression, many Polish families moved out of the industrial area to Polish farming communities in the "Thumb" section of Michigan (Wood 1955:19). The population dropped from a high of 56,268 in 1930 to 49,838 in 1940. Movement of the younger native-born children of the immigrants in the 1940s again dropped the population to 43,455 in 1950 (Wood 1955:10). Agocs's (1971) analysis of the 1960 census data led her to conclude that "the center of Italian, Polish, German and Jewish concentration, for example, have shifted outward in a 'corridor' pattern, to some of the northern and northeastern suburbs" (84).

The Poles remaining in Hamtramck as the blacks move in are older and they are home owners. Most of the wooden houses closely lining the streets that cross the central business artery would not draw a fortune on the modern real estate market; but they are solid, carefully tended, and fairly substantial in size. The main street does not have many buildings over two stories high. Store fronts display bakery goods, sausage, and related meat products; there is an unusual number of shoe stores and podiatric and chiropractic offices (standing for long hours in automobile assembly plants created feet and back problems). Some of the store fronts are vacant, others cater to young black adults.

As of 1960, 63 percent of the Polish-stock people were still living in the metropolitan area of Detroit and its enclaves; the remaining 37 percent had already become the city's suburbanites (Agocs 1971:85). Few Michigan Polish Americans (Agocs 1971:91–92) had turned to higher education as a means of upward mobility. The 1960 median school years completed was 7.0 for the first generation and 10.3 for the second generation. Their overall image is still one of lower or working class. As late as 1971, Musick records a negative attitude toward higher education and there is no evidence of more intelligentsia among the new emigrants in Hamtramck although there are some members in the Detroit area.

Musick (1971) found respondents in Hamtramck still very much oriented toward "hard work," opposed to public welfare programs that would decrease the value of money earned in the traditional way, and rejective of managerial positions for themselves as well as of having wives work for pay. "In Hamtramck, wealth and consumption of material goods are of much less importance than pride in one's property, and concern for neighbor's property" (6). The Polish residents defined themselves as individualistic and had a

> sense of personal identity which is drawn not from the larger society but from the Polish sub-culture of Hamtramck. They have a sense of being apart, of being unique and individual which results from their relationship to the values, norms, and criteria of prestige which are unique to the Polish subculture of Hamtramck and remarkably different from those of the larger society." (6)

Of course, the Polish Americans Musick described were those left behind as the younger generations moved away. The consequences of being left behind are evident in the daily life of Hamtramck's older Polish Americans. Most residents of Hamtramck have lived in the town most of their lives, with their spouses in their own homes, some also housing boarders. The men held blue-collar jobs, identified with the Roman Catholic church, and held peasant-style attitudes toward health and other subjects of daily interest. Their offspring, located elsewhere and enjoying more middle-class lives, were not deeply involved in the life of the community.

The characteristics of the Polish American population in Detroit's areas such as Hamtramck did not change much by the time that Wrobel (1979) moved into one of the neighborhoods and presented his findings in *Our Way*. It was this book that drew so much anger from Polish Americans, as reported in chapter 5, who saw it as contributing to anti-Polish sentiment.

Radzialowski's (1980) historical analysis of the situation of Polish Americans in Detroit from 1921 to 1942 stresses the hardships they were going

through during the depression and the problems of the auto industry. Unemploy-
ment was frequent, so that families had to resort to welfare. Although the figures
were about equal to that of other groups, the fact of having to do so hurt the
individualism and wish for independence of the men. The Polish Americans also
faced discrimination and prejudice, often resulting in violent reaction against
other groups, such as the blacks who were moving into the neighborhoods
(Radzialowski 1980: 202-3).

It is not surprising, in view of the life of similar peoples in other Polonian
communities, to find that Hamtramck had extensive and complex interlocking
social activity at the height of its life.[6] Although recognized in Detroit newspapers mostly in terms of its scandals, criminal and juvenile delinquency rates,
and internal conflict, this working man's community retained a highly developed organizational system enabling a viable status competition. In the absence
of higher education as a basic source of prestige, this competition used land
possession, membership in organizations, and personal reputations to build
status packages. The geographical barriers separating Hamtramck from the rest
of Detroit's population and the stability of the Poles' residential settlement
resulted in the development of a common life-style and a large-scale reproduc-
tion of village life. Political life afforded many opportunities for leadership
roles. Although priests and nuns, small shop keepers, and a few professional
men formed the elite, this social and political life gave other community
residents many occasions for establishing individual records.

Buffalo

The Polonian community of Buffalo, New York has been the subject of
several studies (Carpenter and Katz 1927, 1929; Obidinski 1968; Frysztacki
1986) and appears to have some distinctive features. Obidinski (1968:23) found
the Polonian community to be clustered in several neighborhoods out of its
initial concentration in the "East End". The areas of settlement became more
varied by social class over the years so that upward mobility is possible within
the confines of the city. The initial settlers were part of the immigrant flow that
"passed through Buffalo en route to midwest cities such as Chicago, Detroit,
Milwaukee and Cleveland" (33). Some decided to remain there "for some of
the arrivals, Buffalo was not merely a stop-over point but literally the end of the
line—as the western terminus of some railroads out of New York City—and
accessible to those who could pay the $7.50 fare" (33).

The initial homogeneity of the community (mainly former peasants) was
broken only by the presence of priests and nuns who formed the leadership elite.
They organized not only churches and parishes, but parochial schools, organizations outside of religious confines, and the press. For example, a priest was the
owner and editor of the first Polish language newspaper in Buffalo and was the

cofounder (with another priest) of the Polish Union of America. In fact, Obidinski (1968) attributed the "consolidation of the subcommunity" to Catholicism, the religious leaders, the churches, and their organizations:

> In 1966, when the Buffalo subcommunity was almost 100 years old, many persons and committees planned events and publications in observance of the Polish Millennium commemorating 1,000 years of Christianity among the Polish people. Polish-American clergymen and nuns organized local Millennial events and provided a historical record of the subcommunity. In a literal sense, the Buffalo subcommunity retains its close ties with the church. (62–63)

Although some dispersal had taken place by the 1960s, Obidinski (1968:16) found a definite ethnic subcommunity, persisting over four generations. According to him, "familial and religious institutional patterns are more crucial to subcommunity persistence than are economic or political institutional patterns." In addition,

> the acceptance of traditional ethnic patterns and participation in ethnic associations vary with social class levels within the subcommunity. The Polish-American subcommunity in Buffalo continues to exist despite increased differences among members. Its continued survival, however, is a function of specific institutional practices of persons found at certain class levels. (16)

This refers to the fact that the upper classes tend to live outside the community's territorial boundaries, to participate in organizations of other identity, and to agree less with traditional attitudes than do the lower classes. Their ethnicity is expressed more in familial and religious ties than in total community involvement.

Another significant characteristic of Buffalo's Polonia has been the size of the Polish American segment in proportion to the total population of Buffalo. The Polish Americans of Buffalo are relatively few in number when compared to Chicago or their own past, having dropped from 200,000 foreign stock in 1940 to 82,249 in 1960 (Obidinski 1968:50), but they comprise a high 15 percent of the total Buffalo population, which stood at 533,000 in 1960. Furthermore, the succeeding generations of Polish Americans seem to have influenced the whole city's life on the political and social level. Frysztacki (1986) makes the same observation.

Although Obidinski (1968) concludes that it has been mainly the family and religious interaction that has kept the ethnic community together in the face of increasing internal differences, there seems to be a semblance of a superstructure that may be assisting the process. In the past, a major focal point of Buffalo's social life had been its Dom Polski (Polish Home) which was similar in function to community centers:

> The Dom Polski (Polish Home) in Buffalo was fortunate in having a branch of the municipal public library housed on its first floor; this not only enhanced the character

of a community center, but added to its income, which was augmented further by the rental of space to two dignified businesses—a men's clothing store and a drugstore—enabling it to exist without too much financial stress. In most other cities, however, the Dom Narodowy had to bolster its existence with a saloon and so did not enjoy the patronage of the "better societies." (Zand, as quoted in Obidinski 1968:47)

Although Obidinski (1968) does not refer to an organizational superstructure that could contribute to the preservation of Buffalo's Polonia over the four generations, he took his sample from a list of eighty-four voluntary organizations. Thus, the community was organizationally active beyond the Dom Polski, benefiting also from geographical concentration of its population. Most of Obidinski's respondents of even the third generation lived in neighborhoods that they considered as either "Mostly Polish or Polish-American" (41 percent) or at least "half Polish, half American" (38 percent). Only 29 percent were then living in areas they defined as "neither Polish nor Polish American" (92).

Buffalo's Polonia, therefore, is sociologically interesting because it is able to contain the heterogeneous upwardly mobile second, third, and later generations of Polish Americans. As Obidinski (1968) pointed out, this coexistence is made possible by continued religious and family-centered interaction, which bridges class differences. An interesting subject of future study would be the extent to which voluntary organizations serve as the source of anticipatory and in-role socialization of the descendants of the Polish peasant immigrants who are moving up the socioeconomic ladder. An additional question is the extent to which the ethnic community can provide some of this anticipatory and in-group socialization, and the problems it has of doing so in view of its traditional link with the peasant folk culture. The problems seem less apt to arise in more complex ethnic communities (such as the Polonia of Chicago) because the overlap and openness of the boundaries of companionate circles would make movement possible, if not always pleasant.

Frysztacki (1986), a Polish sociologist, drew the conclusions as to the stages of development of ethnic subcommunities based on geographic changes from his study of Buffalo in the 1980s. However, I am not certain that Buffalo is a typical case of such changes.

Los Angeles

Frysztacki's conclusions, totally applicable to local Polonias of the type represented by Buffalo, does not apply at all to Los Angeles. The Los Angeles Polonian community is the most loosely structured and least demanding of its members of all those that have been studied to date.[7] Sandberg (1974) feels that the people drawn to "the West, many of whom live in Southern California, represent a group of higher socioeconomic status than the national population of Polonia, which is largely working class" (19). He draws this conclusion from the assumption that "those who are better educated are more mobile" (19). The

Los Angeles area Polish American residents moved there from other parts of America; the city was certainly not the port of entry of most immigrants from Poland or other European countries.

The Polish American community of Los Angeles is a perfect illustration of Etzioni's (1959) statement that the web of social relations can exist in spite of residential dispersal even into suburban locations.[8] The dispersal is not just into several settlements or local neighborhoods as in Buffalo. Rather, the families have dispersed and there are only a few clusters of group settlement. The Polish-stock first- and second-generation residents of Los Angeles lived in 632 of the 710 census tracts and were "represented in all of the separately incorporated communities within the SMSA" (Sandberg 1974:19). There were only ten tracts in Los Angeles and one outside the city limits that contained 500 or more people of Polish foreign stock each. In spite of the dispersal, the community was able to maintain both a Roman Catholic parish and a Polish National Catholic church. As of 1950

> a directory indicated that there were 30 Polish American groups in the Los Angeles area, including branches of the major fraternal associations, groups of veterans, labor, business and professional people, the Polish Literary and Dramatic Circle and the Polish University Club. (21)

Because of the initial settlement patterns and the background of the Polish American settlers of the Los Angeles area, it is not surprising that Sandberg (1974) found a much greater weakening of extended family ties than did Obidinski (1968) in Buffalo. Also, as the Los Angeles Polish Americans have become more prosperous and middle-class in their life-styles, in a community with very flexible and nontraditional social structures, the pervasiveness of their ethnicity has

> diminished considerably but continues to be a factor in the lives of many people. The bond of identity is expressed through formal and informal structural associations and maintained by a common history and tradition. It may also be supported by the currently fashionable voicing of ethnic identification and pride, as well as by the emergence of a new militancy resulting from the abrasiveness of intergroup contacts and perceptions. (Sandberg 1974:73)

This continued ethnic identification did not cover all members of the third- and fourth-generation youth, many of whom seemed to be denying identification as Polish Americans in the face of a "comparatively hostile climate" (74). However, the interesting conclusion of this study is that there can be an "emergence of new forms of ethnic identification and communication, which enable the growing numbers of ethnics residing in suburban settings to maintain group continuity" (74). If the shift to higher education as a method of status competition achievement in the broader society is developing, as we hypothesize in this book, then the shift of identification and association from the traditional culture and companionate circles will have to take place all over American Polonia. The Los Angeles model may be one that other local communities will be developing.

The California area still has active Polonian groups. The Polish National Alliance held its 1991 Convention in Garden Grove of that state—the first time the association met west of the Mississippi in its 111 years history (*New Horizon* 1991: 18). Boleslaw Krzeminski, the parson of a Polish parish in Los Angeles, opened a parish school taught by Franciscan sisters in 1943, but had to close it in 1949 for lack of students. The second emigration wave following World War II brought in so many children that a new, Saturday school was opened in 1952. The Polish American Congress placed the school under its care and financial assistance in 1956. As late as 1986-87 the school contained 112 children from 81 families. The school, with the help of the parents observes special Polish occasions attended by others in this dispersed Polonia (*Glos Nauczyciela*, December 1987:4-5). Newport Beach, California is renovating the home of Helena Modjewska, a famous Polish actress, the Board of Supervisors of Orange County having bought her house, "at least partially influenced by thousands of calls and letter from their Pol-Am constituents and organizations" (*Polonia Today*, February 1992b: 2). The presence of active Polish Americans in California can be attested by the fact that the new Republic of Poland established a consulate in Los Angeles (*Polonia Today*, February: 13).

Other Polonian Local Communities

The local Polonian communities range from small towns such as Panna Maria, Texas to large cities such as New York. Panna Maria is known in Polonia as the first town settled entirely by Polish immigrants. Founded in 1854 by 100 Polish families who traveled west, it was named after the mother saint so important to Polish Catholicism.

Abramson (1971) chose four cities in the Connecticut Valley and analyzed their demographic characteristics. He found that 82 percent of the Poles were Catholic, 5 percent were Protestant, and 13 percent were Jewish (19). The socioeconomic resources available to the Polish Americans again reflected the burden of a past lack of education. Only 22 percent of the Polish Catholics were in white-collar occupations, and these people were the least likely of all groups to have attended college, their 18 percent being followed by 20 percent for other East Europeans. The Protestants had a 53 percent college attendance record among the white-collar workers and the Jews had a 49 percent record. Among the blue-collar workers, the French Canadians, the Italians, the blacks, and the Protestants had fewer college attendees that had the Polish Catholics, but even here the Polish total was 13 percent. This would indicate a trend toward status decrystallization, with educational achievement preceding occupational mobility out of the blue-collar world. This conclusion is supported by income figures, in that few Polish Americans in white-collar jobs were as yet living on annual family incomes of $10,000 or more, while almost the same proportion of their blue-collar workers had equivalent incomes (12 percent).

The Connecticut Valley Polish Americans were moving away from total Democratic party affiliation found typical by Abel (1929) in the 1920s—only 64 percent being so identified in 1972, while 15 percent were Republican and 21 percent independent. (The last figure is high in comparison with other groups and the distribution does not vary by blue- and white-collar differences.) Although only 20 percent of the respondents thought that race relations in the United States were getting better, 41 percent saw them as the same and only 35 percent as worse. Interestingly enough, only 8 percent of the blacks saw them as getting worse. Unfortunately, the article describing the Connecticut Valley Polish Americans did not deal with the social structure of their communities. The Polish American Congress had a division in the state and many of its individual members lived in Connecticut (Zmurkiewicz 1972:53).

Polonia Today of February 1992(b), which is published in Chicago but which invites Polonian organizations to send details of their events for inclusion in its Polonia Datebook column announced an Installation Dinner and Dance of Post #12 of the Polish Army Veterans in Eddington, Pennsylvania; Partita chamber ensemble concert at the Kosciuszko Foundation in New York; and a performance of the Polish opera "Halka" and the Old Warsaw Cabaret presented by the Paderewski Female Chorus, both in Philadelphia.

The Polish Americans of Washington, D.C. tend to be of a different background; many came with the new emigration and found jobs with the federal government. A few are elected representatives of their ethnics in other parts of the country. They tend to be active in the cultural and political clubs and companionate circles. There is sufficient cohesion in the community to organize a Polish American Day on the mall at the Washington Monument with the cooperation of the U. S. Park Service. Washington's Polonia is in touch with other communities—visiting groups from other Polish American communities usually get in touch with local organizations. The presence of the Washington office of the Polish American Congress tends to focus political activity there, and the Copernican Year festivities brought together scholars and politicians of many nationalities.

New York contains a great variety of different companionate circles, all trying to work out compromises in their relations with surrounding ethnic groups. John Lindsay (1972), when he was the mayor of New York, reported that in a "section of Brooklyn, Polish-Americans and Puerto Ricans have joined together to start a multi-service community center and plan to push for a day care center as well." In other areas, as reported by Novak (1971), the Polish

Americans and the other blue-collar ethnics were hostile toward the blacks, while themselves developing a "new ethnicity." Both Lindsay (1972) and Novak (1972) reported on a new group of Polish Americans, the children of "white ethnic" families who flooded into "the city's Open Enrollment Program, which guarantees a place in the City University system to every New York high school graduate" (Lindsay 1972:147).

Simultaneously, New York has a highly developed intelligentsia companionate circle centered around the Polish Institute of Arts and Sciences in America, the Kosciuszko Foundation, which arranges for the exchange of students between the United States and Poland and provides stypendiums for students studying here and the Polish American Museum Foundation in the Port Washington Pilsudski Institute for research in the Modern History of Poland (*Informator* 1980:419). New York houses the central administration of the Association of Veterans of the Polish Army in America (SWAP), with soldier's homes in several New York state communities, the Union of Polish Parachutists, the Association of former Political Prisoners, and the Association of Polish Combatants (several circles). Very few of the 83 organizations listed in the *Informator* are located in New York City, some do not give addresses, and 39 can be found in the small area of Greenpoint in Brooklyn. Greenpoint is somewhat similar to Jackowo in Chicago. It is the current and first locale of many of the third-cohort immigrants, from communist Poland and its aftermath. This small Polonia has a miniature institutional completeness, in that there are religious and educational institutions, a number of businesses and professional services, and restaurants where people meet in leisure. Thus, New York and its environs seem to have a pyramidal social structure, more so than is evident in other local communities such as Cleveland, which reports middle-range companionate activities.

Many towns in New York state even have Polish-language radio programs. In 1980, for example, there were radio programs in Auburn, Baldwinsville, Binghamton, Buffalo, Catskill Cheektowaga, Ellensville, Elmira, Fredonia, Fulton, Garden City, Herkimer, Hudson, Kingston, Little Falls, and Londonville.

Summary

Life in Polonia is organized into the activities of various (sometimes overlapping) companionate relationship circles, ranked by social status, size, and flexibility of boundaries. The companionate circles contain different personnel and ranges of activities of interaction. Status crystallization and intercircle differentiation are evident in the demeanor and content of interaction within each companionate circle when viewed from the outside, but status decrystallization and flexibility form an internally important part of the life of Polonia and enable the existence of the circle and status competition.

Local neighborhoods, settlements, or communities and Polonia as a whole can bring together the various circles, or their representatives, for special events but generally most of the circles do not have much in common. The elites form their own circles composed of the intelligentsia, the professional and business leaders, and the political and organizational leaders among the white-collar segment of the population. Within the blue-collar segment of Polonia there are "the Polka World," the local parish, and the local organizational leadership elites. The flow of activity is influenced by seasonal changes, national Polish or American holidays, or local special events. Of recent years some of the special events have been systematized throughout Polonia through the efforts of super-territorial leaders as part of the campaign to change the image of Polish Americans in American society. Thus, special events were clustered around the Copernican Year, the Joseph Conrad Year, the ethnic celebration of America's bicentennial, and the annual Pulaski month and day.

Local Polonias that combine several neighborhoods vary considerably, as we saw from the examples given here. Chicago has been the center of the major multipurpose fraternal and building and loan associations. It is also the head-quarters of the Polish American Congress, a politically active interoganizational group. Its Polonia has been strongly influenced by all three of the immigration cohorts and is still quite active in several companionate circles. Hamtramck, an independent enclave within Detroit, has had a history of internally oriented political activism on the part of a working-class population. However complex its organizational structure, it is not that which has drawn attention of sociologists and anthropologists who are fascinated by that working-class folk culture and its effect on daily life.

Buffalo, New York is seen as a community influenced strongly by its Polish American subcommunity, which formed tight islands only recently dispersing. New York City contains what is identified as a dispersed intelligentsia of all three immigration and emigre cohorts, while Greenpoint has contained Chicago like clusters of temporary residents, similar to that of Milwaukee Avenue and Jackowo. These stereotypes are shared by Polonians in all parts of the country.

Notes

1. Of course the intelligentsia, and the other elites as well, can be involved in interaction on a cosmopolitan Polonian level with similar elites from Canada, England, and other nations in which the Poles have settled, and with the intel-ligentsia or the comparable elites in Poland.

2. Two styles of participation in Polonia's life, in mutually exclusive companionate circles, are demonstrated in two obituaries appearing side by side in the *Dziennik Zwiazkowy* (19 June 1973:6). The first is that of a male doctor in South Bend, Indiana who was a member of the staff of a hospital, a national medical association, the Indiana State Medical Association, the American Academy of Family Physicians,

the Pulaski Post No. 357 of the American Legion, the Schuyler Colfax Post 3194 of the Veterans of Foreign Wars, the Chopin Fine Arts Club, and Group 83 of the Polish National Alliance. His memberships are associated with past veteran's and professional roles, cutting across ethnic lines but with some Polish affiliations ranging from the "cultural" to the fraternal. It is impossible to determine the ethnic composition of some of his groups.

The woman whose obituary happened to be next to the doctor's was typical of older, lower-class parish Polish Americans. She had belonged to the Brotherhood of Women of the Holy Rosary, the Jaslo Club, the Apostleship of Prayer, the Heart of Mr. Jesus, the Soladity of St. Theresa of Infant Jesus, the Society of St. Josef the Protector of the Novitiates of the Congregation C.R., and the Society of the Mother of God of Lourdes and St. Ann.

3. Three meetings held in Poland resulted in enormous volumes (Kubiak and Pilcha 1976, 760pp.; Kubiak and Wrobel 1984, 619pp.; Kubiak, et al. 1988, 848pp.) of chapters reporting research on Polonias all over the world, but mainly in the United States. As the reader can imagine, this is a wealth of information not available when I was writing the first edition of *Polish Americans*, published in 1976.

4. It does not make much sense to present data from locations such as Yankee City (see, for example, Warner and Srole 1945, *The Social Systems of American Ethnic Groups*) since there were so few Poles there at the time of the studies and since the analysis of the community is so badly outdated. There are other studies of Polish Americans, mainly focused on the degree of assimilation of persons rather than on the structure and life of the community. The communities selected here for discussion are described with sufficient detail and are so different from each other that they bear closer attention.

5. For example, the consulate in Chicago can no longer demand that the airline LOT transport books collected by American university faculty for Polish libraries. LOT is now a private firm that must conduct economically advantageous transactions.

6. The composition of Hamtramck's population seems to have been relatively flat in socioeconomic terms, when compared to that of Chicago or New York. In fact, Wood (1955) found the number of professionals very low in 1950, one-fourth of that of neighboring Highland Park, which had very few Polish Americans. There were only half as many proprietors as in Highland Park, which also had a higher educational and combined socioeconomic median achievement.

7. According to Sandberg (1974) the Los Angeles Polonia contains 73,959 Polish foreign-stock residents of whom "31,877 were foreign born and 42,082 were native white of foreign or mixed parentage" (19–20). This is a high ratio of first generation Polish Americans, most of whom are of the new emigration.

8. Specifically, Etzioni (1959:258) states "that a group can maintain its cultural and social integration and identity, without having an ecological basis."

8

Recent Political Action on Behalf of Poland: The Interrelationships among Polonia's Cohorts 1978–1990

Mary Patrice Erdmans

This chapter describes the types of action taken by Polonia's leaders and organizations on behalf of Poland between 1978 and 1990, a period during which the Solidarity union and democratic opposition in Poland emerged and the political and economic communist system began to crumble. While Polonia has a variety of linkages to Poland (e.g., educational, cultural, familial), this chapter focuses on its political linkages and Polonia's actions oriented toward supporting the opposition movement. Polonia centers of political activity in the United States include New York, Washington, D.C., and Southern California; however, this study is mainly limited to activity undertaken by groups located in Chicago. Although New York State has the most Poles, metropolitan Chicago has the largest city concentration. In 1980, 10 percent of the 8 million people in the United States who reported some Polish ancestry lived in Illinois, and roughly 90 percent of these lived in the Chicago metropolitan area (Erdmans 1992a: 39). In addition, Chicago is the headquarters of the Polish American Congress, the Polish National Alliance, the Polish Women's Alliance, the Polish Roman Catholic Union, and several new political organizations founded by members of the new Polish cohort, as well as a Polish consulate. The presence of ethnic and immigrant Poles along with their respective organizations make Chicago's Polonia an ideal setting for the study of political action.

In Chicago, political action was undertaken by a variety of Polonian groups and organizations who at times worked together, but more often worked independently of each other. Although the native-born Polish American community was involved in Poland's struggles for national sovereignty, much of the action undertaken during this period was initiated and carried out by the newest Polish migrants, who began arriving in the mid-1960s.

This chapter first provides a brief overview of the types of Poles within this newest cohort, and how differences among migrants affected participation in political action for the homeland. It then describes the various types of political action undertaken between 1978 and 1990: (1) symbolic and financial support for the opposition; (2) humanitarian aid for the people of Poland; (3) protest activities against the communist regime; (4) lobbying efforts to influence U.S. foreign policy; (5) direct involvement in Poland's elections; and (6) economic support for the free market. Different groups in Polonia had different perceptions of what actions would best help Poland. These perceptions were dependent on the groups' links to Poland, past patterns of political activities, and resource availability. Polish Americans were more likely to send humanitarian aid, lobby, and provide symbolic support. Members of the new Polish cohort provided financial support, protested, and voted. As a result of the diversity of strategies, the groups' actions at times complimented each other and thereby strengthened Polonia's efforts for Poland. Unfortunately, the reverse was also true.[1]

The New Polish Cohort

Only a small percentage of the new Polish cohort was involved in political action for Poland. The factors that affected the level and type of involvement included the legal status of the Pole in the United States and past involvement in the opposition in Poland. The types of Poles who arrived in the United States were influenced by the conditions in Poland and U.S. immigration laws. In the 1970s and 1980s, when economic conditions were poor in Poland and the exchange rate between the dollar and *zloty* was favorable to U.S. currency, there was an increased number of immigrants—some permanent, others temporary— who came to the United States to work and often returned to Poland. In the 1980s, increased political repression in Poland and a favorable policy toward refugees from communist countries led to an influx of Polish refugees to the United States.

The new Polish cohort is composed of three main categories of migrants— quota immigrants, nonimmigrants, and refugees—grouped together according to their status at entry into the United States, and thus the categories are created by an American classification system (see chapter 2). Polish quota immigrants are subject to the numerical limitations set by the 1965 Immigration and Naturalization Act; nonimmigrants refer to Poles who receive temporary visas for the purposes of business, governmental activity, or tourism (in Polonia, tourists are often referred to as *wakacjusze* [vacationers]); and refugees are defined as those who were persecuted or feared persecution in their home country. Refugees compose the smallest percentage within the new cohort, while nonimmigrants represent the largest percentage. A summary of the three types of new Poles is provided in table 8.1, while a more detailed set of numbers is contained in table 2.4.

TABLE 8.1
The New Polish Cohort by Time of Arrival and Status

	Immigrant*	Wakacjusze[#]	Refugees
1965-1979	59,399	293,324	7,924
1980-1989	28,966	374,622	34,903
Totals	88,395	667,946	42,827

Source: U.S. Immigration and Naturalization Services, Annual Reports, 1965-1978, Statistical Yearbook 1979-1989. See also M.P. Erdmans, "Émigrés and Ethnics" (Ph.D. diss., Northwestern University, 1992a), 342-44.
* This refers to immigrants admitted under numerical limitations.
# This refers to nonimmigrants who entered as "temporary visitors for pleasure."

One's legal status in part influences one's intention of returning to Poland, and that intention affects political behavior. Unlike the nonimmigrants, immigrants and refugees have legal permanent residency status in the United States. In general, the wakacjusze were the most likely to say that they intended to return to Poland and the refugees the least likely. Most wakacjusze came with the intention of returning, and the limitations of their visas reinforced this intention. In contrast, most refugees had disposed of their material possessions in Poland before they left, indicating they did not believe they would return. Some refugees escaped from Poland, and this illegal departure reinforced the idea that they could not return. Quota immigrants were between refugees and wakacjusze with respect to intention to return. Most of these immigrants came to the United States in order to reunify with their families. Since they exited Poland and entered the United States legally, they had the option of staying or returning.

The temporary nature of the migrant's stay in the United States influenced the types of political action in which they were involved. I conducted two surveys among Chicago's new Polish cohort—one of voters in Poland's first partially free national election in 1989, and the other of members of a political-economic organization created to support Poland's emerging free market.[2] Those who voted in Poland's national election were mostly temporary residents who planned to return to Poland. In this sample, 4 percent were U.S. citizens, 49 percent had permanent resident status, and 47 percent had temporary resident status (both valid and expired visas). In addition, only 4 percent said they planned to stay in the United States permanently (see table 8.2), although there was variation according to their legal status with temporary residents more likely to plan on returning to Poland. Poles who came from villages were also more likely to plan on returning to Poland; and the older the émigrés, the more likely they were to say they wanted to return to Poland. Finally, the longer they were in America, the less likely they were to return (Erdmans 1992a: 322-24).

TABLE 8.2

Relation between Legal Status and Decision to Return to Poland among Absentee Voters in Chicago for Poland's National Election

	N	% Will Return	% Will Stay	% Uncertain	Totals
U.S. Citizen	17	52.9%	11.8%	35.3%	100%
Permanent resident	221	48.9%	5.4%	45.7%	100%
Temporary resident	215	82.8%	1.9%	15.3%	100%

Source: M.P. Erdmans, "Émigrés and Ethnics" (Ph.D. diss., Northwestern University, 1992a), 207. Data taken from a survey of 464 voters in Chicago who voted in Poland's national election on 3 June 1989.

The Forum respondents look different. Although 45 percent of the sample had arrived in the United States with temporary visas, 44 percent of them were U.S. citizens and another 42 percent were permanent residents by 1989. This contrasts sharply with the election sample, where nearly half of the respondents remained temporary residents. Moreover, 32 percent of the Forum sample said they intended to remain in the United States (Erdmans 1992a: 329-31). Forum members, many of whom were businessmen, had more stable positions in the host country.

Variation in status among members of the new cohort affected the types of political action in which they engaged. Temporary residents were more likely to take actions that led to immediate results, such as voting, while permanent residents were more likely to become involved in actions that required longer-term commitments, such as creating a political organization to support the opposition or making a financial investment in Poland's free market system.

In addition to the legal statuses of the residents, a second factor that influenced the likelihood of involvement in political actions in the United States was past involvement in the opposition in Poland. Data from the Forum sample show a relationship between involvement in Poland and involvement in the United States (see table 8.3). There was a 17 percent increase in activity in the United States based on activity in Poland.

Two reasons are suggested for the influence of political activity in Poland upon the propensity toward political action in the United States. First, involvement in Poland was likely to engender feelings of moral obligation to the political fate of the homeland. This is not to say that all Poles active in the United States had been active in Poland or vice versa. However, those who had been active in Solidarity in Poland were the ones who used expressions like "duty" or "obligation" to the homeland, thereby displaying a moral incentive for their involvement. Second, past affiliation with the opposition in Poland gave émigrés a premigration tie. While a few immigrants and wakacjusze had been involved in the opposition in Poland, all of the refugees had been involved to some degree, for it was by virtue of this involvement that they obtained refugee status. Refugees' primary ties in the United States were generally with other Solidarity refugees. Most of the refugees had not known each other in Poland, but their affiliation with Solidarity tied them to each other. Refugees already living here were aware of new refugee arrivals and often met them at the airport and introduced them to the political circles in Polonia. Thus, participation in Solidarity in Poland created a premigration network for refugees, similar to the way that involvement in World War II created premigration ties for veterans through their military units (e.g., First Airborne Division or Third Armored Division). These premigration ties separated the Solidarity refugees from the quota immigrants (especially the pre-1980 immigrants) and wakacjusze.

TABLE 8.3
The Relation between Political Actions in
the United States and Poland among Members of Forum

	POLITICAL ACTION IN POLAND		
Political Action in America	Yes	No	Total
Yes	86%	69%	84%
No	14%	31%	14%
Totals	100%	100%	100%
	(N=43)	(N=49)	(N=92)

Source: M.P. Erdmans, "Émigrés and Ethnics" (Ph.D. diss., Northwestern University, 1992a), 334. Data taken from a survey of 92 Forum members.

Moreover, previous experience with Solidarity meant that refugees had some connections to the opposition in Poland. Opposition members active in the underground in Poland often communicated with the refugees, informing them of the situation in Poland, and more importantly, about what types of assistance the opposition needed. These ties to the opposition inflamed the feelings of obligation, provided strategic directions to the refugees about how to help the opposition, and gave refugees a network through which resources could flow back to Poland. Thus, previous political involvement begot future political involvement, even while transplanted on foreign land.

Of the three groups—immigrants, refugees, and wakacjusze—the refugees were most likely to organize and take leadership positions in and become members of the new political organizations, especially those formed after 1984. Actions taken before the arrival of the Solidarity refugees were initiated mostly by the early immigrants who arrived in the late 1960s and 1970s. Despite the large number of wakacjusze, they were not well represented in Polonian political organizations or political activity, except for their participation in the absentee ballot. Perhaps the precariousness of the status (some had overstayed their visa limitations, many were illegally employed) discouraged them from becoming involved in any action that could potentially draw attention to themselves. Moreover, most of them were working—often as live-in help six days a week, or as day laborers 12 hours a day, 6 days a week—and had little free time for political activities. Finally, unlike the refugees, most wakacjusze did not have the network to other political activists in Chicago to draw them into political action. Still, those wakacjusze who were connected to other political activists did become involved.

To summarize, the type of émigrés most likely to be engaged in collective action for Poland (i.e., refugees) were not representative of the new cohort, which included mostly wakacjusze (more wakacjusze entered in one year in the mid-1980s than all the refugees together) and quota immigrants (twice as many immigrants as refugees entered the United States between 1965 and 1989). Those Poles who had been involved in the opposition in Poland were more likely to continue this action while in emigration because of moral and concrete ties to the opposition. Prior involvement in the Solidarity movement gave the refugees a network of affiliation in emigration (to other refugees) and a network of affiliation in Poland (to the opposition). In addition, prior involvement gave the refugees political and organizational skills which they used to mobilize sympathizers in Polonia.

Polonia Action for Poland

In the late 1970s, as the opposition movement in Poland emerged, Polonian organizations began to mobilize resources to support basic human rights in Poland (e.g., the right to organize) and national rights (e.g., the right to self-determination). Four uprisings in Poland, in 1956, 1968, 1970, and 1976, laid the foundation for the Solidarity opposition movement. Each successive revolt attracted a greater number and different types of actors and strengthened the opposition's structure within Poland. The 1956 and 1970 revolts were worker-led uprisings directed toward consumer and labor benefits. The 1968 revolt was initiated by intellectuals but failed to arouse the sympathy of the working class.

It was the 1976 revolt that finally brought the two strata together. The imprisonment of the rioters and strikers from the June 1976 disturbances in the cities of Ursus and Radom sparked the formation of the Worker's Defense Committee (known as KOR, from its Polish name *Komitet Obrony Robotnikow*). KOR, founded by a group of intellectuals, defended workers' interests in court by providing lawyers and economic aid. In the late 1970s there was an explosion of organized covert oppositional activity in Poland: the Flying University (underground classes), human rights groups, independent publishing houses, art shows, and critical theaters. In the fall of 1980, the opposition became organized within the trade union *Niezalezny Samorzadny Zwiazek Zawodowy* (Independent Self-Governing Trades Union), known to the world as Solidarity. Solidarity, as a nonviolent social movement, was supported by intellectuals, religious leaders, workers, and professionals within Poland. Solidarity received recognition from the international media and approval from leaders of the Western world and the Roman Catholic church. To support the changes in Poland, Polish American and Polish émigrés provided moral, financial, and political assistance to the opposition movement.

Symbolic Support: Statements and Information

During the 1970s, Poland-oriented actions undertaken by the national Polish American Congress (PAC) toward Poland involved primarily statements of support or denunciation. For example, PAC supported Poland's right to the formerly German territories, it supported the Helsinki agreements, and it objected to Poland's proposed constitutional changes in 1975. In the late 1970s, the national PAC started offering moral support for the budding opposition. PAC praised KOR leaders, backed the striking workers, and offered support to "Polish people seeking full restoration of human national rights and freedom" (*PAC Newsletter*, November 1980). PAC urged the U.S. Congress to support the Gdansk agreements, to recognize the Eastern European countries as sovereign states, and to provide economic assistance to Poland. After martial law was imposed, the PAC sent a statement to the White House asking that the United States demand the removal of martial law, the release of Lech Walesa, and the restoration of the trade union (*PAC Bulletin*, April 1982). Throughout the 1980s the PAC continued to express support for Solidarity and concern for the restrictions of freedom in Poland. PAC's work for Poland was done almost exclusively by members of the post-WWII emigration. The committees on Polish affairs were dominated by post-WWII, or second-cohort, Poles, the memoranda and statements were written by them, and PAC's political stance on U. S.-Poland relations was set by them.

As the events in Poland escalated in the late 1970s, a group of new Polish immigrants decided to organize their resources to support the opposition. In

1979, this new group began to publish a journal called *Pomost Quarterly* for a Polish-reading audience (92 percent of the articles from 1979 to 1984 were in Polish). The impetus for publishing the quarterly came from a Solidarity activist who had stressed the need for publicity as well as for financial support of the opposition movement (*Pomost Quarterly* 1979: vols. 1, 3). *Pomost* founders believed that publicity would provide some security against persecution for opposition leaders in Poland. Between 1979 and 1984, *Pomost* circulated 1500–2000 copies of each quarterly, except during martial law times (1982) when they printed nearly 7000 copies. The quarterly was devoted to Polish issues and often printed articles written by opposition leaders in Poland. Between 1979 and 1984, 52 percent of the articles were about events in Poland, 31 percent of the articles were about Poland-Polonia relations or Poland-U.S. relations, and less than 6 percent of the articles were solely about Polonia.

Pomost became an organization in 1981 and it maintained the journal's goal of helping Poland become an independent nation. During an interview, one Pomost member told me that Pomost attracted supporters because it was "unequivocally intolerant of communism. It was purely political. Whereas some of the other Polish organizations had a lot to do with different things—dances, and banquets and all this—Pomost basically stuck to politics." Although Pomost did attract some young Polish Americans and older post-World War II Poles, it was primarily composed of members of the new cohort—the three founders had immigrated to the United States in the late 1960s, and the majority of its members had arrived in the 1970s and early 1980s.[3]

In the same period, a group of Poles from the WWII emigration as well as younger Polish Americans formed the North American Center for the Study of Polish Affairs (Studium) in Ann Arbor. Established in 1976, the organization was created to educate and inform the United States and Canadian populations about Polish affairs and to assist Polonian organizations in their efforts to help Poland. The majority of Studium's articles in its quarterly were in English, and it primarily informed an educated audience of Poles and Polish Americans in the United States.

PAC, Pomost, and Studium were dedicated to building support for the Polish opposition movement among an audience of sympathizers living in America. Through statements directed at U.S. administrators and politicians, and articles about the opposition movement distributed to both Polish-language and English-language audiences, they educated a broad range of people. Having an informed public helped Polonia activists to secure political and financial support for the opposition in Poland.

Financial Support for the Opposition Movement

Polonia organizations financially supported a variety of opposition organizations in Poland. The established Polish American organizations supported the moderate, national-level opposition, mainly the national Solidarity union, and later, when Solidarity began to fractionalize, Lech Walesa's group. The new organizations composed of members of the new Polish cohort also aided the moderate groups, but they provided additional support to the more radical organizations in the opposition movement (e.g., Confederation for Independent Poland and Fighting Solidarity). Moreover, the new cohort's organizations supported the opposition at the regional and local levels. Which organization each Polonian group supported depended upon the group's ties to Poland. The formal PAC had ties to other formal institutions in Poland, such as Solidarity when it was a legal union and the Roman Catholic church. The organizations of the new Poles, whose members had been involved in the opposition, had informal ties to opposition leaders and organizations operating in the hometowns or regions of their members. Moreover, it was easier for the smaller, less formal organizations of the new Poles to become involved in clandestine activities (e.g., smuggling money and supplies into Poland) than for the larger, formal organizations that were more governed by bureaucratic procedures.

In the late 1970s, Pomost supported several underground publishing houses, striking workers, the union, and other lesser known oppositional groups (see table 8.4). Pomost sent funds and technical aid to 20 different opposition presses (*Robotnik, Bratniak, Glosu, Opinii, Nowa,* and *Spotkania* being the largest recipients) as well as 12 different organizations (e.g., Solidarity, KOR, Confederation for an Independent Poland, Fighting Solidarity, and the Movement for the Defense of Human and Civil Rights).

TABLE 8.4
Pomost Funds Sent to the Opposition Movement, 1979–1983

Destination	Amount Sent
Underground publishing	$6,352
Oppositional organizations	$7,086
Striking workers, political prisoners	$8,448

Source: M.P. Erdmans, "Émigrés and Ethnics" (Ph.D. diss., Northwestern University, 1992a), 110. There was no listing of funds paid out in 1984.

Though the amount of money sent was not large ($21,886 divided, but not equally, among 32 groups), the exchange rate was very favorable at that time (the average monthly salary was roughly U.S.$20). Pomost collected funds primarily through donations from individuals, Polonia organizations, and American labor unions.

In 1976 the Illinois division of the PAC created the Assistance Committee for the Support of Human Rights in Poland (*Komitet Pomocy Obroncom Praw*

Ludzkich i Obywatelskich w Polsce) to collect money for striking workers and their families. This committee sent around $5,000 to the striking workers between 1979 and 1981, and became inactive after 1981. In December 1985, it reappeared as a national PAC committee, with the title National Assistance Committee to Support Democratic Opposition in Poland. The new committee opened an account with over $20,000: the national PAC gave it $10,107; the PAC Illinois Division donated $1,000; and $9,539 came from the elimination of the Moczulski Fund (collected for the medical treatment of Leszek Moczulski). In total they collected over $51,000 from 1985 to 1988, almost half through the Illinois Division of the PAC (*Dziennik Zwiazkowy* 1988: 9). Except for one member from the new cohort, the committee members were all émigrés from the post-World War II cohort.

Shortly after martial law, Solidarity refugees began arriving in the United States, and several new political organizations emerged whose primary purpose was to help the Polish opposition. Freedom for Poland (FFP) was founded in October 1984 after Father Jerzy Popieluszko, a Roman Catholic priest in Poland and a vocal advocate of Solidarity and human rights, was murdered by a communist official. FFP was incorporated in Illinois in March 1985 as a not-for-profit charitable and educational organization directed at fighting communism. Its main activity was to collect money and send it to the underground opposition in Poland. Money was collected outside of churches, at Polonia festivals, political meetings, demonstrations, parades, and other public events in Polonia. Members also paid dues ($5 per month). In addition, FFP members organized demonstrations, circulated petitions, and sponsored opposition leaders to visit America. The organization consisted of roughly 50 members, most of whom were Solidarity refugees.[4] FFP had a working-class tone that came from the occupations of its members (laborers in both Poland and America), the educational level of its members (most had no college education), and its method of fund-raising (collecting small change with tin cans at public functions). The founding president of FFP had been a member of the National Coordinating Commission of Solidarity.

Brotherhood of Dispersed Solidarity Members (Brotherhood) was started in the fall of 1984. The main goals of the organization were to help the opposition in Poland and to unite Solidarity refugees. The organization was never officially incorporated. Brotherhood was a loosely knit group of about 20 people, operating mostly in Chicago. In contrast to FFP members, Brotherhood members had university degrees and had had professional occupations in Poland. In Chicago, leaders of Brotherhood held such positions as president of the Chicago chapter of the Polish University Abroad, Assistant for Immigrant Affairs to U.S. Representative Dan Rostenkowski, journalists for the *Dziennik Zwiazkowy*, editor-in-chief of the magazine *Kurier*, and host of one of the most popular Polish-language radio programs in Chicago. Through these positions, the

Brotherhood leaders became the informal leaders of the new Polish cohort in Chicago. Brotherhood leaders used their institutional and media channels to organize fund-raisers and demonstrations. Several Brotherhood leaders had also held prominent positions in Solidarity: two had been on the National Coordinating Commission of Solidarity; two were regional chairmen; and one was a regional vice chairman. Brotherhood members used their premigration links to help them reorganize themselves in America; in fact, the basis for organization was in part to preserve these premigration links.[5] The ideological ties of Brotherhood to the Solidarity union were evident in how it assessed membership dues. Brotherhood dues were considered union dues. The basis for the dues was set by the same standard used for union dues in Poland—1 percent of annual income (roughly $10–$20 a month in America). In addition to members' union dues, strategies for collecting money included hosting fund-raisers and selling paraphernalia with Solidarity logos (e.g., T-shirts, pins, bumper stickers) at Polonia festivals and events. The money was sent to regional and local underground centers of activity and publishing houses in Poland. Other activities included organizing lectures, demonstrating, and circulating petitions.[6]

The opposition movement in Poland experienced its lowest period from 1984 to 1988. During that time, world attention had turned away from Poland. Martial law had been lifted and the political prisoners for the most part had been released. People in Poland were increasingly affected by deteriorating economic conditions, and they became more preoccupied with economic survival than with working for the opposition. Solidarity, as a union, was illegal, but the movement had not disbanded. It operated underground through the Temporary Coordinating Committee of Solidarity (known as TKK from its Polish name, *Tymczasowa Komisja Koordinacyna*). The TKK had both national and regional organizational units. In addition, other opposition groups (some organized in the pre-martial law period and some organized after martial law) were also working underground. The action of these underground organizations was greatly limited during this repressive period. No new strike activity occurred until the spring of 1988. The most significant action during this period was the proliferation of underground publications supported by these covert organizations and publishing houses. Resources from abroad, sent by organizations like Brotherhood and FFP, helped the underground publishing centers to survive.[7] Because printing supplies could not be easily or cheaply obtained in Poland, the presses had to rely on the expensive black market (which required Western currency) or on materials smuggled into Poland. Also, the Polish government changed its policy toward violators of the censorship code. Instead of imprisonment, violators were fined or had their cars or apartments confiscated. Brotherhood responded to this new policy by setting up an "insurance fund" to provide the activists in Poland with some financial support to continue their activity.

It was more difficult to help the opposition movement in Poland after martial law because the opposition was underground. In order to help the underground presses, Poles abroad needed insider links to the people involved in the publishing movement. The new émigrés had these links, while Polish Americans did not. In 1986, when the national PAC first began to send financial support to the underground opposition movement, the money went mostly to Walesa's mainstream Solidarity. This committee sent funds to Poland through *Kultura* (a Parisian-based literary-political magazine founded by Polish émigrés after WWII), and *Kultura* got the money to the opposition. While Walesa was the largest recipient of PAC aid, this committee also sent some money to non-mainstream groups like Fighting Solidarity, Confederation for Independent Poland, and Rural Solidarity. PAC's funding of smaller nonmainstream organizations in Poland came from the involvement of FFP members working with this committee, who informed the committee about the presence and legitimacy of these organizations.

FFP regularly funded the PAC Committee to Support Democratic Opposition, contributing over $35,000 from 1985 to 1988. FFP also sent money directly to the opposition through its own personal links to the opposition, and over time more of this money was directed at nonmainstream organizations. In 1985–1986, FFP gave 80 percent of its money to Walesa and Solidarity. In 1987 it began to support the Confederation for Independent Poland and Fighting Solidarity, and by 1988, more than 60 percent of FFP's money went to these two organizations. The reason for the shift was twofold. First, the splintering of Solidarity in Poland had a ripple effect in Polonia. By 1988, the Confederation for Independent Poland and Fighting Solidarity were accusing Walesa of bargaining with the communists. These groups wanted a more hard-line, noncompromise approach with the communists—they wanted them out of power. An FFP leader told me that because FFP's statutes stated that the purpose of their organization was to fight against communists, they decided to support those organizations that most upheld that goal—which in their opinion were the Confederation for Independent Poland and Fighting Solidarity.

The second reason that funds were shifted was that Walesa and Solidarity were receiving financial support from other sources around the world. FFP chose instead to support those organizations which did not have as many outside benefactors. As one leader said:

> Fighting Solidarity is one of those groups that doesn't get any money from the State Department. That's why our group decided to support them. We like Morawiecki [the leader of Fighting Solidarity] but apparently the State Department doesn't like him. They consider him too extreme.

By 1988, FFP saw its main goal as supporting Fighting Solidarity. FFP negotiated a special contract with its leader, Kornel Morawiecki: FFP sent money to Fighting Solidarity, and in return received information about the situation in Poland.

Brotherhood supported local and regional activists in the hometowns of its members—Krakow, Wroclaw, Opole, and Gdansk (in that order)—choosing whom to support on the basis of personal ties. A newsletter to Brotherhood members stated that money would be sent to Poland if someone "who is a friend of a member of Brotherhood, informs us that people in his area need money or equipment." The newsletter mentioned that since the bulk of foreign aid to Poland was helping the national and executive committees of Solidarity, Brotherhood would support the regional and local committees. The money went to people Brotherhood leaders knew in Poland and to their friends' organizations and publications. For example, *Wroclaw Journal* was supported for two years because one of the Brotherhood leaders knew the activists who were its publishers. They also sent money to the families of political prisoners and political activists recently released from jail. From 1985 to 1988, friends of Brotherhood carried money to Poland and hand-delivered it to other friends of Brotherhood. Both Brotherhood and FFP used these personal links to smuggle money into Poland while the PAC had to rely on formal organizations, such as *Kultura*, to channel funds to the opposition.

Polonia money was also given to opposition leaders when they were on tour in America. For example, PAC gave money to Leszek Moczulski, leader of the Confederation for Independent Poland when he was touring America in 1988. Regional Solidarity leader Marian Jurczyk, a member of an opposition group that broke with Walesa's mainstream Solidarity in 1988, received support from Pomost during his visit in January 1989. Kornel Morawiecki was supported by FFP when he was in Chicago in July of 1988. Both Pomost and FFP helped to bring these leaders here, housed them while they were here, and helped them raise funds during their tours. In 1988, when the workers started to strike again, the PAC, Brotherhood, and FFP all worked together to help raise money for the Striking Worker's Fund. Together they raised $20,000. This money was handed to Janusz Onyszkiewicz, the national spokesperson for Solidarity, while he was in Chicago in July 1988.

In general, the PAC sent money to the national mainstream Solidarity office while the organizations of new émigrés supported more radical, nonmainstream organizations or local and regional offices of the opposition. The new organizations and PAC supported different strains of the Polish opposition because they had different connections to Poland. PAC knew mostly about Walesa's national organization, and was less informed about particular factions or regional branches. This was because PAC leaders had only formal ties to institutions in Poland. In contrast, the new émigrés, especially the Solidarity refugees, had informal ties to members of the opposition. Brotherhood and FFP members maintained these links while in emigration through mail and electronic hookups.

They also received underground publications that had been either personally carried to the United States, or taken out of Poland and mailed from some other European country. One FFP leader showed me a piece of literature that had a publication date only ten days prior to our interview. In every interview with post-1980 refugees I was given pieces of this underground literature. The native-born Polish Americans and most post-WWII émigrés did not have these informal links to the opposition.

Moreover, as a formal institution, PAC worried about engaging in any illegal activities, such as smuggling money to the underground in Poland. Sending money to *Kultura* was legal and they made the transactions through routine bank transferals. Because PAC preferred to operate through proper channels, its strongest ties to Poland were with legal, legitimate (i.e., noncommunist) institutions, and for most of the 1980s the only institution fitting those requirements was the Roman Catholic church. Thus PAC used the church as its main institutional link in Poland. This linkage conditioned the type of support PAC gave to Poland, humanitarian aid. As the next section discusses, this was the main form of support that PAC gave to Poland in the 1980s.

Humanitarian Aid: PAC Support for the People of Poland

PAC helped the Polish people by supplying humanitarian aid administered through the Polish episcopate. PAC had several humanitarian aid programs for Poland, all directed in Chicago by the PAC Charitable Foundation (PACCF). The Relief Fund for Poland, started in February 1981 on direct request from Solidarity leaders, initially sent food, medicine, and clothing to Poland, and later seeds, books, eyeglass lenses, and baby food, among other things. PAC also initiated the Food For Poland program in early 1981; and, in May of 1981, in response to a specific appeal from Lech Walesa, PAC started the Polonia Medical Bank. The Medical Bank worked in cooperation with Project Hope. PAC delivered $122 million worth of relief goods to Poland between 1981 and 1988 (see table 8.5). PAC's humanitarian aid was distributed by the Roman Catholic episcopate in Poland.[8] The aid was sent through legal shipping agencies and international aid organizations, like Project Hope and CARE.

The PACCF could not use any of the funds it collected for humanitarian aid to support the opposition movement directly. According to the articles of incorporation, the PACCF was "to operate exclusively for religious, charitable, scientific, cultural and educational purposes" (Article 5.A) with no mention made of support for political groups or unions. Also, as one PAC leader told me, "when we advertise we are raising money for one purpose, we can't use it for another." Thus, when people donated money to help needy children, PACCF could not send money to underground publishing houses. Because the formal structure of PAC forced its leaders to be accountable for how the resources were distributed, they chose to support Poland by using legitimate formal institutions such as the Polish episcopate.

TABLE 8.5
PAC Humanitarian Aid: 'Relief for Poland' Program, 1981–1988

Year Sent to Poland	Money Donations Received	Value of Relief Goods
1981	$1,655,261	$5,591,054
1982	$1,929,455	$21,657,700
1983	$185,785	$13,871,884
1984	$172,791	$10,907,241
1985	$698,480	$18,742,768
1986	$275,988	$14,474,997
1987	$68,270	$19,092,110
1988	$79,079	$16,250,000
Totals	$5,065,111	$122,687,754

Source: M.P. Erdmans, "Émigrés and Ethnics" (Ph.D. diss., Northwestern University, 1992a), 112. Data taken from PAC document, "Relief for Poland, General Information on Background and Current Crisis."

Protest Activity: Demonstrations and Boycotts

In August 1980, PAC and Pomost organized a demonstration of 100,000 people in Chicago to show support for the striking workers in Poland, and then organized two other demonstrations together in 1981 before the imposition of martial law. These demonstrations, while large, were peaceful. In the first few demonstrations, the demonstrators marched through the streets of downtown Chicago to the Polish Consulate. It was across from the Polish Consulate that most of the subsequent demonstrations took place, and this grassy area became known as Solidarity Square. From 1979 to 1984, Pomost quarterlies and PAC newsletters chronicled 52 demonstrations in the Chicago area (see table 8.6).

Polonia demonstrated to show support for the striking workers in Poland, and to protest the mass arrests in Poland, the imposition of martial law, and the delegalization of Solidarity. Martial law was imposed in Poland on 13 December 1981; Pomost organized a demonstration of 3,000 people three days later. On 16 December PAC sponsored another demonstration that attracted several thousand protesters, and on 27 December over 50,000 people demonstrated.

Pomost's protests became more disruptive and the PAC became more passive after the imposition of the martial law. Pomost adopted a strategy of guerrilla-style demonstrating—small, frequent, and hostile. At one Pomost demonstration, a protester chained himself to the consulate fence and the Chicago police arrested him for disorderly conduct (*Chicago Tribune*, 19 December 1981: 2). At several demonstrations, Poles threw rocks, eggs, and red paint at the consulate (Briggs and Cordt 1981). This disruptive action began to irritate the wealthy American residents living in the vicinity of the Polish consulate (Shulgasser and Robinson 1981). The president of the PAC Illinois Division said, "I regret the paint throwing. That's hooliganism, and I don't approve of it" (*Chicago Tribune*, 28 December 1981: 17). Eventually, police barricades were set up to keep the protesters away from the consulate. When Pomost planned a demonstration for 31 December 1981, the leader of the PAC Illinois Division actively discouraged people from attending, anticipating that it would be violent (*Pomost Quarterly*, 1983: 54). For several weeks after martial law Pomost held daily protests, and throughout 1982–1984 Pomost continued small (50–100 people) demonstrations in front of the consulate on the 13th of every month, marking the imposition of martial law.

TABLE 8.6
The Organization of Demonstrations in Chicago, 1980–1984*

	Organized by Pomost	Organized by Pomost & PAC	Organized by PAC
1980	0	2	0
1981	7	1	2
1982	18	0	3
1983	13	0	2
1984	4	0	1
Totals	42	3	8

Source: M.P. Erdmans, "Émigrés and Ethnics" (Ph.D. diss., Northwestern University, 1992a), 118. Data taken from Pomost quarterlies, 1979–1984 and PAC newsletters 1979–1984.
* Demonstrations include vigils and rallies. This table only refers to the sponsors. At most demonstrations, both Pomost and PAC members were present. PAC here refers to the Illinois Division.

As an alternative to demonstrating, the PAC supported the more moderate strategy advocated by President Reagan of placing candles in windows during the 1981 Christmas season as a show of support for Solidarity. Moreover, PAC leaders believed that numerous, smaller demonstrations were less effective than a few select demonstrations a year which attracted thousands of supporters. The president of the PAC Illinois division told me he did not think that Pomost's protest strategy was effective because the protesters had lost their ability to attract the American media by demonstrating too often. He said the main purpose of the demonstrations was "not to annoy the Polish consulate," but instead to "bring attention to Poland's cause." While Pomost leaders were also interested in media attraction, the leaders said that another primary reason for protesting was to attract the attention of the Polish consulate. They believed the consulate would inform the Polish government of these actions, and the government might then ease up on its repression of political activists.[9] Both groups wanted to influence governmental policies in Poland, but PAC believed the route was through the American media to the United States government then to Poland. Pomost believed the route to Poland was through the Polish consulates in the United States.

Between 1987 and 1989 there were at least 16 demonstrations in Chicago in front of the consulate. These demonstrations were initiated by members of FFP, Brotherhood, and the PAC Illinois Division. (Internal conflicts made Pomost less active between 1986 and 1989.) At each of the 16 demonstrations from 1987 to 1989, at least 90 percent of the participants were émigrés—members of either the new cohort or the post-WWII cohort. These demonstrations were organized to mark the founding anniversary of Solidarity (31 August) and the anniversary of the imposition of martial law (13 December), and for special events such as to protest the suspect death of a priest in Poland (January 1988), or to support striking workers in Poland (spring 1988).

In addition to demonstrations, other protest activity included boycotts of Polish products. This action was taken solely by Pomost, which was the most radical of all the Polonia organizations. Shortly after the imposition of martial law, Pomost boycotted Polish products (e.g., ham) and Polish performers touring America. While the PAC was careful not to have any relations with the communist *government*, they encouraged contacts with the Polish *nation* through scientific, cultural, and economic linkages. Pomost members objected to these contacts, especially the economic linkages. Polish Americans essentially held the idea that "business was business" and that one could be politically against the communist regime in Poland and still carry on international trade relations. New Poles in Pomost considered business relations with the Polish nation an acknowledgment of the legitimacy of the communist regime. They believed that there should be no economic or cultural relations with Poland. Pomost tried to get PAC to back its boycotts but PAC leaders withheld support, believing the boycotts unfairly hurt the small businesses in Chicago that marketed Polish products or provided Polish entertainment.

In summary, protest behavior in Chicago was tied closely to the situation in Poland. It was primarily the newest cohort of Poles who organized and participated in these protest activities. The PAC was more of an interest group than a social movement organization. As an interest group PAC tried to help Poland through political action as an ethnic lobby. However, as the next section shows, Pomost proved to be a more aggressive organization in this arena as well.

Influencing American Foreign Policy

Two major lobbying efforts oriented toward Poland were undertaken by Polonian organizations in the 1980s. The first focused on the economic sanctions imposed on Poland after martial law and the second on the Yalta treaty. Both PAC and Pomost were involved in these lobbying efforts. The PAC lobbying strategy was to support the State Department and White House in administration policies toward Poland, and to serve as advisors and backers rather than agitators and dissenters. When I examined PAC newsletters for a 20-year period (September 1969 to August 1989), I found 36 events that I classified as "'dialogue with Washington;" and PAC disagreed with White House policy in only three of these dialogues. One occasion for disagreement was PAC's denouncement of the Sonnefeldt Doctrine, which stated that Eastern European countries enjoyed "an organic relationship" with the Soviet Union. For the most part, PAC supported the policies of the White House. The president of the Illinois PAC told me that PAC wanted to work with the State Department; they did not want to be a "counterforce." As he explained:

> It's just good sense to communicate with the State Department and say, "what's your position on this question," rather than create a counterforce. In those instances where we are not satisfied that enough is being done, we would take those [counter] positions. We would do it in a disarming manner, we would not do it in a threatening manner.

Pomost leaders disagreed with this conciliatory strategy. They wanted a lobby that would direct State Department policy, not be directed by it. One Pomost leader believed, "[PAC] simply does whatever those people in the State Department propose. The transmission should be a different way. We should be pressing the State Department to fulfill our will." Pomost leaders wanted a lobby that would demand more for the opposition in Poland and be more aggressive toward the communist regimes in Poland and the Soviet Union.

The conciliatory style of the PAC and the aggressive style of Pomost were evident in how the two groups acted on the issue of lifting economic sanctions. The U.S. administration placed economic sanctions on Poland and the Soviet Union when martial law was imposed in Poland, in December 1981.[10] Initially, Pomost, PAC, and the opposition leaders in Poland all supported the sanctions as a sign of support for the opposition and an act of censure against the communist regime. Almost all segments of Polonia supported the sanctions: the established Polish Americans involved in the PAC, the pro-Solidarity organizations of the newest Polish cohort, members of the post-World War II cohort, the intelligentsia, and the professionals. The only people opposing the sanctions were Polish American businessmen who had trade relations with Poland, some of whom were members of PAC (Krynski 1983).

When in July 1984 a general amnesty released most of the remaining political prisoners (martial law had been lifted in July 1983), the United States decided to remove some of the sanctions (e.g., aviation restrictions and the ban on scientific exchange). PAC leaders agreed with this decision and urged the United States to open discussions on Poland's admission to the International Monetary Fund (IMF) so that Western credits would be extended to Poland and thereby aid in the relief of its economic and ecological problems. PAC leaders argued that the remaining sanctions only hurt the people of Poland. Removing the sanctions would also help Polish American businessmen who had investments in Poland. In Poland, Solidarity leaders (and the communist regime) also agreed with the lifting of the sanctions. Jan Nowak wrote that, in 1985, PAC was on the side of "the Pope, the Polish Episcopate and Lech Walesa" in urging that the remaining sanctions be lifted (1986: 53).

Pomost leaders disagreed with the PAC, the State Department, the church, and Solidarity. Pomost wanted the sanctions to remain in place in order to pressure the Polish government to relegalize Solidarity and to begin a program of social reforms. Pomost leaders felt that IMF membership and subsequent Western aid would only give Poland a face-lift, prolong the process of economic and social decay, and delay the overthrow of the regime (*Pomost Quarterly*, 1984: 49–51). Pomost began to engage in more aggressive efforts, such as trying to embarrass the president of the United States in order to convince the U.S. administration to keep the sanctions in place (Erdmans 1992a: 126).

A second lobbying campaign during this period centered around the Yalta treaty. A "Renounce Yalta" campaign, started in 1982, fought to abolish the Yalta Treaty on the grounds that it had allowed the Soviets to establish totalitarian regimes in Eastern Europe, and that the Yalta agreement itself had been violated, as there had been no free elections in any of the communist satellite countries. In the beginning, PAC worked with Pomost to collect signatures in support of renouncing Yalta. PAC had adopted resolutions in 1983 and 1984 calling on the U.S. Congress to re-examine and renounce the Yalta agreement (*PAC Bulletin*, 4 December 1983; 4 August 1984). However, when it became known that President Reagan and the State Department would not support this campaign, PAC withdrew its support for the "Renounce Yalta" campaign. Dr. Jerzy Lerski, a prominent postWWII émigré and PAC director, wrote, "Polish V.I.P.'s are simply afraid to raise this issue [renouncing Yalta] without the blessing, which seems rather unlikely, of the State Department" (Lerski 1983: 2). PAC took the position, in agreement with the State Department, that the Yalta Treaty need not be renounced, but that its program of free elections should be enforced. Pomost, however, continued to lobby the U.S. Senate to adopt a resolution to renounce Yalta.[11]

Because Pomost felt that the present PAC lobby was not strong enough to be an aggressive spokesperson for Poland's interest, and because Pomost and PAC disagreed on U.S. foreign policy toward Poland, Pomost eventually started their own lobby. Until 1982, most of Pomost's funds were sent to Poland. After 1982 the majority of the funds stayed in the United States to support its lobbying activities (Erdmans 1992a: 128).

Direct Involvement in Poland's Political Process: Elections of June 1989

Between 1986 and 1988, economic conditions in Poland continued to worsen and eventually led to an outbreak of strikes in May and June of 1988. Although the Solidarity union was still outlawed, the failing economy and the labor strikes brought the Polish government back into discussion with Solidarity opposition leaders. The discussions, known as the roundtable talks, resulted in an agreement to hold partially free elections, the first since WWII. Elections were to be held in June 1989 for a two-house parliament. The upper house senate (which had been disbanded after a rigged referendum in 1946) was restored, and all of its 100 seats were open to free election. In the lower house, 35 percent, or 161, of the 460 seats were open for free elections. In addition, Poles were now formally allowed to create free associations and the Solidarity trade union was relegalized. However, a restraining order was placed on the union. Solidarity leaders agreed not to strike until the new congress of union members met and this congress was not slated to meet before fall 1989.

The roundtable agreements were criticized for three primary reasons. First, the elections were not completely free. Groups such as Confederation for Independent Poland and Fighting Solidarity demanded 100 percent free elections in the lower house. Second, many union workers felt that the removal of the right to strike severely crippled the Solidarity union. Third, the critics felt that the elections were designed to coopt members of the opposition into the government to share the responsibility for the economic crisis.

Despite these criticisms, Solidarity leaders accepted the challenge to run for the 261 open seats. Solidarity placed their campaign in the organizational arm of the Citizens' Committee, a group of 120 public figures who served as an advisory council to Walesa. The opposition had only two months to choose candidates, prepare campaign platforms, and disseminate information. Walesa and the Citizens' Committee appealed to Polonia for financial support; and Poles abroad began fund-raising drives to collect money for the technical equipment needed to run a successful campaign.

Both Brotherhood and PAC helped to raise campaign funds for Solidarity. Brotherhood monetarily supported election campaigns in Poland at the local levels rather than the national level. In mid-April, Brotherhood members traveled to Poland with money, video and audio equipment, and fax machines. The cash came from Brotherhood membership dues. The money for the tape recorders and a shot mike came from a special PAC Solidarity Election fund, and the money for the fax machines came from a group of Polish American lawyers. After this initial trip to Poland, Brotherhood's material support for the election was channeled through the PAC. Six weeks before the election, PAC started the Solidarity Election Fund to help organize publicity and buy communications equipment for the Solidarity candidates. PAC state divisions, Polonia organizations, and Polonia radio and newspapers helped raise funds. The PAC Illinois Division raised $4,500, while the national campaign collected over $100,000. The money was sent to the Solidarity's national Citizen Committee. In addition, a group of Polish American lawyers organized Fair Elections in Poland, Inc., which raised money for the Solidarity campaign in Poland and disseminated information to the American public about the elections.[12] All the funds sent to Solidarity were to be used to produce video presentations, to print and distribute election newspapers and campaign literature, and to pay support staff.

In addition to Polonia's financial support, Poles abroad were allowed to vote in the election through absentee ballot. According to Poland's constitution, anyone born in Poland or who at any point in their life had had a Polish passport could vote. Even Poles who had become American citizens could legally vote, according to the Polish constitution. However, it was never certain whether the U.S. constitution gave Poles who had become American citizens the legal right to vote in another nation's elections (Erdmans 1992a: 202–5).

The impetus for mobilizing the absentee vote in America came from Solidarity refugees, particularly in Chicago and Washington, D.C., rather than Solidarity leaders in Poland. As one Solidarity refugee in Chicago explained,

> Solidarity in Poland was too concerned with its own problems to worry about Polonia. We tried to get them to recognize that Polonia's vote was important because we would be voting the day before they voted in Poland, and we could influence the mood of the election in Poland.

The Citizens' Committee in Poland eventually recognized Polonia's value, and supported the campaign by making appeals in the Polonia media asking Poles to vote. Still, the task of mobilizing the voters was primarily undertaken by the émigrés.

Those who organized the absentee vote in Chicago were mostly new cohort Poles grouped together in the Solidarity Election Committee and directed primarily by Brotherhood leaders. This committee nominated ten election judges and two election commissioners to oversee the election in Chicago. All twelve people received individual certificates of approval from the official National Election Commission *(Panstw Wybory Komisjia)* in Warsaw. Strategies for mobilizing voters included teaching Poles abroad how to vote, for whom to vote, and where to vote, in order to insure that Solidarity candidates got elected. This committee put up campaign posters for Solidarity candidates, passed out campaign buttons, and disseminated information about Solidarity candidates and voting procedures. On election day, members of this committee organized the long lines of voters, answered questions, and passed out kielbasa, apples, and tea. They also raised the Polish flag and a Solidarity banner across the street from the consulate. Fair Elections provided shuttle buses to transport voters from the Polish neighborhoods in Chicago to the consulate on election day. The result was that 5361 Chicago Poles came out to vote.[13]

Not all Polonia supported the elections in Poland or in Chicago. Poles living abroad disagreed with the elections basically on the same principles as Poles who opposed the elections in Poland—the elections were not completely free, Solidarity would be scapegoated for the economic problems of the nation, and the union had temporarily lost its ability to strike. FFP and other political organizations conceded that the modified elections were a form of progress but they pushed for 100 percent free elections.[14] The dissenters created a Committee on Behalf of Free Elections in Poland, demanding "free, democratic and non-falsified elections" (*Dziennik Zwiazkowy,* 1989a; 3). This committee included representatives from Polonia (e.g., leaders from FFP, Alliance for Independence, and post-WWII veteran organizations) and Poland (e.g., leaders from Confederation for Independent Poland and Fighting Solidarity). This committee sent a petition to the U.S. Congress urging its members to push the Polish government for completely free elections. They collected petition signatures outside churches, at Polonia meetings, and at Polish American parades. At the May 3rd parade commemorating Poland's 1791 constitution, their placards read, "Democracy not Bargains: Free Elections."

PAC made guarded statements that the elections were "not fully democratic" and that the roundtable agreements "did not completely fill the aspirations of the Polish nation"; however, it maintained that the partially free elections were a move in the right direction, and gave "its full support and trust to the position represented by Lech Walesa" (PAC 1989a: 1; 1989b: 1). Though the PAC supported the elections in Poland, it did not take any actions to help mobilize voters or organize the election in Chicago. The PAC's attitude can be summed up in its statement, "as American Polonia we don't have the opportunity to participate in the elections," but we do "have the opportunity to demonstrate our belief and support in the elections" (PAC 1989d: 1). PAC could ideologically support the elections as a move toward democracy and financially support the campaign in Poland, but they could not participate in the elections in Chicago because they were Americans.

The elections forced émigrés to make a decision on whether they were Poles or Americans, a decision that centered on the question of national loyalties. The most contentious issue was whether Polish émigrés who had taken American citizenship should vote: Was voting in a Polish election an act of disloyalty to one's American citizenship? PAC declared: "According to American law, persons with U.S. citizenship should not vote because that is what they agreed to when they accepted American citizenship" (PAC: 1989d). In fact, very few Poles with American citizenship voted. In my survey only 3.6 percent of the voters were U.S. citizens.

The voters in the sample ranged in ages from 18 to 85 years old, with 57 percent of them in the 30-49 year range. The oldest voter had arrived in the United States in 1939, and had been the last noncommunist consul general in Chicago. The voters resided mostly in Chicago: 99 percent of the sample lived in the Chicago metropolitan area, and 78 percent within the city limits. They tended to be recent arrivals (90 percent had arrived in the United States after 1978, and over 60 percent after 1984). There was a correlation between legal status and length of time in the United States.[15] Those with permanent resident status had been here longer: 84 percent of those who came before 1982 were permanent residents compared with only 20 percent of those who arrived after 1985 (see table 8.7). All of the Poles in the sample with U.S. citizenship arrived before 1981.

TABLE 8.7
Relation between Year of Arrival and Legal Status
of Absentee Voters in Poland's National Election

Arrival	N	% U.S. Citizen	% Permanent Resident	% Temporary Resident	Totals
Before 1982	135	12.6%	84.4%	3.0%	100%
1982-1985	106	0%	62.3%	37.7%	100%
1986-1989	217	0%	20.3%	79.7%	100%

Source: M.P. Erdmans, "Émigrés and Ethnics" (Ph.D. diss., Northwestern University, 1992a), 206. Data taken from survey of 464 voters in Chicago who voted in Poland's national election on 3 June 1989.

The results of the election are now known to the world. Solidarity candidates won in Polonia and Poland. My sample of Poles voted overwhelmingly for Solidarity candidates: 95 percent of the respondents voted for only Solidarity candidates, 4 percent voted for Solidarity and Communist party candidates, and three people voted a straight Communist ticket. Through the absentee ballot, Poles abroad were able to take an active role in shaping Poland's political future.

Involvement in Poland's Emergent Free Market System

Following Poland's political liberation, the new Polish congress began renovating its economic system. To make the transition to a free market system,

Poland needed capital, market skills, and new technology. To promote the process of economic reconstruction, new Polonia organizations were created. Some of these organizations were set up with federal funds from the Support for Eastern European Democracy Act.[16] Other organizations, such as the Polish American Economic Forum (Forum), were grass roots Polonia organizations.

Forum was a business information broker. Organized in Chicago in the fall of 1989, Forum listed its objectives as promoting foreign investments in Poland and Western economic assistance for Poland. Forum attracted small- and medium-sized investors who wanted information about market opportunities, tax laws, and legal procedures. By November 1989, Forum had roughly 450 members, it had secured the appearance of Lech Walesa at its First Annual Convention, it had elected a 27-member board of directors, and it had set up offices in Chicago and Warsaw.

As with the other Polonian organizations discussed in this chapter, Forum was created in response to the changing needs of Poland. The idea for Forum developed in July 1989, soon after the first elections in Poland, when Western aid packages for Poland were being discussed. The founder of Forum was in Poland at the time that President Bush revealed his aid package. He returned to Chicago charged with informal directives from Polish leaders that Polonia had to respond to Poland's economic needs. On his return, he said that a group of new Poles were organizing a "Polish Forum, along the same lines as PUSH, an investment group of about 2000 people to invest in Poland and get together to discuss methods of helping Poland." Poland's leaders gave Forum leaders concrete economic messages. For example, Polish Senator Machalski, a representative of the Economic Campaign (*Akcji Gospodarczej*) asked the Forum leaders to look for capital in the United States to modernize the Polish communications system. Delegates from Poland who attended the Forum Convention brought with them specific investment packages (e.g., a horse breeder who was looking for a foreign partner, a private bank that wanted backers for a joint stock company). Janusz Onyszkiewicz, a national Solidarity spokesman, gave Forum a package of investment proposals from farmers and businessmen in the town of Przemysl (e.g., one man had a castle to sell, another had land he wanted to develop).

The interdependent relationship between the economic and political systems in communist societies meant that activities in one arena directly affected activities in the other. The newly elected government had inherited a crumbling economic system, and its success would be measured by its ability to improve this situation. Forum leaders maneuvered to convince Polonia that economic support of the private market in Poland was a patriotic act. Investment dollars were cast as a form of political demonstration. One leader said that Forum "is nothing more than an idea to make another demonstration—only without the rotten eggs" (*Kurier* 1989: 6). And in fact, most Forum members felt that helping the nation economically was a political act. In a questionnaire completed by 58 percent of the 170 people who attended Forum's Inaugural Meeting, 70 percent of the respondents said they became involved in Forum for political reasons (Kusak 1989: 4). For example, one respondent said, "It's our responsibility to bring help to our nation"; other respondents echoed this sentiment, describing their membership in Forum as an "obligation" in order "to help" Poland, "our fatherland" (Kusak 1989: 4–5). In my survey of 109 Forum members, 73 percent of the respondents indicated that they had joined Forum "to help Poland." Thus, although Forum was oriented toward Poland's economy, because of the inter-twined nature of Poland's political and economic systems, involvement in Forum symbolized political support for the new government.

The majority of Forum members were from the newest cohort. Of the 27 directors, there were 20 new émigrés, 6 Polish Americans, and 1 post-WWII Pole. Forum members were also mostly newcomers. In my survey of members, 92 percent were émigrés, and 77 percent of the respondents had arrived in the United States after 1975. Although the members were overwhelmingly from the new Polish cohort, several people were from the Polish American community, including members from PAC, the Copernicus Foundation, and the Polish American Advocates Society.

In 1990, the Forum organized two business tours in Poland, and it had amassed a data base of over 4,000 investment proposals. However, while the Forum offices had these data on potential investment schemes, tax laws, and legal advice, the office did little to get this information to its members. In the first year of operation, only two newsletters were published—these were the only contact with the members. As a result, by the second year Forum lost more than half of its members, and it survived into 1992 as a skeleton organization. Although Forum was one of the first organizations of its kind in America, numerous organizations developed agendas oriented toward helping Poland move into a free market system, and thereby competed with Forum for resources and members. Still, Forum represents an example of the rapid pace at which Polonia reacted to changes in Poland.

Summary

The new organizations formed in Chicago in the 1980s have either disbanded or altered their strategies in the 1990s as a result of changes in Poland. Pomost developed internal problems in the mid-1980s, changed leadership, and now continues as a radical right-wing organization. Associations such as Brother-hood and FFP were organized to help the Polish underground opposition, which after 1989 had been elected into office. Brotherhood no longer exists, but FFP continues as a small group offering social activities to its members and support for organizations in Poland that have become political parties such as

Confederation for Independent Poland. The Solidarity Election Committee was a temporary association that disbanded after the election. All of these organizations had specific agendas, and when the situation changed in Poland they lost their *raison d'etre*.

The historical trend in Polonia has been that political activists working on behalf of Poland take their cues from Poland. As this chapter shows they orient their activities to compliment the actions of the opposition in Poland. First they supported KOR, then the striking workers, then Solidarity. When Solidarity was forced underground, the Polonian groups funneled money to the underground publishing houses; and when Solidarity began to fractionalize, different groups within Polonia supported different wings of the opposition. When free elections were introduced they worked to mobilize absentee votes, and when the economy opened up to a free market system they began investing and facilitating investments in Poland. Polonian groups do not attempt to direct the changes in Poland, instead they respond to the changes. With the presence of the new Polish cohort, and the exciting changes in Poland, political action for Poland was revived in the 1980s. What action it will take in the 1990s depends on Poland.

Notes

1. The data for this chapter were collected as part of a larger study conducted between 1986 and 1991 on the relations between new émigré organizations and established Polish American organizations in Chicago's Polonia. The study examined the cultural, social, migrational, and biographical differences among Polish émigrés and ethnics that disrupted group solidarity, as well as the organizational strategies, goals, and ideologies that were used to facilitate organizational cooperation. Data for the research were collected through four years of participant observation in Poland and Polonia, interviews with 54 leaders and activists in Chicago's Polonia, archival resources, and surveys. For a fuller description of these methods see Erdmans 1992a, appendix A.
2. I first surveyed 464 Poles in Chicago who voted in Poland's national election through absentee ballot on 4 June 1989. The second survey included 92 Poles who were members of a new economic-political organization, the Polish American Economic Forum (Forum). The participants in both surveys were primarily members of the new Polish cohort—98 percent of the election sample and 92 percent of the Forum sample were Poles who had arrived after 1965, the great majority of them having arrived between 1978 and 1989. In the election survey, nearly 60 percent of the sample came from a provincial capital in Poland, while only 17 percent came from villages; in the Forum data, 67 percent came from provincial capitals and only 13 percent came from small towns with less than 10,000 people. In addition, 82 percent of the voters sampled and 66 percent of the Forum members sampled had university degrees. However, there was also a correlation between education and residence—those from urban areas were more likely to have higher educational levels. (See Erdmans 1992a, appendix B, for a discussion of the surveys.)
3. During its peak years in 1982-1983, Pomost leaders told me they had 6,000 sympathizers nationwide and 900 dues-paying members. The *Pomost Quarterly*

started in Chicago in January 1979. By 1980, Pomost centers were established in Los Angeles, New York City, Stevens Point, Wisconsin, Detroit, Niagara Falls, Ottawa, and Warsaw, as well as in France, England, Japan, and South Africa. The chapters distributed the quarterly, held meetings, organized demonstrations, gathered petitions, and raised funds. Pomost kept its headquarters in Chicago.

4. FFP leaders stated that in 1988 FFP had 100 members in Illinois, with sympathizers in California, New Jersey, Arizona, and Connecticut; but on the average only 25–40 members were active. FFP leaders said that 80 percent of its members arrived in the United States after 1980 the others came in the 1960s and 1970s, and two came in the post-WWII wave.

5. An organizational recruitment letter stated, "The goal of the Brotherhood is to unify the members of NSZZ Solidarity in America." In addition to maintaining Solidarity ties in the United States, Brotherhood tried to maintain its networks with other Solidarity refugees and organizations around the world. Brotherhood was connected to the Solidarity Information Office in Toronto and the larger Conference of Solidarity Support Organizations (CSSO).

6. Brotherhood members also operated through a second group, the Club of Catholic Intellectuals (known as KIK from its Polish name *Klub Inteligentsia Katolickiej*). KIK in Chicago was modeled after KIK in Poland, an organization created in the late 1950s for discussing social, economic, and religious issues. In Chicago, Brotherhood leaders and other new Poles who considered themselves members of the intelligentsia, founded KIK in 1986 to serve as a discussion group. KIK was composed of roughly 30–40 new Polish émigrés. In addition, a half a dozen post-WWII émigrés regularly attended meetings, and some younger Polish Americans were occasionally present. All Brotherhood members were KIK members, but not all KIK members were Brotherhood members. Sometimes Brotherhood conducted its activities under the name of KIK because its purported apolitical agenda was an asset. For example, when Brotherhood invited opposition leaders from Poland to the United States it did so as KIK because it was easier to get a visa for these political leaders while operating as an intellectual discussion group rather than as Brotherhood, which was more of an opposition group. Because of the membership overlap between KIK and Brotherhood, and the informal nature of both organizations, it was difficult at times to separate what was KIK and what was Brotherhood. They shared a common fund, the same leaders, and most members.

7. In addition, to Brotherhood and FFP there were numerous small groups of new Poles organized for the purpose of helping Poland across the United States. An FFP leader estimated that in 1988 there were about 40 political groups of post-Solidarity refugees in the United States. Brotherhood leaders made mention of six other organizations of Solidarity refugees across the United States to which they had connections. Another new organization in Chicago was the Alliance for Independence. Members from this group were interviewed for this study. I also interviewed members of five different new organizations in California. Other organizations were founded in Connecticut, New Jersey, New York, Washington, D.C., and Arizona.

8. The church did not give direct financial aid to the opposition. The church emphasized human rights and criticized the communist regime for imprisoning political activists and using violence to disperse political gatherings. However, the church could not openly give material aid to opposition groups when the groups were illegal. When the organizations were legal the church tried to remain apolitical. PAC did not send money to the church; it sent clothing, food, and medical supplies to the Polish episcopate who then distributed the goods. All of the goods were sent through

legal shipping channels, and the containers could have been checked by state officials before they reached the episcopate. Thus, PAC could not have sent such things as typewriters or copy machines, that is, the type of equipment the underground publishing houses needed. In Poland it was illegal to have an unregistered typewriter in one's possession, and illegal to unofficially send one to a person.

9. One Pomost leader told me:

> We knew for sure that every time we had a demonstration they eased up on the prisoners. I can show you the guy who was in prison for years in Poland, and he said that every time there was something in the West he could feel it—better food, or better treatment, or access to the library. The relation was very simple, they [the Polish government] needed the money, the loans. Up to a point they could suppress the people. And then the West is gonna say, "oh what about human rights."

The fact is that demonstrations did help the political prisoners psychologically. One Polish refugee who had been in jail during martial law told me:

> I remember how important it was, especially when I was in prison, if I had information about some action of Poles abroad. People told me that there was a big demonstration, about 50,000 people just after martial law in Poland. It raises one's spirits.

But he also said that they heard about the demonstrations through Voice of America, the BBC, or Radio Free Europe. Given this, then those demonstrations that were large enough to have media coverage were best able to provide moral support to the opposition activists in Poland.

10. Sanctions that applied to Poland included the suspension of agricultural and dairy surplus shipped to Poland, suspension of major elements of economic relations, no renewal of the Import-Export Bank's line of credit to Poland, suspension of Polish civil aviation privileges, suspension of Polish fishing rights in American waters, and further restrictions on high technology exports to Poland. In October of 1982, when Solidarity was declared illegal, President Reagan also suspended Poland's Most Favored Nation status.

11. In 1984, Pomost was able to enlist the help of Congressman Tom Corcoran who was running as a Republican for an Illinois Senate seat. Corcoran agreed to support the Yalta proposal and in return Pomost supported his Senatorial bid. Pomost initiated and wrote the resolution that called for Congress to formally renounce the Yalta Treaty. Corcoran introduced it as Resolution 435 in the House of Representatives at the 1st session of the 98th Congress in 1983. The joint resolution was referred to the Senate Committee of Foreign Affairs. Corcoran lost the Senate race, but other Congressmen supported the bill. In 1985, Representative Jack Kemp and Senator Robert Kasten sponsored a resolution that was approved by both houses. The resolution did not renounce Yalta, but asked that the provisions of Yalta (free elections and the right to self-determination) be met.

12. Fair Elections made appeals for funds to run the campaigns of Solidarity-backed candidates. The funds they collected were transmitted directly to an official foreign exchange account of the Citizen's Committee of Solidarity in Warsaw. Its activities also included a news blitz about the elections on the local, national and international level. The Honorary Committee included non-Polish politicians, Polish-American

elected officials and prominent Polish émigrés, among others: Bill Bradley, Cecil Partee, Stephen Solarz, William Lipinski, Zbigniew Brzezinski, Czeslaw Milosz, Leszek Kolakowski, and Mike Ditka.

13. Absentee voting also took place in Washington, D.C., and New York City. Poles from 28 midwestern and western states could have voted in Chicago. The consulate in New York was open to Poles living on the East Coast. More than 8,500 Poles voted in New York, where voters came on chartered buses from Pennsylvania, New Jersey, Boston, the western cities of New York, and the northern states on the East Coast. At the embassy in Washington, D.C. less than 500 Poles voted.

14. Several new Poles I interviewed in Northern California were against the election because it was not 100 percent free. One man debated whether the free seats represented a democratic choice when there was "your 40 year enemy on one side, and then those who oppose it all from one party. Of course you have to choose the other, and this again is not like free choice." Another man wrote,

> The idea that democratic elections took place in Poland this June for the first time since World War II is incorrect. Democratic elections will only take place when legally active political parties will be able to advance candidates who in turn will present society with clear, understandable political programs. The elections of June 1989 were a far cry from what we commonly understood as democratic elections. (Dymarski 1989: 143)

Members of an organization known as "Americans for an Independent Poland" were also against the elections. One man was skeptical that the elections represented reform:

> Once all the smoke settles, the regime hopes to continue to reside firmly in the seat of power (with an air of legitimacy hitherto unknown), the discredited Solidarity will be unwittingly co-opted to blame for the economic ruin, the population will lose its heroes, and the West will loosen its purse strings to let billions of dollars trek east to be gobbled up by mankind's most inefficient and inhuman system. (Kruczkowski 1989: 6)

Others wrote about the short amount of time available to prepare the election, and stressed their anger that only 35 percent of the seats in the lower house were open to free elections. One man wrote, "The 'great victory for Walesa' is a defeat for the Polish people" (Cisek 1989: 2).

Despite its criticism of the roundtable talks and agreements, Confederation for Independent Poland announced support for the elections in late April. It stated that although "these elections will not be free" Confederation for Independent Poland had decided to take part in the elections because "we want confrontational elections with the government and not confrontational elections with Solidarity" (*Dziennik Zwiazkowy,* 1989b, 5). Fighting Solidarity also initially boycotted the elections but then some of its members became candidates.

15. The correlation between length of time in the United States and legal status can be accounted for in part by the fact that some legal statuses require a certain period of residency (e.g., citizenship requires five years of permanent residency). In other cases, having been in the United States for a longer period allowed people to gain permanent residency by the Immigration Reform and Control Act 1986. Finally, since most temporary visas are only valid for a few years one would expect the

majority of those with legal temporary visas to have come fairly recently, as was the case. In fact, year of arrival and legal status may be measuring almost the same phenomenon, which could be defined as permanence of one's ties to the host country. This correlation between length of time in the United States and legal status makes it uncertain whether Poles voted because they were recent immigrants or because they were neither U.S. citizens nor planned to become U.S. citizens (see Erdmans 1989).

16. During Walesa's visit to the United States, an $846.5 million package was approved by Congress. The bill, the Support for Eastern European Democracy Act of 1989, was to "facilitate the transition from state-directed controls to a free market economy," to promote democracy, private investment, and the development of a free market in Poland (Pear 1989: 16). The aid was broken down into $125 million in food aid, $240 million in grants to private businesses, up to $200 million to stabilize the Polish currency, and up to $200 million in loans to Polish companies importing American products. The bill also rescheduled Poland's foreign debts, promoted job retraining and unemployment programs, and gave money for cultural and educational exchanges. Moreover, the bill designated $10 million to teach Poles managerial, commercial, entrepreneurial, financial, scientific, and technical skills needed in a market-driven economy. Finally, the package made Poland eligible for programs run by the Overseas Private Investment Corporation and the Import-Export Bank.

9

The Long View

This book has been devoted to an analysis of an ethnic community, locally and superterritorially structured throughout companionate circles, organizations, and the press. This community, Polonia, has been developed in America by three cohorts of emigrating Poles and their descendants with the help of transient Polish nationals, and influenced by its relations with both Poland and America. We have not followed the usual approach to ethnic Americans of tracing the changes in their demographic characteristics, the effects of acculturation, and the problems of assimilation. Rather, our major focus has been Polonia's social structure and the companionate circles of its internal life—the community as created, maintained, and modified over a century of organizational existence.

The Poles who emigrated to the United States in the pre-World War I years were mainly of two social classes. The upper-class immigrants or exiles included political refugees, former members of Poland's governments or armed services, and the intelligentsia. The second group was made up of the peasants in all their subclass, folk, and regional variations. Most came not to stay, but to weather out the political storms in Poland or to accumulate the means for increasing their status back home. The immigrants and emigres brought with them two different views of their own "national character" the *szlachta* (nobility) and the peasant, with overlapping images of individualism and concern for social status. They also brought many different packages of cultural baggage and identity (ranging from cosmopolitan, to nationalistic, to politically patriotic, to folk). Most came as part of a large wave of immigration and settled in relatively concentrated communities that were physically or socially segregated from other national or ethnic groups.

These Poles, as many other entrants who did not plan on staying, dug in to very hard work to gather as fast as possible the means of insuring or improving status back home—money with which to buy land or durable property. While here, they continued seeking community status through acceptable symbols. The peasants turned first to the Roman Catholic church, with the help of a few

243

Polish priests and nuns, to build a complex and status competition satisfying parish system; they formed mutual aid societies providing not only security but opportunities for interaction. The upper strata formed nationalistic groups, the *szlachta* and the peasants (socially isolated in Poland's past) began forming a common community, intermediary rungs of the social status ladder being filled through status decrystallization and mobility of both groups, and repeated waves of newcomers entering with different backgrounds.[1] In fact, the second cohort of World War II displaced persons and ex-combatants as well as the third cohort of communist and independent Poland came mainly from the middle, urban classes that country was developing over time. The emerging ethnic community depended heavily on increased mobility and an expanded status competition as it created new companionate circles and life-styles that could draw second and third generation Polish Americans and, gradually, even the newer emigrations.

As they built their local and superterritorial structures, the Polish Americans were influenced by the fact that Poland constantly fought to regain its independence from foreign occupiers or needed economic aid when it did gain it. Polish political leaders turned to the increasingly affluent Polish Americans in an effort to obtain their financial, and later even military cooperation. These nationalistic leaders were, however, unable to convert the majority of Polish Americans from folk people (with limited formal education and anti-intellectual attitudes) into members of the national culture society. Polonia thus became somewhat of a hybrid of the two types of Polands, folk and national, with an ethnic flavor developed in America. Eventually, efforts to ignite patriotism combined with promises, direct or implied, of status gain and with humanitarian interests in the welfare of friends and relations in Poland resulted in a great deal of assistance to the home country. These efforts drew Polish American attention to events in Europe to such an extent that Polonia began to identify itself as the "fourth province of Poland." It turned this identification into millions of dollars of official and informal help both before and after World War I. Twenty-eight thousand Polish American men even formed a legion joining the Polish armed forces during the war.

Gradually the fervor of war-related activity died down. The Polish Americans became disillusioned with their relations with Poland and the local scene gained their attention. Most realized that they would not return to Poland, being comfortably settled on this side of the ocean. The third or so of the immigrants who went back to the home country often reemigrated when faced with the harshness of life following the war. Polonia's leaders became concerned with building a new ideology justifying the continued existence of the community and its organizations, providing an alternative identity to being the "fourth province of Poland." This they succeeded in doing as early as the 1920s and 1930s by defining American society as pluralistic and Polonia as a necessary component of the mosaic. They thus rejected the melting pot view of this country while simultaneously pushing for activity to benefit themselves and their status vis-a-vis other groups within it.

While these ideological changes were taking place, the vitality and complexity of the status competition, using internally developed criteria and hierarchies, and institutionalizing both cooperation and conflict, continued. The competition allowed for the use of external social control agencies to win the personal, family, or organizational struggle. The ideology simply supplied new hierarchies of status symbols and new activities in which success could be measured. One of the components of the ideology defining identity was the belief in a unique national character that prevented community cooperation and almost guaranteed internal conflict and competition. Armed with this ideology, Polish Americans felt justified in retaining the right to control their own destiny by remaining in the status competition and preventing others from gaining control. Few people have willingly withdrawn from the competition and acquiesced to leadership by someone else who was, after all, no better. Competitive behavior may have prevented cooperation in the community on many occasions and may have made public any conflict, but it has definitely prevented life from being dull or passive throughout Polonia's history.

The community developed not just a web of primary relations, but a whole system of patterned, established social relations, social roles, groups, and companionate circles. The activities of the social units created occasions for repeated contact performing multiple manifest and latent functions. They helped to crystallize, maintain, and then modify the ideology and community identity; they provided the arenas for the status competition and sources of prestige; they contributed to the creation of new groups, as schisms occurred in the established ones; and they offered a very active social life. It is this web of formal and informal interaction that prevented the community from reaching the complete disorganization, and personal or family demoralization predicted by many of its observers (Thomas and Znaniecki 1918-1920). If the hypotheses in this book are correct, the very characteristic which contributed to predictions of community failure was part of the web holding the community together and drawing members' interest inward rather than encouraging a passive adjustment to an acculturated minority status position. The complex competitive social structure of the community served to cushion, dissipate, and even deflect some of the consequences of the intensive change brought about by immigration, and provided the bond needed to create a new social system.

One of the reasons Thomas and Znaniecki (1918-1920) predicted strong social disorganization among the Polish Americans was their view of traditional peasant culture as a total fabric. They assumed it contained a set of stable, interdependent norms, which were being subjected to constant attacks in America from deviation or at least nonconformity, ending in a complete collapse. The history of Polonia over the years, locally or as a superterritorial community, indicates that its cultural fabric was much more flexible and viable, based on the social structure and gradually changing, bending, and modifying as new norms were introduced purposely or through unconscious diffusion by its members. Individuals learned or invented new ways of behaving, which they evaluated as meaningful or useful, and they then convinced others in their companionate circles to modify their behavior. Change occurred as part of an ongoing social process so that many individuals did not have to face it alone, with "demoralizing" consequences that would have been totally disruptive.

Change occurred not only internally and through pressures from the American society but also from the continued entrance of Poles from Poland, a different Poland than the one established Polonians had left behind, and passed on in tales by the ancestors of the Polish Americans of the present time. The life-styles of the newcomers are very different from those of the established Polonia, as evidenced by the language and interests by the places of amusement (night clubs), the press (including slick magazines), and radio and television (not of the Polka world). This does not mean that traditional, folk culture aspects of Polonia's life have been replaced by new "modern" aspects. As Gusfield (1967) pointed out tradition and modernity can exist side by side in cultures. Ethnic communities in America certainly personify the flexibility of cultures.

It would be interesting to trace the changes in an ethnic community's cultural content over time—the items retained and dropped by the different companionate circles and the rhythm of life produced by these changes. Such a study is the proper province of acculturation theorists, but they should not ignore the influence of the home culture which continues upon the community and those people who continue to have contact with it. Polonia has been very conscious of these changes its members face constantly.

Although family status is important at birth, mobility in Polonia has been possible within "decent" boundaries. Members of the community have marshalled resources, including family members, to solidify upward steps and to drop status-demeaning habits or members, watching simultaneously what was happening to neighbors and companionate circle peers, using gossip to establish their own status points and to crystallize their own reputations. Ventures into new means of seeking status that were not part of the traditional folk culture or part of the evolving Polonian life were not frequent on the part of the first two generations of the first cohort because too much was at stake. Sending children to school beyond the required minimum, for example, deprived the family of money that could be immediately converted to status points. Further, education could cause the younger generations to reject the folk culture. Higher education in "foreign" schools that were unconcerned with morality might have been unpredictable effects and was generally to be avoided. For girls it was a waste of time; for boys it was a source of trouble (unless it was in Catholic seminaries in preparation for religious roles).

Daily work for the males, homemaking for the females, and parish schools until "adulthood" for the children continued during the days of Polonia's history. But life had a different flavor in the after-work hours. Meetings were held and elections of officials afforded opportunities for gaining leadership roles that were reflected in status gains for years. Obligations to Poland and the Polish government in exile were met. Polite companionship interaction took place at central congregating places such as restaurants, parish houses, a "Dom Polski" (Polish Home", organizational halls, and theaters. All this activity was available not only to the elites but also to everyone. Seasonal variations in activity added spice to life, and all levels of formality and informality supplied a rich choice for those wishing, and being accepted into, companionship relations. In the meantime, of course, many people who were eligible to form part of this network never became involved.

The community acquired and retained a negative image in America and a low social status in relation to other groups. Many second-generation Polish Americans dropped out of Polonia, often to the extent of changing their names and concealing other visible traces of Polishness. This situation, accentuated by the "Polish jokes," especially affected the members who left Polonia to enter into status competitions with outsiders, but it also bothered those Polish Americans who were active in community affairs. It is doubtful that the Polish jokes could have brought about as concentrated an effort at antidefamation as occurred during the 1970s and even the 1980s, but they certainly had an effect, judging by the constant references to them in the mass media. They have generally phased out by now so that many readers may not even be familiar with them. However, they were sufficiently negative, sufficiently status-depreciating, and sufficiently timely to produce a strong reaction and a mobilization of Polonia's resources into an antidefamation campaign. The main weapons of this campaign were the very aspects of Polish national culture that the intelligentsia, the Polish visitors, and the new emigrants have consistently pushed for in the past: the literary, scientific, artistic national culture, especially those items that were known, or could be made known, to the American society. The intelligentsia, swollen in number by new emigrants, keeps reminding the rest of Polonia of the importance of shifting into a cultural identification more in keeping with the middle-class habits and ideologies of an increasingly affluent, "leisure," and "culture"-oriented American society.

One of the serious sources of conflict in Polonia is over its "true" culture. At least four "subcultures" appear to be competing as representatives of the community, and proponents of each are highly vocal. One, the traditional Polish national culture, is shared by the intelligentsia and those Poles in America who were educated in urban Poland. The second is the folk culture brought by the early immigrants and those persons of the second and third cohort who come from villages and small communities relatively isolated from urban centers. If there is a Polonian culture it is a combination of these, based on folk items woven into a rather American working/lower middle-class fabric. However, there is some question about this typology since the way of life of most members of the newest cohort does not fit any of these categories. They are more middle-class and more Polish than anything else and have created their own world. The wakacjusze blend in with them or with the working class in life style, although it takes years before they are fitted anywhere, and then only if they become legalized.

The argument of whether ethnic identity is based on the folk culture or whether ethnic identity is based on variations of Polish national culture is frequently heard in Polonia.[2] The intelligentsia expresses irritation over the Polish American tendency to either cling to folk culture items, or to move into Americanization while there remains an easily available national literary Polish culture. Of course a major factor in the argument is social class, one that cannot be ignored in any ethnic community, due to original heterogeneity of immigrants and decrystallization of status. Although the Polonian life-styles are varied by "ethclass" and have changed over the decades, there still remains a heavy peasant and blue-collar influence (as sadly commented upon by the intelligentsia, the other elites, or those who are rapidly upwardly mobile).

It is hard to determine how successful Polonia's leadership and elites will be in changing Polish American identity from folk patterns to identification with a Polish national culture, that is foreign to many of the people. Some of the community leaders claim that the only possibility of retaining the identification of the youth lies in that direction. They want formal schooling into this Polish culture, of the kind carried forth in universities or PUNO, rather than having the young depend upon the memories and cultural food-dance-costume-religious items of their parents or grandparents.

Whatever the internal tensions, it is in relation with Poland in recent years that the American flavor of established Polonia becomes apparent. No longer treated as representatives of Poland to the outside world, now that Poland can speak for itself, the Polish American community demands the right to turn its concern inwardly. The Poles in Poland, as reflected by the Polish press the summer and fall of 1992, expressed great disappointment over the refusal of the representatives of the American Polonian groups during the Congress of Polonians from Abroad to coordinate under the banner of the Polish group, Wspolnota Polska. They really did not understand that Polonia sees itself as an independent unit working for itself, seeing and relating to Poland from its own perspective.

The newest cohort of Poles in America identify much more with Poland. Although many members are ambivalent over a return to the home country, they are interested in investing and benefitting from its new economy. Looking at Polonia this cohort resents monopolization of power of the established groups.

The fraternals still continue their existence safe in their financial base and their ability to draw new people because of the obvious benefits. The opportunities to gain social status through office holding or even membership in the numerous groups continue to draw those interested in internal status competition (even if they are simultaneously involved in external status competition). The newest cohort is not part of this life but has been slow to form and maintain its own groups. It does have an active social life with numerous recreational and "cultural" events but lacks the financial base of the old fraternals whose second generation leaders refuse to part with the power.

As the old emigration and its direct descendants die off, many features of peasant, less educated, blue-collar life will vanish. We cannot predict how long the community will last in its present form and how it will change as its composition and American society change. It cannot become a minority status community of the type described by Kramer (1970) unless the national or ethnic flavor vanishes. It could dissolve through the assimilation of individual or family members, or each "ethclass" could break into appropriate class companionship circles outside of its boundaries. The pervasiveness of ethnic identity on the part of individuals is likely to decrease and change content.

The community's life is dependent upon the willingness of sufficient numbers of people to maintain some level of involvement in the web of social relations through the formal groups which it can financially support. This the people could do from suburbs and scattered residences all over the country (Etzioni 1959; Sandberg 1974) while simultaneously leading nonethnic or non-Polish lives in other social relations. An ethnic community need not be geographically concentrated, nor does it require that all of its members participate in all of its institutions in order to perpetuate institutional complexity. Its binding ties of the past could continue in the future through involvement in the status competition, but the cultural folk base is not likely to be retained nor to be sufficiently meaningful to create a revival of interest by younger generations. It certainly turns off the members of the last two cohorts and their children. The question remains as to whether it will be replaced by a Polish national culture base of sufficient viability to retain its social structure. Will the new cohort remain in America? If enough members remain, and are joined by others, will it replace the current leaders of organizations and institutions based on the limited culture of the Polish peasant in America, or will it create its own enduring social structure?

Notes

1. Each person's status "package" in the community is the result of a combination of prestige positions in a variety of hierarchies, including education, occupation, income and how it is spent, association, leadership qualities and life-style. Status

decrystallization refers to the different rates of mobility in these hierarchies. For example, a person can obtain higher education and a white-collar job, but remain on the same income level. In the case of Poles of the first cohort, it was usually the income and possessions such as the home that rose above the educational and occupational levels within the first and second generations.

2. Paul Wrobel's (1977: 67-68) review of the first edition of *Polish Americans* was very critical of my statement that the Polish peasant culture was limited and that the future base for Polonian life lies in increasing identification with the national culture.

Appendices

Appendix A
Polish American Fraternal Associations, Selected Years

FRATERNAL ASSOCIATION	Year Founded	Head-quarters	1924 Members	1924 Groups	1935 Members	1935 Groups	1950 Members	1950 Groups	1973 Members	1973 Groups	1983 Members	1983 Groups	1992-3 Members	1992-3 Groups
Polish Roman Catholic Union	1873	IL	83,326	930	161,769	1,147	175,397	1,095	—		140,000	786	90,000	529
Polish National Alliance	1880	IL	139,137	1,648	272,750	1,869	316,422	1,720	332,962	1,405	306,022	1,271	286,656	965
Polish Falcons of America	1887	PA	12,500	285	—				28,100		29,165		31,035	143
Polish Union in the U.S.	1890	PA	18,520	163	18,153	149	18,742	159	16,226	324	13,600	150	12,005	101
Alliance of Poles in America	1895	OH	7,015	86	—		13,357	100	20,006	89	20,000	73	20,000	63
Polish Assn. of Am. (Northern)	1895	WI	10,272	179	8,740	147	7,614	172	6,543		6,543		6,543	
Polish Women's Alliance of Am.	1898	IL	21,546	235	59,964	618	76,215	1,157	91,000		—		65,000	775
Union of Poles in America	1898	OH	5,850	52	—		11,119	100						—
Polish Beneficial Association	1900	PA	—		—		23,751	132	24,654	132	16,246	105	16,246	105
Association of Sons of Poland	1903	NJ	—		14,879	104	16,763	119	18,000	120	12,000	100	7,000	41
Polish National Alliance of Brooklyn	1905	NY	9,000	131	—		18,700	—					9,713	50
Polish National Union of America	1908	PA	6,192	122	15,211	192	28,065	236	32,550	231	30,000	202	30,000	202
American Federation of Polish Jews	1908	NY							3,000	30	600	50	600	50
Polish Alma Mater of America	1910	IL	6,544	125	6,799	106	7,062	103	5,300	81	5,300	81	Absorbed by PNA	
United Polish Women of America	1912	IL	—		—		—		—		3,000	22	6,000	22
Association of Polish Women of the U.S.	1913	OH	—		—		—		9,379	77	9,379	74	9,379	68
Polish Union of America	1917	NY	21,546	235	35,183	257	24,805	241	—				12,005	120
Mutual Aid Assn. of the New Polish Emigration	1949	IL	—		—		—		750		800		800	—

Sources: H. Z. Lopata. *Polish Americans: Status Competition in an Ethnic Community* (Englewood Cliffs, N.J.: Prentice Hall, 1976), 150–51; Gale Research Companies. *Encyclopedia of Associations* (Detroit, Mich.: Gale Research, 1983, 1992–93).

Appendix B
Nonfraternal Polish-American Voluntary Associations

Category and Name	Year Founded	Head-quarters	Latest Membership	Category and Name	Year Founded	Head-quarters	Latest Membership
Cultural, Political				**Welfare and Relief**			
Polish Singers Alliance	1889	NY	100 GIs	American Relief for Poland	1939	IL	defunct
Pol. Nob. Assn.	1921	MD	–	Catholic League for Rel. Assist. to Pol.	1943	IL	600
Kosciuszko Foundation	1925	NY	4000	P. Am. Immigration and Relief Com.	1947	NY	–
Pol. Museum/Am.	1937	IL	–	Polish Welfare Association	1921	IL	–
Legion of Young Polish Women	1939	IL	150	**Economic, Occupational**			
Polish American Historical Assn.	1941	IL	600	Nat. Medical and Dental Assn.	1900	MI	1000
Pol. Inst. of Arts & Sciences of Amer.	1942	NY	1500	National Advocates Society	1933	IL	1000
Joseph Pilsudzki Institute*	1943	NY	900	Polish-US Economic Council (Chamber of Commerce US)	1974	DC	70
Pol. Amer. Cong.	1944	IL	3000 delegates	**Veterans**			
Amer. Council of Pol. Cultural Clubs	1948	MD	4900	Polish Army Vets Assn. of Amer.	1921	NY	7000
Paderewski Foundation	1948	NY	–	P. Legion of Amer. Veterans	1931	IL	15000
General Pulaski Heritage Foundation	1959	NY	–	Polish Air Force Vets Assn.	1945	NJ	1600
American Institute of Polish Culture	1972	IL	350				

Continued on next page

Appendix B (*continued*)

	Year Founded	Headquarters	Members
Polish American Guardian Society	1945	IL	1,000
Polish Assistance	1956	NY	—
Polish American Numismatic Society	1963	IL	209
Polish Military History Society of America	1973	IL	125
Polish American Library Association	1975		defunct
Polish Genealogical Society	1978	IL	760
Polish Workers' Aid Fund	1980	DC	
Friends of Solidarity	1981	MD	no convention
Committee in Support of Solidarity	1981	NY	inactive
Solidarity International	1982	NY	

Sources: H. Z. Lopata. *Polish Americans: Status Competition in an Ethnic Community* (Englewood Cliffs, N.J.: Prentice-Hall, 1976), 132-33; Gale Research Company. *Encyclopedia of Associations.* (Detroit, Mich.: Gale Research, 1992); Compiled from *Encyclopedia of Associations,* 1992-1993: 13 additional Polish American organizations still named in the *Encyclopedia* are listed as defunct or inactive.

Appendix C
Major Occupation Groups of the Male Population
16 Years Old and Over in 1969 and 25 and over in 1980, by Ethnic Origin (in thousands)

	Total	English	German	Irish	Russian	Spanish	Polish 1969	Polish 1980
Prof., tech., & kindred workers	14.0	16.7	14.8	14.1	13.5	7.9	17.7	18.0
Farmers & farm managers	3.4	4.4	6.7	3.6	0.4	0.6	5.2	2.0
Mgrs., offs., & propsl, exc farm	14.2	16.9	15.4	15.5	14.9	7.4	14.5	15.0
Clerical & kindred workers	7.0	7.3	5.8	8.5	9.1	6.7	9.1	8.0
Sales workers	5.6	6.0	6.1	6.3	5.2	3.3	6.5	9.0
Craftsmen, foremen, & kindred workers	20.4	19.9	21.7	20.8	22.7	18.5	22.8	22.0
Operatives & kindred workers	20.0	17.8	18.2	17.9	20.0	28.6	18.1	20.0
Private household workers	0.1	0.1	—	—	—	—	—	—
Service workers, exc. private household	6.5	5.0	4.7	6.0	7.5	10.5	4.8	7.0
Farm laborers & foremen	1.7	1.2	1.6	1.0	0.2	4.8	—	—
Laborers, exc. farm & mine	7.1	4.9	4.9	6.1	6.4	11.8	1.2	—

1969 Source: U.S. Bureau of the Census, Current Population Reports, Series P-20, No. 221, November 1969, T-15, "Characteristics of the Population by Ethnic Origin," (Washington, D.C.: Government Printing Office, 1971).
1980 Source: Stanley Lieberson and Mary Waters. From Many Strands (New York: Russell Sage Foundation, 1988), 156.

Appendix D

Major Occupation Groups of the Female Population 16 Years Old and Over in 1969 and 25 and Over in 1980, by Ethnic Origin (in thousands)

Subject	Total	English	German	Irish	Russian	Spanish	Polish 1969	Polish 1980
Percent total distributions	100.0	100.0	100.0	100.0	100.0	100.0	100.0	—
Prof., tech., kindred workers	14.4	16.6	16.6	14.9	23.0	8.6	13.1	21
Farmers, farm managers	0.2	0.4	0.4	0.2	—	—	—	1
Mgrs., offs., props., exc. farm	4.3	6.1	4.1	6.0	10.6	1.7	3.4	8
Clerical, kindred workers	34.1	34.9	33.6	35.6	43.6	25.6	35.6	34
Sales workers	7.2	8.4	7.6	7.0	8.8	6.0	8.5	11
Craftsmen, foremen, kindred workers	1.1	1.3	0.9	0.9	2.1	1.1	1.1	T2
Operatives, kindred workers	15.3	13.4	13.0	13.1	6.7	32.8	19.2	11
Private household workers	5.8	3.9	4.5	3.6	0.9	6.4	2.1	—
Service workers, exc. private households	15.8	13.5	15.9	16.9	3.9	17.1	15.5	13
Farm laborers, foremen	1.4	1.3	2.9	1.2	0.3	0.8	1.3	—
Laborers, exc. farm-mine	0.5	0.2	0.3	0.6	—	0.8	0.3	—

1969 Source: U.S. Bureau of Census, Current Population Reports, Series P-20, No. 221, "Characteristics of the Population by Ethnic Origin," November 1969 (Washington, D.C.: Government Printing Office, 1971).
1980 Source: Stanley Lieberson and Mary Waters. From Many Strands (New York: Russell Sage Foundation, 1988), 157.

Appendix E

Highest Grade of School Completed by Persons 25 Years Old and Over, by Ethnic Origin

| Origin | Total (1000s) | PERCENT DISTRIBUTION BY YEARS OF SCHOOL COMPLETED | | | | | | Median School Years Completed |
| | | Elementary | | High School | | College | | |
		0-7 Yrs.	8 Yrs	1-3 Yrs.	4 Yrs.	1-3 Yrs.	4/4+ Yr.	
25 Yrs. Old and Over	106,284	13.8	13.4	17.6	33.9	10.3	11.0	12.2
25-34 Yrs. Old	23,884	4.5	4.8	17.4	43.5	14.7	15.2	12.5
English	2,301	4.3	4.6	15.5	41.2	16.8	17.6	12.6
German	2,848	1.6	4.1	14.8	47.4	14.6	17.5	12.6
Irish	1,670	2.6	3.7	18.8	45.1	15.9	13.9	12.6
Italian	902	5.3	3.3	16.3	50.4	12.7	11.9	12.5
Polish	503	1.3	3.0	10.6	53.8	15.1	16.2	12.7
Russian	209	0.7	0.7	3.7	24.7	17.7	52.5	16.
Spanish	1,239	19.2	10.0	23.5	32.2	9.8	5.3	11.7
Other	11,625	3.6	4.4	17.5	43.3	15.6	15.6	12.6
Not reported	2,585	6.2	7.2	20.3	43.6	10.9	11.8	12.4

Origin	Total (1000s)	0-7 Yrs.	8 Yrs	1-3 Yrs.	4 Yrs.	1-3 Yrs.	4/4+ Yr.	Median School Years Completed
35 Yrs. Old and Over	82,400	16.5	15.9	17.6	31.1	9.1	9.8	12.0
English	9,698	11.9	13.7	17.8	31.7	11.1	13.6	12.2
German	9,977	10.6	22.0	16.1	34.2	8.6	8.5	12.0
Irish	6,960	14.3	16.3	18.8	32.9	8.4	9.3	12.0
Italian	3,780	23.5	17.5	20.0	27.6	5.2	5.9	10.3
Polish	2,266	18.5	19.0	19.2	30.9	5.2	7.2	10.9
Russian	1,375	10.8	12.1	11.9	35.1	11.7	18.4	12.4
Spanish	2,576	43.0	14.4	14.9	17.5	5.7	4.5	8.5
Other	37,661	16.5	14.3	17.8	31.1	9.9	10.4	12.0
Not reported	8,106	20.4	17.3	17.6	30.0	7.4	7.4	11.1

Source: U.S. Bureau of the Census, Current Population Reports, Series P-20, No. 221, "Characteristics of the Population by Ethnic Origin," November 1969 (Washington D.C.: Government Printing Office, 1971).

Appendix F
Educational Attainment of Men and Women Born in the United States,
Aged 25 and Over, 1980 by Ancestry

PERCENT DISTRIBUTION

	Elementary 8 Years or Less		High School 1-3 Years		High School 4 Years		College 1-3 Years		College 4 Years		College 5+ Years		Median Years	
	Men	Women	Men	Women	Men	Women	Men	Women	Men	Women	Men	Women	Men	Women
English	14	12	13	15	30	37	17	18	13	10	13	.07	12.8	12.6
German	12	11	12	13	35	42	17	17	12	0.9	12	0.7	12.7	12.6
Irish	13	11	13	16	33	41	18	18	12	0.8	12	0.6	12.7	12.6
Italian	11	13	16	16	34	45	17	14	11	0.7	11	0.6	12.7	12.5
Polish	12	14	13	15	33	41	17	15	12	0.8	14	0.7	12.8	12.5
Russian	0.5	0.6	0.7	0.7	21	34	18	20	18	16	30	17	15.7	13.4
Other SCE* European	14	13	13	15	35	41	17	17	10	0.7	11	0.7	12.7	12.5
Other NW European	11	09	09	09	29	36	18	22	15	14	19	10	13.3	12.9

Source: Modified from S. Lieberson and M. Waters. *From Many Strands* (Russell Sage Foundation, N.Y., 1988), 107-8.
* South, Central & East

Bibliography

Abel, Theodore. "Sundeland: A Study of Changes in the Group-Life of Poles in New England Farming Community." In *Immigrant Farmers and Their Children*, edited by Edmund De.S. Brunnner, 213-43. Garden City, N.Y.: Doubleday, 1929.

Abramson, Harold J. "Ethnic Pluralism in the Central City." In *Ethnic Groups in the City*, edited by Otto Feinstein, 17-28. Lexington, Mass: Heath Lexington Books, 1971.

_____. *Ethnic Diversity in Catholic America*. New York: John Wiley, 1973.

Agocs, Carol. "Ethnicity in Detroit." In *Ethnic Groups in the City*, edited by Otto Feinstein, 81-106. Lexington, Mass: D.C. Heath, 1971.

Andrews, Wayne, ed. *Concise Dictionary of American History*. New York: Charles Scribner's Sons, 1962.

Babinski, Grzegorz. "Occupational Mobility of Polish Americans in Selected U.S. Cities after World War Two." In *The Polish Presence in Canada and America*, edited by Frank Renkiewicz, 229-67. Toronto: The Multicultural History Society of Ontario, 1982.

Baker, Susan Gonzalez. *The Cautious Welcome: The Legalization Programs of the Immigration Reform and Control Act*. Santa Monica, Calif.: The Rand Corporation, 1990.

Baraniak, Andrzej. "Roofing, Polska Specjalnosc." *Gazeta Polska* (19 September 1992): 10.

Barc, Franciszek, ed. *65 Lat Zjednoczenia Ploskiego Rzymsko-Katolickiego w Ameryce*. Chicago: Polish Roman Catholic Union, 1938.

Baretski, Charles Allan. "How Polonia Reacts to Inadequate Recognition in the Political Arena." *Polish American Studies* 28, 1 (Spring 1971): 45-53.

Barth, Fredrik, ed. *Ethnic Groups and Boundaries*. Boston: Little, Brown, 1969.

Benet, Sula. *Song, Dance and Customs of Peasant Poland*. New York: Roy, 1951.

Bensman, Joseph, and Arthur J Vidich. *The New American Society*. Chicago: Quadrangle Books, 1971.

Bernstein, Carl. "The Holy Alliance. How Reagan and the Pope Conspired to Assist Poland's Solidarity Movement and Hasten the Demise of Communism." *Time* (24 February 1992): 28-35.

Bethell, Nicholas. *Gomulka: His Poland and His Communism*. Middlesex, England: Penguin Books, 1972.

Bialasiewicz, Wojciech. *Czy odzyje koncepcja "wychodzstwo dla wychodztwa"? Dziennik Zwiazkowy* (3 December 1989): 11.

The Black-Polish Conference Newsletter. "Neighbors Unite to Stay Integrated." (June 1973): 2.

Blejwas, Stanislaus A. "Old & New Polonias: Tension within an Ethnic Community." *Polish American Studios* 38, 2(1981): 55–83.

_____. "The Adam Mickiewicz Chair of Polish Culture: Columbia University and the Cold War." *The Polish Review* 36, 3(1991a): 323–37 (1991b): 451–69.

_____. "American Polonia: The Next Generation." Review of *Region USA. Dzialacze Solidarnosci: w Kraju, o Emigracji, o Sobie,* edited by Andrzej Krajewski. *Polish American Studies* 49, 1 (Spring 1992): 81–86.

Bloch, Alfred, ed. *The Real Poland: An Anthology of National Self-Perception.* New York: Continuum, 1982.

Bloch, Harriet. "Changing Domestic Roles among Polish Immigrant Women." *Anthropology Quarterly* 49 (January 1976): 3–10.

Blumer, Herbert. *Critiques of Research in the Social Sciences: An Appraisal of Thomas and Znaniecki's "The Polish Peasant in Europe and America."* New York: Social Science Research Council, 1939.

Bochenkek, Alfred F. *American Polonia: The Cultural Issues.* Detroit: The American Council of Polish Cultural Clubs, 1981.

Bodnar, John. *Immigration and Industrialization: Ethnicity in an American Mill Town, 1870–1940.* Pittsburgh: University of Pittsburgh Press, 1977.

Bogue, Donald J. *The Population of the United States.* Glencoe, Ill.: The Free Press, 1969.

Bolek, Francis. *Who's Who in Polish America.* 3rd ed. New York: Harbinger House, 1943.

_____. *The Polish-American School System.* New York: Columbia Press Corporation, 1948.

Borkowski, Thomas. "Some Patterns in Polish Surname Changes." *Polish American Studies* 20, 1 (January–June 1963): 14–16.

Borun, Thaddeus, comp. *We, the Milwaukee Poles.* Milwaukee: Mowiny Publishing Company, 1946.

Boswell, A. Bruce. "Territorial Division and the Mongol Invasions, 1202–1300." *The Cambridge History of Poland to 1696,* edited by W.F. Reddaway, J.H. Penson, O. Halecki, and R. Dyboski, 85–107. Cambridge, England: University Press, 1950.

Bott, Elizabeth J. *Family and Social Network.* London: Tavistock, 1957.

Bowler, Alida C. "Recent Statistics on Crime and the Foreign Born." National Commission on Law Observance and Enforcement, *Report on Crime and the Foreign Born,* pt. 2, 83–193. Washington, D.C.: Government Printing Office, 1931.

Breton, Raymond. "Institutional Completeness of Ethnic Communities and the Personal Relations of Immigrants." *American Journal of Sociology* 70, 2 (September 1964): 193-205.

Briggs, Michael, and Michael Cordt. "Envoys Hit 'Vandals' in Polish Protest." *Sun Times* 29 (3 December 1981).

Brozek, Andrzej. *Polonia Amerykanska, 1854-1939. Warszawa Wydawnictwo Interpress,* 1977.

Bruckner, A. "Polish Cultural Life in the Seventeenth Century." In *The Cambridge History of Poland,* edited by W.F. Reddaway, J.H. Penson, O. Halecki and R. Dybowski, 557-69. Cambridge, England: University Press, 1950.

Brunner, Edmund De.S. *Immigrant Farmers and Their Children.* Garden City, N.Y.: Doubleday, 1929.

Buczek, Daniel S. "Polish-Americans and the Roman Catholic Church." In *The Polish Americans,* edited by Eugene Kleban and Thaddeus V. Gromada, 39-61. *The Polish Review Bicentennial Issue* 21, 3 (1976): 39-61.

Bugelski, B.R. "Polish Americans." Speech delivered at a meeting of the American Council of Polish Cultural Clubs. Mimeo. 1952.

Bukowczyk, John J. *And My Children Did Not Know Me: A History of the Polish-Americans.* Bloomington: Indiana University Press, 1987.

_____. "Factionalism and the Composition of the Polish Immigrant Clergy." In *Pastor of the Poles,* edited by Stanislaus Blejwas and Mieczyslaw Biskupski, 37-47. New Britain, Conn.: Polish Studies Program Monographs, 1992.

Burton, Ronald. "Status Consistency and Secondary Stratification Characteristics in an Urban Metropolis." Ph.D. diss., Michigan State University, 1972.

Bush, George. "Remarks by President Bush." *New Horizon* (March 1991a): 5-6.

_____. "General Pulaski Memorial Day. *Polish-American Heritage Month, 1991 Proclamations." New Horizon* (October 1991b): 4-5.

Butturini, Paula. "Poland's Communists Trying to Learn New Skill: Campaigning." *Chicago Tribune* 30 (8 April 1989).

Carpenter, Niles, and Daniel Katz. "The Cultural Adjustment of the Polish Group in the City of Buffalo: An Experiment in the Technique of Social Investigation." *Social Forces* 6 (September 1927): 76-90.

_____. "A Study of Acculturation of the Polish Group of Buffalo, 1926-1928." *The University of Buffalo Studies* 7 (June 1929): 103-31.

Cassel, Andrew. "Chicago's Poles are Key Players in Polish Vote." *The Philadelphia Inquirer* 2 (8 June 1989).

Chicago Sun-Times Magazine. "Poland: Reaching for the Good Life." (23 September 1983).

Chicago Tribune. "Seven Centuries Ago a Polish King Knew that Men Could Differ, Yet Live Together Productively. He Did Something About It" (Advertisement). (5 December 1973): section 1, 8.

_____. (19 December 1981).

_____. (28 December 1981).

Chrobot, Leonard. "The Effectiveness of the Polish Program at St. Mary's College, 1958-1968." *Polish American Studies* 26, 2 (Autumn 1969): 31-33.

Cisek, Andzej M. "Polish Elections Won't Be Free." *Gannett Westchester Newspapers.* (Philadelphia) (8 April 1989).

Claghorn, Kate Holladay. *The Immigrant's Day in Court. Americanization Series,* edited by W.S. Bernard. Montclair, N.J.: Patterson, Smith, 1971.

Conderacci, Greg. "Polish Americans Hit Ethnic Slurs, Praise Their Culture in Ads." *Wall Street Journal* (12 October 1971): 1.

Coser, Lewis A. *Masters of Sociological Thought.* New York: Harcourt Brace Jovanovich, 1977.

_____. *Refugee Scholars in America: Their Impact and Their Experiences.* New Haven, Conn.: Yale University Press, 1984.

Crane, Diana. "Social Structure in a Group of Scientists: A Test of the 'Invisible College' Hypothesis." *American Sociological Review* 34, 3 (June 1968): 335-52.

Cross, Robert D. "How Historians Have Looked at Immigrants to the United States." *International Migration Review* 7, 1 (Spring 1973): 4-22.

Curti, Merle, and Kendall Birr. "The Immigrant and the American Image in Europe, 1860-1914." *Mississippi Valley Historical Review* 37, 2 (September 1950): 203-30.

Czerwinski, Edward J. "Notes on Polish Theatre in the United States." In *Studies in Ethnicity: The East European Experience in America,* edited by Charles A. Ward, Philip Shashko, and Donald E. Pienkos, 211-24. Boulder: East European Monographs, 1980.

Daniels, Roger. *Coming to America: A History of Immigration and Ethnicity in American Life.* New York: Harper Collins, 1990.

Davies, Norman. *God's Playground: A History of Poland: 1975 to the Present,* vol. 2. New York: Columbia University Press, 1984.

Davis, Allison, Burleigh B. Gardner, and Mary R. Gardner. *Deep South.* Chicago: University of Chicago Press, 1941.

Davis, Michael M. J. *Immigrant Health and the Community, Americanization Series,* edited by W.S. Bernard. Montclair, N.J.: Patterson, Smith, 1921/1971.

Declaration: The May 3rd Manifestation. *Dziennik Zwiazkowy* (14 March 1989): 3.

deVise, Pierre. "Ethnic Shifts in Chicago." Working paper 5.5, Chicago Regional Hospital Study, 1973.

Diamont, Stanley. "Kibbutz and Shtetl: The History and Idea." *Social Problems* 2 (Fall 1957): 71–99.

Diaz, May M., and Jack M. Potter. "The Social Life of Peasants." In *Peasant Society*, edited by Jack M. Potter, May M. Diaz, and George M. Foster. Boston: Little, Brown, 1967.

Dingell, John. "Blast State Department on Polish Visas Policy." *Polish American Journal* 63, 1 (January 1974): 1.

Drachsler, Julian. *Democracy and Assimilation*. New York: Macmillan, 1920.

Drozdowski, Marian Marek. "The Role of Polish Parishes in the United States in the Struggle for Independence." *Przeglad Poloijny* 16, 1 (1990): 39–50.

Dulczewski, Zygmund. *Florian Znaniecki: Life and Work*. Poznan: Wydawnictwo Nakom, 1992.

Duncan, Beverly, and Otis Dudley Duncan. "Minorities and the Process of Stratification." *American Sociological Review* 33, 3 (June 1968): 356–64.

Dunin-Markiewicz, Alexsandra Maria. "Occupational and Educational Aspirations of Minority Group Adolescents in Face of an Unfavorable Ethnic Stereotype." Ph.D. diss. Wayne State University, 1972.

Durkheim, Emile. *The Elementary Forms of Religious Life*. New York: Free Press, 1915/1965.

Dymarski, Lech. "The Polish Search for Democracy." *Studium Papers* 13 (3) 1989: 141–43.

Dziennik Zwiazkowy (Chicago: The Alliance Printers). "Obituaries." (19 June 1973): 6.

———. "Poszukiwanie Danych o Stosunkach Polsko-Zydowskich." (13–14 October 1973): 12.

———. 12-letnia Sluzba Ruchom Semocratycznym w Polsce. (9 December 1988): 2–3.

———. "Do Polakow na Emigracji." (3 March 1989a.) 6.

———. "Apel do Polakow w Kraju i na Obczynie." (24 April_): 5. Reprinted (18 May 1989b.): 5.

———. "Oswiadcznie Freedom for Poland." (10 October 1989): 3.

———. "Amerykanski Centrum Kultury Polskiej Otwarte Zostalo w Waszyngtonie." (31 July – 2 August 1992): 1, 7.

Ehrenpreis, Viktor J., in cooperation with Manfred Kridl. "Poland up to 1918," and "Poland, 1918–1945." In *Central Eastern Europe: Crucible of the World Wars*, edited by Joseph S. Roucek. Englewood Cliffs, N.J.: Prentice-Hall, 1946.

Ehrenreich, Barbara. *Fear of Falling: The Inner Life of the Middle Class*. New York: Harper. 1989.

Eisenstein, Sarah. *Give Us Bread, Give Us Roses: Working Women's Conscious-ness in the United States, 1890 to the First World War*. Boston: Routledge & Kegan Paul, 1983.

Emmons, Charles F. "Economics and Political Leadership in Chicago's Polonia: Some Sources of Ethnic Persistence and Mobility." Ph.D. diss., University of Illinois Circle Campus, 1971.

Erdmans, Mary. "Who Can Poland Count On?" *Studium Papers* 13, 3: 3-4. 1989.

_____. "Émigrés and Ethnics: Patterns of Cooperation between New and Established Residents in Chicago's Polish Community." Ph.D. diss., Northwestern University, 1992a.

_____. "The Social Construction of Emigration as a Moral Issue." *Polish American Studies* (Spring 1992b.): 5-25.

Etzioni, Amitai. "The Ghetto." *Social Forces* 37, 3 (March 1959): 258-62.

Fallers, L.A., ed. *Immigrants and Associations*. The Hague: Mouton, 1967.

Fallows, Marjorie R. *Irish Americans: Identity and Assimilation*. Englewood Cliffs, N.J.: Prentice-Hall, 1979.

Feinstein, Otto, ed. *Ethnic Groups in the City*. Lexington, Mass.: Heath Lexington Books, 1971.

Finestone, Harold. "A Comparative Study of Reformation and Recidivism among Italians and Polish Adult Male Criminal Offenders." Ph.D. diss., University of Chicago, 1964.

_____. "Reformation and Recidivism Among Italian and Polish Criminal Offenders." *American Journal of Sociology* 72, 6 (May 1967): 575-88.

Fishman, Joshua, and John E. Hofman. "Mother Tongue and the Nativity in the American Population." In *Language Loyalty in the United States*, edited by Joshua Fishman, Vladimir C. Nahirny, John E. Hofman, and Robert G. Hayden. The Hague: Mouton, 1966.

Fishman, Joshua A., Robert G. Hayden, and Mary E. Warshauer. "The Non-English and Ethnic Group Press, 1910-1960." In *Language Loyalty in the United States*, edited by Joshua A. Fishman, Vladimir C. Nahirny, John E. Hofman, and Robert Hayden, 51-74. The Hague: Mouton, 1966.

Fishman, Joshua, and Vladimir Nahirny, "Organizational and Leadership Interests in Language Maintenance." In *Language Loyalty in the United States*, edited by Joshua Fishman, Vladimir Nahirny, John Hofman and Robert Hayden, 156-89. The Hague: Mouton, 1966.

Fleis-Fava, Sylvia. "The Relationship of Northwestern University Settlement to the Community." Master's thesis, Northwestern University, 1950.

Form, William H., and Gregory P. Stone. "Urbanism, Anonymity and Status Symbolism." In *Neighborhood, City and Metropolis*, edited by Robert Gutman and David Papenoe. New York: Random House, 1970.

Fox, Paul. *The Polish National Catholic Church.* Scranton, Pa.: School of Christian Living, 1957.

The Fraternal Field. *The Fraternal Compend Digest.* 1950.

The Fraternal Monitor (Rochester, N.Y.). *The Consolidated Chart of Insurance Organizations* 63, 10 (May 1953).

Frysztacki, Krzysztol. *Polonia w Duzym Miescie Amerykanskim.* Warszawa: Ossolineum. 1986.

Gale Research Company. *Encyclopedia of Associations.* Detroit: Gale Research Company, 1959–1973, 1992–1993.

Galusz, William J. "Faith and Fatherland: Dimensions of Polish-American Ethnoreligion, 1875–1975." In *Immigrants and Religion in Urban America,* edited by Randall M. Miller, 84–102. Philadelphia: Temple University Press, 1977.

Gans, Herbert. *The Urban Villagers: Group and Class in the Life of Italian-Americans.* New York: Free Press, 1962.

Gavin, Palmer John. *Americans by Choice.* In *Americanization Series,* edited by W.S. Bernard. Montclair, N.J.: Patterson, Smith, 1971.

Gerson, Louis. *Woodrow Wilson and the Rebirth of Poland, 1914–1920.* Hamden, Conn.: The Shoe-String Press, 1972.

Giergielewicz, Mieczyslaw, ed. *Polish Civilization: Essays and Studies.* New York: New York University Press, 1979.

Glastris, Paul. "Stepping Lively in Immigrant Politics." *U.S. News and World Report* (19 October 1992): 23.

Glazer, Nathan, and Daniel P. Moynihan. *Beyond the Melting Pot: The Negroes, Puerto Ricans, Jews, Italians, and Irish of New York City.* 2nd ed. Cambridge, Mass.: M.I.T. Press, 1970.

Glos Niezalenznych. "Stop Helping Communists." (16 June 1989): 3.

Glos Nauczyciela. 1985–1992.

Goffman, Irving. "Role Distance." In *Encounters,* edited by Irving Goffman. Indianapolis: Bobbs-Merrill, 1961.

Goldfarb, Jeffrey C. *On Cultural Freedom: An Exploration of Public Life in Poland and America.* Chicago: University of Chicago Press, 1982.

Goldstein, Sidney, and Calvin Goldscheider. *Jewish and Americans: Three Generations in a Jewish Community.* Englewood Cliffs, N.J.: Prentice Hall, 1968.

Gordon, Milton M. *Assimilation in American Life.* New York: Oxford University Press, 1964.

Gould, K. H. "Social Role Expectations of Polonians by Social Class, Ethnic Identification and Generational Positioning." University of Pittsburgh, 1966.

Greeley, Andrew. "The Alienation of White Ethnic Groups." Paper presented at the National Unity Conference held at Sterling Forest Gardens, New York, 19-20 November 1969a.

_____. *Why Can't They Be Like Us?* New York: Institute of Human Relations Press, 1969b.

_____. "Ethnicity as an Influence on Behavior." In *Ethnic Groups in the City*, edited by Otto Feinstein. Lexington, Mass.: Heath Lexington Books, 1971.

_____. "Making it in America: Ethnic Groups and Social Status." *Social Policy* (September-October 1973): 21-29.

_____. "The Ethnic and Religious Origins of Young American Scientists and Engineers: A Research Note." *Ethnicity in the United States.* New York: John Wiley, 1974a: 282-87.

_____. *Ethnicity in the United States.* New York: John Wiley, 1974b.

_____. Review of "Our Way" by Paul Wrobel. *Polish American Studies* 33 (1976).

Greeley, Andrew M., and Peter H. Rossi. *The Education of Catholic Americans.* Garden City, N.Y.: Doubleday, 1968.

Greene, Victor. *For God and Country: The Rise of Polish and Lithuanian Ethnic Consciousness in America, 1860-1910.* Madison: University of Wisconsin Press, 1975.

Greene, Victor R. *The Slavic Community on Strike: Immigrant Labor in Pennsylvania Anthracite.* South Bend, Ind.: University of Notre Dame Press, 1968.

_____. "The Polish American Worker to 1930: The 'Hunky" Image in Transition." *The Polish Review* 21 (1976): 63-78.

Gromada, Thaddeus. "Annual Report of the Acting Director and Secretary General." *Information Bulletin* (New York: Polish Institute of Arts and Sciences in America). 10, 1 (Summer 1973): 2-5.

Gross, Felix. "The American Poles." A research project submitted by the Polish Institute of Arts and Sciences in America. New York: City University of New York, n.d.

Gusfield, Joseph R. "Tradition and Modernity: Misplaced Polarities in the Study of Social Change." *American Journal of Sociology* 72 (January 1967): 351-62.

_____. "The Nature of Deference and Demeanor." In *Interaction Ritual*, edited by Irving Goffman. Garden City, N.Y.: Doubleday, 1967.

_____. *Relations in Public.* New York: Basic Books, 1971.

_____. *Community: A Critical Response.* New York: Harper Colophon Books, 1975.

Gwiazda Polarna (Stevens Point, Wis.). 16 February 1974.

Haiman, Mieczyslaw. *Zjednoczenie Polskie Rzymsko-Katolickie, 1873–1948.* (Polish Roman Catholic Union.) Chicago: Polish Roman Catholic Union, 1948.

Hall, Richard H. *Occupations and the Social Structure.* 2nd ed. Englewood Cliffs, N.J.: Prentice-Hall, 1975.

Hauser, Philip M., and Evelyn Kitagawa, eds. *Local Community Fact Book for Chicago, 1950.* Chicago: Community Inventory, University of Chicago, 1953.

Heaps, Willard. *The Story of Ellis Island.* New York: Seabury Press, 1967.

Heberle, Rudolf. "Displaced Persons in the Deep South." *Rural Sociology* 16, 4 (December 1951): 362–77.

Heller, Celia Stopnicka. "Assimilation: A Deviant Pattern among Jews of Inter-war Poland." *Jewish Journal of Sociology* (December 1973): 213–17.

_____. "Anti-Zionism and the Political Struggle within the Elite of Poland." *Jewish Journal of Sociology* 11, 2 (December 1969): 133–50.

Herberg, Will. *Protestant-Catholic-Jew.* New York: Doubleday, 1955.

Hertzler, J. O. *American Social Institutions.* Boston: Allyn & Bacon, 1961.

Horowitz, Irving Louis. "Race, Class and the New Ethnicity: The Holy Ghost of Social Stratification." In *The American Working Class: Prospects for the 1980's,* edited by Irving L. Horowitz, John Leggett, and Martin Oppenheimer, 43–69. New Brunswick, N.J.: Transaction Publishers, 1979.

Hourwich, Isaac A. *Immigration and Labour.* New York: Putnam's, 1912.

Hughes, Everett C. *French Canada in Transition.* Chicago: University of Chicago Press, 1934.

_____. *The Sociological Eye.* Chicago: Aldine-Atherton, 1971.

_____., and Helen McGill Hughes. *Where People Meet.* Glencoe, Ill.: The Free Press, 1952.

Hunter, Albert. *Symbolic Communities.* Chicago: University of Chicago Press, 1974.

Hutchinson, Edward P. "Immigration Policy since World War I." *Annals of the American Association of Political and Social Science* 262 (March 1949): 15–21.

_____. *Immigrants and Their Children, 1850–1950.* New York: John Wiley, 1956.

Informator Polonii w USA, 1980–81. New York: News Daily, 1980.

Informator PUNO. Chicago: Polski Instytut Naukii Kultury, Oddzial w Chicago. 1988/89.

Jadlecki, Waclaw. "The Role of the Polish Intellectual in America." *The Polish Review* 12 (Spring 1967): 3–10.

Janowitz, Morris. "Introduction." In *W.I. Thomas on Social Organization and Social Personality, Selected Papers,* edited by Morris Janowitz, vii–lvii. Chicago: The University of Chicago Press, 1966.

Janta, Alexander. "Barriers into Bridges: Notes on the Problem of Polish Culture in America." *The Polish Review* 2 (Spring-Summer 1957): 79-97.

Jarmakowski, Andrzej T. "O pieniadzach any slowa: Po zjezdzie Polonii." *Dziennik Chicagowski* (3-5 September 1992a): 7.

_____. "Po Zjezdie w Krakowie—Polonia w Glebokim Konflikcie." *Dziennik Chicagowski* (3-5 September 1992b):20.

Jaroszynska, Anna Dorota. "The American Committee for Resettlement of Polish Displaced Persons (1948-68) in the Manuscript Collection of the Immigration History Research Center." *Polish American Studies*. 44 (Spring 1987): 67-74.

Johnson, Ruth. *The Assimilation Myth: A Study of Second Generation Immigrants in Western Australia*. The Hauge: Martinus Nijhoff, 1969.

_____. *Immigrants' Assimilation: A Study of Polish People in Western Australia*. New York: Perth, Paterson and Brokensha, 1965.

Jones, Madwyn Allen. *American Immigration*. Chicago: University of Chicago Press, 1960.

Jurczak, Chester Andrew. "Ethnicity, Status and Generational Positioning: A Study of Health Practices among Polonians in Five Ethnic Islands." Ph.D. diss., University of Pittsburgh, 1964.

Kamm, Henry. "Israel Honors 12 Polish Heroes." *New Horizon* (April 1991): 11.

Kantowicz, Edward R. "Polish Chicago: Survival through Solidarity." In *Ethnic Chicago*, edited by Melvin G. Holli and Peter d'A. Jones, 214-38. Grand Rapids, Mich.: William B. Eerdmans, 1984.

Kapiszewski, Andrzej. *Stereotyp Amerykanow Polskiego Pochodzenia*. Warszawa: Ossolineum, 1976.

_____. "Stosunki Polsko-zydowskie w Stanach Zjednoczonych Ameryki." In *Polonia Amerykanska: Przeszlosc i Wspolczesnosc*, edited by Hieronim Kubiak, Eugeniusz Kusielewicz, and Tadeusz Gromada, 609-71. Warszawa: Ossolineum, 1988.

Karlowiczowa, Jadwiga. *Historia Zwiazku Polek w Ameryce*. Chicago: Sziasek Polek w Ameryce, 1938.

Karski, Jan. *Story of a Secret State*. Boston: Houghton Mifflin, 1944.

Keil, Charles. "Class and Ethnicity in Polish-America." *Journal of Ethnic Studies* 7 (Summer 1979): 37-45.

Kennedy, John F. *A Nation of Immigrants*. New York: Popular Library, 1964.

Kennedy, Ruby Jo Reeves. "Single or Triple Melting Pot: Intermarriage in New Haven." *American Journal of Sociology* 58, 1 (July 1952) 55-66.

Kirkpatrick, Clifford. *Intelligence and Immigration*. Baltimore: Williams and Wilkins (Mental Measurement Monographs, Serial 2), 1926.

Kivistro, Peter, and Dag Blanck, eds. *American Immigrants and Their Generations: Studies and Commentaries on the Hansen Thesis After Fifty Years.* Urbana: University of Illinois Press, 1990.

Kobelinski, Michael, Anthony J. Fornelli, and David G. Roth. "The Executive Suite." Reported in various mass communication media by the American Jewish Committee. Mimeo. 1974.

Kobylanski, Julia. "Demonstrations." *Pomost Quarterly* 8 (1980): 52.

Kokicki, Jarosiaw. "Wakacjusze' na Jackowie i Inni. Szkic o Sytuacji Wspolczesnych Polskich Emigrantow Zarobkowych w Chicago." *Przeglad Polonijny* 15, 3 (1989): 105-18.

Kolm, Richard. "The Change of Cultural Identity: An Analysis of Factors Conditioning the Cultural Integration of Immigration." Ph.D. diss., Wayne State University, 1966.

_____. "The Identity Crisis of Polish-Americans." *The Quarterly Review* 21, 2 (April-June 1969): 1, 4.

_____. "Ethnicity in Society and Community." In *Ethnic Groups in the City*, edited by Otto Feinstein. Lexington, Mass.: Heath Lexington Books, 1971a.

_____. Ethnicity." *Perspective* 1, 3 (July-Sepbember 1971b): 1, 6-7.

Kos, Rabcewicz-Aubkowski Ludwig. *The Poles in Canada.* Toronto: Polish Alliance Press, 1968.

Kosinski, Jerzy. *The Painted Bird.* New York: Bentham Books, 1972a.

_____. *Steps.* New York: Bentham Books, 1972b.

Kostrzewski, T. "Polish Americans." *Polish Medical and Dental Bulletin* (November 1938).

Kotlarz, Robert J. "Writings about the Changing of Polish Names in America." *Polish American Studies* 20, 1 (January-June 1963): 1-4.

Kowall, Mark. "Polonia's Respose." *Pomost Quarterly* 13 (1982): 46-50.

Kowalski, Thaddeus. *Anti-Defamation Guide.* Chicago: Polish American Congress, n.d.

Krakowska, Constance. "The Polish American Associations and the Liberation of Poland." *Polish American Studies* 12, 1-2 (January-June 1955): 11-18.

Kraly, Ellen Percy, and Robert Warren. "Long-term Immigration to the United States: New Approaches to Measurement." *International Labor Review* 25 (Spring 1991): 60-79.

Kramer, Judith R. *The American Minority Community.* New York: Thomas Y. Crowell, 1970.

Kromkowski, John A. "Eastern and Southern European Immigrants: Expectations, Reality and a New Agenda." *The Annals of the American Academy of Political and Social Sciences* 487 (September 1986): 57-78.

Kruczkowski, Zenon. "The Story Behind Poland's Reforms." *Transcript-Telegram* (Holyoke, Mass.: 18 (6 March 1989).

Krynski, Magnus. "Answer to the Memorandum." *Pomost Quarterly* 19 (1983): 9.

_____. "The Economy as a Component of Foreign Policy: The Need for a Long-range Trade Buildown with the Soviet Bloc." *Pomost Quarterly* 21 (1984): 45–51.

Kubiak, Hieronim, and Andrzej Pilcha, eds. *Stan i Potzeby Badan nad Zbioros-ciami Polonijnymi.* Warszawa: Ossolineum, 1976.

Kubiak, Hieronim, and Janusz Wrobel, eds. *II Congress Uczonych Polskiego Pochodzenia.* Warszawa: Ossolineium, 1984.

Kubiak, Hieronim, Eugeniusz Kusielewicz, and Taddeusz Gromada, eds. *Polonia Amerykanska: Przeszlosci Wspolczesnosc.* Warszawa: Os-solineum, 1988.

Kula, Witold, Nina Assorodobraj-Kula, and Marcin Kula. *Writing Home: Im-migrants in Brazil and the United States, 1890–1891,* edited and translated by Josephine Wtulich. New York: Columbia University Press (Boulder, East European Monographs), 1986.

Kuniczak, Wieslay. *The Silent Emigration.* Chicago: Polish Arts Club, 1968.

Kurjer. "Jeden cel-pomoc Polsce." (26 September 1989): 4–7.

Kusak, Teresa. Results of Kusak questionnaire from the inaugural meeting of the Polish American Economic Forum. Unpublished document, 1989.

Kusielewicz, Eugene. "Reflections on the Cultural Condition of the Polish American Community." In *The Poles of America, 1608–1972,* edited by Frank Renkiewicz, 97–132. Dobbs Ferry, N.Y.: Oceana Publications, 1973.

_____. "Polski Wklad do Literatury i Sztuki w Ameryce. Wprowadzenie." In *Polonia Amerykanska: Przeszloc i Wspolczesnosc,* edited by Hieronim Kubiak, Eugeniusz Kusielewicz, and Taddeusz Gromada, 487–504. Warszawa: Ossolineum, 1988.

Kuznets, Simon, and Ernest Rubin. "Immigration and Foreign Born," oc-casional paper no. 46. New York: National Bureau of Economic Research, 1954.

Lard, Ann Gdab. *The Polish American Community of Philadelphia 1870–1920.* Ann Arbor: University of Michigan Microfilm, 1971.

Laumann, Edward O. "The Social Structure of Religious and Ethno-religious Groups in a Metropolitan Community." *American Sociological Review* 34 (April 1969): 182–97.

Lenski, Gerhard. *The Religious Factor.* New York: Doubleday, 1961.

Lerski, Jerzy. "Co o Jalcie Pamietac Nalezy?" *Pomost Quarterly* 18 (1983): 2–6.

Les, Barbara. *Kosciol w Procesie Asymilacji Polonii Amerykanskiej.* Warszawa: Ossolineum, 1981.

Lewandowski, Robert. "Chicago impresje." *Dziennik Zwiazkowy* (28–30 August 1992a: 8, part 1; 4–7 September 1992a: 9, part 2; 11–13 September 1992a: 9).

_____. Personal interview, 1992b.

Lewis, Flora. "Us and Them in Poland." *New York Times*. (3 April 1989): 23E.

Lieberson, Stanley. *Ethnic Patterns in American Cities*. New York: Free Press, 1963.

_____. *A Piece of the Pie: Blacks and White Immigrants Since 1880*. Berkeley: University of California Press, 1980.

Lieberson, Stanley, and Mary C. Waters. *From Many Strands: Ethnic and Racial Groups in Contemporary America*. N.Y.: Russel Sage Foundation, 1988.

Lindsay, John V. "New York's Ethnic Boom." In *Pieces of a Dream*, edited by Michael Wenk, S. M. Tomasi, and Geno Baroni. New York: Center for Migration Studies, 1972.

The Link, "Survey offers Snapshot of Chicago's Polish Community." 1992.

Linton, Ralph. *The Science of Man*. New York: Appleton-Century-Crofts, 1936.

Lopata, Helena Znaniecka. "The Function of Voluntary Associations in an Ethnic Community: Polonia." Ph.D. diss., University of Chicago, 1954.

_____. "The Function of Voluntary Associations in an Ethnic Community: Polonia." In *Contributions to Urban Sociology*, edited by Ernest W. Burgess and Donald J. Bogue, 203-23. Chicago: University of Chicago Press, 1964a.

_____. "A Restatement of the Relations between Role and Status." *Sociology and Social Research* 49, 1 (October 1964b): 58-68.

_____. "Loneliness: Forms and Components. *Social Problems* 17, 2 (Fall 1969a): 248-62.

_____. "The Social Involvement of American Widows." *American Behavior Scientist*. (Fall 1969b): 41-57.

_____. *Occupation: Housewife*. New York: Oxford University Press, 1971a.

_____. "Roles, Status and Acculturation: Dimensions of Ethnic Identity." Paper presented at the Southern Sociological Association Meeting, Miami, Florida, 1971b.

_____. The Effect of Schooling on Social Contacts of Urban Women." *American Journal of Sociology* 59, 3 (November 1973a): 604-19.

_____. "Self-identity in Marriage and Widowhood." *Sociology Quarterly* 14, 3 (Summer 1973b): 407-18.

_____. "Social Relations of Black and White Widowed Women in a Northern Metropolis." *American Journal of Sociology* 78, 4 (January 1973c): 241-48.

_____. *Widowhood in an American City*. Cambridge, Mass.: Schenkman Publishing Company, General Learning Press, 1973d.

_____. "Life Styles of Elderly Urbanites: Chicago of the 1970s." *The Gerontologist* 15, 1 (February 1975): 35-41.

_____. "Polish Immigration to the United States of America: Problems of Estimation and Parameters." *The Polish Review* 21, 4 (1976a): 85-108.

_____. "Members of the Intelligentsia as Developers and Disseminators of Cosmopolitan Culture." In *The Intelligentsia and Intellectuals*, edited by Aleksander Gella, 59–78. London: Sage Publications, Sage Studies in International Sociology. 1976b.

_____. *Polish Americans: Status Competition in an Ethnic Community.* Englewood Cliffs, N.J.: Prentice-Hall 1976c.

_____. "Florian Znaniecki: The Creative Evolution of a Sociologist." *Journal of the History of the Behavioral Sciences* (1976d): 203–15.

_____. "Widowhood in Polonia." *Polish American Studies* 34, 2 (Autumn 1977) : 7–25.

_____. "Funkcja Stowarzyszen Dobrowolnych w Polonij Wspolnocie Etnicznej." *Studia Poloniine* Lublin: Towarzystwo Naukowe Katolickiego Universytetu Lubelskiego (1978): 83–112.

_____. "Widowhood and Husband Sanctification." *Journal of Marriage and the Family* 43 (2 May 1981): 439–50.

_____. "Polska Intelligentcja za Granica i jej Wplyw na Rozwoj Nauki." In *II Congress Uczonych Polskiego Pochodzenia*, edited by Hieronim Kubiak and Janus Wrobel. Warszawa: Ossoleum, 1984.

_____. "The Polish Intelligentsia as Émigrés." In *Sociology and Society. The Collection of Papers in Honour of Professor Jan Szczepanski*, 295–308. Warszawa: Zaklad Narodowy Imienia Ossolinskich, 1985.

_____. "The Polonia Families." In *Polonia Amerykanska: Prezeszlosc i Wspolczesnosc*, edited by Hieronim Kubiak, Eugeniusz Kusielewicz and Taddeusz Gromada, 343–69. Warszawa: Zaklad Narodowy Imienia Ossolinskich, 1988a.

_____. "Women's Family Roles in Historical Perspective." In *Analyzing Gender: A Handbook of Social Science Research*, edited by Beth Hess and Myra Marx Ferre. Beverly Hills, Sage, 1988b.

Loyola World. "Niles College Once was Home for Polish American Orphans." (21 November 1992): 7.

Lukas, Richard C. *The Forgotton Holocaust: The Poles Under German Occupation 1939–1944.* Lexington: University Press of Kentucky, 1986.

Lynd, Helen Merrell. *On Shame and the Search for Identity.* New York: Science Editions, 1974.

MacIver, R. M. *Society.* New York: Farrar and Rinehard, 1937.

Makowski, William Boleslaus. *History and Integration of Poles in Canada.* Niagra Peninsula, Canada: The Canadian Polish Congress, 1967.

Manning, Caroline. *The Immigrant Woman and Her Job.* Washington, D.C.: Government Printing Office, 1930.

Martineau, Harriet. *Society in America*, edited by Seymour Martin Lipset. Garden City, New York: Anchor Book, Doubleday, 1834/1962.

Mazewski, Alojzy. "Excellent Speech of President Mazewski." *Dziennik Zwiaz-kowy* (19 September 1973a): 2.

_____. "The Poles—a National Group Full of Dynamism and Individualism." *Dziennik Zwiazkowy* (17 October 1973b): 5.

Miaso, Josef. "Z Dziejow Oswiaty Polskiej w Stanach Zjednoczonych." *Problemy Polonii Zagranicznej* 4, (1971): 19-42.

Michalski, Wojciech. "Migracje Ludnosci Miedzy Polska i Francja w Latach 1980-1986." *Przeglad Polonijny* 16, 1 (1990): 111-21.

The Michigan State Chamber of Commerce. *Michigan's Challenge: The Polish Americans of Michigan.* Lansing, Michigan: The Michigan State Chamber of Commerce, April 1971.

Mierzynska, Zofia. *Wakacjuszka.* Warszawa: Wydawnictwo Polonia, 1990.

Mikos, Michael J. "Polish in the United States: A Study in Language Change." In *Studies in Ethnicity: The East European Experience in America*, edited by Charles A. Ward, Philip Shashko, and Donald Pienkos, 15-26. Boulder: East European Monographs, 1980.

Miller, Commissioner. *Monthly Review* (Immigration and Naturalization Service) 6, 3 (September 1948): 48.

Milosz, Cheslaw. *Native Realm: A Search for Self-Definition*, translated by Catherine E. Leach. Garden City, N.Y.: Doubleday, 1968.

Mindel, Charles H., Robert Habenstein, and Roosevelt Wright, Jr. *Ethnic Families in America.* New York: Elsevier, 1988.

Miodunka, Wladyslaw. "Polonia Research as the Polish Form of Ethnic Studies in Historical Perspective." *Przeglad Polonijny* 15, 2 (1989): 5-17.

Morawska, Ewa. *For Bread and Butter: The Lifeworlds of East Central Europeans in Johnstown, Pennsylvania, 1890-1940.* New York: Cambridge University Press, 1985.

Moseley, Ray. "The Pope Triumphant: Experts Debate Vatican Role in Communism's End." *Chicago Tribune* (26 July 1992).

Moskal, Edward. "Wrazenia z Polski." *Dziennik Zwiazkowy* (July 1992): 1, 3, 25.

Moskos, Charles C. *Greek Americans: Struggle and Success.* Englewood Cliffs, N.J.: Prentice-Hall, 1980.

_____. *Greek Americans: Struggle and Success.* New Brunswick, N.J.: Transaction Publishers, 1990.

Mostwin, Danuta. "Post World War II Polish Immigrants in the United States." *Polish American Studies* 26, 2 (Autumn 1969): 5-14.

_____. "The Transplanted Family: A Study of the Social Adjustment of the Polish American Family to the United States after the Second World War." Columbia University, School of Social Work, University Microfilms of Dissertations, 1971.

_____. *Emigranci Polscy w USA*. Lublin: Redakcja Wydawnictwo Katolick-
iego Uniwersytetu Lubelskiego, 1991.

Mullan, Eugene. *The Mentality of the Arriving Immigrant*. New York: Arno
Press, 1917.

Musick, John. "Ethnicity and the Economic Squeeze." The University of
Michigan School of Social Work. Mimeo. April 1971.

Myers, Linnet. "Coalition Eludes 4th Polish Premier." *Chicago Tribune* (5
July1992): 1, 5.

Nam, Charles B. "Nationality Groups and Social Stratification." *Social Forces*
37, 4 (May 1959): 328–33.

Napolska, Sister Mary Remigia. *The Polish Immigrant in Detroit to 1914*.
Chicago: Polish Roman Catholic Union Archives and Museum, 1945–
1946).

New Horizon: Polish American Review. "Bush Cancels $2.6 Billion of Poland's
Debt." (March 1991a): 9.

_____. "Polish American Congress." (April 1992b)): 17.

_____. "U.S. Assistance to Poland, Recent Economic Developments." (March
1991b): 25–27.

_____. "Poland Lifts Visa Requirements." (April 1991c): 18.

_____. "PNA Convention in California." (September 1991d): 18.

_____. "Summer Sessions of the Kosciuszko Foundation." (October 1991e):
21–22.

_____. "Jews Honor Polish Catholic Rescuer." (January 1992a): 17.

_____. "LDPa Rutgers Program." (February 1992b): 10–11.

_____. "Purposes and Objectives of the Polish American Congress." (May–
June 1992d): 4.

Newman, Barry. "Solidarity's Legacy: Underground Culture Pervades Polish
Life, But Can It Survive Lack of Repression?" *Wall Street Journal* 68
(1987): 1.

Newman, Katherine S. *Falling from Grace: The Experience of Downward
Mobility in the American Middle Class*. New York: The Free Press, 1988.

Nickerson, Matthew. "Spertus Scholar Talks Peace to Poles, Jews." *Chicago
Tribune* (September 1992: sections 2, 8).

Novak, Michael. *The Rise of the Unmeltable Ethnics*. New York: Macmillan,
1973.

_____. "New Ethnic Politics vs. Old Ethnic Politics." In *Pieces of a Dream*,
edited by Michael Wenk, S.M. Tomasi, and Geno Baroni. New York: Center
for Migration Studies, 1972.

Nowak. "Pomost." *Pomost Quarterly* (5 January 1980): 3–4.

_____. "The Polish American Congress and the U.S. Policy of Sanctions."
Studium Papers 10 (1986): 50–56

Nowak, Stefan. "Values and Attitudes of the Polish People." *Scientific American* (July 1981): 45-53.

Nowakowski, Stefan. "Tendencje Rozwojowe Polonii Americanskiej." *Problemy polonii Zagranicznej.* III Warszawa: Wydawnictwo Polonia, 1964.

Nowicka, Bozena. Interviews (15 June 1 and 6 October 1992).

Obidinski, Eugene. "Ethnic to Status Group: A Study of Polish Americans in Buffalo." Ph.D. diss., State University of New York, 1968.

_____. "Polish American Social Standing: Status and Stereotypes." *Polish Review: Bicentennial Issue* (1976):79-101.

_____. "The Polish American Press: Survival through Adaptation." *Polish American Studies* 34 (Autumn 1977): 38-55.

_____. "Duma, Uprzedzenia i stereotypy Polonii." In *Polonia Amerykanska: Przeszlosc i Wspolczesnosc,* edited by Hieronim Kubiak, Eugeniusz Kusielewicz and Taddeusz Gromada, 541-53. Warszawa: Ossolineum, 1988.

Obidinski, Eugene and Helen Stankiewicz Zand. *Polish Folkways in America: Community and Family.* New York: Lanham, 1987.

Ocytko, Adam. "Stanowisko Zwiazku Klubow Polskich wobec Zjazdu Polonii z Zagranicy w Krakowie." (19 September 1992): 6.

Orbach, Harold L. "Znaniecki's Contributions to the Polish Peasant." In *The Contribution of Florian Znaniecki to Sociological Theory,* edited by Renzo Gubert and Luigi Tomasi, 142-58. Milano, Italy: Franco Angeli, 1993.

Orzechowski, Emil. *Theatr Polonijny w Stanach Zjednoczonych.* Warszawa: Ossolineum, 1989.

PAC Bulletin. 18 vols. Chicago: Polish American Congress, 1981-1990.

PAC Bulletin (December 1983): 4, (August 1984): 4.

PAC Illinois Division Bulletin. Chicago: Illinois Division of the Polish American Congress, 1974-1981.

PAC Newsletter. 15 vols. Chicago: Polish American Congress, 1969-1984.

_____."Anti-Defamation off to a Good Start." (15 July 1969).

_____. "The Accomplishment of the Agreement in Poland Requires Prudence and Modernation: Declaration of PAC." *Dziennik Zwiazkowy* 24 (February 1989a): 1.

_____. "Decision Defines New Socio-political Relations in Poland: Declaration of PAC." *Dziennik Zwiazkowy* (6 April 1989b): 1.

_____. "For Solidarity's Election Fund." *Dziennik Zwiazkowy* (19 April 1989c): 3. E.

_____. "Kto Moze Glosowac?" *Dziennik Zwiazkowy* (22 May 1989d): 3.

_____. "Kongres Polski Amerykanskiej na Wybory." *Dziennik Zwiazkowy* (2 June 1989e): 1.

Packard, Vance. *The Status Seekers.* New York: Cardinal Pocket Books, 1959.

_____. *The Pyramid Climbers*. Greenwich, Conn.: Fawcett, 1962.

_____. *A Nation of Strangers*. New York: McKay, 1972.

Pacyga, Dominic A. "Villages of Steel Mills and Packing-houses: The Polish Worker on Chicago's South Side, 1880-1921." In *The Polish Presence in Canada and America*, edited by Frank Renkiewicz, 19-27. Toronto: The Multicultural History Society of Ontario, 1982.

_____. "Polish Americans in Transition: Social Change and Chicago's Polonia, 1945 to 1980." *Polish American Studies* 44 (1987): 38-55.

_____. *Polish Immigrants and Industrial Chicago: Workers on the South Side, 1880-1922*. Columbus: Ohio State University Press, 1991a.

_____. "To Live amongst Strangers: Polish Americans and Their Neighbors in the Industrial United States." Presented at the Polish American Historical Association 50th Anniversary Conference, Chicago, December 1991b.

Park, Robert. *The Immigrant Press and its Control*. New York: Harper & Row, 1922.

_____. "Human Migration and the Marginal Man." *American Journal of Sociology* 33 (May 1928): 81-93.

Park, Robert, and E. W. Burgess. *The City*. Chicago: University of Chicago Press, 1925.

Parot, Joseph John. *The American Faith and the Persistence of Chicago Polonia, 1870-1920*. Ann Arbor: University Microfilms (A Xerox Company), 1970.

_____. "The Serdeczna Matko' of the Sweatshops: Marital and Family Crises of Immigrant Working-Class Women in the Late Nineteenth-Century Chicago." In *The Polish Presence in Canada and America*, edited by Frank Renkiewicz, 155-82. Toronto: The Multicultural History Society of Ontario, 1980.

Passel, Jeffrey S. "Undocumented Immigration." *Annals of the American Academy of Political and Social Science* 487 (1986): 181-200.

Pastusiak, Longin, Stanislaw Przywarski, and Bohdan Bielewicz. "Polonia w Organach Wladzy Politycznej Stanow Zjednoczonych Ameryki (na Szczeblu Federalnym,Stanowym i Lokalnym)." In *Polonia Amerykanska: Przeszlosc i Wspolczesnosc*, edited by Hieronim Kubiak, Eugeniusz Kusielewicz, and Taddeusz Gromada. Warszawa: Ossolineum, 1988.

Pear, Robert. "Congress Approves Aid Plan of $852 Million for Poland." *New York Times* (19 November 1989): 16.

Petras, John W. "Polish American in Sociology and Fiction." *Polish American Studies* 21, 1 (January-June 1964): 16-32.

Pienkos, Donald E. "Dimensions of Ethnicity: A Preliminary Report on the Milwaukee Polish American Population." *Polish American Studies* 30 (Spring 1973): 5-19.

_____. *PNA: A Centennial History of the Polish National Alliance of the United States of North America*. New York: Columbia University, 1984.

_____. *One Hundred Years Young: A History of the Polish Falcons of America, 1887–1987.* Boulder: East European Monographs. 1987.

_____. *For Your Freedom through Ours: Polish American Efforts on Poland's Behalf, 1863–1991.* Boulder: East European Monographs, 1991.

Piwowarski, Stanislaw. "Conference Underscores the Difference between Polish Nation and Communist Regime." *Polish American Congress Newsletter* 1, 2 (20 July 1970): 7–8.

The Polish American Congress. *Purposes and Achievements.* Chicago: Polish American Congress, 1971, 1972.

Polish American Guardian Society. "An Urgent Call for Unified Action." *Polonia Today* (April 1993): 9.

The Polish Institute of Arts and Sciences in America. *Information Bulletin* 10, 1 (Summer 1973).

The Polish-Italian Conference. *Program of the Saint Joseph's Day Reception.* Chicago, (19 March 1973).

Polish Pageant. *The Poles of Chicago, 1837–1937: Their Contributions to a Century of Progress.* Chicago: Polish Day Association, 1937.

Polish Welfare Association. "Pastoral Outreach Program for Polish Speakers." Mimeo. 1989.

_____. *Annual Reports.* Chicago: Polish Welfare Association, 1990, 1991.

Polonia Today. "The Heritage Club of Polish Americans Announces the Formation of a Teen Chapter," (1991).

_____. "Founding New Alliance College," (4 February 1992a).

_____. Calendar of Events (February 1992b).

_____. "English Classes for Children." (May 1992): 3.

_____. "Polkabration Festival," June 1992): 19

_____. "Polka Radio" (May 1992): 18–19.

Polzin, Theresita. "English for Children" *The Polish Americans: Whence and Whither.* Pulaski, Wis.: Franciscan Publishers, 1973.

_____. "The Polish American Family—I the Social Aspects of the Families of Polish Immigrants to America before World War II and Their Descendants." *Polish American Review* 21, 3 (1976): 103–22.

Pomost Quarterly. 24 vols. Chicago: Pomost Social-Political Movement, 1979–1984.

_____. "Kroniku Pomostu." 5(1983):52–55.

_____. "Skandal w Sprawie Sankcji." 23 (1984): 49–51.

Przezdziecka, Barbara. "Immigration Reform of 1990." *The Link* 4 (1 December 1990): 2–3.

Przyloski, Jerzy. "Polska i Polonia Amerykanska." *Dziennik Zwiazkowy* (15–17 May 1992): 1–3.

Puacz, Edward. "Uwagi o Ofiarnosci Polonii Amerikanskiej." *Kultura*, Nr. 10/301. Paris: Instytut Literacki (October 1972): 103–12.

Pula, James, and Eugene E. Dziedzic. *United We Stand, the Role of Polish Workers in the New York Mills Textile Strikes, 1912 and 1916.* Boulder: East European Monographs 286, 1990.

The Quarterly Review. (January–March 1972): 8.

_____. American Council of Polish Cultural Clubs.: Falls Church, Va.: 1972–74.

Radzialowski, Thaddeus. "A View from a Polish Ghetto. Some Observations on the First One Hundred Years in Detroit." *Ethnicity* 1, 2 (July 1974): 125–50.

_____. "Reflections on the History of the Felicians." *Polish American Studies* 32 (Spring 1975): 19–28.

_____. "Immigrant Nationalism and Feminism: Glos Polek and the Polish Women's Alliance in America, 1898–1917." *Review Journal of Philosophy and Social Science* 2 (1977): 183–203.

_____. "Polish American Institutions of Higher Learning." In *Poles in America*, edited by Frank Mocha, 461–96. Stevens Point, Wis.: Worzalla, 1978.

_____. "Ethnic Conflict and the Polish Americans of Detroit, 1921–1942." In *The Polish Presence in Canada and America*, edited by Frank Renkiewicz, 195–207. Toronto: The Multicultural History Society of Ontario, 1980.

_____. "Class, Ethnicity and Community: The Polish Americans of Detroit and the Organization of the CIO." Paper presented at the annual meeting of the American Association for the Advancement of Slavic Studies, 1984.

_____. "The Second Generation: The Unknown Polonia." *Polish American Studies* 43, 1 (Spring 1986): 5–13.

_____. "Historia Stosunkow Pomiedzy Murzynami i Polska Grupa Etniczno w Stanach Zjecnoczonych Ameryki." In *Polonia Amerykanska: Przeszlosc i Wspolczesnosc*, edited by Hieronim Kubiak, Eugeniusz Kusielewicz, and Taddeusz Gromada. Warszawa: Ossolineum, 1988.

_____. "Immigrant Women and Their Daughters." The Fiedorczyk Lecture in *Polish American Studies.* New Haven, Conn.: Central Connecticut and Yale University, April 1990.

The Random House Dictionary of the English Language. Unabridged edition. New York: Random House, 1966.

Reddaway, W. J., J. H. Penson, O. Halecki, and R. Dyboski, eds. *The Cambridge History of Poland.* Cambridge, England: The University Press, vol. 1, 1950; vol. 2, 1951.

Renkiewicz, Frank. "Language Loyalty and Ethnic Culture." *Polish American Studies* 26, 2 (August 1969): 57–61.

_____, ed. *The Poles in America 1608–1972: A Chronology and Fact Book.* Dobbs Ferry, New York: Oceana, 1973.

_____. "The Uses of the Polish Past in America." *Polish American Studies* 34, 1 (Spring 1977): 70–79.

_____. "Polish American Workers, 1880-1980." In *Pastor of the Poles: Polish American Essays Presented to Right Reverend Monsignor John P. Wodarski*, edited by Stanislaus A. Blejwas and Mieczyslaw B. Biskupski, 116-36. New Britain, Conn.: Polish Studies Program Monographs, 1982a.

_____, ed. *The Polish Presence in Canada and America*. Toronto: The Multicultural History Society of Ontario, 1982b.

_____. "Organizowanie sie Robotnikow Polskiego Pochodzenia w Stanach Zjednoczonych Ameryki w Latach 1880-1980." In *Polonia Amerykanska*, edited by Heironim Kubiak, Eugeniusz Kusielewicz, and Thaddeusz Gromada, 449-85. Warszawa: Ossolineum, 1988.

Reymont, Ladislas. *The Peasants: Fall, Winter, Spring, Summer*. 4 vols. New York: Knopf, 1925.

Rokicki, Jaroslaw. "Wakacjusze' na Jackowie i Juni. Szkico Sytuacji Wspolczesnych Polskich Emigrantow Zarobkowych w Chicago." *Przeglad Polonijny* 15, 3 (1989): 105-18.

Rooney, Elizabeth. "Polish Americans and Family Disorganization." *The American Catholic Sociological Review* 18 (March 1957): 47-51.

Rosenblum, Gerald. *Immigrant Workers*. New York: Basic Boosk, 1973.

Rosenmayr, Leopold, and Eva Kockeis. "Propositions for a Sociological Theory of Aging and the Family." *International Social Science Journal* 15, 3 (1963: 410-26.

Roucek, Joseph S. *Poles in the United States of America*. Gdynia, Poland: Baltic Institute, 1937.

_____, ed. *The Slavonic Encyclopedia*. New York: Philosophical Library, 1949.

Ruggiero, Mary. "The Executive Suite Study." Chicago: Joint Civic Committe of Italian Americans. Mimeo. 1970.

Rurasz, Zdzislaw. "The True Meaning of Yalta." *Pomost Quarterly* 21 (1984): 42-44.

Sacrum Polonian Millenium 6. "The Contributions of the Poles to the Growth of Catholicism in the United States." Rome (1959).

St. Hyacinth Jubilee Committee. *St. Hyacinth Parish: The Past, the Present, the Future, 1894–1969*. Chicago: St. Hyacinth Parish, 1969.

Sakson, Andrzej. "Problem Masowej Emigracji z Polski w latach Osiemdziesiatych." *Przeglad Polonijny*. 1989.

Sanday, Peggy. "Female Status in the Public Domain." In *Women, Culture and Society*, edited by M. Z. Rosaldo and L. Lamphere, 189-205. Stanford, Calif.: Stanford University Press, 1974.

Sandberg, Neil C. *Ethnic Identity and Assimilation: The Polish American Community*. New York: Praeger, 1974.

Schermerhorn, Richard A. *These Our People*. Boston: D.C. Heath, 1949.

Schodolski, Vincent. "In Fredom, Disunity Threatens Lithuania." *The Chicago Tribune*. (28 June 1992): section 1, pp. 1-6.

Schwartz, Barry. *George Washington: The Making of an American Symbol.* New York: The Free Press. 1987.

Sennett, Richard. "Genteel Backlash: Chicago, 1886." In *Marriages and Families,* edited by Helena Z. Lopata. New York: Van Nostrand, 1973.

Shanas, Ethel, and Gordon Streib, eds. *Social Structure and the Family.* Englewood Cliffs, N.J.: Prentice-Hall, 1965.

Shaw, Clifford R., and Henry D. McKay. *Juvenile Delinquency and Urban Areas.* Chicago: University of Chicago Press, 1942.

Shriver, R. Sargent. Speech to the 9th Conference of the Polish National Congress. Quoted by Wlodzimierz Zmurkiewicz. "Protokol Dziewiatej Krajowej Konwencji Kongresu Polonii Amerykanskiej," 1972: 66–81.

Shulgasser, Barbara, and David S. Robinson. "Enough Protests, Polish Consulate Neighbors Say." *Sun Times* (30 December 1981): 5.

Smith, William Carlson. *Americans in the Making.* New York: Appleton-Century-Crofts, 1939.

Solidarity Election Committee. "Do Wszystkich Polakow na Emigracji." [To all Poles in Emigration.] *Kurier* (9 May 1989): 5.

Squier, D. Ann, and Jill S. Quadagno. "The Italian American Family." In *Ethnic Families in America,* edited by Charles Mindel, Robert Habenstein, and Roosevelt Wright, Jr., 109–37. New York: Elsevier, 1988.

Starzynski, F. "Polish Americans." *Polish Medical and Dental Bulletin* (November 1938).

Statistics of Fraternal Benefit Societies. National Fraternal Congress of America. 1937.

Steven, Stewart. *The Poles.* New York: Macmillan, 1982.

Stonequist, E. V. *The Marginal Man.* New York: Scribner's, 1937.

Studium Papers. 14 vols. (From 1976 to 1982 published as Studium News Abstracts.) Ann Arbor: The North American Study Center for Polish Affairs, 1976–1989.

Stypulkowski, Zbigniew. "Polish-American Relations with Poland." Orchard Lake, Mich.: Orchard Lake Center for Polish Studies and Culture Monograph No. 3, (November 1970).

Super, Paul. *The Polish Tradition.* London: Maxlove, 1939.

Suttles, Gerald. *The Social Order of the Slum.* Chicago: University of Chicago Press, 1968.

_____. *The Social Construction of Communities.* Chicago: University of Chicago Press, 1972.

Symmons-Symonolewicz, Konstantin. "The Polish-American Community Half a Century After *The Polish Peasant.*" *The Polish Review* 40, 3 (1966): 1–7.

_____. "The Polish Peasant in Europe and America: Its First Half a Century of Intellectual History (1918–1968)." *The Polish Review* 31, 2 (Spring 1968): 14–27.

_____. "Polonia Amerykanska." *Kultura* (Paris), No. 7/255-8/226 (July-August 1969): 105-35.

Synak, Brunon. "Polish Society, Integration and Anomie." Paper presented at the first Bremen-Gdansk Symposium, Bremen, Germany, December 1990.

Szawleski, Mieczyslaw. *Wychodztwo Polskie w Stanach Zjednoczonych Ameryki.* Warszawa: Zaklad-Narodowego Im. Ossolinskiego, 1924.

Szczepanski, Jan. "The Polish Intelligentsia, Past and Present." *World Politics* 16, 3 (April 1962): 406-20.

_____. *Polish Society.* New York: Random House, 1970.

Taeuber, Alma F., and Karl E. Taeuber. "Recent Immigration and Studies of Ethnic Assimilation." *Demography* 4, 2 (1967): 798-808.

Taft, Donald. "Nationality and Crime." *American Journal of Sociology* 1, 4 (August 1936): 724-36.

Taft, Donald, and Richard Robbins. *International Migrations: The Immigrant in the Modern World.* New York: The Ronold Press, 1955.

Tagliabue, John. "For Many, the Accord Seems to be a Nonevent." *New York Times* (7 April 1989a): 4.

_____. "Jaruzelski Wins Polish Presidency by Minimum Votes." *New York Times* (20 July 1989b): 1.

_____. "Support for Jaruzelski Splits Solidarity." *New York Times* (21 July, 1989c): 3.

_____. "Poles Approve Solidarity Led Cabinet." *New York Times* (13 September 1989d): 3.

Tec, Nechama. *When Light Pierced the Darkness: Christian Rescue of Jews in Nazi-Occupied Poland.* New York: Oxford University Press, 1986.

Theoharis, Athan. "The Republican Party and Yalta: Partisan Exploitation of the Polish American Concern over the Conference, 1945-1960." *Polish American Studies* 28, 1 (Spring 1971): 5-19.

Thomas, John L. "Marriage Prediction in the Polish Peasant." *American Journal of Sociology* 55 (May 1950): 573.

Thomas, William I. "Comment on Blumer's Analysis in Herbert Blumer *Critiques of Research in the Social Sciences: An Appraisal of Thomas and Znaniecki's The Polish Peasant in Europe and America.*" New York: Social Science Research Council, 1949.

Thomas, William I., Robert E. Park, and Herbert A. Miller. *Old World Traits Transplanted.* Montclair, N.J.: Patterson, Smith, 1921/1971.

Thomas, William I., and Florian Znaniecki. *The Polish Peasant in Europe and America.* New York: Dover Publications, Inc., 1918-1920/1958.

Thrasher, Frederick M. *The Gang: The Study of 1,313 Gangs in Chicago.* Chicago: University of Chicago Press, 1927.

Thurner, Arthur W. "Polish Americans in Chicago Politics, 1890-1920." *Polish Amierican Studies* 28, 1 (Spring 1971): 20-42.

deTocqueville, Alexis. *Democracy in America*, edited by J. P. Mayer. Garden City, New York: Doubleday Anchor Books, 1835/1969.

Tomczak, Anthony C. *The Poles in America: Their Contribution to a Century of Progress*. Chicago: Polish Day Association, 1933.

Townsend, Peter. *The Family Life of Old People*. London: Routledge and Kegan Paul, 1967.

Tryfan, Barbara. "The Role of Rural Women in the Family." *Warsaw, W.D.N.* 365/9/72. Paper presented at the 3rd World Congress of Rural Sociology, Baton Rouge, Louisiana, 1972.

_____. "Polska i Polonia: Spotkanie." *Tygodnik Kulturalny* 1 (8 July 1973): 1, 9.

_____. "Polonia i Polska: Potomkowie Emigrantow" 2 (22 July 1973): 3, 11.

_____. "Changes in the Situation of Country Women in Poland." In *Rural Social Change in Poland*, edited by Jan Turowski and Lili Maria Szwengrug. Warszawa: Ossolineum, 1976.

Tschan, Francis J., Harold J. Grimm, and J. Duane Squire. *Western Civilization*. Philadelphia: Lippincott, 1942.

Tullia, Sister Mary. "Polish American Sisterhoods and Their Contribution to the Catholic Church in the United States." In *Sacrum Poloniae Millennium: The Contribution of the Poles to the Growth of Catholicism in the United States* 5-6, Rome (1959): 255-369.

U.S. Bureau of Census. *Prisoners in State and Federal Prisons and Reformatories: 1933*, p. 29, table 25. Washington, D.C.: Government Printing Office, 1935.

_____. *Historical Statistics of United States Colonial Times to 1957*. Washington, D.C.: Government Printing Office, 1960.

_____. "Census of the Population." *Detailed Characteristics*, Final Report P.C. (1)-01. *United States Summary*. Washington D.C.: Government Printing Office, 1970a.

_____. *Special Reports: National Origin and Language*. P.C. (2)-la. Washington, D.C.: Government Printing Office, 1970b.

_____. *Marital Status*. P.C. (2)-4C, table 2, 1970c.

_____. *Current Population Reports*. Series P-20, November, 1969. N. 221, Characteristics of the Population by Ethnic Origin." N. 220, "Ethnic Origin and Educational Attainment." N. 226, "Fertility Variations by Ethnic Origin" (November, 1971). N. 249, "Characteristics of the Population by Ethnic Origin." Washington, D.C.: Government Printing Office, 1971, 1972.

_____. *Statistical Abstracts of the United States*. 93rd ed. Washington, D.C.: Government Printing Office, 1972; 94th ed. Washington, D.C.: Government Printing Office, 1973.

U.S. Bureau of Justice, Immigration Commission. *Immigration and Crime.* Report 26. Washington, D.C.: Government Printing Office, 1910; Report 36, 1911.

U.S. Commission on Civil Rights. *Civil Rights Issues of Euro-Ethnic Americans in the United States: Opportunities and Challenges.* Washington, D.C.: U.S. Commission on Civil Rights, 1980.

U.S. Department of Justice. *Annual Report to the Commissioner of Immigration and Naturalization.* Washington, D.C.: Government Printing Office, 1902–1972.

U.S. Department of Justice, Immigration and Naturalization Service. 1977–1989. *Statistical Yearbook of the Immigration and Naturalization Service.* Washington, D.C.: Government Printing Office, 1902–72.

U.S. National Commission on Law and Enforcement. *Report on Crime and Foreign Born*, p. 29, table 25. Washington, D.C.: Government Printing Office, 1935.

U.S. Poland Chamber of Commerce. *U.S. Poland Connection* 1 (Fall 1991).

Wachtl, Karol. *Polonia w Ameryce.* Published by the author in Philadelphia, 1944.

Wagner, Stanley P. "The Polish American Vote in 1960." *Polish American Studies* 21, 1.

Walaszek, Adam. "Migracja Powrotna z Stanow Zjednoczohnych Ameryki do Polski" In *Polonia Amerykanska: Przeszlosc i Wspolczesnosc Pieszlosci Wrpokzesnosc*, edited by Heironim Kubiak, Eugene Kusielewicz, and Thaddeus Gromada. Warszawa: Ossolineum, 1988: 745-56.

_____. "Krnabrni Przybysze: Przemysl Amerykanski, Polscy Immigranci, Praca i Zwiazki Zawodowe na Poczatku XX w." *Przeglad Polonijny* 15, 3 (1989): 5-24.

_____. "Preserving or Transforming Role?: Migrants and Polish Territories in the Era of Mass Migration." Paper presented at the Fiftieth Anniversary International Congress, Polish Institue of Arts and Sciences in America, New Haven, Connecticut, 18-20 June 1992.

Walesa, Lech. *A Way of Hope.* New York: Henry Holt and Company, 1987.

_____. "Ezekalismy na was Bardzo Dlugo." *Dziennik Zwiazkowy* (21-23 August 1992)

Ward, Charles A., Philip Shashko, and Donald E. Pienkos, eds. *Studies in Ethnicity: The East European Experience in America.* Boulder: East European Monographs, 72, 1980.

Ware, Caroline. "Ethnic Communities." In *Encyclopedia of Social Sciences*, vol. 11, edited by Edwin R. A. Seligman. New York: Macmillan, 1931.

Warner, W. Lloyd, and Leo Srole. *The Social Systems of American Ethnic Groups*, Yankee City Series, vol. 3. New Haven, Conn.: Yale University Press, 1945.

Waters, Mary C. *Ethnic Options: Choosing Identities in America*. Berkeley: University of California Press, 1990.

Watson, Jerome. "For Polish Hero, an American Farewell." *Chicago Sun Times* (27 June 1992): 1, 8.

Webster's Seventh New Collegiate Dictionary. Springfield, Mass.: Merriam, 1965.

Weed, Perry L. *The White Ethnic Movement and Ethnic Politics*. New York: Prager, 1973.

Wenk, B., Michael, S.M. Tomasi, and Geno Baroni, eds. *Pieces of a Dream; The Ethnic Worker's Crisis with America*. New York: Center for Migraion Studies, 1972.

Wespiec, Jan. *Polish American Serial Publications, 1842–1966*. Published by the Author in Chicago, 1968.

Whyte, William Foot. *Street Corner Society: The Social Structure of an Italian Slum*. Chicago: University of Chicago Press, 1955.

Wicislo, Aloysius. "New Americans of Polish Descent." *Polish American Studies* 16, 3–4 (July–December 1959): 85–89.

Wierzewski, Wojciech. "Skad Nasz Rod: Po Swiatowym Zjezdzie Polakow i Polonii w Krakowie." *Dziennik Zwiazkowy* (4–7 September 1991): 1, part 1; 1–4, part 2.

_____. "Zjazd Pieknych Intencji." *Dziennik Zwiazkowy* (20–30 August 1992): 1, 4, 5, 12.

Wilke, David. "Public Relations: An Important Tool." *Pomost Quarterly 1653–55* (1982).

Willis, Paul. *Learning to Labor: How Working Class Kids Get Working Class Jobs*. New York: Columbia University Press, 1977.

Wirth, Louis. *The Ghetto*. Chicago: University of Chicago Press, 1928.

_____. "Urbanism as a Way of Life." 1–24. In *Neighborhood, City and Metropolis*, edited by Robert Gutman and David Popenoe, 54–84. New York: Random House, 1938/70.

_____. "Morale and Minority Groups." *The American Journal of Sociology* 47, 3 (1942): 415–33.

_____. "The Problem of Minority groups." In *The Science of Man in the World Crisis*, edited by R. Linton. New York: Columbia University Press, 1945.

Wirth, Louis, Eleanor Bernert, and Margaret Furez, eds. *Local Community Fact Book of Chicago*. Chicago: University of Chicago Press, 1938.

Wlodarczyk, Wlademar. "Pomost after One Year." *Pomost Quarterly* 6 (1980): 40–42.

Wood, Arthur Evans. *Hamtramck: Then and Now*. New York: Bookman Associates, 1955.

Worwag, Mike. "The Legal Profession and the Immigration Solo Practitioner." Unpublished paper, Loyola University, 1992.

Wrobel, Paul. "Review of H. Z. Lopata's *Polish Americans. Polish American Studies* 83 (1976): 65–68.

_____. *Our Way: Family, Parish and Neighborhood in Polish-American Community*. Notre Dame: University of Notre Dame Press, 1979.

Wygocki, Zygmund. "Emigracja czy Odmowa Powrotu?" *Dziennik Zwiazkowy* (21–23 August 1992): 3, section 2.

Wyman, Mark. "Emigranci Wracaja z Ameryki, 1880–1930." *Przeglad Polonijny*. 15 (1989): 31–43.

Wytrwal, Joseph A. *Poles in America*. Minneapolis: Lerner Publications, 1969a.

_____. *Poles in American History and Tradition*. Detroit: Endurance Press, 1969b.

Yaffe, James. *The American Jews*. New York: Paperback Library, 1969.

Zagraniczny, Stanley J. "Some Reasons of Polish Surname Changes." *Polish American Studies* 20, 1 (January–June 1963): 12–14.

Zand, Helen Sankiewicz. "Polish Family Folkways in the United States." *Polish American Studies* 13, 3–4 (July–December 1956): 77–88.

_____. "Institutional Folkways in the United States." *Polish American Studies* 14, 1–2 (January–June 1957): 24–32.

_____. "Polish American Weddings and Christenings." *Polish American Studies* 16, 1–2 (January–June 1959): 24–33.

Zawodny, J. K. *Death in the Forest*. Notre Dame, Ind.: University of Notre Dame Press, 1962.

Zborowski, Mark, and Elizabeth Herzog. *Life is with People: The Culture of the Shtetl*. New York: Schocken Books, 1952.

Zeranska, Alina. "Goals and Purpose of the Polish Scholars Convention." *Perspectives* 1, 4 (October–December 1971): 6.

Zmuda, James. "Facing the Consequences". *Pomost Quarterly* 13 (1982): 43–45.

Zmurkiewicz, Wlodzimierz. *Protokol Dziewiatej Krajowej Konwencji Kongresu Polonii Amerykanskiej*. No date, no publishing information, probably 1972.

Znaniecki, Florian. "Intellectual America, by a European." *The Atlantic Monthly* (February 1920): 188–199 (anonymous but identified).

_____. *Modern Nationalities*. Urbana, Ill.: University of Illinois Press, 1952.

_____. *Social Relations and Social Roles*. San Francisco: Chandler, 1965.

Zolkowski, Anna. "Immigration Reform of 1990." *Link* 4 (December 1990): 2–3.

Zorbaugh, Harvey W. *The Gold Coast and the Slum*. Chicago: University of Chicago Press, 1929.

Zubrzycki, Jerzy. *Polish Immigrants in Britain*. The Hague: Martinus Nijhoff, 1956.

Zwiazek Narodowy Polski. *60-ta Rocznica: Pamietnik Jubieleuszowy, 1880–1940.* Chicago: Dziennik Zwiazkowy, 1948.

Index

A

ABC Emigranta, 88
Abel, Theodore, 56
Abramson, Harold J., 153, 208
African-American-Polish relations, 135-36
Agocs, Carol, 202
Alexander III, 22
Alfa, 88
America, characteristics of society in, 35-36, consequences of immigration, 32-34, history of migration to, 28-32, Polish immigration to, 36-49, population composition in, 34, social class structure and mobility in, 34-35
American Council of Polish Cultural Clubs, 123
A Nation of Immigrants (Kennedy), 28
Annual Report (U.S. Immigration Bureau), 37, 39-40
Anti-intellectualism, 147, 244
Anti-Polishness, 116-22
Anti-Semitism, 21-22, 135
Associations, 77, interorganizational, 82-83, multipurpose, 79-82, single interest groups, 78-79
Atlantic Monthly, 134

B

Benet, Sula, 75
Black-Polish relations, 135-36
Blejwas, Stanislaus A., 189
"Brain drain," 95
Brotherhood, 222-23, 232
Buczek, Daniel S., 89
Buffalo, NY, 204-6
Bukowczyk, John J., 160
Business elites, 186-87

C

Chicago, 197-202
Chinese Exclusion Act of 1882, 30
Civil Rights Issues of Euro-Ethnic Americans in the United, States, 33
Columbia University, 64-65
Communist party, 106, 127
Companionate circles, 180-83, 211, cooperative events among, 196, intelligentsia, 183-86, interaction among circles, 191-96, local community life and, Buffalo, 204-6, Chicago, 197-202, Hamtramck, MI, 202-4, Los Angeles, 206-8, other Polonian communities, 208-10, parish life, 188, political and organizational elites, 187-88, professional and business elites, 186-87, religious personnel, ex-combatants, and polka world, 190-91, *Solidarnosc* and other third cohorts, 188-90
Connecticut Valley, 208-9
Coser, Lewis A., 116-17
Country, 4
Culture, 65-67

D

Deportation cases, 168
Discrimination, 116-22
Displaced persons, 9, 103-4, 160-62
Displaced Persons Act of 1948, 160
District ethnic community, 55
Divorce rates, 158
Domestic workers, 169
Duchy Period, 17
Dulczewski, Zygmund, 27
Duncan, Beverly, 151
Duncan, Otis Dudley, 151